NEW PERSPECTIVES ON
MIMBRES ARCHAEOLOGY

EDITED BY
BARBARA J. ROTH,
PATRICIA A. GILMAN,
AND ROGER ANYON

NEW PERSPECTIVES ON
MIMBRES
ARCHAEOLOGY

*Three Millennia of Human Occupation
in the North American Southwest*

THE UNIVERSITY OF
ARIZONA PRESS
TUCSON

The University of Arizona Press
www.uapress.arizona.edu

ISBN-13: 978-0-8165-3856-0 (cloth)

Cover design by Leigh McDonald
Cover illustrations by Will G. Russell

Library of Congress Cataloging-in-Publication Data
Names: Roth, Barbara J., 1958– editor. | Gilman, Patricia A., editor. | Anyon, Roger, 1952– editor.
Title: New perspectives on Mimbres archaeology : three millennia of human occupation in the North American
    Southwest / edited by Barbara J. Roth, Patricia A. Gilman, and Roger Anyon.
Description: Tucson : The University of Arizona Press, 2018 | Includes bibliographical references and index.
Identifiers: LCCN 2018014005 | ISBN 9780816538560 (cloth : alk. paper)
Subjects: LCSH: Mimbres culture—Southwest, New. | Excavations (Archaeology)—Southwest, New. | Pueblo
    Indians—Antiquities.
Classification: LCC E99.M76 N49 2018 | DDC 979/.01—dc23 LC record available at
    https://lccn.loc.gov/2018014005

Printed in the United States of America
♾ This paper meets the requirements of ANSI/NISO Z39.48-1992 (Permanence of Paper).

CONTENTS

NEW PERSPECTIVES ON
MIMBRES ARCHAEOLOGY

Introduction

New Perspectives on Mimbres Archaeology

BARBARA J. ROTH, PATRICIA A. GILMAN,
AND ROGER ANYON

THE CHAPTERS IN THIS VOLUME derive from a 2014 Society for American
Archaeology symposium organized to celebrate the fortieth anniversary of the
Mimbres Foundation's pioneering research in the Mimbres Valley of southwestern
New Mexico in the mid- to late 1970s. The Mimbres Foundation's work was fundamental in documenting the nature of the prehistoric occupation of the Mimbres
region, and it provided the investigative framework for today's researchers throughout
the southwestern United States and northern Mexico. Prior to the Mimbres Foundation's work, most of what was known about the Mimbres region was based on excavations conducted in the early 1900s at large and predominantly pueblo sites along
the Mimbres River and on studies of the elaborate black-on-white ceramics made and
used during the Mimbres Classic (pueblo) period (Anyon and LeBlanc 1984; Bradfield 1931; Cosgrove and Cosgrove 1932; Fewkes 1914; Haury 1936a; Nesbitt 1931).
The Mimbres Foundation expanded this research agenda to study the breadth of the
prehistoric occupation in the Mimbres Valley, encompassing work at large pueblo
sites, but also including work at smaller Classic period pueblos, earlier Pithouse sites,
and later Postclassic pueblo sites. The major goal of this work was to gain a better
understanding of the long-term occupation of the Mimbres region and its place in
southwestern prehistory. We organized the SAA session to both celebrate the important work that had been done by director Steven LeBlanc and the Mimbres Foundation archaeologists and to highlight and discuss more recent data that have built on
the understanding of the Mimbres region and people that the earlier work provided.

This volume presents these current data and interpretations of the Mimbres region's
prehistoric occupations. In this sense, much like the Mimbres Foundation's work, it
builds on and moves beyond a focus on ceramics and pueblos to encompass studies of

the Archaic, Pithouse, Classic, and Postclassic occupations. The authors discuss the range of material culture variability present in the Mimbres region, documenting continuities and breaks in behavior and material culture over time as groups committed to agriculture, became increasingly sedentary, and developed distinct and sometimes disparate social groupings and ritual practices that played key roles in the development of societal structures over three millennia.

We see this volume as important for several reasons. Despite being written off as an archaeological wasteland for research because of widespread looting, this region still contains much information about its occupation, as the Mimbres Foundation's investigations, later research, and the studies reported in this volume show. The chapters use a wealth of data from new excavations, studies of archaeological collections, advances in archaeological dating and other analytic techniques, and reinterpretations and new syntheses of old and new data to explore issues of fundamental concern to archaeologists working in the Southwest and worldwide today.

One essential aspect of Mimbres archaeology is that most of the fieldwork is and has been done by private foundations and university researchers, often in collaboration with government agencies. Thus, one factor that has significantly affected our knowledge of Mimbres prehistory is the lack of cultural resource management (CRM) work in the region, unlike other portions of the Southwest, where large-scale contract projects have contributed substantially to our understanding of the prehistoric occupation, particularly in the Jornada area to the east and the Hohokam region to the west. Even so, it is CRM work that has greatly enhanced our understanding of the Mimbres region's Archaic period.

In this introduction, we first discuss Mimbres chronology and culture history for those readers who are not familiar with them. We begin with the Middle Archaic period at 4000 B.C., then describe the Late Archaic, Pithouse, and Classic periods, and end with the Postclassic period at A.D. 1400. We go on to consider the Mimbres ceramic typology, and our final section focuses on common themes among the chapters. These include diversity within continuity, social and ritual organization, and population aggregation and dispersal.

Mimbres Chronology and Culture History

The Mimbres region as defined in this volume is situated predominantly within what is now southwestern New Mexico (figure I.1). In this area are three major river valleys: the Mimbres River, an internal drainage that flows from the Black Range to south of Deming (figure I.2); the Gila River, located west of the Continental Divide (figure I.3); and the Rio Grande, east of the Black Range and east of the Continental Divide (figure I.4). This region encompasses basin and range topography, riverine

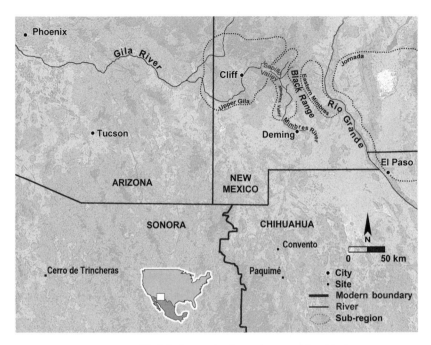

FIGURE I.1 The Mimbres region in southwestern New Mexico.

valleys, and mountains ranging from 4,000 to 10,000 ft above sea level, and it includes the lower and upper Chihuahuan Deserts and coniferous forests.

Archaeologists have developed the chronology of the Mimbres region's prehistoric occupation during two periods of work: the first in the early 1900s at major Classic pueblos and pithouse sites, and the second by the Mimbres Foundation and contemporary researchers at a variety of site types in the 1970s. A third phase of research, currently ongoing (Anyon et al. 2017), is likely to result in some changes in the ways we view the chronology and ceramic sequence through time, and the beginnings of that research are provided in this volume. Because this work is still being compiled and interpreted, the chapters in this volume use the traditional phase sequence and ceramic typology developed by the Mimbres Foundation and other researchers (table I.1; Anyon et al. 1981; Hegmon et al. 1999). In this section, we present basic information on each period, which is then expanded in the succeeding chapters.

Middle and Late Archaic Periods (4000 B.C.–A.D. 200)

The Archaic period is one of the least understood times in the Mimbres region, in part because few researchers have focused on it until recent CRM projects uncovered Archaic occupations as a result of fiber optic and highway construction projects

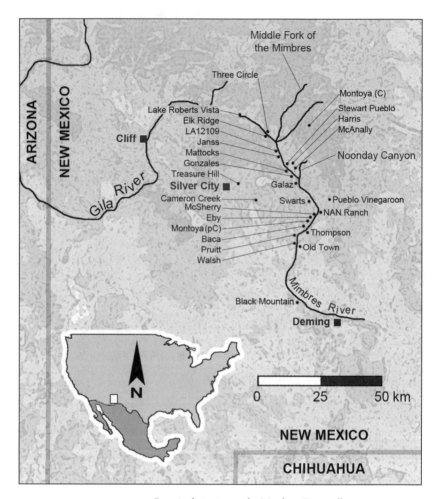

FIGURE I.2 Post-Archaic sites in the Mimbres River valley.

(chapter 1). Even so, our knowledge of the Archaic period occupation in the Mimbres region remains less comprehensive than that of later periods.

Data from southwestern New Mexico reveal little about the Early Archaic period (before 4000 B.C.) but have added to our understanding of the Middle Archaic and especially the Late Archaic/Early Agricultural periods (chapter 1). These data point to processes similar to those occurring across the southern Southwest, with Middle Archaic occupations representing primarily mobile hunter-gatherers who were increasingly focused on specific environmental zones, especially resource-rich biomes such as ciénegas and playa margins. Elsewhere in the Southwest, some Archaic foragers had adopted maize agriculture by 2000 B.C. and possibly earlier, and it is likely that

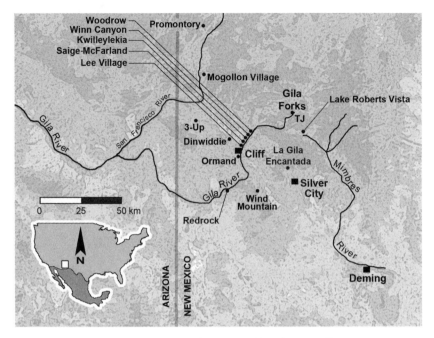

FIGURE I.3 Post-Archaic sites in the Gila River valley.

groups living along playa lake margins in the Mimbres region began experimenting with maize during this same time (Roth 2016). The sustained adoption of maize by Archaic period foragers, coupled with an increased focus on agriculture by some of these groups, continued for the next fifteen hundred years, and by 500–300 B.C., farmers living in seasonally occupied pithouses were present throughout the lower deserts of southwestern New Mexico (chapter 1). These occupations predate the Early Pithouse period, during which we have the best evidence for early maize farmers in the mountain valleys of the Mimbres region, but given the widespread occurrence of earlier maize farmers in the broader region, it seems likely that these farmers also used the well-watered alluvial floodplains of the three major rivers (e.g., O'Laughlin 1980; Wallace 1998).

Pithouse Period (A.D. 200–1000)

The Pithouse period occupation in the Mimbres region was first identified by excavations conducted in the early 1900s at the major Classic pueblo sites in the Mimbres Valley, such as Swarts (Cosgrove and Cosgrove 1932), Mattocks (Nesbitt 1931), Galaz (Anyon and LeBlanc 1984), and Cameron Creek (Bradfield 1931), all of which

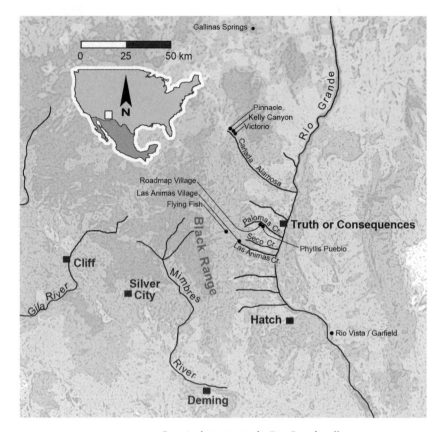

FIGURE I.4 Post-Archaic sites in the Rio Grande valley.

revealed underlying pithouse components. It was not until Haury's (1936a) work at the Harris site and Mogollon village, however, that the Pithouse period was formally defined. Haury identified three phases of the Pithouse period—Georgetown, San Francisco, and Three Circle—and dated the Georgetown phase prior to A.D. 800 and the Three Circle phase between A.D. 900 and 1000. The Mimbres Foundation termed this the Late Pithouse period, dating Georgetown to A.D. 550–650, San Francisco to A.D. 650–750, and Three Circle to A.D. 750–1000 (Anyon et al. 1981).

Haury did not identify the Early Pithouse period as he focused on pithouses associated with painted ceramics. The Mimbres Foundation established the Early Pithouse period, dating it between A.D. 200 and 550 (Anyon et al. 1981). This period was first systematically investigated as part of the Mimbres Foundation's work at the McAnally and Thompson sites (Diehl and LeBlanc 2001) in the Mimbres Valley and Fitting's (1973) work at the Winn Canyon site in the Gila Valley. It is generally characterized by the presence of small sites (usually with fewer than fifteen houses) often located on isolated knolls and ridges. Pithouses were circular with ramp entries. Ceramics were undecorated and composed of a brown paste, which by the end of the period sometimes included a red slip. People were still seasonally mobile, and maize agriculture formed a critical component of a diet that also relied on hunting and gathering. Debate continues as to the reason why many sites were located on hilltops. LeBlanc ties this to defensive strategies, while Diehl argues that it was for resource monitoring (Diehl and LeBlanc 2001). LeBlanc continues his consideration of Early Pithouse site locations in chapter 13.

One of the most significant changes dividing the Georgetown phase of the Late Pithouse period from the Early Pithouse period is the shift in site locations from knoll and ridge settings to river terraces adjacent to floodplains, a shift generally regarded as indicating an increased commitment to agriculture. Pithouses were circular or D shaped with ramp entries, and some large pithouses are thought to have been structures for community-wide use. Ceramics include both plain and polished red-slipped (San Francisco Red) pottery.

During the succeeding San Francisco phase, major settlement locations remained on the first terrace above floodplains, a pattern that continued through the Mimbres Classic period. Pithouses were rectangular with rounded corners, while communal structures remained circular but were significantly larger than domestic structures (Anyon and LeBlanc 1980). Site size increased, and Roth and Baustian (2015) argue that the first extended family corporate groups are present at some of the larger sites in the Mimbres River valley by this time. This phase also witnessed the first production of painted ceramics, Mogollon Red-on-brown.

During the Three Circle phase, substantial changes occurred in Mimbres pithouse communities, likely in response to increasing agricultural dependence and population increase. Site sizes continued to increase, with large sites present adjacent to productive agricultural settings, such as at Old Town (Creel 2006a), NAN Ranch (Shafer 2003), Swarts (Cosgrove and Cosgrove 1932), Galaz (Anyon and LeBlanc 1984), Harris (Haury 1936a; Roth 2015), and Woodrow (Sedig 2015). Pithouses were rectangular with ramp entries and often exhibited evidence of remodeling, suggesting greater longevity of use. Burials were placed beneath house floors by the end of this phase. Changes in site layout have been documented by the mid– to late Three Circle phase and include clusters of contemporary pithouses at several sites such as Old Town (Creel 2006a, 2006b; Lucas 2007), NAN Ranch (Shafer 2003), and the Harris site (Roth 2015), which have been interpreted as representing extended family groups (Roth and Baustian 2015). Ceramic designs also changed during the Three Circle phase, beginning with the shift to red-on-white (Three Circle Red-on-white) and then black-on-white (Style I Black-on-white and Style II Black-on-white) ceramics.

TABLE 1.1 Traditional Mimbres Temporal Periods

Period	Phase	Date Range A.D.	Subregion	Archaeological Characteristics
Late Archaic		2000 B.C.–A.D. 200		Small, circular pithouses; no ceramics
Early Pithouse		200–550	Mimbres Valley, Eastern Mimbres, and upper Gila	Circular pithouses; plain and a few red-slipped ceramics
Late Pithouse		550–1000		Pithouses; definite communal structures; increased elaboration of ceramic decoration
	Georgetown	550–650	Mimbres Valley, Eastern Mimbres, and upper Gila	Circular pithouses; plain and San Francisco Red pottery
	San Francisco	650–750	Mimbres Valley, Eastern Mimbres, and upper Gila	Rectangular pithouses with rounded corners; Mogollon R/b pottery; increased communal structure size
	Three Circle	750–1000	Mimbres Valley, Eastern Mimbres, and upper Gila	Rectangular pithouses with squared corners; Three Circle R/w, Mimbres Style I (Boldface) B/w pottery; increased communal structure size. A.D. 900–1000: rooms with shallow floors and thin adobe walls; Mimbres Style II (Transitional) B/w pottery
Mimbres Classic		1000–1130	Mimbres Valley, Eastern Mimbres, and upper Gila	Aboveground masonry pueblos; Mimbres Style III (Classic) B/w and corrugated pottery; large aggregated sites.
Early Postclassic		1130–1300		Aboveground adobe or masonry architecture; a diversity of ceramics
Terminal Classic Mimbres		1130–late 1100s	Mimbres Valley	Continued occupation in Classic sites; small amounts of Mimbres B/w with Chupadero B/w, El Paso Polychrome, Playas Red, and Tularosa and Chihuahuan Corrugated

Period	Phase	Date	Region	Characteristics
	Reorganization	1130–early 1200s	Eastern Mimbres	Small masonry hamlets; Mimbres B/w, Chupadero B/w, El Paso Polychrome, Playas Red, White Mountain Red Wares, and Tularosa Corrugated
	Tularosa	late 1100s–1300	Mogollon Highlands east to the Rio Grande	Tularosa B/w, White Mountain Red Wares, and Tularosa Fillet Rim
	Black Mountain	late 1100s–1300	Mimbres Valley	Adobe architecture; White Mountain Red Wares, Chupadero B/w, Playas Red, El Paso Bi/Polychrome, and corrugated
	Early Animas	1150–1300	Animas Valley and southeast Arizona	Adobe architecture including plazas; Roosevelt Red Wares, Chihuahuan polychromes, and Cloverdale Corrugated
	Late Doña Ana	1150–1300	Jornada Mogollon and portions of the Rio Grande	Rectangular pithouses; El Paso Bi/Polychrome, Chupadero B/w, Playas Red Ware, and Three Rivers Red-on-terracotta
Late Postclassic		1300–1450		Aboveground adobe or masonry architecture; a diversity of ceramics
	Cliff/Salado	1300–1450	Upper Gila, Mimbres Valley	Aboveground adobe or masonry architecture; Roosevelt Red Wares, late El Paso Polychrome, and Chihuahuan polychromes
	Magdalena	1300–1450	Magdalena Mountains and surrounding areas	Aboveground slab masonry architecture; Magdalena B/w, El Paso Polychrome, Reserve Indented Corrugated, and Seco Corrugated
	Late Animas	1300–1450	Animas Valley and southeast Arizona	Aboveground adobe architecture including plazas; Roosevelt Red Wares, Chihuahuan polychromes, and Cloverdale Corrugated
	El Paso	1300–1450	Jornada Mogollon and portions of the Rio Grande	Aboveground adobe architecture; late El Paso Polychrome, Chupadero B/w, Three Rivers Red-on-terracotta, White Mountain Red Wares, Roosevelt Red Wares, and Chihuahuan polychromes

Another major change that occurred during the Three Circle phase was the construction of large rectangular community structures identified as great kivas. These structures were substantially larger than the domestic structures and sometimes included features like benches, floor grooves, and sipapus. Many of them, especially those at the larger sites, opened onto central plazas containing burials and cremations (Creel and Anyon 2003; Creel et al. 2015; Creel and Shafer 2015; Shafer 2003).

Toward the end of the Three Circle phase, Shafer (2003) sees a shift to roof entries in pithouses, the use of slab-lined instead of basin hearths, and the placement of burials beneath pithouse floors as reflecting ideological changes in Mimbres society. This proposed ideological shift occurred at a time when great kivas were being phased out of community use (Creel and Anyon 2003; Creel et al. 2015). These changes, among others, culminated in the pithouse-to-pueblo transition.

The transition between pithouses and pueblos, that is, between the Late Pithouse and the Classic periods, occurred between A.D. 900 and the early 1000s. Few tree-ring dates are available from this time (Anyon et al. 2017), and so the timing of the transition is poorly understood. However, Sedig's (2013, 2015; Sedig and Lekson 2012) recent research at the Woodrow site in the Gila Valley and Roth's (2015) investigations at the Harris site in the Mimbres Valley are beginning to illuminate the diversity in the ways that people made the transition (chapter 3).

Classic Period (A.D. 1000–1130)

The Classic is the best known of the various periods in the Mimbres region. The Classic rock-walled pueblos and the Style III Black-on-white pottery with detailed geometric, human, or animal designs have attracted archaeologists, avocationalists, and looters for more than one hundred years, and the pottery accounts for our relatively extensive knowledge of this period.

Characteristics of the Classic period include aboveground, rock-walled rooms clustered into room blocks, with several room blocks present on larger sites. Although the room blocks might suggest population aggregation, it is not clear that the regional population increased from the Late Pithouse to the Classic period (Gilman and LeBlanc 2017). Room function varied by size: small rooms were apparently used for storage and larger rooms for habitation and some other functions including granaries and partly or fully enclosed plazas. Great kivas appear to have been out of commission by the early A.D. 1000s, and open plazas between room blocks may have replaced them, although we have little evidence for the use of these open areas. Most large (more than one hundred rooms) Classic pueblos show evidence of much rebuilding in the form of superimposed rooms and multiple room floors (Creel 2006a; Shafer 2003). The Mattocks site, however, has little such evidence (Gilman and LeBlanc 2017), suggesting that Classic site histories vary in their start and end dates, social organization, and relationships with people internal to and external to the Mimbres region. Differences among sites might account for why Shafer (2003) and Creel (2006b) interpret some Classic sites as having corporate groups, while Gilman and LeBlanc (2017) suggest that only households and not corporate groups were present at the Mattocks site.

Classic occupation included small and medium-sized sites in addition to large sites. Stokes and colleagues (chapter 5) focus on small Classic sites, demonstrating that not all small pueblo sites were used for agriculture but instead had different functions. While these small sites may seem less significant than the contemporary large pueblos, Stokes and colleagues show that the diversity within this category is important for understanding Mimbres communities, which include more than just the large sites.

Style III Black-on-white pottery is the item that draws most people to the Classic period because its exquisite painted designs set it apart from most other ceramics in the southwestern United States and indeed around the world. One hundred years after Fewkes (1914) first introduced this pottery to archaeologists, we still know little about why ancient people in the Mimbres region painted such designs or what those designs might have meant. We are making progress on these issues, however, as evidenced by several chapters in this book. Creel and Speakman (chapter 6) discuss neutron activation analysis (NAA) of Mimbres pottery production and distribution, a baseline necessary for understanding where painted vessels were made and where they ended their use lives. Gilman and colleagues (chapter 4) note that while Style III Black-on-white pottery was the only painted ceramic type made in the Mimbres region during the Classic period, the designs are extremely varied, leading them to suggest that the overall style helped hold people together and form their "Mimbres" identity. Despite the variability in designs, Creel and Speakman (chapter 6) and Hegmon and colleagues (chapter 7) show that the distribution of painted designs at Classic sites throughout the Mimbres region was homogeneous. These ceramic studies support the concept of social diversity within overall Mimbres societal conformity that we discuss later in this introduction.

In chapter 11, Nelson and Minnis discuss the connectivity of people during the Mimbres Classic period to the people in the Chaco and Hohokam regions and particularly with those to the south in Mexico. They are interested in whether apogees to the south in Mesoamerica affected the beginning or end of the Classic period, and they conclude that such events did not. They do support the idea that some people from the Mimbres region may have made their way to the Postclassic site of Paquimé in northern Mexico. LeBlanc (chapter 13) also discusses the similarities in the Chacoan and Mimbres systems during the Classic period, as well as the parallels between Mimbres and Casas Grandes painted pottery and the relationships between people in the Mimbres and those farther south in Mesoamerica.

Postclassic Period (A.D. 1130–1400)

The Postclassic period was a time of substantial changes in settlement locations, architecture, ceramics, and burials. We divide the Postclassic into early and late periods. The Early Postclassic dates from A.D. 1130/1150 to 1300, and the Late Postclassic from A.D. 1300 to 1400/1450. Several contemporary phases characterize the Early Postclassic depending on location within the Mimbres region, including the Black Mountain phase in the south end of the Mimbres Valley, the Reorganization phase in the Eastern Mimbres, and the Animas phase in the Bootheel of New Mexico. The Late Postclassic encompasses the Cliff phase, the easternmost manifestation of the Salado phenomenon.

During the Early Postclassic period, settlement locations changed in the Mimbres Valley, and populations focused their occupation in the southern portion. Areas of Classic occupation north of the Galaz site were essentially depopulated. It appears that some people moved to the east, where Nelson (1999) and Hegmon and colleagues (1999) have documented the Reorganization phase, during which people lived in small, dispersed farming hamlets and used Style III ceramics in conjunction with other pottery types common in Postclassic sites (chapter 9). In the southern Mimbres Valley, people often built Black Mountain phase pueblos adjacent to disused Mimbres Classic pueblos but not on top of them, such as at NAN Ranch and Old Town (chapter 10). The new pueblos were of adobe construction, a fundamental change from Classic period rock and adobe walls. Changes in burial practices also occurred and show more diversity than was present previously, including a decrease in burials having bowls with "kill holes" punched in them and an increase in cremations. During the Black Mountain phase, different pottery types replaced Style III Black-on-white and nonpainted types, including Chupadero Black-on-white, El Paso Polychrome, Playas Red, and Tularosa Fillet Rim Corrugated, suggesting closer social ties with groups to the east, south, and north than previously. The nature and extent of contact with Paquimé, a very large multistory adobe walled site in northern Chihuahua, during both the Early and Late Postclassic periods is one topic among others that is addressed further in chapters 9, 10, and 11.

The Late Postclassic, which is the final occupation of the prehistoric Mimbres region, postdates A.D. 1300 and is characterized by a variety of pueblo construction styles and painted ceramic types including polychrome ceramics collectively referred to as Salado polychromes or Roosevelt Red Ware. Late El Paso Polychrome and Chihuahuan polychromes are also present. As with the Early Postclassic period, different material culture assemblages occur in different areas and sometimes at contemporary sites that are geographically very close to one another.

Sites in the Mimbres Valley fall on the eastern edge of the Salado phenomenon. LeBlanc and Nelson (1976:5) note that the Mimbres Valley was "exceedingly peripheral" during this phase, and the Gila Valley to the west appears to have been more densely populated. The nature of the Salado phenomenon is a subject of varying interpretations (Clark et al. 2013; Crown 1994; Dean 2000). Current work in the Gila Valley by Archaeology Southwest may help to clarify the nature and meaning of Salado in this area. Late Postclassic occupations in the Rio Grande valley are not thought of as Salado and are much more complex in terms of their varied material culture, which may indicate divergent populations living side by side.

Mimbres Ceramic Typology

Fewkes (1914) originally illustrated Classic (Style III) Black-on-white ceramics, while Haury (1936a, 1936b) initially described the basic painted pottery sequence for the Pithouse period. Cosgrove and Cosgrove (1932), based on their work at the Swarts site, were the first to attempt to differentiate between black-on-white types, but it was not until work by the Mimbres Foundation (Anyon and LeBlanc 1984) and the NAN Ranch project (Shafer and Brewington 1995) that the ceramic typology was revised to essentially its modern form. Because the current ceramic typology serves as a kind of lingua franca for researchers in the Southwest, the chapters in this volume use this traditional typology, including Styles I, II, and III for the Mimbres Black-on-white types.

The earliest painted ceramics were present during the San Francisco phase, represented by Mogollon Red-on-brown, which developed from the earlier San Francisco Red and is characterized by a brown slip with polished red designs. Designs are usually rectilinear, and the bowl exteriors are often red slipped, polished, and dimpled, similar to San Francisco Red. Haury (1936b) defined an earlier type that he called San Lorenzo Red-on-brown, but we and most other Mimbres researchers subsume this rare type under Mogollon Red-on-brown.

During the Three Circle phase, ceramic styles changed rapidly, first with the production of Three Circle Red-on-white with a creamy white slip and polished red designs that exhibit an increase in curvilinear motifs. This was quickly followed by a sequence of black-on-white decorated styles. The earliest black-on-white was initially called Boldface (Cosgrove and Cosgrove 1932) and later essentially classified as Style I (Anyon and LeBlanc 1984). Style I is characterized by a true white slip with bold black curvilinear designs, usually large scrolls, wavy lines as hachure, and very few representational designs of animals and people. Style II Black-on-white (first called Transitional by the Mimbres Foundation) spans the pithouse-to-pueblo transition and has more linear and representational designs and thin brushwork in which fine lines are framed by thicker lines. Style III (Classic) Black-on-white reveals the continued evolution of design styles, with geometric and most of the well-known animal and human designs. It is also characterized by fine brushwork with fine lines framed by fine lines. Shafer and Brewington (1995) have further defined microstyles for Styles II and III based on their research at the NAN Ranch site.

The Mimbres sequence ends at about A.D. 1130/1150 with a cessation of use of Style III Black-on-white in most areas. Style III extends for several decades into the Early Postclassic Reorganization phase in the eastern Black Range. One of the defining characteristics of the Postclassic is the plethora of pottery types noted previously, none of which seem to evolve from the Mimbres Black-on-white series.

Themes in Mimbres Prehistory

The authors in this volume discuss the chronological sequence, current data and interpretations, and other issues associated with three millennia of occupation in the Mimbres region. While directly pertinent to Mimbres archaeology, these topics also have important implications for researchers working on problems in other regions, including the impact of the adoption and intensification of agricultural production (chapters 1 and 8), village formation (chapter 2), the causes and consequences of population aggregation and dispersal (chapters 2, 5, 9, and 10), social identity (chapters 4, 6, and 7), the role of ritual in community integration (chapters 2 and 4), and the role of connectivity with other regions (chapter 11). In this section, we discuss some of the major themes that emerge from the volume and their significance for the Mimbres region and the greater Southwest, as well as for our understanding of Neolithic societies in general. The themes include diversity within continuity and conformity, social and ritual organization, and population aggregation, dispersal, and redistribution.

Diversity within Continuity and Conformity

One theme that emerges from an examination of the Mimbres region archaeological record is the considerable diversity across time and space, and yet within that diversity, at least prior to A.D. 1150, is an underlying continuity that appears to be a key factor in being "Mimbres." For example, Sedig and colleagues (chapter 3) discuss the variability present across the pithouse-to-pueblo transition in terms of organizational complexity while documenting continuity between the two periods. They show that in the A.D. 900s people built and used a range of architectural forms and that the transition from pithouses to pueblos was not uniform. The results of the transition, however, were uniformly Mimbres Classic in that they included cobble-walled pueblos and a continuation of the Mimbres Black-on-white pottery tradition.

Gilman and colleagues (chapter 4) document the variations in Classic period site and room-block layouts, site histories, and the presence or absence of ritual areas, as well as differences in Style III Black-on-white pottery designs, and they relate these differences to social diversity. They note that only one painted pottery style, Style III Black-on-white, is present during the Classic period and that some of the iconography painted on those ceramics may symbolize the religious and ritual practices that supported conformity and held the society together. Social conformity within diversity is apparent in several other ceramic studies in this volume. Creel and Speakman (chapter 6) discuss the general similarity of pottery designs among the many compositional groups determined by NAA. Hegmon and colleagues (chapter 7) use design analyses to show the homogeneity of ceramic design distribution during the Classic period. All sites have common motifs, and designs are distributed evenly among and within sites and across age and sex in burials. Hegmon and colleagues suggest that people must have deliberately created such a distribution. It certainly could have been one of the factors that held Mimbres society together in terms of a common identity (see the next section for more on this topic).

Social and Ritual Organization

The chapters in this volume present new insights that have implications for understanding social and ritual change in general and illustrate that often these two aspects of society were intertwined. Anyon and Roth (chapter 2) discuss variations in the way that Pithouse period sites were organized, with extended family corporate groups present at the larger sites in the Mimbres Valley associated with large great kivas that were essential for ritual and community integration (Creel et al. 2015). This occurred while other contemporary groups lived in smaller, less integrated settings (Roth 2010; Swanson et al. 2012).

Gilman and colleagues (chapter 4), Stokes and colleagues (chapter 5), and Schollmeyer and colleagues (chapter 8) examine the diverse ways that Classic period pueblo groups were organized. They document differences in rooms and room suites, site sizes, site layouts, locations of small pueblo sites on the landscape, and subsistence strategies that signify distinctions in social organization.

Ritual integration likely changed following the ritual retirement of great kivas at the major pithouse sites in the Mimbres River valley in the mid– to late A.D. 900s, possibly tied to changes in ideology (Gilman et al. 2014). By the Mimbres Classic period, great kivas were replaced with smaller kivas and large central plazas serving as loci for community integration. Gilman and colleagues (chapter 4) discuss the religious and ritual practices that developed during the Classic period and that focused on scarlet macaws and the Hero Twins.

As noted earlier, decorated ceramics have been of key concern to researchers studying the Mimbres, and they remain a major source of information, especially about social and ritual organization. Many of the chapters in this volume use ceramic data, but they illustrate how new approaches, new analytical techniques, and the reanalysis of existing data have strengthened our interpretations not just of ceramic use, but of their role in the social and ritual aspects of Mimbres society. For example, ceramics appear to have been important components in intersite exchange. Creel and Speakman (chapter 6), using NAA results on the floor vessels from contemporary pithouses, show that people living in each of those structures had very different social ties to pottery producers at other sites. Similarly, by examining NAA results from virtually all Swarts-site vessels, they suggest that people in the two Classic period room blocks had varying social relationships with those from other sites.

Ceramics were also important in solidifying Mimbres identity (chapter 7) and in symbolizing and strengthening ideological views (chapter 4). That these ceramics are still today clearly recognizable markers of Mimbres society indicates the significant role that they played in Mimbres identity formation and perpetuation, representing a distinction from Hohokam and northern Puebloan groups that extended beyond ceramics. In this sense, ceramics served as important social boundary markers. The fact that painted ceramic designs may have represented ideological views reinforces their importance in Mimbres society.

Changes in ceramic types during the Postclassic period (chapters 9 and 10), tied with new site locations, architecture, and burial practices, mark a shift that we are only beginning to understand, but they appear to represent a fundamental reorganization of the social, ritual, and ideological worlds after A.D. 1130/1150. Although sometimes linked to drought in the early A.D. 1100s, the abandonment of some sites, the discontinuation of Style III Black-on-white (except for the Eastern Mimbres area) in favor of ceramic styles that were widespread across the southern Southwest, and the shift in architectural styles indicate that social and ideological factors were also likely at play. Putsavage and Taliaferro (chapter 10) discuss both continuity with the previous Mimbres Classic period and the substantial changes that occurred during the Black Mountain phase in the southern Mimbres region. Schollmeyer and colleagues (chapter 9) document a change in site structure from villages, which were larger and more permanently occupied, to smaller hamlets, which were used intermittently, in the Eastern Mimbres region during the transition from Mimbres Classic to Reorganization phase. This surely denotes changes in social organization.

Population Aggregation, Dispersal, and Redistribution

The Mimbres region presents an important case study of the factors influencing population aggregation and the reasons why it ultimately did not work. Aggregation and dispersal of populations are not mutually exclusive phenomena. In general, populations prior to the Three Circle phase tended to be dispersed, but during the Three Circle phase and the Mimbres Classic period, aggregation occurred in large sites alongside dispersed populations living in smaller settlements. Anyon and Roth (chapter 2) see aggregation occurring as early as the Three Circle phase and link this to population growth and the labor and organizational demands of irrigation agriculture in the well-watered Mimbres Valley and likely in the Gila Valley. The presence of aggregated Classic period pueblos dating to the early A.D. 1000s in resource-rich portions of the Mimbres and Gila Valleys with access to large expanses of arable land has also been argued to be tied to agricultural intensification, rising populations, and ideological changes (chapter 4; Shafer 1995, 2003, 2006).

Population dispersal is also a major characteristic of the Mimbres region. Small dispersed sites are present throughout the Pithouse and Classic periods and were linked to the larger sites in varying ways (Stokes 2003; Stokes and Roth 1999; chapter 5). Stokes and colleagues (chapter 5) argue that some of the small pueblos found in the side drainages and canyons that feed into the Mimbres River represent offshoots of groups from larger riverine sites who did not have access to prime agricultural land. In addition, Anyon and Roth (chapter 2) note that people dispersed from the Harris site in the late A.D. 900s and that no subsequent puebloan occupation was present. Sedig and colleagues (chapter 3) also mention the possible movement of people from the upper Gila to the Mimbres Valley during the pithouse-to-pueblo transition.

Population aggregation, dispersal, and distribution during the Late Pithouse and Classic periods differ from those following the end of the Classic period. Previous research has shown that resource depletion (Cannon 2000; Minnis 1985) and drought played major roles in the shift from Classic to Postclassic periods. Postclassic populations were primarily aggregated in medium to large pueblos, with the exception of the eastern Black Range, where small hamlets were predominant. During the Early Postclassic, populations were distributed mainly in the lower river valley elevations and in the lower Chihuahuan desert. By the late Postclassic period, populations were once again living along the major watercourses.

Conclusions

It is clear from reading these chapters that the persistence of researchers can pay off tremendously, even in a region that many southwestern archaeologists had written off because of the extensive looting and vandalism. The chapters in this volume illustrate that much is still to be learned, not only from an examination of large looted sites, but also from smaller sites, subsistence data, legacy collections, and the application of innovative analytical techniques. Steven LeBlanc had this vision when he started the Mimbres Foundation research, and the authors of the chapters in this volume have built on this legacy.

We do not see this volume as the final statement on Mimbres archaeology by any means. Instead, we see it as part of a pathway that extends from the earliest work in the region through that of the Mimbres Foundation and others and on to the application of current method, theory, analyses, and interpretation. The chapters presented here incorporate new data based on advances in analytical techniques that have enhanced our understanding of the Mimbres region archaeological record, just as new techniques will further expand our understanding of this significant southwestern region. We see this volume as providing a current baseline and foundation for future work not only in the Mimbres region, but also in Neolithic societies worldwide.

References Cited

Anyon, Roger, Darrell Creel, Patricia A. Gilman, Steven A. LeBlanc, Myles R. Miller, Stephen E. Nash, Margaret C. Nelson, Kathryn J. Putsavage, Barbara J. Roth, Karen Gush Schollmeyer, Jakob W. Sedig, and Christopher A. Turnbow. 2017. Re-evaluating the Mimbres Region Prehispanic Chronometric Record. *Kiva* 83:316–343.

Anyon, Roger, Patricia A. Gilman, and Steven A. LeBlanc. 1981. A Re-evaluation of the Mogollon-Mimbres Archaeological Sequence. *Kiva* 46:209–225.

Anyon, Roger, and Steven A. LeBlanc. 1980. The Architectural Evolution of Mogollon-Mimbres Communal Structures. *Kiva* 45:253–277.

———. 1984. *The Galaz Ruin: A Prehistoric Mimbres Village in Southwestern New Mexico*. University of New Mexico Press, Albuquerque.

Bradfield, Wesley. 1931. *Cameron Creek Village: A Site in the Mimbres Area in Grant County, New Mexico*. Monograph No. 1. School of American Research, Santa Fe, New Mexico.

Cannon, Michael D. 2000. Large Mammal Relative Abundance in Pithouse and Pueblo Period Archaeofaunas from Southwestern New Mexico: Resource Depression Among the Mimbres Mogollon? *Journal of Anthropological Archaeology* 19:317–347.

Clark, Jeffrey, Deborah L. Huntley, J. Brett Hill, and Patrick D. Lyons. 2013. The Kayenta Diaspora and Salado Meta-identity in the Late Precontact U.S. Southwest. In *The Archaeology of Hybrid Material Culture*, edited by Jeb J. Card, pp. 399–424. Occasional Paper No. 39. Center for Archaeological Investigations, Southern Illinois University, Carbondale.

Cosgrove, H. S., and C. B. Cosgrove. 1932. *The Swarts Ruin: A Typical Mimbres Site in Southwestern New Mexico*. Papers of the Peabody Museum of American Archaeology and Ethnology Vol. 15(1). Harvard University, Cambridge, Massachusetts.

Creel, Darrell. 2006a. Excavations at the Old Town Ruin, Luna County, New Mexico, 1989–2003. U.S. Bureau of Land Management, New Mexico State Office, Santa Fe.

————. 2006b. Social Differentiation at the Old Town Site. In *Mimbres Society*, edited by Valli S. Powell-Martí and Patricia A. Gilman, pp. 32–44. University of Arizona Press, Tucson.

Creel, Darrell, and Roger Anyon. 2003. New Interpretations of Mimbres Public Architecture and Space: Implications for Cultural Change. *American Antiquity* 68:67–92.

Creel, Darrell, Roger Anyon, and Barbara Roth. 2015. Ritual Construction, Use and Retirement of Mimbres Three Circle Phase Great Kivas. *Kiva* 81:201–219.

Creel, Darrell, and Harry J. Shafer. 2015. Mimbres Great Kivas and Plazas During the Three Circle Phase, ca. AD 850–1000. *Kiva* 81:164–178.

Crown, Patricia L. 1994. *Ceramics and Ideology: Salado Polychrome Pottery*. University of New Mexico Press, Albuquerque.

Dean, Jeffrey S. (editor). 2000. *Salado*. University of New Mexico Press, Albuquerque.

Diehl, Michael W., and Steven A. LeBlanc. 2001. *Early Pithouse Villages of the Mimbres Valley and Beyond: The McAnally and Thompson Sites in their Cultural and Ecological Contexts*. Papers of the Peabody Museum of Archaeology and Ethnology Vol. 83. Harvard University, Cambridge, Massachusetts.

Fewkes, J. Walter. 1914. *Archaeology of the Lower Mimbres Valley, New Mexico*. Smithsonian Miscellaneous Collections Vol. 63(10). Smithsonian Institution, Washington, D.C.

Fitting, James E. 1973. An Early Mogollon Community: A Preliminary Report on the Winn Canyon Site. *Artifact* 11(1–2):1–94.

Gilman, Patricia A., and Steven A. LeBlanc. 2017. *Mimbres Life and Society: The Mattocks Site of Southwestern New Mexico*. University of Arizona Press, Tucson.

Gilman, Patricia A., Marc Thompson, and Kristina C. Wyckoff. 2014. Ritual Change and the Distant: Mesoamerican Iconography, Scarlet Macaws, and Great Kivas in the Mimbres Region of Southwestern New Mexico. *American Antiquity* 79:90–107.

Haury, Emil W. 1936a. *The Mogollon Culture of Southwestern New Mexico*. Medallion Papers No. 20. Gila Pueblo, Globe, Arizona.

————. 1936b. *Some Southwestern Pottery Types, Series IV*. Medallion Papers No. 19. Gila Pueblo, Globe, Arizona.

Hegmon, Michelle, Margaret C. Nelson, Roger Anyon, Darrell Creel, Steven A. LeBlanc, and Harry J. Shafer. 1999. Scale and Time-Space Systematics in the Post–A.D. 1100 Mimbres Region of the North American Southwest. *Kiva* 65:143–166.

LeBlanc, Steven, and Ben Nelson. 1976. The Salado in Southwestern New Mexico. *Kiva* 42:71–79.

Lucas, Jason. 2007. Three Circle Phase Architectural Variability Among the Mimbres-Mogollon. In *Exploring Variability in Mogollon Pithouses*, edited by Barbara J. Roth and Robert Stokes, pp. 71–80. Arizona State University Anthropological Research Papers No. 58. Arizona State University, Tempe.

Minnis, Paul. 1985. *Social Adaptation to Food Stress: A Prehistoric Southwestern Example*. University of Chicago Press, Chicago.

Nelson, Margaret C. 1999. *Mimbres During the Twelfth Century: Abandonment, Continuity, and Reorganization*. University of Arizona Press, Tucson.

Nesbitt, Paul. 1931. *The Ancient Mimbreños: Based on Investigations at the Mattocks Ruin, Mimbres Valley, New Mexico*. Logan Museum, Beloit College, Beloit, Wisconsin.

O'Laughlin, Thomas C. 1980. *The Keystone Dam Site and Other Archaic and Formative Sites in Northwest El Paso, Texas*. Publications in Anthropology No. 8. El Paso Centennial Museum, University of Texas, El Paso.

Roth, Barbara J. 2010. *Archaeological Investigations at La Gila Encantada (LA 113467), Grant County, New Mexico*. Report submitted to the Archaeological Conservancy, Southwest Division, Albuquerque, New Mexico.

———. 2015. *Archaeological Investigations at the Harris Site, LA 1867, Grant County, Southwestern New Mexico*. Report on file, Department of Anthropology, University of Nevada, Las Vegas.

———. 2016. *Agricultural Beginnings in the American Southwest*. Rowman and Littlefield, Lantham, Maryland.

Roth, Barbara J., and Kathryn M. Baustian. 2015. Kin Groups and Social Power at the Harris Site, Southwestern New Mexico. *American Antiquity* 80:1–22.

Sedig, Jakob W. 2013. Recent Research at Woodrow Ruin. In *Collected Papers from the 17th Biennial Mogollon Archaeology Conference*, edited by Lonnie C. Ludeman, pp. 95–107. Friends of Mogollon Archaeology, Las Cruces, New Mexico.

———. 2015. The Mimbres Transitional Phase: Examining Social, Demographic, and Environmental Resilience and Vulnerability from A.D. 900–1000 in Southwest New Mexico. PhD dissertation, Department of Anthropology, University of Colorado, Boulder.

Sedig, Jakob W., and Stephen H. Lekson. 2012. *Archaeological Investigation of Woodrow Ruin (LA 2454), Grant County, New Mexico, June 6th–June 11th, 2011*. Report submitted to the New Mexico Cultural Properties Review Committee, Santa Fe.

Shafer, Harry J. 1995. Architecture and Symbolism in Transitional Pueblo Development in the Mimbres Valley, SW New Mexico. *Journal of Field Archaeology* 22:23–47.

———. 2003. *Mimbres Archaeology at the NAN Ranch Ruin*. University of New Mexico Press, Albuquerque.

———. 2006. Extended Families to Corporate Groups: Pithouse to Pueblo Transformation of Mimbres Society. In *Mimbres Society*, edited by Valli S. Powell-Martí and Patricia A. Gilman, pp. 15–31. University of Arizona Press, Tucson.

Shafer, Harry J., and Robbie L. Brewington. 1995. Microstylistic Changes in Mimbres Black-on-white Pottery: Examples from the NAN Ruin, Grant County, New Mexico. *Kiva* 61:5–29.

Stokes, Robert J. 2003. Aspects of Land Tenure in an Ancient Southwestern Farming Society in the Mimbres Valley, New Mexico. PhD Dissertation, Department of Anthropology, University of Oklahoma, Norman. UMI Dissertation Services, Ann Arbor, Michigan.

Stokes, Robert J., and Barbara J. Roth. 1999. Mobility, Sedentism, and Settlement Patterns in Transition: The Late Pithouse Period in the Sapillo Valley, New Mexico. *Journal of Field Archaeology* 26:423–434.

Swanson, Steve, Roger Anyon, and Margaret C. Nelson. 2012. Southern Mogollon Pithouse Period Settlement Dynamics, Land Use, and Community Development, A.D. 200–1000. In *Southwestern Pithouse Communities, A.D. 200–900*, edited by Lisa C. Young and Sarah A. Herr, pp. 95–109. University of Arizona Press, Tucson.

Wallace, Laurel T. 1998. *The Ormand Village: Final Report on the 1965–1966 Excavations*. Archaeology Notes No. 229. Office of Archaeological Studies, Museum of New Mexico, Santa Fe.

1

First Farmers of the Mimbres Region

CHRISTOPHER A. TURNBOW, JOHN R. RONEY,
AND ROBERT J. HARD

IN THE DECADES SINCE the Archaic syntheses conducted by Minnis (1980) and Lekson (1992), archaeologists have generated important new data on preceramic farming societies in the Mimbres region, centered on the Mimbres and upper Gila River drainages of southwestern New Mexico (figure 1.1). Research now challenges the old paradigm that Archaic populations continued a seasonally mobile hunting and foraging lifestyle until around A.D. 200 (Anyon and LeBlanc 1984; LeBlanc 1983; Minnis 1980). Instead, the introduction and intensification of maize farming among these groups led, at least at times, to reduced mobility, new technologies, and profound transformations to their social structure.

This chapter examines the accumulating archaeological evidence for preceramic farmers in the Mimbres region during the late Middle Archaic and Late Archaic periods and considers how farming influenced the cultural fabric of these populations. We use the term *Early Agricultural*, as defined by Huckell (1996), to classify these groups. We argue that early farming began in the region by at least 2000 B.C. and that some populations may have reached the tipping point from incipient to more intensive farming at least a millennium before the Early Pithouse period.

Early Agricultural Research in the Mimbres Region

Early Agricultural period populations in the Mimbres region left behind a rich cultural landscape that reflects their changing land-use patterns and social organization in response to food production. Yet the period has received scant attention compared

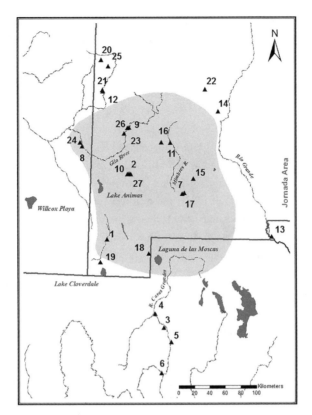

FIGURE 1.1 Archaic sites discussed in this chapter: 1. Animas Cienega, 2. Beargrass, 3. Cerro El Canelo, 4. Cerro Juanaqueña, 5. Cerro Los Torres, 6. Cerro Vidal, 7. Duke, 8. Duncan Donut, 9. Eaton, 10. Forest Home, 11. Harris, 12. HO-Bar (WS-17), 13. Keystone Dam, 14. LA 53488, 15. LA 75993, 16. LA 107539, 17. LA 159879, 18. LA 162023, 19. Lake Cloverdale, 20. Luna sites, 21. Mogollon village, 22. Monticello Canyon and Victorio Arroyo, 23. Ormand, 24. Round Mountain, 25. SU, 26. Winn Canyon, 27. Wood Canyon. The shading is the Mimbres core area as used in this chapter.

with archaeological investigations in the adjacent Jornada (Miller 2018) and southeast Arizona (Mabry 2005a) regions.

Research in the Mimbres region from the 1930s to the 1950s focused on establishing culture histories of the ceramic periods but did report on aceramic bell-shaped storage pits, middens, and artifacts that would later be recognized as associated with the Archaic and Early Agricultural periods (Cosgrove 1947; Haury 1936; Martin et al. 1949). The development of the three-stage Cochise Complex in nearby southeastern Arizona offered a temporal framework to examine changes in forager populations, but Archaic maize farming was not confirmed until the 1940s and 1950s with excavations and later reanalyses of stratified deposits at Bat Cave and other sites in the Mogollon Highlands north of the Mimbres region (Dick 1965; Martin et al. 1952; Wills 1988a, 1988b, 1989).

The advent of cultural resource management projects and increased university research led to the excavation of more Archaic components in the Mimbres region in the 1960s and 1970s. Early highway salvage excavations revealed Archaic deposits at Gila Hot Spring, reported at the time as a Cochise San Pedro phase camp (Honea 1963), and at Ormand, a Salado phase village overlying eleven purportedly aceramic pit structures (Hammack et al. 1966; Wallace 1998). Fitting of Case Western Reserve University conducted research on the transition from the Archaic to the Early Pit-house period in the Gila River drainage. His excavations targeted the Eaton site, a Late Archaic settlement (Hemphill 1983), and nearby Winn Canyon, an Early Pithouse site that also produced a possible Late Archaic structure (Fitting 1973). Collectively, these projects were plagued by a lack of time, money, or methods to systematically recover botanical remains. Although the sites may contain cultigens, few, if any, archaeobotanical samples were collected, and the presence of maize at these Archaic components remains unconfirmed.

Since the 1980s, detection of preceramic farming sites has greatly benefited from new technologies for the extraction, identification, and interpretation of plant remains and the direct accelerator mass spectrometry (AMS) dating of maize. With these new tools, research-driven excavations began to generate a wealth of new data on the Early Agricultural period in the Mimbres region. Investigations by universities and foundations specifically targeted Archaic midden sites in the Bootheel of New Mexico (Roney et al. 2012) and the Black Range (Laumbach 2013, 2014, 2015), as well as *cerros de trincheras* sites along the Gila River (Roney et al. 2015) and on the southern border of the Mimbres region (Hard and Roney 1998, 1999, 2005). University excavations at later Pithouse period sites have also revealed late Middle Archaic and Late Archaic components at WS-17, also known as the HO-Bar site (Neely and Brunnemann 1988; Peck 1991); Mogollon village (Linse 1997; Mauldin et al. 1996); and SU (Wills 1988a, 1989). Cultural resource management projects have documented Archaic occupations across diverse geographic settings and have conducted large-scale excavation and analysis of Archaic components that would not otherwise have been studied (Brown 1998; Chapman et al. 1985; Duran and Manning 1993; Jones et al. 2012; Kirkpatrick 2016; Kugler 1994; Kurota and Cohen 2009; Lentz et al. 2013; Oakes and Zamora 1999; Turnbow et al. 2000).

Chronology

Despite increased research on the Early Agricultural period, tight chronological frameworks for these first farmers have yet to be established for the Mimbres region.

Of the 547 Archaic sites currently listed from southwestern New Mexico in the New Mexico Archaeological Records Management System, only 43 have received even limited excavation, and fewer have botanical studies. Deeply stratified alluvial and rock-shelter sites suitable for chronology building are rare, and a paltry 134 radiocarbon determinations exist for the entire Archaic sequence. This stands in sharp contrast to the 3,295 radiocarbon dates from Archaic and Early Formative sites in the Jornada region or the numerous extensively excavated sites in the Tucson Basin. As a consequence, archaeologists have simply assigned Early Agricultural components to the Middle and Late Archaic periods based on diagnostic projectile-point types and radiocarbon dates or have borrowed phase-based temporal sequences defined in southeastern Arizona (Mabry 2005a; Sayles 1983; Sayles and Antevs 1941) and south-central New Mexico (Lehmer 1948; MacNeish and Beckett 1987; Miller 2018; see table 1.1 for a comparison of Mimbres, Jornada, and southeastern Arizona chronologies).

Indeed, the southeastern Arizona Late Archaic San Pedro and Cienega phases are applicable in the western Mimbres region of the Gila River drainage and the Bootheel area, while the material culture and settlement patterns from the southeastern portion of the Mimbres region closely parallel the Jornada Archaic phase sequence. Unfortunately, given the paucity of Early Agricultural period research over most of the Mimbres region, it is difficult to correlate either sequence through much of the Mimbres basin country or the mountainous area to the north.

Given these problems, the Early Agricultural period discussed in this chapter is divided into three broad temporal horizons that are roughly contemporaneous with the defined phases to the east and west. The periods include the introduction of maize during the late Middle Archaic (2000–1300 B.C.), the rise of incipient farming during the early Late Archaic (1300–800 B.C.), and intensified farming during the late Late Archaic (800 B.C.–A.D. 150/175), ending with the general appearance of large well-made cooking and storage ceramic vessels. Unless otherwise noted, all specific site dates cited in this chapter are calibrated using InCal13 and presented as two-sigma ranges or the calibrated intercept.

Late Middle Archaic Period (2000–1300 B.C.)

Over much of the southern Southwest, the Middle Holocene interval between 5500 and 2500 B.C. witnessed heightened aridity associated with greater temperatures and less effective precipitation than at present (Mabry and Stevens 2014). For the Mimbres region, those harsh conditions may have supported only sparse populations that left very few archaeological components. Greater effective moisture and lower temperatures during the ensuing interval of 2000 B.C. to B.C./A.D., however, caused populations to be drawn to the reliable water and rich biotic resources around ciénegas, floodplains, and other alluvial settings. It was during this period that Doolittle

TABLE 1.1 Early Agricultural Chronology of the Southern Southwest United States

		Jornada Mogollon	Mimbres	Southeastern Arizona
	Late Holocene (2500 B.C.–present)			
	A.D. 300			
	A.D. 200			
	A.D. 100	Hueco		
	A.D./B.C.			
	100 B.C.			
	200 B.C.			
	300 B.C.		late Late Archaic	
	400 B.C.			Cienega
	500 B.C.	Arenal		
	600 B.C.			
	700 B.C.			
	800 B.C.			
Late Archaic	900 B.C.			
	1000 B.C.			
	1100 B.C.	Fresnal	early Late Archaic	San Pedro
	1200 B.C.			
	1300 B.C.			
	1400 B.C.			
	1500 B.C.			
	1600 B.C.		late Middle Archaic	
	1700 B.C.			Unnamed
	1800 B.C.			
	1900 B.C.			
	2000 B.C.	Keystone		
Middle Archaic	2100 B.C.			
	2200 B.C.			
	2300 B.C.			
	2400 B.C.			
	2500 B.C.			
	Middle Holocene (5500–2500 B.C.)			

Source: Miller 2018 (Jornada); Mabry 2005a (southeastern Arizona)

and Mabry (2006) have suggested conditions allowed the Middle Archaic foragers to reduce mobility and possibly begin cultivating native plants and cultigens in an incipient form of farming.

The earliest evidence of maize in the North American Southwest occurs around 2600 to 2200 B.C. in the Arizona desert, the Mogollon Highlands, and the Colorado Plateau (Gregory 1999, 2001; Huber 2005; Huckell 2006; Mabry 2005a; Merrill et al. 2009). Initially, people simply incorporated maize into the existing subsistence-settlement system and farmed on floodplains and alluvial fans using flood and water-table farming practices (Mabry 2005b; Wills 1988b). Pepo squash was added sometime prior to 1200 B.C. (Merrill et al. 2009).

Occupations between 2200 and 1200 B.C. in southeastern Arizona (Mabry 2005a) and the contemporaneous Keystone phase (2500–1200 B.C.) in the Jornada region (Miller 2018) developed during these more favorable climatic conditions. Both are marked by significant increases in sites and features and the appearance of the first village settlements. While the Arizona sites showed evidence of incipient farming, poor preservation of plant remains at the Keystone phase site near El Paso, Texas, limited their value for assessing farming activities. Currently, evidence for farming comes from just a single feature from Keystone 33, where maize pollen was associated with a date of 2085 to 1895 B.C.

Contemporaneous occupations in the Mimbres region are only vaguely known, primarily recognized by Middle Archaic San Jose/Pinto, Gypsum contracting stem, and Cortaro dart points. Site numbers do dramatically increase over the preceding Early Archaic components with concentrations in the vicinity of lake shorelines (Formby 1986:102; Roney et al. 2012; Turnbow et al. 2008). These sites vary in size but have produced grinding implements, diagnostic dart points, and cutting and scraping tools. One of the largest sites, located along Lake Cloverdale, was a likely base camp strategically situated next to a fertile alluvial fan suitable for early farming endeavors (Turnbow et al. 2008).

The earliest dated maize in the Mimbres region came only a few centuries after its initial appearance in the Southwest. Laumbach (2013, 2014) reported direct AMS dates of 1925 and 1973 B.C. on maize recovered during test excavations near the Montoya site (LA 88891), located on Cañada Alamosa in the Black Range (table 1.2). Maize production in this well-watered tributary of the Rio Grande is probably not an isolated occurrence. Unfortunately, few Middle Archaic sites have been excavated, and besides the Montoya dates, only ten radiocarbon determinations from four sites fall between 2200 and 1300 B.C. Cerro Juanaqueña, located on the southwestern edge of the Mimbres region in northern Chihuahua, had six AMS dates on maize with intercept dates in the decades before 1300 B.C. (to be discussed in more detail) and another date on a *Cucurbita* seed of 1745 to 1450 B.C. The HO-Bar site (WS-17)

TABLE 1.2 Pre-ceramic Radiocarbon Dates on Maize or Maize Contexts from the Mimbres Region

Site Name/Number	[14]C Age[a]	Cal B.C./A.D. Range[b]	Number of Dates	References
Beargrass	1840±50	A.D. 60–330	1	Turnbow et al. 2000
Wood Canyon (late)	2000±60	170 B.C.–A.D. 125	1	Turnbow et al. 2000
Cerro Vidal	2100±40	345 B.C.–A.D. 0	1	Hard and Roney 1999
Harris	2170±30	360–120 B.C.	1	Roth 2015
Duncan Donut	2150±30	360–60 B.C.	1	Roney et al. 2015
Cerro Juanaqueña	2140±40 to 2315±60	360–180 B.C.	3	Hard et al. 2001
Forest Home	2270±40 to 2240±50	390–210 B.C.	3	Turnbow et al. 2000
Duke	2330±40	540–230 B.C.	1	Kirkpatrick 2016
Alamosa Canyon	not available	740–440 B.C.	1	Laumbach 2015
Cerro Vidal	2340±55	745–210 B.C.	1	Hard et al. 2001
SU	2290±110	760–90 B.C.	1	Wills 1989
LA 159879	2460±30	760–430 B.C.	1	Lentz et al. 2013
LA 53488[c]	2360±80	770–210 B.C.	1	Kugler 1994
Wood Canyon (early)	2650±50 to 2480±40	805–770 B.C.	3	Turnbow et al. 2000
Cerro Los Torres	2920±55	1275–935 B.C.	1	Hard and Roney 1999
Cerro Juanaqueña	2870±50 to 3080±70	1280–1130 B.C.	13	Hard et al. 2001
Animas Cienega[c]	3030±80	1450–1030 B.C.	1	Davis et al. 2002
Cerro Juanaqueña	3130±55	1540–1255 B.C.	1	Hard et al. 2001
Montoya	3610±30	2110–1890 B.C.	2	Laumbach 2013, 2014
	3640±30	2135–1920 B.C.		

[a]Conventional ^{14}C age B.P. If multiple dates were available, both upper and lower bounding maize dates are given.
[b]Two-sigma calibrated dates using OxCal 4.2.
[c]Dated deposits containing maize.

yielded a single date from this period with such large standard errors that its signifi-cance is questioned (Neely and Brunnemann 1988). Two other dates were obtained from short-term camps characterized by a few extramural roasting and fire pits (Oakes and Zamora 1999). These two components produced no evidence of cultigens, large storage pits, or associated structural remains.

Early Late Archaic Period (1300–800 B.C.)

Beginning around 1300 B.C., both the San Pedro phase (1200–800 B.C.) of south-eastern Arizona (Huckell 1996; Mabry 2005a) and the Fresnal phase (1300–700 B.C.) of the Jornada region (Miller 2018) were characterized by the expansion of settlements and an increased use of maize. Miller, however, considers maize farming only a minor component in the Fresnal phase economy, and Diehl (2005) refers to the San Pedro populations as "farmagers" since a greater portion of their subsistence base was still derived from foraging.

The use of the term *San Pedro phase* seems applicable across the western half of the Mimbres region. Miller (2018:138) also contends that "similarities in the timing of broad-scale subsistence trends and technological traits suggest the Jornada could be considered an eastern correlate and variant of the San Pedro phase and Early Agricul-tural period of the southern Southwest." San Pedro settlements exhibit middens with an abundance of fire-cracked rock and artifacts, shallow oval pit structures, hearths and large bell-shaped storage pits, burials, San Pedro projectile points, and, at least in southeastern Arizona, ceramic figurines and the first appearance of incipient ceramic wares (Heidke et al. 1998; Huckell 1996; Roth 2014).

In the Mimbres region, this period is best recognized by an abundance of San Pedro points in both camps and larger midden sites, but excavations are rare and we currently have little evidence of farming. Only sixteen radiocarbon determinations from six sites date to this period. Three components are camps containing roasting and fire pits (Jones et al. 2012; Oakes and Zamora 1999). Three other thick aceramic middens that appear to have their origins during this period include LA 53488, situated along the Cuchillo Negro Creek in the Black Range (Kugler 1994); LA 162023, located in the Bootheel just west of Laguna de las Moscas (Roney et al. 2012); and LA 159879, along the Mimbres River near Deming. While the first two are primarily known from exploratory excavations, more intensive highway excavations at LA 159879 produced three separate Late Archaic components, including two dating between 1000 and 800 B.C. that revealed shallow pit structures and thermal features. The midden sites are located adjacent to reliable water and arable land. Even so, no evidence of maize production, large storage pits, or incipient ceramics has yet been identified, although LA 159879 produced cotton pollen in deposits dating between 835 and 795 B.C. (Lentz et al. 2013).

However, indirect evidence of maize farming does occur at the Animas Creek ciénega in the southwesternmost corner of New Mexico. Core samples from the ciénega revealed maize pollen associated with a radiocarbon determination of 1270 B.C. (Davis et al. 2002). Although the relationship between the pollen and the date is tenuous at best, it suggests that farming may have been practiced along Animas Creek at this time.

Much stronger evidence of farming has emerged from the cerros de trincheras sites located only 65 km southwest of Animas Creek in northern Chihuahua (Hard et al. 2008; Hard and Roney 1998, 2005, 2007; Hard et al. 2001; Roney and Hard 2002, 2003, 2004). This distinctive site type is characterized by complexes of hill terraces, rock rings, and stone walls. Cerro Juanaqueña and three other cerros de trincheras sites in northern Mexico were occupied over two brief episodes during the Early Agricultural period. The earlier and most intensive lasted for approximately two hundred years from 1300 to 1100 B.C. Hard and Roney (1998, 2007) postulate that farming populations had existed in the adjacent fertile valleys until around 1300 B.C., when the settlements shifted to hilltop locations.

Cerro Juanaqueña, the largest known example of this site type, is a 10 ha aggregated settlement with 99 rock rings and 550 terraces representing almost 8 km of wall. Mostly constructed on the upper third of the hillslope, the rock rings are interpreted as dwellings with circular or oval configurations and a mean diameter of 2.63 m.

Although faunal and wild plant resources were important subsistence resources, maize was a significant dietary staple at Cerro Juanaqueña. It occurred in 51 percent of the flotation samples, including sterile samples ($N = 157$). Cheno-am was the next most frequent charred taxon, including both nondomesticated *Chenopodium* and possibly domesticated amaranth (Hard et al. 2008; Hard and Roney 2005). Some rock rings on the summits of these hills may have been footings for aboveground storage facilities.

Construction of these cerros de trincheras sites implies a degree of sedentism, community organization and planning, and a large population. Hard and his colleagues (1999) suggest that thirty person-years of labor was needed to construct Cerro Juanaqueña, and life on these hilltops, some rising to 150 m above the surrounding landscape, required considerable caloric expenditures to support the occupations. Based on a worldwide cross-cultural study of forty-two ethnographic groups, as well as other arguments, Hard and Roney (2007) conclude that this commitment was almost certainly motivated by concerns about raiding and warfare (also see McGuire and Villalpando 2015).

Late Late Archaic Period (800 B.C.–A.D. 150/175)

The last Early Agricultural occupations in the Mimbres region are characterized by a significant increase in more sedentary residential settlements and the widespread presence of maize (see table 1.2). When excavated, these settlements have shallow oval or circular pit structures, roasting and fire pits, large-capacity storage pits, and burials. Supported by a mixed farming, gathering, and hunting economy, these communities were established near well-watered, arable lands in mountain highlands, river valleys, and desert basins. Collectively, they reflect reduced mobility; increased labor investments for the construction of large storage pits, structures, and mortuary facilities; and fundamental changes in social organization and technology that in part reflect the intensification of maize in the diet.

The current sample of seventy-six radiocarbon determinations for this period is derived from thirty sites. Of those, fifty-six dates are from nineteen middens that could represent residential farming sites and repeatedly occupied logistical procurement camps. The remainder are from seven small camps with roasting or fire pits and three brief camps with ephemeral structures.

In terms of cultural traits, sites on the western half of the Mimbres region easily fall into the Cienega phase (800 B.C.–A.D. 50) as defined by Huckell (1995) and Mabry (2005a). Tool assemblages include Cienega and San Pedro dart points, oval or circular one-hand manos, basin-shaped metates, and rare cruciforms and ground-stone vessels (bowls, trays, mortars) like those identified on Cienega phase sites in southeastern Arizona and northern Sonora (Ferg 1998; Hemphill 1983; Huckell 1995; Huckell et al. 1995; Knight 2003; Mabry 1998; Turnbow et al. 2000; Wallace 1998).

Phase affiliations for the rest of the Mimbres region are less clear, although components in the southeastern area may fit into the Jornada Arenal (700–200 B.C.) and Hueco (200 B.C.–A.D. 300/500) phases defined by Miller (2018) and earlier researchers (Lehmer 1948; MacNeish 1993; MacNeish and Beckett 1987). Miller (2018:133) has described the Arenal phase as "distinctly non-agricultural" with a marked reduction in the evidence of maize, a decline in radiocarbon dates and plant-baking pits, and a shift in settlements to playa basins. By 200 B.C., however, Miller contends that southeastern Arizona and the Jornada were similar in terms of the use of maize, the expansion and intensification of settlements, and population growth.

SETTLEMENTS While it may be premature to discuss population demographics for this period, intensive midden-forming occupations are more common than during the previous period (table 1.3). They appear to be particularly concentrated in the Gila River drainage (Duncan et al. 1991; Fitting 1973; Hammack et al. 1966; Hemphill 1983; Lekson 1992; Linse 1997; Mauldin et al. 1996; Roney et al. 2015; Wallace 1998; Wills 1988a, 1995). Although not excavated or dated, eighteen purportedly aceramic pithouse sites documented during a survey of Gila River tributaries also suggest increased residential densities (Chapman et al. 1985). Nearby in the Big Burro Mountains, four farming settlements of this period were discovered during excavations along a 9 km highway improvement project (Turnbow et al. 2000). Other midden sites have been excavated in the Mimbres Valley (Brown 1998; Kirkpatrick 2016; Lentz et al. 2013), along tributaries of the Rio Grande in the Black Range (Kugler 1994; Laumbach 2015), along Cooks Canyon at the base of Cooks Peak (Duran and Manning 1993), and in the Bootheel in the southwestern corner of New Mexico (Kurota and Cohen 2009; Roney et al. 2012).

Excavations of these middens, when combined with robust archaeobotanical sampling and budgets, often reveal evidence of at least semisedentary residential occupations with maize, community planning, and increased labor investments for the construction of structures, storage facilities, and burials. Among the more fully excavated farming settlements of this period are the Forest Home and Wood Canyon sites in the Big Burro Mountains, the latter containing spatially discrete components. These settlements had small pit structures surrounded by large extramural bell-shaped or cylindrical storage pits and ground-stone caches, all associated with thick (0.3–0.6 m) cultural deposits and dense concentrations of burned rock and artifacts (Turnbow et al. 2000). Burials were either interred in recycled storage pits or in more elaborate facilities near the edge of the components. Hearths and small roasting pits were more widely scattered. Based on direct AMS dates of annual seeds, including maize, the settlements date from around 805 B.C. to probably no later than A.D. 200 (see table 1.2).

Intensified farming implies reduced mobility and increasingly complex land-tenure systems and territories. Control over prime farmland and stored foods, as well as changing natural conditions (climate, food resources) and social factors (sociocultural values, political ideology, population trends), likely led to increased tension and hostilities in the Mimbres region. This may be the case for the construction or reoccupation of cerros de trincheras sites in northwestern Chihuahua and the Gila River drainage between 500 and 150 B.C. (Hard and Roney 2007; Roney et al. 2015). If such sites were defensive in origin as proposed by Hard and Roney (2007), then cerros de trincheras sites like Round Mountain (Roney et al. 2015) and possibly Canador (Roney 1999) and Gomez Peak, all in the western Mimbres region, were probably built in response to persistent threats of raiding or attempts to drive populations from developed agricultural lands.

Not all thick midden sites are interpreted as farming settlements. LA 107539, located in the Mimbres River drainage, contained stratified components dating to this period with no indication of cultigens, structures, or storage pits (Brown 1998). Resinous substances found in a roasting pit and midden may have derived from processing agave or other succulents. In the absence of cultigens, the site was interpreted as a seasonal base camp related to wild resource procurement. Similarly, LA 159888 and LA 162023, both located in the Bootheel area, exhibit thick middens located adjacent to playa basins and fertile soils but have not yet produced maize or other cultigens.

Current interpretations suggest that these middens accumulated from repeated occupations that exploited the area's rich environmental zones.

ARCHITECTURE Residential architecture of this period is characterized by shallow circular or, less commonly, oval pits similar to contemporary structures identified elsewhere in the Southwest (Hemphill 1983; Lentz et al. 2013; Turnbow et al. 2000; Wills 1988a; Woosley and McIntyre 1996). Ranging up to 3.2 m in diameter, they varied from 6 to 12 m² in floor space and around 15 to 50 cm in depth. In some cases, small peripheral posts encircled the pits, and internal posts suggest roof support. Intramural hearths were either simple basin-shaped pits or informal surface facilities. Given their size, the structures could accommodate only a small nucleated family or household, and the relative absence of floor artifacts indicates that most domestic activities were performed outside or in other structures. According to pithouse attributes examined by Diehl (1997), these structures score rather low for architectural investment and residential commitment but were better constructed than the brush shelters found on more temporary camps.

Although poorly dated, purported Archaic structures at the Winn Canyon, Wind Mountain, and Ormand sites are slightly larger and deeper than most Early Agricultural structures, and Ormand Village has a confusing array of characteristics (i.e., deep vertical walls, clay or plaster floors, adobe-lined hearths, and, in one case, a short ramped entrance) more reminiscent of Early Pithouse dwellings. The structures at Winn Canyon and Wind Mountain had one radiocarbon date each that fell into the Early Agricultural temporal span. At Ormand, Hammack and his colleagues (1966) assumed that the eleven pit structures underlying a Salado village dated to the Archaic period given the lack of pottery on their floors (Wallace 1998). Of additional interest, surveys near the Ormand and Winn Canyon sites found eighteen other sites with one to twelve aceramic pithouse depressions ranging from 3 to 10 m in diameter (Chapman et al. 1985). If these structures are indeed Early Agricultural in age, then they probably fall late in the transition to the Early Pithouse period, perhaps around A.D. 100 to 150.

MORTUARY AND RITUAL BEHAVIOR Thus far, the earliest firmly dated human and animal burials in the Mimbres region occur within residential sites of this period (Duran and Manning 1993; Hemphill 1983; Kirkpatrick 2016; Turnbow et al. 2000). Although only eleven human burials have been confirmed, the construction of the graves, associated objects, and their placement within the settlements suggest mortuary and ritual behaviors related to family lineages, social memory, and a significance of place. All undisturbed burials were flexed, primary inhumations, except for one cremation from the Eaton site. Five were placed in recycled bell-shaped or cylindrical pits at the Wood Canyon, Duke, and Forest Home sites. At Wood Canyon, a bell-shaped pit contained the articulated remains of a tightly flexed adult and disarticulated elements of two subadults mixed throughout the fill with sixty-two shell disk beads and a bone tube. All three may have been interred at the same time, but it is also plausible that the pit was reopened for each burial. This scenario implies group knowledge of the original burial location and a kin-based desire to place those remains together.

Three more elaborate, labor-intensive mortuary facilities may signify some degree of social status within the communities. The Wood Canyon settlements constructed two facilities on the outer edge of the occupations (Turnbow et al. 2000). In one case, an adult male was buried in a simple oval pit covered by large rocks and metates that conforms to the milling-stone-cairn mortuary complex from southern Arizona (Mabry 1998). As such, it currently represents the only burial of this kind confirmed in the Mimbres region. Two other individuals, a child and an adult male, were buried in small oval pits dug into the sides of the largest nonstructural pit on the site. A metate was positioned over each burial. The large pit was then backfilled with midden refuse containing a complete Cienega point, a quartz crystal, and abundant deer remains that could all represent graveside rituals. Equally elaborate was a primary cremation from the Eaton site associated with a flat-cobble grinding slab covered in red hematite, two vesicular basalt oval bowls, two projectile points, and a burned tubular bead (Hemphill 1983).

Besides human interments, the articulated remains of a red-tailed hawk were unearthed close to three complete San Pedro and Cienega points in a bell-shaped storage pit at Wood Canyon. Its purposeful burial may indicate totemism or animism among these populations.

FOOD PRODUCTION Evidence for intensified food production during this period is supported by the more frequent and widespread occurrence of maize, squash, and other potential cultigens and large storage pits (see tables 1.2, 1.3). Thus far, twenty direct AMS dates have been derived from maize, and other dates have come from maize-bearing aceramic deposits. Where more robust macrobotanical, pollen, and phytolith sampling occurred, maize has often been ubiquitous, commonly occurring in structures, hearths, and storage pits. Even with poor botanical preservation, maize was found in half of the eighteen sampled early Wood Canyon features but in all of the structures and bell-shaped pits. Around 450 years later, the Forest Home component had 95 percent ubiquity ($n = 20$ of 21 sampled features). Likewise, maize pollen occurred in 50 percent ($n = 8$) of the samples from early Wood Canyon and 100 percent of those from Forest Home ($n = 6$) and late Wood Canyon ($n = 3$). A tobacco seed and squash pollen and phytoliths were also identified at Forest Home. These results indicate that unlike the Arenal phase (700–200 B.C.), which was described as distinctly nonagricultural, contemporary Early Agricultural populations in the Mimbres region likely had a greater reliance on farming.

Stable carbon isotope ratios in skeletal tissues provide another measure of maize consumption. Stable $^{12}C/^{13}C$ isotope analyses of human remains primarily from the Jornada region also included a burial recovered from Early Agricultural deposits at LA 75993 in the Mimbres region northeast of Deming (Duran and Manning 1993). The study concluded that this individual, buried in midden deposits dating between 560 and 175 B.C., was consuming maize in quantities similar to later El Paso phase pueblo populations further east. At the time, Duran and Manning (1993) questioned whether the skeletal remains were in fact associated with the dated deposits. However, in light of present evidence, these data lend support to the idea of greater maize dependency during the Early Agricultural period.

STORAGE FACILITIES Farming may have generated enough surplus food to account for the increased size and number of storage pits after 800 B.C. Large bell-shaped and cylindrical storage pits were identified at the early and late Wood Canyon components, Forest Home, Duke, SU, and Eaton and, although undated, in aceramic contexts at Mogollon village (Haury 1936) and the Ormand site (Wallace 1998). Most occurred in extramural contexts, although Forest Home, Eaton, and Ormand also revealed storage pits in the floors of pit structures.

Bell-shaped pits at the early Wood Canyon component were similar in size to those from Duke, Mogollon village, and Ormand; had a mean volume of 1364 L; and consistently contained maize remains. Huckell and colleagues (1995) developed a formula to estimate the storage capacity of bell-shaped pits based on Early Agricultural cob size. Using their assumptions, a pit of this size could hold 16,647 ears of maize.

Conclusions

In their study of the Mimbres Early Pithouse period, Diehl and LeBlanc (2001:4) noted that the "preceramic occupation of the Mimbres area is poorly documented and in fact so little evidence is available that a discussion of the preceramic occupations of the Mimbres Valley is not warranted." Considering those data gaps, we have synthesized the current knowledge of preceramic farming populations in the Mimbres region and concluded that those groups followed the same general pattern of Early Agricultural food production reported elsewhere in the American Southwest. For centuries following its introduction by 2000 B.C., maize farming probably had only a minor impact on Archaic hunter-gatherers who spent most of the year in small residentially mobile groups. Following 1300 B.C., more aggregated settlements and major

TABLE 1.3 Major Early Agricultural Midden and Residential Sites in the Mimbres Region

	2-Sigma ^{14}C	Midden	Maize	Structures	Large Storage Pits	Burials	References
Gila River Area							
Beargrass	A.D. 70–215	x	x	x			Turnbow et al. 2000
Wood Canyon (late)	A.D. 30–220	x	x	x	x	x	Turnbow et al. 2000
Ormand	no date	x		x	x	x	Hammack et al. 1966; Wallace 1998
WS 17	95 B.C.–A.D.135	x		x			Peck 1991
Duncan Donut	360–60 B.C.	x	x	x			Roney et al. 2012
Forest Home	390–210 B.C.	x	x	x	x	x	Turnbow et al. 2000
Round Mountain	510–395 B.C.			x			Roney et al. 2012
Eaton	540–205 B.C.	x		x	x	x	Hemphill 1983
Wind Mountain	730 B.C.–A.D. 130			x			Woosley and McIntire 1996
SU	760–90 B.C.	x	x	x	x		Wills 1989
Winn Canyon	805 B.C.–A.D. 65	x		x			Fitting 1973
Wood Canyon (early)	805–770 B.C.	x	x	x	x	x	Turnbow et al. 2000
Mimbres River Drainage							
LA 107539	20 B.C.–A.D. 400	x					Brown 1998
Harris	360–115 B.C.		x				Roth 2015
Duke	540–230 B.C.	x	x		x	x	Kirkpatrick 2016
LA 159879	770–535 B.C.	x	x	x			Lentz et al. 2013

Site	Date					Reference
LA 159879	835–795 B.C.	x		x		Lentz et al. 2013
Duke	895–550 B.C.	x			x	Kirkpatrick 2016
LA 159879	975–840 B.C.	x		x		Lentz et al. 2013
LA 107539	830–545 B.C.	x				Brown et al. 1998
Black Range						
LA 53488	770–210 B.C.	x	x			Kugler 1994
Victorio Arroyo	740–440 B.C.	x	x			Laumbach 2015
LA 75993	750–175 B.C.	x			x	Duran and Manning 1993
LA 53488	1385–900 B.C.	x				Kugler 1994
Chihuahua						
Cerro Vidal	345–210 B.C.	x	x			Hard et al. 2001
Cerro Juanaqueña	360–180 B.C.	x	x			Hard et al. 2001
Cerro Juanaqueña	1280–1130 B.C.	x	x			Hard et al. 2001
Cerro Juanaqueña	1605–1415 B.C.	x	x			Hard et al. 2001
New Mexico Bootheel						
LA 159888	A.D. 1–130	x				Kurota and Cohen 2009
LA 159888	350–50 B.C.	x				Kurota and Cohen 2009
LA 162023	520–390 B.C.	x				Roney et al. 2015
LA 162023	920–810 B.C.	x				Roney et al. 2015

shifts in social organization are evidenced by the construction of sophisticated irrigation and field systems along the major watercourses of the southern basin and range
country, as well as the appearance of cerros de trincheras sites along the periphery of
the Mimbres in northwestern Chihuahua and the Tucson Basin. We think that these
changes reflect the first subsistence economies that were dependent upon agriculture.
However, in the Mimbres core area we have yet no strong evidence of similar shifts
until after 1000 B.C. and probably not until about 800 B.C., when a tipping point
occurred to more intensified farming.

With the onset of this intensified agriculture, farming settlements expanded across
much of the Mimbres region, situated along well-watered drainages suitable for farming in both upland and desert lowland settings. Increased food production and storage
capacities at these sites suggest farming was contributing a more significant portion
of the diet. Where sufficient data exist, we see that maize ubiquity was between 50
and 95 percent, comparable to the figures recorded for many Early Pithouse sites. It
is beyond this study to evaluate the differing opinions regarding Early Agricultural
or, for that matter, Early Pithouse dependence on food production, but the settlements do argue for fundamental changes in land use related to increased reliance on
farming.

While residential mobility likely decreased with intensified farming, the longevity
of any settlement was probably not more than a few years. Structures showed little,
if any, remodeling or subsequent refuse disposal by Early Agricultural inhabitants,
but the settlements survived long enough to produce dense middens, discreet ash
dumps, multiple burials, ground-stone caches, numerous roasting and other cooking
pits, and structures. Questions remain as to whether these farming sites were occupied
sporadically in a seasonal settlement cycle or whether populations were seasonally
sedentary over multiple seasons or, following Mabry's (1998) definition, sedentary
over the entire year with some portion of the population leaving for logistical procurement sites. Clearly, farming requires people to be present in the spring to pre-
pare and plant fields, in summer to reduce animal predation, and in fall to harvest,
consume, and store surpluses. Wild plant foods from these settlements also suggest
spring to fall occupations. Although not as deep, large, or as thermally insulated as
later pit structures, Early Agricultural dwellings in the farming settlements were better
constructed than those brush shelters typical of temporary camps, and the presence
of interior fire hearths could make them comfortable for cooler weather habitation.
Hunter-Anderson (1986), Whalen (1994), and Huckell et al. (2002) have proposed
that large-scale, on-site storage could support an overwintering strategy with groups
leaving in the spring after the stores had been consumed. On the other hand, ethnographic data from the Eastern Woodlands and Great Plains indicate that subterranean
storage pits were built primarily to conceal food surpluses from pillagers, particularly

during periods of village abandonment in the winter (DeBoer 1988). If that were the case, then Early Agricultural populations would have hidden their crops before leaving for winter hunts, returning in the lean spring season to subsist on their food stocks while preparing fields for planting.

Finally, people living in the Mimbres region seem to have continued a basically Early Agricultural period lifeway for another two hundred years after functional storage and cooking ceramics were introduced around A.D. 175. Diehl and LeBlanc (2001) noted this pattern for the Mimbres region as did Gilman (1995) for the San Simon branch to the west and Wills (1995) for the Reserve area to the northwest, so it may represent a region-wide pattern.

References Cited

Anyon, Roger, and Stephen A. LeBlanc. 1984. *The Galaz Ruin: A Prehistoric Mimbres Village in Southwestern New Mexico*. Maxwell Museum of Anthropology, University of New Mexico Press, Albuquerque.

Brown, Gary M. 1998. *Archeological Data Recovery in the Tailings Pond Enlargement Area at the Continental Mine, Grant County, New Mexico*. Western Cultural Resource Management, Farmington, New Mexico.

Chapman, Richard C., Cye W. Gossett, and William J. Gossett. 1985. *Class II Cultural Resources Survey, Upper Gila Water Supply Study, Central Arizona Project*. Deuel and Associates, Albuquerque, New Mexico. Report submitted to the Bureau of Reclamation, Phoenix, Arizona.

Cosgrove, C. B. 1947. *Caves of the Upper Gila and Hueco Areas in New Mexico*. Papers of the Peabody Museum of Archaeology and Ethnology Vol. 24(2). Harvard University, Cambridge, Massachusetts.

Davis, Owen K., Tom Minkley, Tom Moutouz, Tim Jull, and Bob Kalin. 2002. The Transformation of Sonoran Desert Wetlands Following the Historic Decrease in Burning. *Journal of Arid Environments* 50:393–412.

DeBoer, Warren. 1988. Subterranean Storage and the Organization of Surplus: The View from Eastern North America. *Southeastern Archaeology* 7(1):1–20.

Dick, Herbert W. 1965. *Bat Cave*. Monograph No. 27. School of American Research, Santa Fe, New Mexico.

Diehl, Michael W. 1997. Changes in Architecture and Land Use Strategies in the American Southwest: Upland Mogollon Pithouse Dwellers, AC 200–1000. *Journal of Field Archaeology* 24:179–194.

——— (editor). 2005. *Subsistence and Resource Use Strategies of Early Agricultural Communities in Southern Arizona*. Anthropological Papers No. 34. Center for Desert Archaeology, Tucson, Arizona.

Diehl, Michael W., and Steven A. LeBlanc. 2001. *Early Pithouse Villages of the Mimbres Valley and Beyond: The McAnally and Thompson Sites in their Cultural and Ecological Contexts.* Papers of the Peabody Museum of Archaeology and Ethnology Vol. 83. Harvard University, Cambridge, Massachusetts.

Doolittle, William E., and Jonathan B. Mabry. 2006. Environmental Mosaics, Agricultural Diversity, and the Evolutionary Adoption of Maize in the American Southwest. In *Histories of Maize: Multidisciplinary Approaches to the Prehistory, Linguistics, Biogeography, Domestication, and Evolution of Maize,* edited by John E. Staller, Robert H. Tykot, and Bruce F. Benz, pp. 109–121. Elsevier Academic Press, Boston.

Duncan, Marjorie, Patricia A. Gilman, and Raymond P. Mauldin. 1991. *Mogollon Village Archaeological Project, 1991: Preliminary Report.* Report submitted by the University of Oklahoma to the USDA Forest Service, Gila National Forest, Silver City, New Mexico.

Duran, Meliha S., and Maureen Manning. 1993. *Report on an Archaic Burial Recovered from Site LA 75993, Fort Cummings, Luna County, New Mexico.* Report No. HSR 8600. Human Systems Research, Tularosa, New Mexico.

Ferg, Alan. 1998. Rare Stone, Fired Clay, Bone and Shell Artifacts. In *Archaeological Investigations of Early Village Sites in the Middle Santa Cruz Valley,* edited by Jonathan B. Mabry, pp. 545–654. Anthropology Papers No. 19. Center for Desert Archaeology, Tucson, Arizona.

Fitting, James E. 1973. An Early Mogollon Community: A Preliminary Report on the Winn Canyon Site. *Artifact* 11(1–2).

Formby, Donald E. 1986. Pinto-Gypsum Complex Projectile Points from Arizona and New Mexico. *Kiva* 51:99–127.

Gilman, Patricia A. 1995. Multiple Dimensions of the Archaic–to–Pit Structure Period Transition in Southern Arizona. *Kiva* 60:619–632.

Gregory, David A. (editor). 1999. *Excavations in the Santa Cruz River Floodplain: The Middle Archaic Component at Los Pozos.* Anthropological Papers No. 20. Center for Desert Archaeology, Tucson, Arizona.

———. 2001. *Excavations in the Santa Cruz River Floodplain: The Early Agricultural Occupation at Los Pozos.* Anthropological Papers No. 21. Center for Desert Archaeology, Tucson, Arizona.

Hammack, Laurens C., Stanley D. Bussey, and Ronald Ice. 1966. *The Cliff Highway Salvage Project.* Laboratory of Anthropology Notes No. 41. Museum of New Mexico, Santa Fe.

Hard, Robert J., Karen R. Adams, John R. Roney, Kari M. Schmidt, and Gayle J. Fritz. 2008. The Emergence of Maize Farming in Northwest Mexico. In *Case Studies in Environmental Archaeology,* 2nd ed., edited by Elizabeth Reitz, C. Margaret Scarry, and Sylvia J. Scudder, pp. 315–333. Springer Science and Business Media, New York.

Hard, Robert J., and John R. Roney. 1998. A Massive Terraced Village Complex in Chihuahua, Mexico, 3000 Years Before Present. *Science* 279:1661–1664.

———. 1999. *An Archaeological Investigation of Late Archaic Cerros de Trincheras Sites in Chihuahua, Mexico.* Center for Archaeological Research Special Report No. 25. University of Texas, San Antonio.

———. 2005. The Transition to Farming on the Rio Casa Grandes and in the Southern Jornada Mogollon Region. In *The Late Archaic Across the Borderlands*, edited by Bradley J. Vierra, pp. 141–186. University of Texas Press, Austin.

———. 2007. Cerros de Trincheras in Northwestern Chihuahua: The Arguments for Defense. In *Trincheras Sites in Time, Space, and Society*, edited by Suzanne K. Fish, Paul R. Fish, and Maria Elisa Villalpando, pp. 11–52. University of Arizona Press, Tucson.

Hard, Robert J., José E. Zapata, Bruce K. Moses, and John R. Roney. 1999. Terrace Construction in Northern Chihuahua, Mexico: 1150 B.C. and Modern Experiments. *Journal of Field Archaeology* 26:129–146.

Hard, Robert J., José E. Zapata, and John R. Roney. 2001. *Una investigación arqueológica de los sitios cerros con trincheras del Arcaico tardío en Chihuahua, México*. Center for Archaeological Research Special Report No. 27-S. University of Texas, San Antonio.

Haury, Emil W. 1936. *The Mogollon Culture of Southwestern New Mexico*. Medallion Papers No. 19. Gila Pueblo, Globe, Arizona.

Heidke, James, Elizabeth J. Miksa, and Michael K. Wiley. 1998. Ceramic Artifacts. In *Archaeological Investigations of Early Village Sites in the Middle Santa Cruz River Valley: Analysis and Synthesis Pt. II*, edited by Jonathan B. Mabry, pp. 471–544. Anthropological Papers No. 19. Center for Desert Archaeology, Tucson, Arizona.

Hemphill, Claudia B. 1983. The Eaton Site: Late Archaic in the Upper Gila. Master's thesis, Department of Anthropology, University of Oregon, Eugene.

Honea, Kenneth. 1963. *The Diablo Complex of the San Pedro Stage at Gila Hot Springs, New Mexico*. Manuscript on file at the Laboratory of Anthropology, Museum of New Mexico, Santa Fe.

Huber, Edgar K. 2005. Chapter 36: Early Maize at the Old Corn Site (LA 137258). In *Fence Lake Project: Volume 1. Introduction and Site Descriptions*, edited by Edgar K. Huber and Carla R. Van West, pp. 36.31–36.33. Technical Series No. 84. Statistical Research, Tempe, Arizona.

Huckell, Bruce B. 1995. *Of Marshes and Maize: Preceramic Agricultural Settlements in the Cienega Valley, Southwestern Arizona*. University of Arizona Anthropological Papers No. 59. University of Arizona Press, Tucson.

———. 1996. The Archaic Prehistory of the North American Southwest. *Journal of World Prehistory* 10:305–373.

Huckell, Bruce B., Lisa W. Huckell, and Karl K. Benedict. 2002. Maize Agriculture and the Rise of Mixed Farming-Foraging Economies in Southeastern Arizona During the Second Millennium B.C. In *Traditions, Transitions, and Technologies: Themes in Southwestern Archaeology*, edited by Sarah H. Schlanger, pp. 137–246. University Press of Colorado, Boulder.

Huckell, Bruce B., Lisa W. Huckell, and Suzanne K. Fish. 1995. *Investigations at Milagro, a Late Preceramic Site in the Eastern Tucson Basin*. Technical Report No. 94–5. Center for Desert Archaeology, Tucson, Arizona.

Huckell, Lisa W. 2006. Ancient Maize in the American Southwest: What Does It Look Like and What Can It Tell Us? In *Histories of Maize: Multidisciplinary Approaches to the*

Prehistory, Biogeography, Domestication, and Evolution of Maize, edited by John E. Staller, Robert H. Tykot, and Bruce F. Benz, pp. 97–107. Elsevier Academic Press, Boston.

Hunter-Anderson, Rosalind L. 1986. *Prehistoric Adaptation in the American Southwest*. Cambridge University Press, New York.

Jones, Joshua G., Timothy M. Kearns, and Janet L. McVickar (editors). 2012. *Archaeological Investigations for the AT&T NEXGEN/Core Project: New Mexico Segment*. Western Cultural Resource Management, Farmington, New Mexico.

Kirkpatrick, David T. 2016. The Duke Site (LA 135139), Luna County, NM. Manuscript on file, Human Systems Research, Las Cruces, New Mexico.

Knight, Brian D. 2003. Early Hunter-Gatherer Occupations in the Southern Playas and Animas Valleys, Hidalgo County, New Mexico. Master's thesis, Department of Anthropology, New Mexico State University, Las Cruces.

Kugler, Chris. 1994. Chapter 13: LA 53489. In *On the Periphery of the Mimbres Mogollon: The Cuchillo Negro Archaeological Project, Volume 1*, edited by Jeanne A. Schutt, Richard C. Chapman, and June-el Piper, pp. 339–346. Office of Contract Archaeology, University of New Mexico, Albuquerque.

Kurota, Alexander, and Leslie Cohen (editors). 2009. *The Border Fence Project: Excavations at 11 Sites near Cloverdale Playa and the U.S.-Mexico Border (HV 1–3), Hidalgo County, New Mexico*. OCA/UNM Report No. 185–1004B. Office of Contract Archeology, University of New Mexico, Albuquerque.

Laumbach, Karl W. 2013. *Cañada Alamosa Project: A Preliminary Report on the 2011 Research Season*. Human Systems Research Report No. 2011–20. Human Systems Research, Las Cruces, New Mexico.

———. 2014. Serendipity and Old Corn. *NewsMAC* 3:21–23.

———. 2015. Canada Alamosa Project. Electronic document, http://www.canadaalamosaproject.org/, accessed December 12, 2015.

LeBlanc, Steven A. 1983. *The Mimbres People: Ancient Pueblo Painters of the American Southwest*. Thames and Hudson, New York.

Lehmer, Donald J. 1948. *The Jornada Branch of the Mogollon*. Bulletin No. 17. University of Arizona, Tucson.

Lekson, Stephen H. 1992. *Archaeological Overview of Southwestern New Mexico*. Human Systems Research, Las Cruces, New Mexico.

Lentz, Stephen C., Robert D. Dello-Russo, Pamela J. McBride, Donald Tatum, Linda Scott Cummings, and Chad L. Yost. 2013. Evidence for Early Domesticates at LA 159879: An Early Agricultural Site in the Mimbres Bolson near Deming, Luna County, New Mexico. In *Collected Papers from the 17th Biennial Mogollon Archaeology Conference*, edited by Lonnie C. Ludeman, pp. 19–30. Friends of Mogollon Archaeology, Las Cruces, New Mexico.

Linse, Angela R. 1997. *Excavations at Mogollon Village and Survey of Surrounding Areas: University of Washington Archaeology Field School 1993*. Report submitted by the University of Washington to the USDA Forest Service, Gila National Forest, Silver City, New Mexico.

Mabry, Jonathan B. 2005a. Changing Knowledge and Ideas About the First Farmers in Southeastern Arizona. In *The Late Archaic Across the Borderland: From Foraging to Farming*, edited by Bradley J. Vierra, pp. 41–83. University of Texas Press, Austin.

———. 2005b. Diversity in Early Southwestern Farming and Optimization Models of Transitions to Agriculture. In *Subsistence and Resource Use Strategies of Early Agricultural Communities in Southern Arizona*, edited by Michael M. Diehl, pp. 113–152. Anthropological Papers No. 34. Center for Desert Archaeology, Tucson, Arizona.

——— (editor). 1998. *Archaeological Investigations of Early Village Sites in the Middle Santa Cruz Valley*. Anthropological Papers No. 19. Center for Desert Archaeology, Tucson, Arizona.

Mabry, Jonathan B., and Michelle N. Stevens. 2014. Beyond the Cochise Culture: New Views of Archaic Foragers and Early Farmers in Southeastern Arizona. In *Between Mimbres and Hohokam: Exploring the Archaeology and History of Southeastern Arizona and Southwestern New Mexico*, edited by Henry D. Wallace, pp. 115–164. Anthropological Papers No. 52. Archaeology Southwest, Tucson, Arizona.

MacNeish, Richard S. (editor). 1993. *Preliminary Investigations of the Archaic in the Region of Las Cruces, New Mexico*. Historic and Natural Resources Report No. 9. Directorate of Environment, U.S. Army Air Defense Artillery Center, Fort Bliss, Texas.

MacNeish, Richard S., and Patrick H. Beckett. 1987. *The Archaic Chihuahua Tradition*. Monograph 7. COAS Bookstore, Las Cruces, New Mexico.

Martin, Paul Sidney, John B. Rinaldo, and Ernst Antevs. 1949. *Cochise and Mogollon Sites, Pine Lawn Valley, Western New Mexico*. Fieldiana: Anthropology Vol. 38, No. 1. Chicago Natural History Museum, Chicago.

Martin, Paul Sidney, John B. Rinaldo, A. Bluhm Elaine, Hugh C. Cutler, and Roger Grange Jr. 1952. *Mogollon Cultural Continuity and Change: The Stratigraphic Analysis of Tularosa and Cordova Caves*. Fieldiana: Anthropology Vol. 40. Chicago Natural History Museum, Chicago.

Mauldin, Raymond, Patricia A. Gilman, and Christopher M. Stevenson. 1996. Mogollon Village Revisited: Recent Chronometric Results and Interpretations. *Kiva* 61:385–400.

McGuire, Randall H., and Maria Elisa Villalpando. 2015. War and Defense of Cerros de Trincheras in Sonora, Mexico. *American Antiquity* 80:429–450.

Merrill, William L., Robert J. Hard, Jonathan B. Mabry, Gayle J. Fritz, Karen R. Adams, and John R. Roney. 2009. The Diffusion of Maize to the Southwestern United States and Its Impacts. *PNAS* 106(50):21019–21026.

Miller, Myles R. 2018. Archaic Transitions and Transformations in the Jornada Mogollon Region of Southern New Mexico and Western Texas. In *The Archaic Southwest: Foragers in an Arid Land*, edited by Bradley J. Vierra, pp. 119–144. University of Utah Press, Salt Lake City.

Minnis, Paul E. 1980. The Archaic of Southern New Mexico. In *An Archeological Synthesis of Southcentral and Southwestern New Mexico*, edited by Steven A. LeBlanc and Michael E.

Whalen, pp. 64–102. OCA/UNM Report No. 185–14A. Office of Contract Archeology, University of New Mexico, Albuquerque.

Neely, James A., and Eric J. Brunnemann. 1988. *Field Report, 1986 Season of the HO-Bar (WS-17) Site Project: The Study of a Prehistoric Occupational Sequence at an Archaic and Early Mogollon Village in West Central New Mexico*. Report prepared by the Department of Anthropology, University of Texas, Austin, for the Gila National Forest, Silver City, New Mexico.

Oakes, Yvonne, and Dorothy A. Zamora (editors). 1999. *Archaeology of the Mogollon Highlands: Settlement Systems and Adaptations*. Office of Archaeological Studies Archaeology Notes 232. Museum of New Mexico, Santa Fe.

Peck, Jay Richard. 1991. A Comparative Analysis of Chipped Stone Artifacts Recovered in Test Excavations at Mogollon Village and WS-17, Two Pithouse Period Mesatop Sites in the Middle San Francisco River Valley, West Central New Mexico. Master's thesis, Department of Anthropology, University of Texas, Austin.

Roney, John R. 1999. Acanador Peak, an Early Pithouse-Period Cerro de Trincheras in Southwestern New Mexico. In *La Frontera: Papers in Honor of Patrick H. Beckett*, edited by Meliha S. Duran and David T. Kirkpatrick, pp. 173–184. Archaeological Society of New Mexico 25. Archaeological Society of New Mexico, Albuquerque.

Roney, John R., and Robert J. Hard. 2002. Early Agriculture in Northwestern Chihuahua. In *Traditions, Transitions, and Technologies: Themes in Southwestern Archaeology: Proceedings of the 2000 Southwestern Symposium*, edited by Sarah Schlanger, pp. 160–177. University Press of Colorado, Boulder.

——. 2003. Late Archaic Villages on the Rio Casas Grandes. *Archaeology Southwest* 17(2):11.

——. 2004. A Review of Cerros de Trincheras in Northwestern Chihuahua. In *Surveying the Archaeology of Northwest Mexico*, edited by Gillian E. Newell and Emiliano Gallaga, pp. 127–147. University of Utah Press, Salt Lake City.

Roney, John R., Robert J. Hard, and Lori Barkwill Love. 2012. *Archaeological Investigations in Southwestern New Mexico 2011*. Report submitted to the Bureau of Land Management, Las Cruces, New Mexico.

Roney, John R., Robert J. Hard, A. C. MacWilliams, and Mary E. Whisenhunt. 2015. Recent Test Excavations at an Early Agricultural Period Cerro de Trincheras Site on the Upper Gila River, Arizona. Paper presented at the 80th Annual Meeting of the Society of American Archaeology, San Francisco.

Roth, Barbara J. 2014. Foragers, Farmers, and In Between: Variability in the Late Archaic in the Southern Southwest. In *Archaeology in the Great Basin and Southwest: Papers in Honor of Don D. Fowler*, edited by Nancy J. Parezo and Joel C. Janetski, pp. 98–108. University of Utah Press, Salt Lake City.

——. 2015. *Archaeological Investigations at the Harris Village (LA 1867), Grant County, New Mexico*. University of Nevada, Las Vegas.

Sayles, E. B. 1983. *The Cochise Cultural Sequence in Southeastern Arizona*. Anthropological Papers No. 42. University of Arizona, Tucson.

Sayles, E. B., and Ernst Antevs. 1941. *The Cochise Culture*. Medallion Papers 29. Gila Pueblo, Globe, Arizona.

Turnbow, Christopher A., Alexander Kurota, Leslie Cohen, and Brian Cribbin. 2008. *A Cultural Resources Survey of Proposed Vehicle Fence Corridors, Access Roads, and Staging Areas (HV 1 to 3) On and Near the U.S.-Mexico Border in the Boot Heel Region, Hidalgo County, New Mexico*. UNM/OCA Report No. 185–966B. University of New Mexico / Office of Contract Archeology, Albuquerque.

Turnbow, Christopher A., Jonathan E. Van Hoose, Lori Stephens Reed, Lisa W. Huckell, Jim A. Railey, Richard M. Reycraft, Gwyneth A. Duncan, Richard D. Holmes, John C. Acklen, Timothy G. Baugh, Grant D. Smith, Catherine Heyne, Steven Bozarth, M. Steven Shackley, A. Russell Nelson, Andrea Carpenter, Joell Grant, and Hector Neff. 2000. *A Highway Through Time: Archaeological Investigations Along NM 90, in Grant and Hidalgo Counties, New Mexico (U.S. Forest Service Report 03-06-98-005b)*. Technical Report 2000–3. TRC, Albuquerque, New Mexico.

Wallace, Laurel T. 1998. *The Ormand Village: Final Report on the 1965–1966 Excavations*. Office of Archaeological Studies Archaeology Notes 229. Museum of New Mexico, Santa Fe.

Whalen, Michael E. 1994. *Turquoise Ridge and Late Prehistoric Residential Mobility in the Desert Mogollon Region*. University of Utah Anthropological Papers No. 118. University of Utah Press, Salt Lake City.

Wills, Wirt H. 1988a. Early Agriculture and Sedentism in the American Southwest: Evidence and Interpretations. *Journal of World Prehistory* 2:445–488.

———. 1988b. *Early Prehistoric Agriculture in the American Southwest*. School of American Research Press, Santa Fe, New Mexico.

———. 1989. Patterns of Prehistoric Food Production in West-Central New Mexico. *Journal of Anthropological Research* 45:116–137.

———. 1995. Archaic Foraging and the Beginning of Food Production in the American Southwest. In *Last Hunters, First Farmers: New Perspectives on the Prehistoric Transition to Agriculture*, edited by T. Douglas Price and Anne Birgitte Gebauer, pp. 215–242. School of American Research Press, Santa Fe, New Mexico.

Woosley, Anne I., and Allan J. McIntyre. 1996. *Mimbres Mogollon Archaeology: Charles C. Di Peso's Excavations at Wind Mountain*. University of New Mexico Press, Albuquerque.

2

Changing Perspectives on Pithouse Period Occupations in the Mimbres Region

ROGER ANYON AND BARBARA J. ROTH

WHEN THE MIMBRES FOUNDATION began its research program four decades ago, little more was known about pithouse occupations in the Mimbres region than what Haury had published in 1936. Haury's pioneering work at the Harris site and Mogollon village established the basic ceramic and architectural sequence for the period prior to A.D. 1000, a culture history that has remained essentially unchanged over the ensuing decades. A wealth of data coming from both the Mimbres Foundation's work and research at the NAN Ranch, Wind Mountain, Old Town, Harris, and Woodrow sites, among others, is providing new insights into the Pithouse period that are expanding and sometimes challenging our views of this important time.

In this chapter, we discuss accumulating data and our changing views of the Pithouse period (ca. A.D. 200–1000) in the Mimbres region, with a brief review of early work, including the impact of the Mimbres Foundation, and the results of work conducted in the last few decades. This body of work has enhanced our knowledge of the temporal sequence, subsistence and settlement practices, and social changes that occurred during this period. In addition, the recent data allow us to better understand two major transitions: first, the changes that occurred as a result of ceramic production that began around A.D. 175 following the aceramic pithouse occupations discussed by Turnbow and his colleagues in the previous chapter; and second, the important role that these developments played in the transition to the subsequent Mimbres Classic pueblo period.

History of Research

By the time Haury began his excavations at the Harris site in 1934, it was well estab-lished that pithouses preceded Mimbres pueblos (Bradfield 1931; Cosgrove and Cos-grove 1932). Bradfield followed his fieldwork at Cameron Creek, a site with pit struc-tures underlying pueblo rooms, with 1927 and 1928 excavations at the Three Circle pithouse site, which remained unpublished until well after his untimely death (Everett 1992). The Cosgroves excavated at the Swarts site, also a Classic period pueblo super-imposed over pit structures.

Haury (1936) focused on pithouse sites with no later pueblo occupation and used his findings to provide the first coherent temporal and material culture framework for the Pithouse period. After Haury's work and prior to the mid-1970s, few pithouses were excavated in the Mimbres region, apart from several highway salvage projects along the Gila River, most of which remain unpublished. One notable exception to this dearth of activity was the work of Fitting, who produced several papers on his excavations in the Gila Valley, the most germane of which was the publication of his work at the Winn Canyon site (Fitting 1973), in which he demonstrated the existence of a pithouse settlement with only plain ceramics that predated the earliest occupa-tions in the Mimbres region as defined by Haury. In addition, Bussey's (1975) work at Lee village as part of a highway salvage project established that the growth of Late Pithouse period sites in the Gila River valley paralleled that of the Mimbres Valley.

In the late 1970s, the Mimbres Foundation substantially advanced our knowledge of the Pithouse period through comprehensive surface survey (Blake et al. 1986) and sample excavations at sites located throughout the Mimbres Valley, including the Galaz, McAnally, and Thompson sites, among others (figure 2.1; Anyon and LeBlanc 1984; Diehl and LeBlanc 2001). Complementary data were derived from Shafer's (2003) NAN Ranch project in the southern portion of the valley in the late 1970s and 1980s, which focused primarily on NAN Ranch, a large pithouse and pueblo site.

The state of our knowledge of the Pithouse period in the early 1980s supported an occupational sequence similar to that defined by Haury (1936), with the addition of an Early Pithouse period occupation associated with plain ceramics. Anyon and colleagues (1981) affirmed Haury's architectural and ceramic sequence, as well as his three sequential phases of pithouse occupation, the Georgetown, San Francisco, and Three Circle phases, all of which were incorporated into the Late Pithouse period. The architectural development of large great kivas was refined (Anyon and LeBlanc 1980), which reflected Haury's (1950) Forestdale region great-kiva sequence. New chronometric dates and more refined stylistic divisions of black-on-white ceramics resulted in a modified phase chronology (Anyon et al. 1981). Anyon and LeBlanc

FIGURE 2.1 The Mimbres River valley with an overview of the Galaz site location.

(1984) convincingly documented the practice of burying individuals below in-use pit-house floors during the Three Circle phase, a practice that previously had been linked only with the Mimbres Classic pueblo period. Blake and colleagues' (1986) survey and work by Shafer (2003) on the NAN Ranch property documented Pithouse period occupations in tributary drainages to the Mimbres River, demonstrating that pithouse settlements were present in a range of ecological niches in addition to the major sites located adjacent to perennial watercourses and large tracts of floodplain land. Survey (Blake et al. 1986) and excavation data (Anyon and LeBlanc 1984) showed that Three Circle phase populations were substantial, and some of the larger sites such as Galaz had an estimated two hundred inhabitants. Subsistence studies and fuel-wood use indicated that domesticated crops were critical foods, to such a degree that by the late Three Circle phase the riverine environment was being adversely impacted (Minnis 1985) and hunting had shifted from artiodactyls to rabbits around some of the larger sites (Cannon 2000, 2003).

This work culminated in the development of a model of Pithouse period cultural change that involved gradually increasing sedentism and agricultural dependence from the Early Pithouse through the end of the Late Pithouse period. Pithouse period sites were interpreted as sedentary settlements occupied year-round, and the focus of the subsistence base was agriculture. Social distinctions were recognized in some burials, but these were not seen as substantial and were not considered to be associated with the development of social hierarchy. Instead, researchers saw Mimbres Pithouse period groups as essentially egalitarian, with social integration at the larger sites maintained primarily by the use of great kivas. The end of the Pithouse period, marked by the pithouse-to-pueblo transition, was viewed as the result of a change from family-based groups living in pithouses to larger extended family corporate groups living in the pueblos.

Changing Interpretations of the Pithouse Period

Research in the Mimbres region since the end of the Mimbres Foundation's work and recent reevaluations of previous work have both supported and challenged some Mimbres Foundation interpretations, leading to new questions about the role of agricultural production, population increase, and social change in the pithouse-to-pueblo transition. In this section, we summarize critical aspects of this recent work and discuss the advances in our knowledge that have come from it.

Several projects are most pertinent to our changing views of the Pithouse period: the NAN Ranch, Old Town, and Harris sites in the Mimbres drainage and the Wind Mountain and Woodrow sites in the Gila drainage. Although the NAN Ranch fieldwork began at the end of the Mimbres Foundation's work, the multiyear excavations were published later after considerable reflection (Shafer 2003), and thus we include that research here. The situation was similar at Wind Mountain, which was excavated by Di Peso in the late 1970s and published by Woosley and McIntyre in 1996. More recent projects at Old Town (Creel 2006a), Harris (Roth 2015; Roth and Baustian 2015), and Woodrow (Sedig 2013) have each provided new insights into Pithouse period developments. In addition, reevaluations of existing data combined with new data have also proved valuable (cf. Creel and Anyon 2003).

Extensive excavations at the NAN Ranch revealed a pithouse component beneath the large Classic period pueblo, with occupation starting during the Georgetown phase. Shafer (1995, 2003) documented changes in architecture, ceramics, burial practices, and communal architecture over the course of the Late Pithouse period and into the Classic period. By the late Three Circle phase, lateral entryways in pithouses had been replaced by roof entries, basin hearths had been replaced with slab-lined rectangular hearths, and some burials had been placed beneath house floors. Shafer (1995, 2003) saw this shift as having symbolic and ideological implications, with the "inward" architectural focus associated with ancestor veneration related to changes in land tenure. He tied these changes to the development of land-holding corporate groups, which he linked to a greater reliance on irrigation agriculture. He further suggested that the continuity in occupation observed at NAN Ranch across the pithouse-to-pueblo transition was related to the fact that core households established the initial pueblo room blocks to maintain their rights to prime agricultural land.

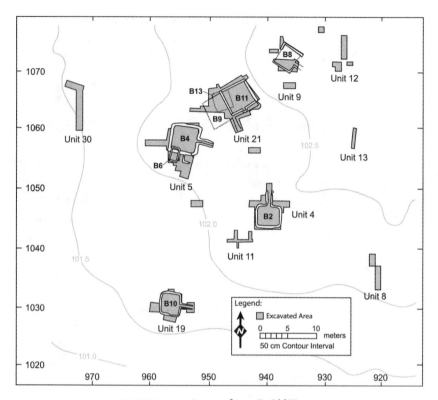

FIGURE 2.2 A map of Area B, Old Town.

Creel's work at Old Town, a large and heavily looted Classic period pueblo in the southern Mimbres Valley, has documented a substantial Pithouse period component and has provided further insights into great kiva use during the Pithouse period (Creel and Anyon 2003; Creel 2006a). Portions of several San Francisco and Three Circle phase structures were excavated beneath pueblo rooms, but the Pithouse period occupation is best documented in Area B, a part of the site not superimposed by Classic pueblo rooms, where several late Three Circle phase (post–A.D. 900) pit structures with masonry or coursed adobe walls were identified (figure 2.2; Creel 2006a; Lucas 2007). Creel (2006b) and Lucas (2007) posit that these late Three Circle phase structures were organized around small courtyards and represent the development of extended family corporate groups akin to those documented in the Hohokam region. Like Shafer (2003), they see the pithouse-to-pueblo transition as related to the construction of pueblos by landholding corporate groups practicing irrigation agriculture.

Data from Old Town and Galaz show that communal architecture also changed during the Three Circle phase. Creel and Anyon (2003) note that sometime in the early to mid–A.D. 900s, great kivas at many large sites in the Mimbres Valley, including

Old Town, Galaz, Harris, NAN Ranch, and perhaps Swarts, were ritually retired through dramatic fires, spectacular events that would have been visible throughout the Mimbres Valley (Creel and Anyon 2003, 2010; Creel et al. 2015).

Recent excavations at the Harris site have been conducted north of the portion of the site excavated by Haury (1936) and include pithouses, associated extramural features, and portions of a Three Circle phase kiva (Roth 2015; Roth and Baustian 2015). Roth has identified two forms of household organization at the site: pithouse clusters that were spatially distinct and shared particular architectural and artifact traits, which are interpreted as the remains of extended family corporate groups; and autonomous households that were contemporary with the pithouse clusters and integrated into the site via the central plaza and great kivas. The development of pithouse clusters in the San Francisco phase and the subsequent expansion of the site in the Three Circle phase suggest that changes in household organization were associated with agricultural intensification, most likely irrigation agriculture, increased sedentism, and associated changes in land tenure. The role of the central plaza in site integration was further developed during the A.D. 800s, when two sequentially used, increasingly elaborate Three Circle phase great kivas were built, culminating in the construction of House 10 (excavated by Haury) in the A.D. 870s (figure 2.3). This great kiva was ritually retired in a major fire similar to those observed at Old Town and Galaz (Creel

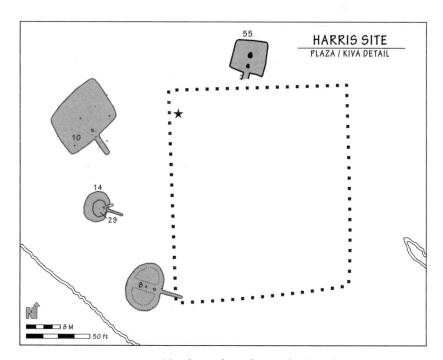

FIGURE 2.3 The plaza and great kivas at the Harris Site.

and Anyon 2003). An archaeomagnetic date from the kiva wall indicates that it was burned in the mid–A.D. 900s, and this event was followed by a dispersal of extended family households from the site. No pueblo was built on top of the pithouses at the Harris site, an unusual situation, and it appears that social changes possibly in concert with the retirement of House 10 may have led to community dispersal.

New Interpretations of Pithouse Period Social Developments

These new excavation data and ongoing research on the assemblages recovered from Late Pithouse period contexts provide important insights into this period in the Mimbres region. In this section, we highlight some of these insights and the challenges that remain in reconstructing Pithouse period social dynamics, in particular sedentism and community integration, interactions and connections with adjacent regions, and the end of the Pithouse period.

Sedentism and Community Integration

The issue of sedentism and village formation is, as elsewhere in the Southwest, very much a topic of concern, since it is during the Late Pithouse period that we see some major transformations in society that are linked by most researchers to increasing sedentism and growing agricultural dependence. Researchers no longer assume that the combination of maize, ceramics, and pithouses equates with sedentary populations; they are now asking more nuanced questions and examining the degree of sedentism and how this changed over time. It is currently thought that populations were mobile for at least part of the year during the Early Pithouse period and the Georgetown phase, when red slip was added to plain ceramics. Prior to the inception of painted ceramics, populations do not appear to have been fully invested in any one location on the landscape, and social structure was relatively fluid. Even so, most of what later became substantial Three Circle phase pithouse sites were established during the Georgetown phase, suggesting some degree of sedentism.

With the advent of painted pottery, Mogollon Red-on-brown, we see an increase in site size and a change in domestic architecture to more substantial and more rectangular structures. From the A.D. 700s onward, it appears that most if not all of the major sites along perennial watercourses were occupied year-round. Even so, a portion of each site population may have moved to small settlements in nearby nonriverine areas during part of the year. In the A.D. 800s, during the Three Circle phase, increases in site size and a greater expansion of pithouse settlements into tributary drainages indicate that the overall population was rising quite dramatically (Swanson et al. 2012).

Change intensified and the pace of change increased in the A.D. 800s. By the mid–A.D. 800s, people in the Mimbres Valley and likely elsewhere were living in markedly different ways than a century previously. After centuries of incremental change, ceramics exhibited a rapid design evolution from Mogollon Red-on-brown through Three Circle Red-on-white to Mimbres Black-on-white (Anyon and LeBlanc 1984; Shafer and Brewington 1995), possibly within thirty years or less. Domestic houses also changed from a variety of sizes and shapes to more standardized square and rectangular houses with lateral entryways. People increasingly invested in domestic pithouses, and we see evidence of more effort being put into their maintenance as livable structures (Diehl 1992, 1997). At some of the larger sites, inhumations placed beneath pithouse floors became a regular aspect of burial placement by the late A.D. 800s, first of infants and children and then quickly of adults. Individuals not buried beneath house floors were sometimes buried in specific extramural areas within each site, and at some large sites, plazas were used to bury substantial numbers of cremations along with inhumations (Creel and Shafer 2015). More burials had accompanying funerary objects, primarily ceramics or shell. Researchers have interpreted all of these traits as representing significant social changes. In particular, the placement of burials beneath house floors has been linked to maintaining ties with ancestors, likely the result of establishing land tenure (Roth and Baustian 2015; Shafer 2003). Shafer (2003), Creel (2006b), and Roth and Baustian (2015) all see this as tied to a growing emphasis on irrigation agriculture, resulting in changes in labor organization and land tenure practices.

Changes also occurred at the level of site organization. It has long been assumed that autonomous households, represented by pithouses and associated extramural features in the archaeological record, were the basis of site organization during the Pithouse period throughout the Mimbres region (Hegmon et al. 2000; Roth 2010a). Recent research at Old Town, NAN Ranch, and Harris, however, indicates that this was not the case. What we now see is that at the larger sites extended family households became established at about the time or slightly after painted ceramics appeared. These households may well have been the initial full-time sedentary families at each site. By the late A.D. 800s, these households appear to have functioned as corporate groups, probably in response to the labor needs associated with agricultural intensification (Creel 2006b; Roth 2015; Shafer 2003). Pithouse clusters at the Harris site, for example, shared distinct architectural and artifact characteristics; surrounded communal work areas containing large storage structures, processing areas, and sometimes burials; and may have represented extended family corporate groups (Roth 2015; Roth and Baustian 2015). Each cluster had one pithouse that is understood to be the domicile of the founding household, somewhat akin to the core households identified by Shafer at the NAN Ranch site (Roth and Baustian 2015; Shafer 2003). These pithouse clusters appeared during the San Francisco phase at the Harris site and continued through the late Three Circle phase into the mid–A.D. 900s. At Old Town, the pithouse cluster in Area B could be another manifestation of an extended family corporate group. These developments presage the shift to corporate groups reflected in the core rooms noted by Shafer (2003) in the Mimbres Classic pueblo at the NAN Ranch site. The shift into Classic pueblo architecture that had previously been assumed to be linked with the inception of corporate social groups clearly has a long history of development in the Mimbres region, connected to the changing needs associated with population growth and an increased reliance on agriculture.

Changes are also apparent in intersite integration. During the San Francisco phase, communal structures—that is, great kivas—became markedly larger than domestic houses, developed more stylized architecture, and evidenced fairly standardized ritual dedications and retirements (Creel and Anyon 2003; Creel et al. 2015). This is a dramatic change from the Georgetown phase and earlier, when communal structures were less standardized and less distinct from domestic architecture. With the shift to black-on-white ceramics, we see a concomitant increase in great kiva size and architectural standardization, which became particularly pronounced in the mid–A.D. 800s, when great kivas were constructed in a number of sites. These changes in great kivas were likely the result of site growth and the increased need to integrate the extended core households and autonomous households. Evidence from the Harris site indicates that certain households and individuals within the site were responsible for sponsoring rituals, which in turn led to differences in social power (Roth and Baustian 2015).

During the A.D. 800s, the increased investment in domestic architecture, changes in burial locations and practices, establishment and longevity of core households, rapid evolution of ceramic styles, and standardization, size, and ritual importance of community integrative great kivas all reveal the complex nature of developments in the Mimbres region. Fundamental changes in social organization were most likely tied to the interplay between population increase and agricultural intensification.

This sequence of site development does not hold true for sites located in nonriverine settings, however. Swanson and colleagues (2012) found that Pithouse period settlements away from perennial streams were generally short-term occupations that exhibited more episodic use than the continuous occupations observed along perennial rivers such as the Mimbres and the Gila. Research at Lake Roberts Vista (Roth 2007) and La Gila Encantada (Roth 2010b) has shown that Pithouse period groups in nonriverine settings remained mobile through the San Francisco phase, with a relatively rapid shift to a more sedentary, year-round occupation during the Three Circle phase in the A.D. 800s. Roth has tied this shift to an increased focus on agriculture in these upland settings, where agriculture was likely riskier than in the broad alluvial expanses adjacent to the Mimbres and other perennial rivers. The role of communal structures in these nonriverine settings also appears to differ from that at major sites in riverine settings. Stokes and Roth (1999) have argued that the great kiva at Lake Roberts Vista served more than the residents of the site and was constructed to serve a larger community of pithouse sites in that portion of the Sapillo Valley. No great kiva was found at La Gila Encantada, and Roth (2010b) thinks that the residents were attending ceremonies elsewhere as a way for them to link to and integrate with other sites in the region.

Interactions and Connections with Adjacent Regions

Haury (1936) hinted at social connections beyond the Mimbres after about A.D. 700, but he was, we think, somewhat reticent to make much of a case for this interpretation because his primary goal was to show that the Mogollon culture was distinct and separate from neighbors to the west and north. The Mimbres Foundation also focused on the internal dynamics of the Mimbres region during the Late Pithouse period. Recently, however, connections with the Hohokam have been more concretely considered (Creel 2014), although the actual nature of the interactions remains unclear. Shell items appear to have been manufactured in the Hohokam region and imported into the Mimbres region as finished pieces (Heacock 2015). But palettes were manufactured in the Mimbres region and not imported from the Hohokam area (Garcia de Quevedo 2004). Mimbres palettes are not as elaborate as those in the Hohokam region, and their use in the two regions does not appear to be equivalent. Hohokam palettes were predominantly ritual objects, whereas in the Mimbres region they have been found in both ritual and domestic contexts. Hohokam-like painted pottery designs, especially naturalistic designs, appear on Mimbres Black-on-white ceramics, but very little exchange of the ceramics themselves occurred between the Mimbres and Hohokam regions (Creel 2014). Cremations have been found in central plazas at several large Pithouse period sites in the Mimbres Valley (Creel and Shafer 2015), even though inhumation was the predominant burial practice. It is possible that these represent an entirely different practice than the cremations in the Hohokam area, where cremation was the primary burial practice for much of the cultural sequence and was associated with distinct artifacts such as palettes and censors, which are thought to be part of the Hohokam cremation ritual (Wallace 2014). Large community-level architectural structures, standardized great kivas in the Mimbres area and ballcourts in the Hohokam, developed at about the same time, but to date no great kivas have been documented in the Hohokam region, and no ballcourts have been found in the Mimbres. This suggests that the level of interaction was different than simple trade or emulation, but its actual nature is unclear.

Mimbres regional connections with populations to the north in the Reserve area are also being reassessed. While a small amount of northern white wares has long been known to be present in Late Pithouse period ceramic assemblages, research at the Harris site suggests that some internal architectural details in domestic pithouses could also indicate connections with the north, at least for some inhabitants of the site (Roth 2015).

Familial and trade connections beyond the Mimbres region may well have been much greater and more fluid than previously understood. We suspect that some individuals in each Pithouse period site had connections with people living in adjacent regions and that some intermarriage and possibly migration occurred between regions, though on a limited scale. It is also possible that people at different sites had connections that focused more on one particular adjacent region than others.

The End of the Pithouse Period

While information about developments within the Three Circle phase has increased substantially, our knowledge about the end of the Pithouse period is less clear. Much of what we do know is derived from research at the Harris, Woodrow, and NAN Ranch sites (see chapter 3). Tree-ring and archaeomagnetic data show that many pithouses constructed in the latter part of the A.D. 800s were burned in the early to mid–A.D. 900s, as was also the case for a number of great kivas built in the mid–A.D. 800s, which were the most intensely burned great kivas of the Pithouse period. At the Harris site, the burning of great kiva House 10 appears to mark the end of the occupation by many of the extended core households, although several autonomous households continued living there for perhaps another generation or so. This burning took place in the mid–A.D. 900s, apparently a generation later than the burning of similar great kivas at other sites. Of note is that the Harris site had no successor great kiva to House 10, no superimposed Mimbres Classic pueblo, and surprisingly little Style II Black-on-white pottery (Stokes 2015). Other sites that have superimposed pueblos, such as Galaz and NAN Ranch, have substantial amounts of Style II ceramics and a successor great kiva that was not burned with anything like the intensity of the great kivas built in the late A.D. 800s. We can only speculate about the meaning of this, but we suspect that if Gilman and colleagues (2014) are correct and a new religion swept into the Mimbres region around the beginning of the Mimbres Classic period, then perhaps the prodigious burnings of great kivas in the early A.D. 900s and the events that resulted in the depopulation at the Harris site in the mid–A.D. 900s are some indication of a religious and societal upheaval at that time. This may suggest that a new religious order began to develop in the century before the start of the Mimbres Classic period.

In other respects, the A.D. 900s, particularly the latter half of the century, appear to be an unsettled time. Domestic architecture at large sites became quite varied, ranging from the continued use of pithouses to semisubterranean cobble-walled rooms with roof entryways to ephemeral adobe-walled structures (chapter 3; Creel 2006a; Shafer 2003). What had been a series of well-structured pithouse sites became less homogeneous and seemingly less structured. In addition, we suspect that at least in the Mimbres Valley, the population may have decreased at some of the larger sites, although the continuity of occupation documented at sites like NAN Ranch and Galaz indicates that such a drop was not a valley-wide phenomenon. At many settlements, the great kivas built in the mid–A.D. 900s were smaller than their predecessors. Recent work at the Woodrow site in the Gila Valley shows that populations there were likely at their apex in the A.D. 900s (chapter 3). In any event, by the A.D. 1030s the Mimbres Valley population was once again growing rapidly, this time in large pueblo sites.

Conclusion and Future Prospects

When the Mimbres Foundation began its work in the mid-1970s, many archaeologists assumed that the region had been so heavily devastated by looting that nothing could be learned by further archaeological research. Not only did the Mimbres Foundation show this to be inaccurate, but the foundation demonstrated the potential of such research for the future. Recent projects have taken full advantage of the framework and knowledge derived from the Mimbres Foundation's work. We can state that the Mimbres Foundation provided a solid footing on which more recent research has been based, much as the Mimbres Foundation relied on Haury's work of the 1930s. We have progressed from the culture history of the 1930s, through the processual framework of the Mimbres Foundation and its continued chronology building and subsistence and environmental studies, to household studies and a more nuanced understanding of population dynamics and social relations during the Late Pithouse period.

Recent advances in our knowledge of the Pithouse period have raised many new questions that open future research possibilities. Building a Pithouse period chronology based on chronometric samples remains a basic research goal. Demographics also remain elusive, as seen in the current divergence in Pithouse period population estimates, from very low (Gilman 2010) to substantial (Anyon and Le Blanc 1984; Roth 2015). Swanson and colleagues' (2012) study of Pithouse period land use in the Mimbres region showed that most Pithouse period sites were small short-term occupations. Despite this assessment, few studies of small pithouse sites have been conducted, and the role of these small sites is thus not clear. Were they autonomous households living away from the larger sites as Roth (2010b) has proposed for La Gila

Encantada; were the occupants of these sites participating in rituals and fully integrated into life at the larger sites; or were some of them seasonal farmsteads connected to the larger riverine sites? We need additional research to elucidate the interactions and connections between people in the Mimbres and adjacent regions, the role of population movements within the Mimbres region, and the nature of the events and change in the A.D. 900s that culminated in the construction and occupation of Mimbres Classic pueblos.

References Cited

Anyon, Roger, Patricia A. Gilman, and Steven A. LeBlanc. 1981. A Re-evaluation of the Mogollon-Mimbres Archaeological Sequence. *Kiva* 46:209–225.

Anyon, Roger, and Steven A. LeBlanc. 1980. The Architectural Evolution of Mogollon-Mimbres Communal Structures. *Kiva* 45:253–277.

———. 1984. *The Galaz Ruin: A Prehistoric Mimbres Village in Southwestern New Mexico*. University of New Mexico Press, Albuquerque.

Blake, Michael, Steven A. LeBlanc, and Paul E. Minnis. 1986. Changing Settlement and Population in the Mimbres Valley, SW New Mexico. *Journal of Field Archaeology* 13:439–464.

Bradfield, Wesley. 1931. *Cameron Creek Village: A Site in the Mimbres Area in Grant County, New Mexico*. Monograph No. 1. School of American Research, Santa Fe, New Mexico.

Bussey, Stanley D. 1975. *The Archaeology of Lee Village: A Preliminary Report*. Monograph No. 2. COAS Publishing and Research, Las Cruces, New Mexico.

Cannon, Michael D. 2000. Large Mammal Relative Abundance in Pithouse and Pueblo Period Archaeofaunas from Southwestern New Mexico: Resource Depression Among the Mimbres Mogollon? *Journal of Anthropological Archaeology* 19:317–347.

———. 2003. A Model of Central Place Forager Prey Choice: An Application to Faunal Remains from the Mimbres Valley, New Mexico. *Journal of Anthropological Archaeology* 22:1–25.

Cosgrove, H. S., and C. B. Cosgrove. 1932. *The Swarts Ruin: A Typical Mimbres Site in Southwestern New Mexico*. Papers of the Peabody Museum of American Archaeology and Ethnology Vol. 15(1). Harvard University, Cambridge, Massachusetts.

Creel, Darrell. 2006a. Excavations at the Old Town Ruin, Luna County, New Mexico, 1989–2003. U.S. Bureau of Land Management, New Mexico State Office, Santa Fe.

———. 2006b. Social Differentiation at the Old Town Site. In *Mimbres Society*, edited by Valli S. Powell-Martí and Patricia A. Gilman, pp. 32–44. University of Arizona Press, Tucson.

———. 2014. The Hohokam, The Mimbres, and the Land Between: A Mimbres Perspective. In *Between Mimbres and Hohokam: Exploring the Archaeology and History of Southeastern Arizona and Southwestern New Mexico*, edited by Henry D. Wallace, pp. 535–549. Archaeology Southwest, Tucson, Arizona.

Creel, Darrell, and Roger Anyon. 2003. New Interpretations of Mimbres Public Architecture and Space: Implications for Cultural Change. *American Antiquity* 68:67–92.

——. 2010. Burning Down the House: Ritual Architecture of the Mimbres Late Pithouse Period. In *Mimbres Lives and Landscapes*, edited by Margaret C. Nelson and Michelle Hegmon, pp. 29–37. School for Advanced Research Press, Santa Fe, New Mexico.

Creel, Darrell, Roger Anyon, and Barbara Roth. 2015. Ritual Construction, Use and Retirement of Mimbres Three Circle Phase Great Kivas. *Kiva* 81:201–219.

Creel, Darrell, and Harry J. Shafer. 2015. Mimbres Great Kivas and Plazas During the Three Circle Phase, ca. AD 850–1000. *Kiva* 81:164–178.

Diehl, Michael W. 1992. Architecture as a Material Correlate of Mobility Strategies: Some Implications for Archaeological Interpretations. *Behavior Science Research* 26:1–35.

——. 1997. Changes in Architecture and Land Use Strategies in the American Southwest: Upland Mogollon Pithouse Dwellers, A.C. 200–1000. *Journal of Field Archaeology* 24:179–194.

Diehl, Michael W., and Steven A. LeBlanc. 2001. *Early Pithouse Villages of the Mimbres Valley and Beyond: The McAnally and Thompson Sites in Their Cultural and Ecological Contexts.* Papers of the Peabody Museum of Archaeology and Ethnology 83. Harvard University, Cambridge, Massachusetts.

Everett, Robert F. 1992. The Three Circle Site: A Late Pithouse Period Settlement in the Upper Mimbres Valley of Southwestern New Mexico. Master's thesis, Department of Anthropology, University of Texas, Austin.

Fitting, James E. 1973. *Four Archaeological Sites in the Big Burro Mountains of New Mexico.* Monograph No. 1. COAS Publishing and Research, Las Cruces, New Mexico.

Garcia de Quevedo, Susan L. 2004. Trade, Migration, or Emulation: A Study of Stone Palettes from the Mimbres Region. Master's thesis. Department of Anthropology, University of Oklahoma, Norman.

Gilman, Patricia A. 2010. Substantial Structures, Few People, and the Question of Early Villages in the Mimbres Region of the North American Southwest. In *Becoming Villagers: Comparing Early Village Societies*, edited by Mathew S. Bandy and Jake R. Fox, pp. 119–139. University of Arizona Press, Tucson.

Gilman, Patricia A., Marc Thompson, and Kristina C. Wyckoff. 2014. Ritual Change and the Distant: Mesoamerican Iconography, Scarlet Macaws, and Great Kivas in the Mimbres Region of Southwestern New Mexico. *American Antiquity* 79:90–107.

Haury, Emil W. 1936. *The Mogollon Culture of Southwestern New Mexico.* Medallion Papers No. 20. Gila Pueblo, Globe, Arizona.

——. 1950. A Sequence of Great Kivas in the Forestdale Valley, Arizona. In *For the Dean, Essays in Anthropology in Honor of Byron Cummings*, edited by Erik K. Reed and Dale S. King, pp. 29–39. Southwest Parks and Monuments Association, Santa Fe, New Mexico.

Heacock, Erika. 2015. Shell Use in the Mimbres Region: Not so Black and White. Master's thesis, School of Anthropology, University of Arizona, Tucson.

Hegmon, Michelle, Scott Ortman, and Jeanette Mobley-Tanaka. 2000. Women, Men, and the Organization of Space. In *Women and Men in the Prehispanic Southwest: Labor, Power, & Prestige*, edited by Patricia L. Crown, pp. 43–90. School of American Research Press, Santa Fe, New Mexico.

Lucas, Jason. 2007. Three Circle Phase Architectural Variability Among the Mimbres-Mogollon. In *Exploring Variability in Mogollon Pithouses*, edited by Barbara J. Roth and Robert Stokes, pp. 71–80. Arizona State University Anthropological Research Papers No. 58. Arizona State University, Tempe.

Minnis, Paul. 1985. *Social Adaptation to Food Stress: A Prehistoric Southwestern Example*. University of Chicago Press, Chicago.

Roth, Barbara J. 2007. The Late Pithouse Period Occupation of the Lake Roberts Vista Site. In *Exploring Variability in Mogollon Pithouses*, edited by Barbara J. Roth and Robert Stokes, pp. 5–11. Arizona State University Anthropological Research Papers No. 58. Arizona State University, Tempe.

———. 2010a. Engendering Mimbres Mogollon Pithouses. In *Engendering Households in the Prehistoric Southwest*, edited by Barbara J. Roth, pp. 136–152. University of Arizona Press, Tucson.

———. 2010b. *Archaeological Investigations at La Gila Encantada (LA 113467), Grant County, New Mexico*. Report submitted to the Archaeological Conservancy, Southwest Division, Albuquerque, NM.

———. 2015. *Archaeological Investigations at the Harris Site, LA 1867, Grant County, Southwestern New Mexico*. Report on file, Department of Anthropology, University of Nevada, Las Vegas.

Roth, Barbara J., and Kathryn M. Baustian. 2015. Kin Groups and Social Power at the Harris Site, Southwestern New Mexico. *American Antiquity* 80:1–22.

Sedig, Jakob W. 2013. Recent Research at Woodrow Ruin. In *Collected Papers from the 17th Biennial Mogollon Archaeology Conference*, edited by Lonnie C. Ludeman, pp. 95–107. Friends of Mogollon Archaeology, Las Cruces, New Mexico.

Shafer, Harry J. 1995. Architecture and Symbolism in Transitional Pueblo Development in the Mimbres Valley, SW New Mexico. *Journal of Field Archaeology* 22:23–47.

———. 2003. *Mimbres Archaeology at the NAN Ranch Ruin*. University of New Mexico Press, Albuquerque.

Shafer, Harry J., and Robbie L. Brewington. 1995. Microstylistic Changes in Mimbres Black-on-White Pottery: Examples from the NAN Ruin, Grant County, New Mexico. *Kiva* 61:5–29.

Stokes, Robert J. 2015. Decorated Ceramics and Red Wares. In *Archaeological Investigations at the Harris Site, LA 1867, Grant County, Southwestern New Mexico*, edited by Barbara J.

Roth, pp. 115–177. Report on file, Department of Anthropology, University of Nevada, Las Vegas.

Stokes, Robert J., and Barbara J. Roth. 1999. Mobility, Sedentism, and Settlement Patterns in Transition: The Late Pithouse Period in the Sapillo Valley, New Mexico. *Journal of Field Archaeology* 26:423–434.

Swanson, Steve, Roger Anyon, and Margaret C. Nelson. 2012. Southern Mogollon Pithouse Period Settlement Dynamics, Land Use, and Community Development, A.D. 200–1000. In *Southwestern Pithouse Communities, A.D. 200–900*, edited by Lisa C. Young and Sarah A. Herr, pp. 95–109. University of Arizona Press, Tucson.

Wallace, Henry. 2014. Ritual Transformation and Cultural Revitalization: Explaining Hohokam in Pre–A.D. 1000 Southeastern Arizona. In *Between Mimbres and Hohokam: Exploring the Archaeology and History of Southeastern Arizona and Southwestern New Mexico*, edited by Henry D. Wallace, pp. 433–499. Archaeology Southwest, Tucson, Arizona.

Woosley, Anne I., and Allan J. McIntyre. 1996. *Mimbres Mogollon Archaeology: Charles C. Di Peso's Excavations at Wind Mountain*. University of New Mexico Press, Albuquerque.

3

Making the Transition

Using New Data to Reassess the Mimbres Pithouse-to-Pueblo Period

JAKOB W. SEDIG, STEPHEN H. LEKSON,
AND BARBARA J. ROTH

ORK BY THE MIMBRES FOUNDATION helped define the Late Pithouse period in the Mimbres region. Yet while the distinctions between the Late Pithouse and later Classic period were clear by the end of the foundation's work, the archaeological signature of the terminal Late Pithouse–Early Classic period remained somewhat muddled. Much has already been written about this "Mangas phase" or "pithouse-to-pueblo transition" in Mimbres prehistory, which occurred during the latter portion of the A.D. 900s (Anyon et al. 1981; Fitting et al. 1982; Hegmon 2002; LeBlanc 1983; Lekson 1988, 1990, 1999; Shafer 2003).

Originally, the Mangas phase, placed between pithouse and pueblo architecture, was defined as small, surface cobble-adobe room blocks associated with Mimbres "Boldface" (now termed Style I) ceramics (Gladwin and Gladwin 1934). In the years following this original designation, archaeologists working in the upper Gila argued strongly for the Mangas phase (Fitting et al. 1982; Lekson 1988), while archaeologists primarily studying the Mimbres River valley observed little evidence of it (Anyon et al. 1981; Anyon and LeBlanc 1984). Subsequently, the Mimbres Foundation, in its seminal chronology, omitted the phase, positing a very rapid shift from pithouse-to-pueblo sites. However, new research since the Mimbres Foundation's investigations has uncovered much about this contentious period. Work in the Mimbres Valley at NAN Ranch and the Harris site has revealed that the pithouse-to-pueblo transition was more diverse than originally thought. Additionally, sites such as Saige-McFarland have provided substantial evidence of this transitional period in the upper Gila (Lekson 1990). Recent research at the Woodrow site (also referred to as Woodrow Ruin), also on the upper Gila, has provided new insights as well. These new data suggest that a reanalysis of the pithouse-to-pueblo transition is warranted because Mimbres archaeologists now have new information with which to better delineate the characteristics of this transition and its significance.

An opening comment regarding vocabulary is necessary. At this point in time, arguing for the appellation "Mangas" for the period we examine in this chapter (A.D. 900–1020) would be a quixotic task. In fact, as we contend, "Mangas" as it was originally conceived is itself a relic and needs to be retired. We therefore abandon the word (although we do use it in reference to previous research) and use the less controversial "pithouse-to-pueblo transition" instead.

This chapter is divided into three sections. We begin by reviewing the history of research on the pithouse-to-pueblo transition in the Mimbres region. This is followed by a discussion of new findings on the pithouse-to-pueblo transition at the Woodrow and Harris sites. We conclude with an examination of our revised understanding of the pithouse-to-pueblo transition and why Mimbres archaeologists have offered such varied interpretations of this segment of time.

History of Research

Early Mimbres archaeologists suggested a phase or stage of Anasazi-like, small "unit pueblos" associated with what was then called Boldface Black-on-white pottery. This stage fell chronologically between the Pithouse and Pueblo periods and was called the "Mangas" phase (Gladwin and Gladwin 1934). The Mangas phase was established at a time when few Mimbres sites had been excavated, and so revisions to this original definition should have been expected. Yet different sides of the Mangas debate became entrenched based on this original definition, with researchers vehemently arguing either yea or nay for the existence of this division of time.

After nearly a half-century hiatus in Mimbres research in the mid-1900s, the Mangas phase was emphatically rejected in the mid-1970s by Mimbres Foundation archaeologists (e.g., Anyon et al. 1981; LeBlanc 1983). Their rejection, however, overlooked substantial evidence—for example, Room Block A at the Saige-McFarland site, a large Mimbres site in the Gila Valley (Fitting et al. 1971). Room Block A was a small six-room masonry "pueblo." The painted ceramics were predominantly Boldface with a relatively small amount of Mimbres Classic Black-on-white. Later reanalysis using the I-II-III typology tallied about 60 percent Style II (approximately A.D. 900–1020) and earlier types and 39 percent Style III (approximately A.D. 1000–1130)—ratios perhaps to be expected at a site with substantial Pithouse and Classic components. Additional "Mangas" evidence was found in Room Block B at Saige-McFarland, where a single subfloor adult burial was found with "a spectacular cache of [eighteen]

Mimbres Boldface Black-on-white vessels" (Fitting et al. 1971:21). Most of the vessels were partial (about half of each), a few were whole, and almost all were later reassigned to Style II (Lekson 1990). The burial was clearly associated with the masonry room block, which therefore was evidently built or begun in Style II times before the Classic period. Other ceramic evidence, such as indented corrugated jars and a Style III seed jar found on the floors of several rooms, indicated that the rooms continued to be used well into the Classic period.

Subsequently in the Mimbres Valley, "Transitional" (or "Late Three Circle") room blocks very similar to Room Block A were found at the NAN Ranch site under the later Classic period pueblo (Shafer 2003:40–54; described further in what follows). Room 104, for example, was nearly identical to the rooms of Room Block A in that subfloor burials had funerary pots "spanning early to late Style II" (Shafer 2003:47). Shafer's work at the NAN Ranch site demonstrated that a unique transitional phase could indeed be identified in the Mimbres River valley and that a diversity of structures was built during this phase. Shafer (1995, 2003) noted several forms of significant change during the pithouse-to-pueblo transition, including architecture and associated features such as hearths and entryways, special function rooms such as granaries, an increased production of painted ceramics and the incorporation of new ceramic motifs, and the shift to subfloor burials. Concerning architecture, Shafer (2003:43) found that early pueblo-style structures had freestanding cobble-adobe or puddled adobe walls and floors formed of, or into, the hardpan surface. Excavations at NAN Ranch found floors of sixteen structures that were constructed by either leveling or excavating 10–30 cm into the underlying hardpan. These rooms were superimposed over deeper and earlier pithouses and lay beneath later Mimbres Classic rooms. The ceramics found in the transitional rooms at NAN Ranch included Style II Black-on-white, Three Circle Neck Corrugated, Mimbres Red-slipped, and plain brown (Shafer 2003:52). A similar architectural feature, containing the same ceramic types, was identified at Woodrow and will be discussed.

Overall, Shafer's (1995, 2003) work demonstrated that a definable pithouse-to-pueblo transition existed in the Mimbres River valley, at least at NAN Ranch. For him, the transformations that occurred during the pithouse-to-pueblo transition, especially those associated with burial practices, reflected dramatic changes in world view and beliefs. Shafer hypothesized that architectural transformations corresponded with an ideology that focused on emergence from the underworld. Exiting structures through the roof were the physical manifestation of this ideology. Shafer (2003:43) also noted that similar "transitional" architecture was recognized a half century earlier at the Swarts site. This meant that what archaeologists had previously assumed was a rapid transformation between pithouses and pueblos was in fact gradual and distinct (Shafer 2003:40). Despite these data, the term *Mangas* has effectively vanished from recent Mimbres literature.

The original objections to the Mangas phase stemmed, at least in part, from its Anasazi population roots or referents. Mimbres archaeologists in the 1970s and 1980s rejected old ideas of "Anasazi swamping" as the reason for Mimbres pueblos (Haury 1936), and the "unit pueblos" of the Mangas phase brought Anasazi population baggage. Because the earliest cohort of Mimbres-Mogollon archaeologists viewed the contemporaneous appearance of black-on-white ceramics and aboveground pueblo architecture as the results of outside influence from the northern Southwest, it seemed important in the 1970s and 1980s to establish the Mimbres region as a free and independent entity, unentangled with neighbors north (Anasazi/Ancestral Pueblo) or west (Hohokam). This, in addition to the apparent absence of transitional data at sites such as Galaz and Cameron Creek (Anyon et al. 1981:169), resulted in the dismissal of the Mangas phase. We will discuss other reasons, but the hint of Anasazi entanglements surely colored early conclusions.

Thus, an old, seemingly arcane disagreement actually matters. Decades after attempts in the 1970s to establish Mimbres autonomy, it is becoming increasingly clear that Mimbres was deeply engaged with Hohokam during the Pithouse period and with the Anasazi during the Early Pueblo period (e.g., Lekson 2009:133–136). Recognizing the Mangas phase (or something like it) does not require a return to "Anasazi swamping." Influences and ideas from outside the Mimbres region were reinterpreted and reconstructed in Mimbres ways. But it is important to reconnect Mimbres with the larger world of its times, and the Mangas phase (or something like it) well describes Mimbres at a critical juncture between Late Pithouse and Early Pueblo periods, when Mimbres populations shifted their attention from the Hohokam to the Anasazi region (Lekson 2006) and when new ritual practices emerged (Gilman et al. 2014; see also Sedig 2015). We now know that during the transition from pithouse to pueblo a range of architectures appeared: small "unit pueblos," perhaps owing something to the north, and shallow rectangular pithouses, possibly reflecting traditions to the west. As we will argue, new evidence suggests that the shift from pithouses to pueblos began in the early A.D. 900s, but it was not uniformly accomplished, nor should we expect it to have been.

New Understandings of the Pithouse-to-Pueblo Transition

The Mangas debate in Mimbres archaeology has centered on whether the pithouse-to-pueblo transition consisted of either a direct switch from stone-lined pithouses to pueblos or from pithouses to small stone-surface rooms to large stone pueblos. Our reevaluation of the "Mangas" phase stems largely from recent research that Sedig and the University of Colorado have conducted at the Woodrow site in the upper Gila

River valley and that Roth and the University of Nevada–Las Vegas have done at the Harris site in the Mimbres River valley. Research at these sites has revealed that both sides of the Mangas debate were lacking key data needed to fully evaluate the Mimbres pithouse-to-pueblo transition.

The Woodrow Site

The Woodrow site is located on the upper Gila, approximately 10 km north of Cliff, New Mexico. Although archaeologists have known of Woodrow since at least 1929 (Cosgrove and Cosgrove 1929), no professional excavations were conducted at the site until 2012 (Sedig 2013; Sedig and Lekson 2012). Woodrow is one of the largest archaeological sites in the Mimbres region. Prior to Sedig's research, perhaps the most well-known components of Woodrow were the numerous visible surface room blocks and the two prominent great kivas. In fact, some researchers (Danson 1957; Fitting et al. 1982; Lekson 1988) speculated that as many as five hundred surface rooms, along with numerous pithouses (Fitting et al. 1982:48), were present at Woodrow. Sedig's research has revealed that while Woodrow does have numerous surface rooms associated with the Classic period, the apex of occupation was during the pithouse-to-pueblo transition.

Surface survey, mapping, and excavation have provided basic information about the occupation of Woodrow, while helping to redefine the pithouse-to-pueblo transition. Structures ranging in date from the San Francisco phase to the Classic period were uncovered during two seasons of excavation at the site. In this chapter, we focus on Structures 2a–c and Structure 3, the most salient to our examination of the pithouse-to-pueblo transition (figure 3.1).

Architectural Complex 2

Architectural Complex 2 consists of three domiciles—a deep pithouse (Structure 2a), a shallow pithouse with thin adobe walls (Structure 2b), and a cobble room (Structure 2c)—stacked one upon the other in the southwest section of the Woodrow site (figures 3.2 and 3.3). These structures were built and occupied consecutively and provide clear evidence of the changes in architecture between the Mimbres Late Pithouse and Classic periods.

Structure 2a was the first built in this architectural complex and appears to have been a "typical" pithouse from the Three Circle phase. The floor of this pithouse was almost 2 m below modern ground surface. Numerous artifacts were found on the floor, including a plain brown bowl, a Style I bowl, and a large subfloor olla. Structure 2a was burned after it had ceased to be used, as evidenced by the multiple burned beams uncovered during excavation. Accelerator mass spectrometry (AMS) analysis

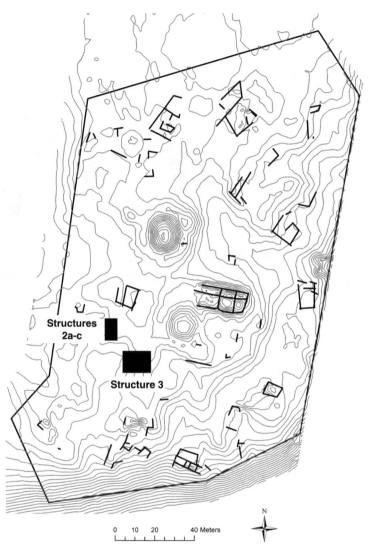

FIGURE 3.1 The location of Structures 2a–c and Structure 3 at the Woodrow Site (not to scale).

of burned roof material and maize cupules excavated in 2012 and 2013 returned dates between A.D. 690 and 870 at the two-sigma level (Sedig 2015).

While the AMS date range for Structure 2a is broad, the slipped ceramic assemblage from Structure 2a suggests the pithouse was occupied sometime in the early to mid–A.D. 800s (table 3.1). Style I was the most common ceramic type, with San

FIGURE 3.2 A plan view of Structures 2a–c.

Francisco Red, Mogollon Red-on-brown, and Three Circle Red-on-white composing at least 10 percent each of the structure's painted/slipped assemblage.

Structure 2a was filled with trash after its ritual burning. Structure 2b was then constructed in the trash-filled depression of Structure 2a. The first step in construction of Structure 2b was the excavation of an approximately 1.5–2.0 × 3.0–4.0 m cavity in the trash fill of 2a. This cavity was then covered with an approximately 5–10 cm thick coat of adobe that served as the walls for the structure. The floor, like most floors identified at Woodrow, was informally prepared by the placement of a thin wash of adobe on a hard-packed surface. Approximately 75 cm of fill separated the floors of Structures 2a and 2b, and the floor of Structure 2b was approximately 110 cm below modern ground surface. Poles lining the adobe walls supported the roof of Structure 2b (figure 3.4). The roof consisted of tree beams capped with adobe; the beams were likely removed and reused once use of Structure 2b ceased. Adobe debris from the roof was left on the floor of the structure after the beams were removed. Unlike the earlier Structure 2a, Structure 2b had no evidence of ritual closure through burning. Like Structure 2a, Structure 2b was filled with trash upon its closure.

FIGURE 3.3 A profile view of Structures 2a–c, facing north.

Overall, Structure 2b was most similar to Structure 3, as we will describe, in that it was a shallow pithouse (or, more accurately, a house in a pit) with thin adobe walls. The ceramic assemblage in Structure 2b differed from that of 2a (see table 3.1). While virtually no Style II or later ceramics were found in Structure 2a, those types comprised 3 percent of Structure 2b's slipped ceramic assemblage. There was also a noticeable increase in Style I ceramics in Structure 2b (53 percent compared to 37 percent). The increased amount of Style I ceramics, along with the presence of Style II or later sherds, indicates that Structure 2b was used around the late ninth to early

TABLE 3.1 Percentages of Slipped and Painted Ceramics from Structures 2a–c and Structure 3

Structure	% SF Red	% Mogollon R/b	% 3 Circle R/w	% Indet. White Slip[a]	% Style I[b]	% Style II[c]	% Indet. II/III[d]	% Style III[e]	Total Number of Painted/Slipped Ceramics from Structure
2a	20	18	10	14	37	<1	0	0	484
2b	8	9	6	20	53	3	1	0	1876
2c	7	8	3	34	39	5	4	<1	2775
3	11	11	3	37	25	6	6	1	3404

Note: Ceramics percentages and counts derived from room-fill and floor contexts.

[a] Indeterminate white-slipped ceramics. These sherds have a slip, but there is not enough painted design present to determine a type.

[b] Also referred to as "Mimbres Boldface."

[c] Also referred to as "Mimbres Transitional."

[d] Indeterminate Style II/III ceramics. These sherds are clearly not Style I, but they did not have enough painted design present to determine clearly if they were Style II or III.

[e] Also referred to as "Mimbres Classic."

FIGURE 3.4 A posthole in the thin adobe wall of Structure 2b.

tenth century. Unfortunately, no features containing dendrochronological or archaeomagnetic material were encountered during excavation. While botanical material was
recovered, none of it was from contexts suitable for radiocarbon dating.

Structure 2c, a surface-cobble room, was the third and last domestic building constructed in Architectural Complex 2. Although Structure 2c was undoubtedly built
on top of Structure 2b after use of the latter ended, the exact process of construction
was difficult to define. It appears that the cobble wall for Structure 2c was built by
people placing foundation stones (upright cobbles often referred to as *cimientos*) into

the trash fill of Structure 2b, stacking cobbles on top of those cimientos, and then coating the interior of the wall with adobe plaster. Excavation identified part of the north wall and northwest corner of Structure 2c (see figure 3.2). The topmost remaining cobbles in the wall were only a few centimeters below modern ground surface. The wall is a single course, with large cobbles ranging from 10 to 25 cm in diameter. Only the foundation of the wall was discovered intact during excavation. No evidence of a formally prepared floor was found in Structure 2c.

Whether Structure 2c was an isolated stone-walled room or part of a room block could not be determined during excavation. No additional rooms were attached to the north cobble wall, and the northwest corner indicates that no rooms were attached to the west. However, the possibility of additional rooms to the south and east cannot be discounted.

Architecturally, Structure 2c appears to be a typical "Mangas" small stone pueblo. Ceramics from the structure also fit the traditional "Mangas" (see table 3.1) model. Style II or later ceramics constitute 10 percent of the structure's painted/slipped assemblage (compared to 4 percent in Structure 2b). As we would expect, the percentage of Style I dropped in Structure 2c (to 38 percent of painted/slipped ceramics), indicating the type's waning popularity. San Francisco Red, Mogollon Red-on-brown, and Three Circle Red-on-white also decreased, but not substantially, from Structure 2b. This assemblage is like those found in other "Mangas/Transitional" phase structures (Lekson 1990; Shafer 2003).

Like Structure 2b, Structure 2c was not ritually closed through fire. Roof beams were apparently removed from Structure 2c upon its closure. Only Structure 2a had its roof beams left in place, likely to serve as fuel for its conflagration. While the removal and likely reuse of the beams in Structures 2b and 2c could indicate decreasing availability of beams, possibly from overexploitation of nearby trees, the burning of 2a and not 2b and 2c could also indicate significant social and ideological changes. Yet even if significant social and ideological changes did occur between the construction of Structure 2a and Structure 2c, it seems that Structure 2a remained important and closed. After it burned, it was left undisturbed, even though two structures were built on top of it. This was not the case for Structures 2b and 2c. With Structures 2b and 2c, fill was removed and redeposited, roofs were demolished and beams removed, floors were left exposed upon closure, and no complete artifacts were left in situ. The change in closing practices between Structure 2a and Structures 2b–c suggests a transformation in domestic ritual practices during the pithouse-to-pueblo transition.

Structures 2a–c reveal the evolution of domestic architecture from pithouses to aboveground room blocks. At Woodrow, the transition consisted of a transformation from deep pithouses to shallow pithouses with thin adobe walls to aboveground room blocks. The identification of Structure 2b was crucial in delineating the changes between the Late Pithouse period and transitional domiciles. Finding Classic period room blocks on top of pithouses is nothing new in Mimbres archaeology (Anyon and LeBlanc 1984; Cosgrove and Cosgrove 1932; Creel 2006; Shafer 2003). However, the excavations at Woodrow have demonstrated how easy it is to "miss" transitional structures during excavation. Had it not been for carefully controlled excavation techniques (and admittedly, a little luck with the placement of the excavation units), Structure 2b would have been completely missed or removed during fieldwork, and thus, the transition from pithouses to aboveground room blocks would have seemed rapid and direct. The thin adobe that comprised the walls of Structure 2b could easily have been dug through, and because of the absence of a floor and roof beams, it was hard to differentiate the fill of Structure 2b from that of 2a and 2c. Finally, the cobble wall of Structure 2c was not visible on the surface of the site, and Architectural Complex 2 left no signature in the magnetometry survey conducted in 2012. In fact, the only reason the wall was discovered, even though it was only 5 cm below ground surface, was because excavation expanded north and not east, south, or west.

Structure 3

Structure 3 was another shallow thin adobe–walled pithouse excavated at the Woodrow site, located southeast of Architectural Complex 2 (see figure 3.1). Overall, its architecture is most like Structure 2b's. However, Structure 3 was stratigraphically isolated; no structures were found above or below it, making it easier to define stratigraphically than Structure 2b and perhaps sparing it from looting (looters focus on cobble room blocks). Thus, Structure 3 provided an undisturbed snapshot of a domicile constructed during the pithouse-to-pueblo transition and helped confirm that shallow thin adobe–walled pithouses were a form of architecture built between the Late Pithouse and Classic periods.

Approximately 75 percent of Structure 3 (figure 3.5) was uncovered during fieldwork. Structure 3 was approximately 2.5 × 4.0 m in dimension, with its floor about 80 cm below modern ground surface. To construct Structure 3, people first dug a shallow pit into the locally derived conglomerate and sandstone, which is characterized by red sediment and medium-sized gravels. Thin, puddled adobe walls were then placed against the pit. Adobe was also used to create the floor of Structure 3. Although disturbed in some areas, the floor was present and exposed across most of Structure 3. The only artifacts on the floor were flat-laying sherds and chipped-stone flakes; all floor artifacts were secondary trash deposits. No in situ tools, vessels, or other artifacts were present. The most notable feature of the structure was a remodeled stone-lined hearth (figure 3.6). No hearths were encountered during the excavation of Structure 2b, and so the remodeled hearth in Structure 3 provides the only example of a transitional hearth at Woodrow.

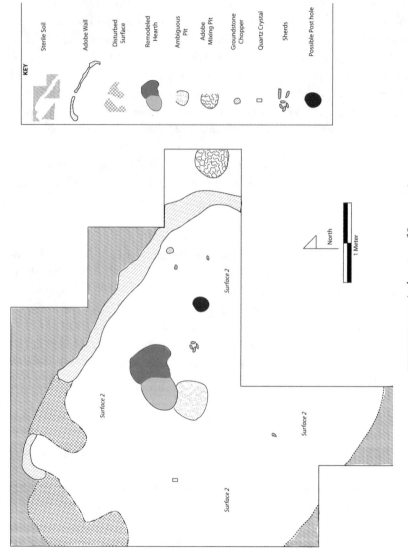

KEY

Sterile Soil

Adobe Wall

Disturbed
Surface

Remodeled
Hearth

Ambiguous
Pit

Adobe
Mixing Pit

Groundstone
Chopper

Quartz Crystal

Sherds

Possible Post hole

Surface 2

Surface 2

Surface 2

Surface 2

North

1 Meter

FIGURE 3.5 A plan view of Structure 3.

FIGURE 3.6 Remodeled hearths in Structure 3.

Unfortunately, no preserved postholes were identified during excavation; thus, the design of the roof cannot be described. However, like Structure 2b, several pieces of adobe with roof-beam and thatching impressions were found in the fill of Structure 3. It therefore appears that Structure 3 was also unburned and its roof beams were removed once use of the structure ceased. The roof of Structure 3 was likely very similar to Structure 2b's roof and almost certainly consisted of posts that supported beams covered with thatching and adobe. As with Structure 2b, the posts that supported the roof of Structure 3 would have lined the adobe walls.

Structure 3 was most like Structure 2b in terms of architecture, but the ceramic assemblage was most comparable to that of Structure 2c (see table 3.1). In fact, Structure 3 had the highest percentage of Style II or later ceramics (13 percent) of the Woodrow structures discussed in this chapter. It also had the lowest percentage (25 percent) of Style I ceramics. Like Woodrow structures described previously and the transitional buildings at NAN Ranch discussed by Shafer (2003:52), Structure 3 also had a mixture of Three Circle Red-on-white and red-slipped ceramics.

Ceramics and radiocarbon analysis provided dates for Structure 3. Three AMS samples put its occupation in the early A.D. 900s (Sedig 2015). Although ceramics from the fill and on the floor were mixed, the presence of Style II ceramics corroborates an early tenth-century date for Structure 3.

In summary, of all the structures excavated at Woodrow, Structure 3 is most similar to Structure 2b. Both structures consisted of thinly puddled adobe placed against the wall of a pit excavated into cultural fill or local sediments and gravels. Both structures were also "shallow pithouses"; they were not nearly as deep as Structure 2a. Both had the beams of their roofs removed once their use ceased.

Woodrow Site Summary

Taken together, Architectural Complex 2 and Structure 3 indicate that the transition from pithouses to pueblos took longer and was more diverse than previously suspected. The architecture of Structures 2b and 3 at Woodrow suggests that shallow pithouses with thin adobe walls preceded the small stone-surface room blocks previously termed "Mangas." While very similar architecturally to Structure 2b, Structure 3's ceramic assemblage more closely matched that of Structure 2c, with an increased density of Style II or later ceramics. The presence of these later ceramics could indicate that Structures 2c and 3 were used later in the transition from pithouses to pueblos, while Structure 2b was constructed earlier. While the different densities of Style II or later ceramics in Structures 2b, 2c, and 3 are minor, they help demonstrate the truly transitional nature of the pithouse-to-pueblo period in the Mimbres region, when people experimented with new forms of architecture over the course of several decades. In sum, Architectural Complex 2 and Structure 3 at Woodrow demonstrate that both sides of the Mangas debate were lacking information and that people used a variety of architectural forms between A.D. 900 and 1020.

The Harris Site

We can gain additional insights into the nature of the pithouse-to-pueblo transition from recent excavations at the Harris site in the Mimbres River valley. The Harris site was one of the largest in the region during the Late Pithouse period. Haury (1936) first conducted excavations at the site in the 1930s, and more recently archaeologists from the University of Nevada–Las Vegas (Roth 2015) excavated at the site from 2007 to 2013. Most of the pithouses excavated at the site during both projects date to the Three Circle phase. Unlike other large pithouse sites along the Mimbres River, Harris does not have a pueblo component built over the pithouses, indicating that it was abandoned by the Classic period. Dates on structures excavated during recent fieldwork suggest that a substantial population lived there in the A.D. 900s, however (Roth 2015).

Roth (2015) has argued that most of the Harris site occupants dispersed after the ritual retirement (burning) of the large Three Circle phase great kiva in the mid–A.D. 900s. Archaeomagnetic dates indicate that several of the pithouses associated with the great kiva were burned at the same time. Roth sees the retirement of the great kiva as causing social stress that resulted in the movement of long-standing extended family corporate groups to other sites in the valley.

A small pithouse-to-pueblo-phase population remained at the site after these events. The best evidence for this comes from House 52, an adobe surface structure (figure 3.7). This was a shallow (30 cm below ground surface) square structure located on the far west side of the site. Only the northwest portion of the house was excavated, defining parts of the structure's north and west walls, and so its dimensions are not known. One large posthole in the northwest corner was found, along with a smaller wall post along the west wall, and extensive adobe melt was found around these postholes. The floor was plastered, but the plaster had decomposed in much of the excavated area except around the hearth and near the walls. A circular plastered adobe–collared hearth was found near the north wall. Charcoal from the main post yielded a radiocarbon date of 1020 ± 30 B.P. (A.D. 980–1030; two sigma), indicating a late pithouse-to-pueblo-phase date for this structure. Only one piece of decorated pottery was recovered from the floor fill, an indeterminate Style I/II Black-on-white sherd. The presence of a surface adobe structure and a date in the late A.D. 900s fits well with the transitional structures documented at NAN Ranch (Shafer 2003).

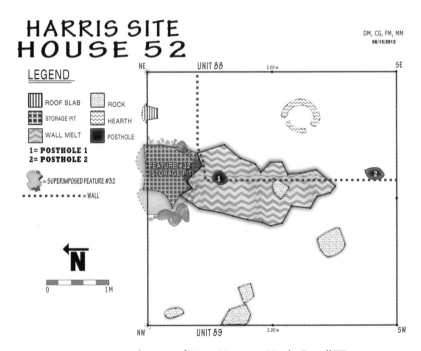

FIGURE 3.7 A plan view of Harris House 52. Map by Russell Watters.

Haury's 1934 excavations at Harris recovered three possible pithouse-to-pueblo transitional structures: Houses 7, 17, and 23. House 17 is perhaps the best candidate for this period because it is a shallow masonry-lined house with a short entryway. According to Haury's (1934) field notes, the ceramics included "Mangas" Black-on-white (now called Styles I and II Black-on-white), red-slipped, Alma Plain, and Three Circle Neck Corrugated. The house yielded a noncutting tree-ring date of A.D. 856, but it stratigraphically postdates House 10, the large Three Circle phase communal structure, discussed previously, that was burned in the mid–A.D. 900s, suggesting a late A.D. 900s date for this house. Haury (1934) stated in his field notes that the house was "a clear step in the evolution towards the stone pueblos" given its square corners, shallow depth, masonry lining, and short entryway. House 23, located east of House 10, was also shallow (the floor was 25 cm below ground surface) and masonry lined. It was built above three earlier structures and yielded two noncutting tree-ring dates of A.D. 836 and 838. Haury referred to it as a "late stone structure." He wrote that "the Mangus black-on-white strikes me as being somewhat later than the average we have been getting." House 7 is also a candidate for a pithouse-to-pueblo transitional structure because it is masonry lined; contains primarily black-on-white, red-slipped, Alma Plain, and Three Circle Neck Corrugated ceramics; and is one of the only structures on the site with a subfloor burial.

In sum, the reevaluation of Haury's work and new excavations at Harris have uncovered evidence of the pithouse-to-pueblo period in the Mimbres River valley. These data not only help to substantiate what previously appeared to be an ephemeral occupation in the Mimbres River valley during the A.D. 900s, but also reveal why this period has been so difficult to define archaeologically, as we will discuss.

Discussion

The data we have presented demonstrate that the pithouse-to-pueblo transition was in fact a distinct, definable segment of time between A.D. 900 and 1020 in the Mimbres region, particularly in the upper Gila, but also at some sites (Harris and NAN Ranch) in the Mimbres River valley. Thus, it seems that the pithouse-to-pueblo transition was much more important in Mimbres chronology than previously suspected.

Mimbres archaeologists should not be surprised by the existence of a definable pithouse-to-pueblo period; instead, we argue that it should be expected. Archaeologists, whether supportive of a "Mangas" phase or not, have long noted the dramatic differences between the Late Pithouse and Classic periods. During the Late Pithouse period, most people in the Mimbres region lived in small villages that housed one to five families (Anyon and LeBlanc 1984; Blake et al. 1986; LeBlanc 1989). Still, several large pithouse villages existed. Woodrow appears to have had a substantial population, perhaps as many as five hundred people (Sedig 2015). Roth estimates that the Harris site had over one hundred people at the height of its occupation during the Three Circle phase and Galaz (Anyon and LeBlanc 1984:91–95), and NAN Ranch also likely had large populations, possibly in the hundreds (Shafer 2003:22–23). Some of the pithouses in these sites were organized into courtyard groups, with three to five structures surrounding an open central area (Creel and Anyon 2003:81; Lekson 2009:92; Roth and Baustian 2015; Shafer 2003:26). Each large community had a sub-terranean communal structure where ceremonies and rituals were held. By A.D. 850, inhabitants of the pithouse sites had created black-on-white ceramics with prominent, bold designs.

Life in the Mimbres region was substantially different by A.D. 1050. Large towns consisting of clusters of aboveground room blocks had replaced pithouse sites. Great kivas had been burned and abandoned, and plazas served as ritual and ceremonial gathering places (Creel and Anyon 2003; Gilman et al. 2014:93). Numerous families lived in Classic period towns. People also made black-on-white pottery, but the designs were noticeably different and included finer painting, many more human and animal figures, and Mesoamerican-inspired iconography (Gilman et al. 2014:93). In a recent article, Gilman and colleagues (2014:94) argue that the adoption of Mesoamerican imagery and the end of great kiva use suggest a major change in the structure of Mimbres religious practices. By the Classic period, people had abandoned Late Pithouse traditions. The rate at which these traditions were abandoned (rapidly or gradually) is up for debate, although it probably varied and was not consistent throughout the region. However, most people likely did not wake up one day and simply discard many generations' worth of tradition, ideology, and cosmology.

We argue that the change from the Late Pithouse to the Classic should be, and is, definable. What we hope to have demonstrated in this chapter is that, short or long, there is a distinct, definable segment of time between the Late Pithouse and Classic periods throughout the Mimbres region. Previously, debates about the change from pithouses to pueblos focused on small stone-surface rooms: "Mangas" architecture. However, new data from Woodrow and Harris suggest that the change from pithouses to pueblos began before these stone structures, sometime in the early to mid–A.D. 900s, when people constructed shallow structures with thin adobe walls. Small cobble rooms, previously referred to as "Mangas" architecture, followed these structures; this evolution was clearly demonstrated by Structures 2a–c at Woodrow. Thus, the pithouse-to-pueblo transition began sometime in the early A.D. 900s and concluded in the early A.D. 1000s. Roth's work at Harris also makes it increasingly apparent that evidence for the pithouse-to-pueblo transition is not limited to the upper Gila Valley, as some previously suspected.

These new data on the pithouse-to-pueblo transition lead to questions about why this particular period has been so hard to define in Mimbres archaeology. While clearly evident at some sites (Woodrow, NAN Ranch, and Harris), the pithouse-to-pueblo transition appears to be absent or greatly obfuscated at others (particularly Galaz, Mattocks, and other Mimbres River valley sites). In what follows, we provide three explanations—the demolition of transitional structures, excavation and sampling bias, and diffusion of ideas—for the presence or absence of clear pithouse-to-pueblo evidence in the Mimbres region.

Demolition of Transitional Structures

It seems likely that at many Mimbres sites, especially those with large Classic period occupations like Galaz, people destroyed or modified transitional architecture as they built more and more rooms and room blocks. Shafer (2003) found direct evidence of this destruction and modification at NAN Ranch. We know that structures were built directly on top of each other, disturbing earlier occupations. Structures 2a–c at Woodrow perhaps best demonstrate how easily adobe transitional architecture, sandwiched between pithouses and cobble room blocks, can be missed during excavation. Structures 2a (the deep pithouse) and 2c (the cobble room) were easily definable during excavation. However, Structure 2b (the shallow pithouse/early transitional room) was not. In fact, it was not until the last week of excavation in 2013 that Structure 2b was defined, although part of it had been encountered during the previous field season. Had Structure 2b not been defined (and Structure 3 not excavated), and only the stone room block imposed on the deep pithouse identified, the architectural evolution at Woodrow would have seemed to fit the rapid transition model. The switch from pithouses to pueblos would have appeared direct.

Looting of Mimbres sites has also undoubtedly made the pithouse-to-pueblo transition harder to define archaeologically. Mimbres archaeologists have done superb work recovering data from sites once thought to be lost due to looting (e.g., Anyon and LeBlanc 1984; Creel 2006). Yet the impacts from looting cannot be avoided. Looters are skilled at what they do, and they know exactly where to dig to find the bowls associated with burials—in corners below the floors of Classic period rooms. Many burials would have been in the same level as transitional architecture. Looting would certainly damage or destroy the thin, fragile adobe walls of transitional structures, while perhaps not damaging even deeper pithouses. Once again, this creates a picture of easily definable (if disturbed) Classic period rooms and easily definable (if deep) pithouses, as well as a rapid transition between the two.

Even at sites such as Harris and Woodrow, which are better preserved than most Mimbres sites, transitional structures are difficult to define and easy to miss. The authors of this chapter almost overlooked transitional structures while excavating at their respective sites. Because these structures are shallow, built primarily with adobe, disturbed by looting (or rodents), and for the most part unexpected, they may have been misclassified or not recognized as transitional structures. House 52 at Harris, because of its shallow depth and lack of definable walls, was almost missed during excavation. Fortunately, the large posthole on the northwest corner of the structure was found relatively early during the excavation of the unit, and so it was possible to trace the structure from that point. It is thus highly likely that other transitional structures at sites across the Gila and Mimbres River valleys have been missed because of the difficulty in identifying them. Additionally, excavation procedures in the early part of the twentieth century were not as precise as current methods, and it is possible that early archaeologists dug through transitional structures without noticing thin adobe walls.

Excavation and Sampling Bias

This second explanation is related to the first. The pithouse-to-pueblo transition is exceedingly difficult to define at multicomponent sites with Classic period occupations. NAN Ranch is an exception to this rule in the Mimbres River valley. Woodrow is another of the few multicomponent sites with much evidence for the pithouse-to-pueblo transition. However, evidence of the pithouse-to-pueblo transition likely is present at Woodrow for three primary reasons: its location on the upper Gila River (where sites were looted but not as extensively as those in the Mimbres River valley), its relatively good preservation, and the fact that its population peaked during the pithouse-to-pueblo transition. The Harris site is unique because, as noted, it is a Late Pithouse site in the Mimbres River valley that does *not* have a large superimposed Classic period occupation, thus preserving transitional material. Many previous Mimbres archaeological projects have rightfully focused on Classic period room blocks in the Mimbres River valley due to the extensive looting that has occurred there. Yet as we have demonstrated, these Classic room blocks are places where delineating transitional period architecture is most difficult due to prehistoric demolition or destruction through looting, hence the apparent lack of a definable pithouse-to-pueblo transition.

A focus on Classic room blocks may have also caused Mimbres researchers to miss some transitional structures that were located apart from Classic period architecture. Extramural areas of Mimbres sites have received much less excavation than intramural areas. At Woodrow and Harris, the best-preserved and easiest to define transitional structures were found isolated from room blocks (and other structures in the case of Harris), where they are less prone to various disturbances.

Diffusion of Ideas

Experimentation with aboveground structures would have occurred before the cobblestone room block of the Mimbres Classic period was perfected. Shallow, semisubterranean, thin adobe–walled rooms and puddled adobe/cobble room blocks (i.e., small "Mangas" room blocks) were all steps along the way to Mimbres Classic architecture. Although the different forms of pre–Classic period architecture are found in both the upper Gila and Mimbres River valleys, the Mimbres Classic stone room blocks may have developed, and gained popularity, in the upper Gila first. The idea of diffusion goes hand in hand with research that indicates people moved from the upper Gila to the Mimbres River valley between the Late Pithouse and Classic periods (Lekson 1988; Nelson and Anyon 1996). If aboveground stone pueblos first developed in the upper Gila and then diffused to the Mimbres River valley, then we should expect to see less evidence of experimentation and refinement of this architectural form in the Mimbres River valley and thus the seemingly higher amount of transitional architecture in the upper Gila.

Of the three explanations offered for the varying degrees of evidence for the pithouse-to-pueblo material in the Mimbres region, diffusion is the weakest, especially with increasing evidence in the Mimbres River valley. More research is needed to help confirm this hypothesis. In particular, excavation of surface room blocks at Woodrow will help establish if those room blocks do indeed precede similar structures in the Mimbres River valley.

Likely, it is not a single factor but a combination of the three that explains the presence or absence of transitional material at archaeological sites in the Mimbres region. Work by the Mimbres Foundation greatly influenced archaeological knowledge of the prehistoric Mimbres region. Mimbres Foundation researchers argued against the "Mangas" phase because they saw no evidence for it. Yet the bulk of the work conducted by the project focused on sites where we would expect evidence of the pithouse-to-pueblo transition to be destroyed, disturbed, or missed.

Conclusion

The Mangas debate has been one of the longest lasting issues in Mimbres archaeology. Although the definition of "Mangas" has been modified since the Gladwins coined the term, the original definition—small room blocks with Style I pottery—has largely stuck. Critics of the Mangas phase rejected this definition due to what seemed like an implicit recognition of "Anasazi" influence in the Mimbres region and apparent lack of architectural evidence, particularly in the Mimbres River valley.

However, recent research, particularly at Woodrow, Harris, and NAN Ranch, has revealed that although small stone pueblos with Boldface pottery were present during the A.D. 900s, these characteristics should not solely define the pithouse-to-pueblo transition.

While the focus of this chapter, and the Mangas debate in general, has been on architecture, architecture is only a small part of the suite of changes that occurred in the Mimbres region during the tenth century. With increasing evidence that the pithouse-to-pueblo transition was a distinct, definable period, Mimbres archaeologists need to examine it closely to elucidate larger, more important questions. What caused the transition? What other social or ideological changes occurred? How does the transition articulate with contemporary events in other parts of the Southwest? In this chapter we have demonstrated how evidence for the pithouse-to-pueblo transition can be identified archaeologically. We hope this will lead to the delineation of more transitional occupations. Yet it is already apparent that the pithouse-to-pueblo transition was a critical part of Mimbres prehistory. With these new data, archaeologists can more accurately examine the social, ideological, and demographic transformations that occurred through time in the Mimbres region.

Acknowledgments

Research at Woodrow Ruin was supported by a National Science Foundation Doctoral Dissertation Research Improvement Grant (#1220059) and grants from the Arizona Archaeological and Historical Society, Colorado Archaeological Society, and Grant County Archaeological Society. Multiple individuals also supported research at Woodrow Ruin through a GoFundMe campaign. Research at the Harris site was supported in part by a grant from the National Science Foundation (#1049434).

References Cited

Anyon, Roger, Patricia A. Gilman, and Steven A. LeBlanc. 1981. A Reevaluation of the Mogollon-Mimbres Archaeological Sequence. *Kiva* 76:159–175.

Anyon, Roger, and Steven A. LeBlanc. 1984. *The Galaz Ruin: A Prehistoric Mimbres Village in Southwestern New Mexico.* Maxwell Museum of Anthropology and University of New Mexico Press, Albuquerque.

Blake, Michael, Steven A. LeBlanc, and Paul E. Minnis. 1986. Changing Settlement and Population in the Mimbres Valley, SW New Mexico. *Journal of Field Archaeology* 13:439–464.

Cosgrove, Harriet B., and Cornelius B. Cosgrove. 1929. Mimbres Valley Expedition Field Notes: Gila Valley and Duck Creek. Manuscript on file, Arizona State Museum, Tucson.

————. 1932. *The Swarts Ruin: A Typical Mimbres Site in Southwestern New Mexico*. Papers of the Peabody Museum of Archaeology and Ethnology Vol. 15(1). Harvard University, Cambridge, Massachusetts.

Creel, Darrel. 2006. *Excavations at the Old Town Ruin, Luna County, New Mexico, 1989–2003*. Vol. 1. Bureau of Land Management, New Mexico State Office, Santa Fe.

Creel, Darrell, and Roger Anyon. 2003. New Interpretations of Mimbres Public Architecture and Space: Implications for Cultural Change. *American Antiquity* 68:67–92.

Danson, Edward Bridge. 1957. *An Archaeological Survey of West Central New Mexico and East Central Arizona*. Papers of the Peabody Museum of Archaeology and Ethnology Vol. 44(1). Harvard University, Cambridge, Massachusetts.

Fitting, James E., Claudia B. Hemphill, and Donald R. Abbe. 1982. *The Upper Gila Water Supply Study. A Class I Cultural Resources Overview*. Prepared for the U.S. Department of the Interior, Department of Reclamation, Lower Colorado Region, Boulder City, Nevada. Hemphill Associates, Springfield, Oregon.

Fitting, James E., James L. Ross, and B. Thomas Gray. 1971. *Preliminary Report on the 1971 Excavations at the Saige-McFarland Site (MC146)*. Southwestern New Mexico Research Reports 4. Department of Anthropology, Case Western Reserve University, Cleveland, Ohio.

Gilman, Patricia A., Marc Thompson, and Kristina Wyckoff. 2014. Ritual Change and the Distant: Mesoamerican Iconography, Scarlet Macaws, and Great Kivas in the Mimbres Region of Southwest New Mexico. *American Antiquity* 79:90–107.

Gladwin, Winifred, and Harold S. Gladwin. 1934. *A Method for Designation of Cultures and Their Variations*. Medallion Paper No. 15. Gila Pueblo, Globe, Arizona.

Haury, Emil W. 1934. Harris Site Excavation Field Notes. On file at the Arizona State Museum, Tucson.

————. 1936. *The Mogollon Culture of Southwestern New Mexico*. Medallion Papers No. 20. Gila Pueblo, Globe, Arizona.

Hegmon, Michelle. 2002. Recent Issues in the Archaeology of the Mimbres Region of the North American Southwest. *Journal of Archaeological Research* 10:307–357.

LeBlanc, Steven A. 1983. *The Mimbres People: Ancient Pueblo Painters of the American Southwest*. Thames and Hudson, London.

————. 1989. Cultural Dynamics in the Southern Mogollon Area. In *Dynamics of Southwest Prehistory*, edited by Linda S. Cordell and George S. Gumerman, pp. 179–207. Smithsonian Institution Press, Washington, D.C.

Lekson, Stephen H. 1988. The Mangas Phase in Mimbres Archaeology. *Kiva* 53:129–145.

————. 1990. *Mimbres Archaeology of the Upper Gila, New Mexico*. Anthropological Papers No. 52. University of Arizona Press, Tucson.

————. 1999. Unit Pueblos and the Mimbres Problem. In *La Frontera: Essays in Honor of Patrick H. Beckett*, edited by Meliha Duran and David Kirkpatrick, pp. 105–125. Archaeological Society of New Mexico, Albuquerque.

————. 2006. *Archaeology of the Mimbres Region, Southwestern New Mexico, USA*. BAR International Series, 1466. Archaeopress, Oxford.

————. 2009. *A History of the Ancient Southwest*. School for Advanced Research Press, Santa Fe, New Mexico.

Nelson, Ben A., and Roger Anyon. 1996. Fallow Valleys: Asynchronous Occupations in Southwestern New Mexico. *Kiva* 61:275–294.

Roth, Barbara J. (editor). 2015. *Archaeological Investigations at the Harris Site (LA 1867), Grant County, New Mexico*. Manuscript on file, Department of Anthropology, University of Nevada, Las Vegas.

Roth, Barbara J., and Kathryn M. Baustian. 2015. Kin Groups and Social Power at the Harris Site, Southwestern New Mexico. *American Antiquity* 80:1–22.

Sedig, Jakob W. 2013. *Summary of 2012 Testing and Excavation at Woodrow Ruin, LA 2454, Grant County, New Mexico*. Report submitted to the New Mexico Cultural Properties Review Committee, Santa Fe.

————. 2015. The Mimbres Transitional Phase: Examining Social, Demographic, and Environmental Resilience and Vulnerability from A.D. 900–1000 in Southwest New Mexico. PhD dissertation. Department of Anthropology, University of Colorado, Boulder.

Sedig, Jakob W., and Stephen H. Lekson. 2012. *Archaeological Investigation of Woodrow Ruin (LA 2454), Grant County, New Mexico, June 6th–June 11th, 2011*. Report submitted to the New Mexico Cultural Properties Review Committee, Santa Fe.

Shafer, Harry J. 1995. Architecture and Symbolism in Transitional Pueblo Development in the Mimbres Valley, SW New Mexico. *Journal of Field Archaeology* 22:23–47.

————. 2003. *Mimbres Archaeology at the NAN Ranch Ruin*. University of New Mexico Press, Albuquerque.

4

Mimbres Classic Period Architecture, Ceramics, and Religion

Maintaining Social Cohesion in the Face of Social Diversity

PATRICIA A. GILMAN, DARRELL CREEL,
AND THOMAS E. GRUBER

BUILDING ON DECADES OF archaeological research in the Mimbres region, we now know that large Classic period pueblo sites (A.D. 1000–1130), which followed the pithouse-to-pueblo transition (chapter 3), were diversely organized, as seen in site and room-block layouts, differences in site histories, and the presence of at least two sites with special ritual components and people. We also know that Style III (Classic) Black-on-white painted pottery designs were similarly diverse. Conversely, archaeologists have described the Classic period as a time and place separate from neighboring culture history designations, and so we recognize the commonalities in pueblo architecture and the single pottery type used during this time in the Mimbres "culture area." We thus see clear evidence for social cohesion, what we call Mimbres, even though architecture and ceramics vary from site to site and between the different subareas. We contend that people were actively maintaining social cohesion even as they were producing this organizational (architectural) and individual vessel-design diversity.

The use of only one decorated ceramic type, Style III Black-on-white (figure 4.1), suggests an ideological unity that provided social cohesion for people who simultaneously demonstrated their differences with architectural variations (Hegmon 2010). On the other hand, although a few are quite similar, no two painted designs are exactly the same at the individual vessel level, a point that also could relate to the social diversity of the painters. LeBlanc's (2004, 2006, 2010) research suggests that only a very few individuals painted pottery in any site during the Classic period, which is another form of social diversity in that people would have been divided into painters and non-painters. Similarly, Creel and colleagues' (2012, 2014; Speakman 2013) instrumental

FIGURE 4.1 A Mimbres Style III Black-on-white bowl showing the Hero Twins. The older twin is on the right, has a larger right arm, and is wearing a male sash. The younger twin is on the left, has a larger left arm, and is wearing a string apron in his feminine guise. MimPIDD 198. Illustration by Kristina C. Wyckoff.

neutron activation analysis (INAA) investigations imply that Classic ceramics were produced only at sites from the NAN Ranch north in the Mimbres Valley, perhaps where adequate fuel for firing pottery could be found. The provisional linkage of a compositional group to a specific site or to multiple sites in close proximity is based largely on the compositional group that has the highest proportion at a particular site or sites. To some extent, petrographic analyses support these linkages (Schriever 2008; also, indirectly, Ownby et al. 2014). Gruber's (2015) research using the minute details of geometric designs (technological style) on Style III Black-on-white pottery shows that distinct ceramic-painting production groups were present at some large Classic sites (although we do not know whether these groups included few or many painters), while at others the production groups overlapped much more. Thus, Classic ceramics potentially represent many dimensions of social differences.

We argue that in the face of all of this social diversity, a set of religious and ritual practices that focused on Hero Twins iconography and scarlet macaws from the east coast of Mexico held people together for the century or so of the Classic period. Even with the social diversity that the architecture and the ceramic designs suggest, individuals with special roles, perhaps using the ideological unity that the Mimbres painted pottery designs suggest, may have helped maintain community cohesion and social integration. We currently have a rich foundation of data with which to examine social differences and similarities in this "egalitarian" society, that is, a society without elites or a strong centralized authority and one in which social differences were diffused or masked.

Mimbres Classic Period Research—The Background

The spectacular Style III Black-on-white pottery has focused archaeological attention on the Classic period pueblos with which these vessels are associated (see figure I.1). Fewkes's (1914, 1915, 1916a, 1916b, 1923, 1924) initial reports on and purchase of the pottery for the Smithsonian in the 1910s and 1920s, especially from Old Town and other southern Mimbres Valley sites, fueled both archaeological interest and the market for the ceramics. Excavations at six of the thirteen large Classic pueblos in the Mimbres Valley followed in the 1920s and 1930s. These sites were Mattocks (Nesbitt 1931; Gilman 2006; Gilman and LeBlanc 2017), Galaz (Anyon and LeBlanc 1984), Swarts (Cosgrove and Cosgrove 1932), Cameron Creek (Bradfield 1931), Eby, and McSherry (Carlson 1965). The reports from these projects formed the basis for future research, which unfortunately did not happen until the 1970s, perhaps because archaeologists thought that the sites had been so looted that no useful information remained.

Fitting (1971a, 1971b, 1972, 1973) conducted survey and excavations on Mimbres and post-Mimbres sites in the upper Gila drainage in 1971–72 (Baker 1971; Burns 1972). Unfortunately, some of the most important results and interpretations pertaining to the Classic period were not available to researchers until much later (Lekson 1978, 1990), if at all, and so the differences in the architecture and pottery between the Gila and the rest of the Mimbres region were not noted. We discuss these differences in what follows.

The Mimbres Foundation began research in the Mimbres Valley in 1974. Mattocks was the large Classic site on which the investigators focused to contextualize Mimbres Style III painted pottery and to provide modern excavated samples that would address questions about site and social organization. Although the Mattocks site had been excavated (Nesbitt 1931) and looted, the Mimbres Foundation demonstrated that archaeologists could gain information from such sites because they often contained sections that neither the looters nor the professionals had touched.

The Mimbres Foundation examined research questions current in the 1970s, such as those related to changing subsistence and demographics, but also did much chronology building because only a basic time line from Haury's (1936a, 1936b) and the Cosgroves' (1932) research in the 1930s existed. Hundreds of tree-ring samples yielded many dates, including the first chronometric dates for Classic pueblos. Also, seriation and a stylistic analysis of Mimbres painted pottery provided a new type—Transitional Black-on-white (now Style II) between the previously defined Boldface (Style I) and Classic (Style III) Black-on-white—that allowed finer temporal distinctions. This was the first formal definition of a distinction that Haury had recognized in the 1930s (Lehmer 1948:27). To answer subsistence questions, Mimbres Foundation personnel collected many flotation and pollen samples and conducted paleoethnobotanical, faunal, and chipped- and ground-stone analyses (Cannon 2000, 2001, 2003; Halbirt 1985; Lancaster 1984, 1986; Minnis 1985; Nelson 1984, 1986). They also recorded the building sequences of Mattocks site room blocks in terms of doorways, vents, and bond-abut patterns of wall corners to understand the building order and therefore the numbers of people in a room block and on the site at any given time (Gilman and LeBlanc 2017). Augmenting this work was a survey that recorded site sizes, dates, and settlement patterns (Blake et al. 1986). From these analyses, it became clear that the highest number of people lived in the Mimbres Valley during the Classic period. Minnis (1985), working with the Mimbres Foundation, addressed the depopulation of the valley at the end of the Classic period, largely in response to environmental changes away from better than average conditions.

Other projects overlapped with and followed the Mimbres Foundation in their investigation of large Classic pueblos, particularly at the NAN Ranch (Shafer 2003, 2006) and Old Town (Creel 2006a, 2006b) sites. The Texas A&M University NAN Ranch Project, directed by Harry Shafer, focused on the NAN Ranch site, where an extensive multiyear effort excavated numerous pit structures and Classic period pueblo rooms. The project also conducted excavations at other sites, most notably at the late Classic pueblo Vinegaroon (LA 73824), several miles from the NAN Ranch site up an eastern tributary of the Mimbres River. Survey in the Mimbres Valley and this tributary provided context for the excavations. The NAN Ranch Project resulted in numerous analyses of the sort conducted by the Mimbres Foundation, one of which led to a refinement of the painted pottery sequence (Shafer and Brewington 1995). Importantly, the NAN Ranch Project performed numerous INAA studies of Mimbres pottery (Brewington et al. 1996; Dahlin 2003; Dahlin et al. 2007; Gottshall et al. 2002; James et al. 1995), creating a composite suite of data that comprises a large and critical portion of the overall Mimbres area INAA data set. Equally important, the work involved an intensive analysis of the human remains (Holliday 1996; Marek 1990; Olive 1989; Patrick 1988), including their use in a recent DNA analysis (Snow et al. 2011).

The Old Town Project, with field seasons most years from 1989 to 2007, investigated various parts of the large Old Town site (LA 1113) on the lower Mimbres River. Much of the effort focused on the latest areas of the Classic period pueblo but also made a significant investigation of the Late Pithouse period (Creel 2006a, 2006b) and the Black Mountain phase pueblo remains (Taliaferro 2014). In terms of the Classic period, the Old Town Project demonstrated that all the immediate post-Mimbres pottery types, such as Chupadero Black-on-white, Playas Incised, El Paso Polychrome, and Three Rivers Red-on-terracotta, actually first occur in very late Classic contexts.

In the remainder of this chapter, we build on the work of these earlier projects to consider how people maintained social cohesion in the face of much social diversity. We use data on room-block and site organization and Style III Black-on-white pottery to address this issue.

Social Cohesion and Diversity in
Room-Block and Site Organization

Several measures, including room-block size, number, and layout; site histories; and presence or absence of ritual aspects such as great kiva complexes, roads, and scarlet macaws, show some large-scale social cohesion but much small-scale diversity in Mimbres Classic architecture. Classic sites in the Mimbres region suggest an overarching cohesion in that they all have surface room blocks, but the layouts of rooms of various sizes, with size probably relating to function, vary within and among room blocks. Site histories differ among the large pueblo sites: some are long lived (that is, having long occupations in the preceding pithouse periods) and others not. The presence of at least one great kiva just before the Classic period, however, appears to be a commonality among large pueblos, although each great kiva is unique in size and features. The Galaz and Old Town sites have ritual areas with related characteristics that set them apart from all other large Classic sites. We discuss each of these points in turn.

Many Classic room blocks, as we see them today, are the end products of perhaps several generations of construction. Others are Late Classic (about A.D. 1100–1130) and seem to have been built and occupied over just one or two generations. At the Swarts site, Cosgrove and Cosgrove (1932:13) proposed that each room block began as a nucleus of rooms that was expanded as the population grew. The result was two large room blocks. More recent analysis of Swarts architecture indicates that multiple small room groups likely merged to form each of the two excavated room blocks (Hill

1997). At the Mattocks site, each of the eight room blocks started as a small set of rooms, perhaps one to four, to which the inhabitants added other room suites as the household grew (figure 4.2; Gilman 2006; Gilman and LeBlanc 2017). That is, one household probably built and occupied each room block, which is not the same as the process that resulted in two large room blocks at Swarts. The differences in how room blocks developed highlight the diversity in Classic period pueblo architecture.

Based on their analyses of room blocks at the Mattocks and the NAN Ranch sites, Gilman (2006; Gilman and LeBlanc 2017) and Shafer (2003) have argued for different kinds of social arrangements at those sites. Gilman has suggested that room blocks at the Mattocks site represent households that built and used sequential room suites in a room block through time. Shafer (1999, 2003), in contrast, posited that corporate groups—large extended families—built and used the room blocks on the NAN Ranch site.

Room-block and site organization shows another kind of diversity. To the west in the Gila Valley and in the Eastern Mimbres region along the drainages on the east side of the Black Range (see figure I.1), both room-block organization and site organization during the Classic period are different from those in the Mimbres Valley. In the Gila Valley, there are three large Classic sites with more than one hundred rooms each (Fitting 1972; Lekson 1978, 1982; Sedig 2015), and each has between ten and twenty-five small room blocks. Rooms are not aggregated into large room blocks. At Woodrow, one of the three large sites, for example, they form blocks of two to fourteen rooms, with an average of six to eight rooms. In the Eastern Mimbres region, archaeological survey data show a few twenty- to thirty-room Classic pueblos with many one- to seven-room sites (Schollmeyer 2009:275–276) that are likely special-use locations such as outlying farmsteads (Nelson 1999:55–65). The largest sites include three at the mouth of the Palomas drainage with thirty-six, fifty, and sixty-five rooms each (Schollmeyer 2009:275–276), Las Animas in the Las Animas drainage with a Classic component of thirty to fifty rooms in eleven room blocks (Hegmon 2017:abstract), and Rio Vista/Garfield on the Rio Grande with more than one hundred rooms (Mayo 1994:1). Unlike Classic sites in the Gila Valley and more like those in the Mimbres Valley (Schollmeyer 2009:23), sites in the Eastern Mimbres region have three to four room blocks on the larger sites and one or two on the smaller ones.

Some of the architectural variation is certainly due to differences in household sizes and stages in the lives of the households, but some of it also results from differences in social organization among households and communities. Creel (2006a:178–179) suggests that some variation at Classic sites is due to substantial modification of Early and Middle Classic rooms and room suites, which were sometimes split, sometimes expanded, and sometimes destroyed almost entirely. In part, this was probably because of changes in household size and structure over time. Rooms built later naturally had

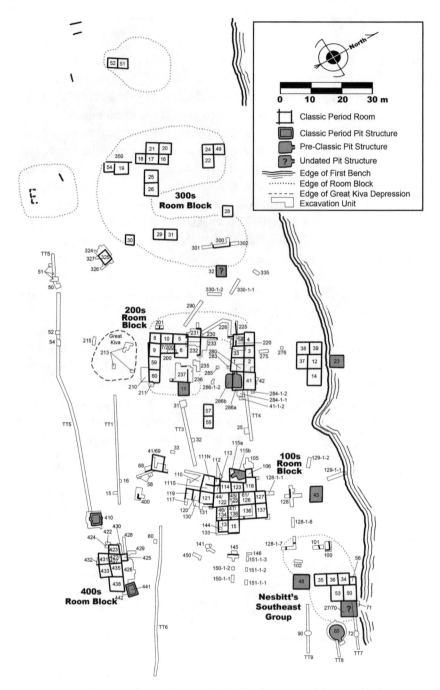

FIGURE 4.2 The Mattocks site, showing the final configuration of the room blocks. Finalized by Will Russell. From *Mimbres Life and Society* by Patricia A. Gilman and Steven A. LeBlanc. © 2017 The Arizona Board of Regents. Reprinted by permission of the University of Arizona Press.

less modification, and the latest built rooms were larger, usually in two-room suites that were sometimes interconnected (Creel 2006a:178–179). Suites with unusually large rooms may have had special functions and were probably not used for habitation. Overall, then, some of the variation is temporal and related to household changes.

Shafer (1982) and Hegmon et al. (2006) have shown that room suites (sets of contemporary rooms that a single social group used) contain much variation within and among sites, including both large and small Classic pueblos. Building on initial research by the Mimbres Foundation (Gilman and LeBlanc 2017; LeBlanc 1976) and Shafer (1982), Hegmon and colleagues (2006) suggest that some households occupied a flat, which was a single habitation room with one or two attached storage rooms. Other households lived in duplexes, which had two linked habitation rooms, both with hearths. Hegmon and colleagues propose that the presence of large suites and nonsuite architecture hints that some people may not have lived in household units. They conclude that the room-suite architecture and room-size ratios from each site are different, and so the social processes and organization producing the rooms and room blocks at the sites may also have been different (Hegmon et al. 2006:63–64). Hegmon (2010) later noted that people who built these varied architectural forms had the autonomy to design them in response to their household needs.

Some sites were used rather heavily through time while others were not, a fact that also implies social diversity. That is, most Classic period pueblos superimpose a good number of earlier pit structures, suggesting two hundred or more years of intensive site use before the Classic period. In contrast, probably no more than one or two families lived on the Mattocks site until about A.D. 1080. Clearly, these different site histories represent diverse social contexts.

In contrast, one commonality among site histories is that all the large Classic sites for which we have such information had at least one great kiva dating to the preceding Pithouse period (Creel and Anyon 2003). Even the Mattocks site, with only one or two families, had such a great kiva. One of the functions of the great kiva was presumably to integrate people at the site with those from other sites and perhaps to attract others to the ceremonies performed at a site. Importantly, though, each great kiva was different from every other one (Gilman and Stone 2013).

A measure of organizational diversity is the presence or absence of ritual areas at large Classic sites. Among the approximately twenty-five Classic period sites with more than one hundred rooms in the Mimbres region, the Galaz and Old Town sites are substantially different from the others. Galaz is near the north end of the Mimbres Valley, while Old Town is in the south end. Both sites had ceremonial complexes composed of adjacent great kivas used sequentially through time until the beginning of the Classic period (Creel 2006a, 2006b; Creel and Anyon 2003). The Old Town site had a road segment, a cleared linear pathway with low berms on both sides, which came from the north into the site at the location of the ceremonial complex. Apparently, special people, perhaps religious leaders, were buried within the complex. Old Town also had three or four macaws, brightly colored birds from at least 1000 km away, and some evidence, specifically four unusually small rooms along a courtyard edge, that the large birds were kept during the Late Classic period (Cannon et al. 2015).

At the Galaz site, Hegmon and colleagues (2006) noted very few small probable storage rooms compared to other large Classic sites, hinting perhaps that fewer "ordinary" activities occurred there. The Galaz site had more macaws and parrots than any other Mimbres site (Creel and McKusick 1994; Gilman et al. 2014; Wyckoff 2009). A military macaw, one of the few in the U.S. Southwest before A.D. 1150, was wrapped in hundreds of shell and turquoise beads and buried below a green stone in the floor of the latest Galaz great kiva. As noted in the next section, the Galaz site also was a special place in terms of ceramic production and macaws painted on Style III Black-on-white bowls.

In sum, building on earlier research, we now know that no standardized Mimbres room blocks or sites existed either within the Mimbres Valley or between sites there and in other parts of the Mimbres region. There were many differences and much flexibility in domestic arrangements, and this flexibility reflected and produced different social contexts for people's daily lives. As well, some sites had longer and more complicated use histories, and Galaz and Old Town were different in terms of their apparent focus on religion and ritual. Although we know of some overarching points of social cohesion—the presence of room blocks and earlier great kivas at all large Classic sites—the differences in room-block and site organization also suggest social diversity among people in the Mimbres Valley and the region.

Social Cohesion and Diversity in Style III Black-on-white Pottery

From the first painted pottery through the end of the Classic period in the Mimbres region, only one type of painted pottery was regionally produced, starting with Mogollon Red-on-brown and continuing with Three Circle Red-on-white and then Style I (Boldface), Style II (Transitional), and Style III (Classic) Black-on-white. Even though the pottery designs varied west and east of the Mimbres Valley from the earliest types on (Gruber 2007; Powell 1991, 1996), the pottery, starting with Style I, was always clearly Mimbres Black-on-white. That single overarching type may have helped maintain social cohesion through the similarities of practice (also see Hegmon 2010).

Building on previous small pilot projects (chapter 6), Creel and colleagues (2014; Creel and Speakman 2012; Speakman 2013) suggest that the one type of Mimbres painted pottery per time period was made in many places. During the Classic period in the Mimbres Valley, people apparently only made it at sites from NAN Ranch north, and the Galaz site appears to have been a center of painted pottery production. However, the fact that people at all other sites in the valley accepted and used it suggests that it might have promoted social cohesion. Substantial quantities of Style III Black-on-white pottery were also made at locations beyond the Mimbres Valley, minimally from the Rio Grande on the east to the Gila Valley on the west.

Despite repeated efforts to find patterned associations between painted designs and room blocks or sites, including a detailed analysis by Hegmon and colleagues (chapter 7), no painted representational pottery designs that associate only with one room block or site have been identified, again suggesting an acceptance of Style III Black-on-white pottery and its many designs across sites in the Mimbres Valley. Powell-Martí (Powell 2000; Powell-Martí and James 2006) specifically examined Middle Classic (A.D. 1060–1110) representational designs from several large Mimbres Valley sites (Galaz, Old Town, NAN Ranch, and Cameron Creek) and found that while fish and birds are most common, neither motif ever composes more than 26 percent of all designs at any site. Hegmon and colleagues' chapter in this volume supports the conclusion that no specific representational design associates with any one site, any one room, any age, or either sex. However, using newer INAA data, Creel and Speakman (2012) suggest that turtle images may associate with the Swarts site and were most probably produced there. Nevertheless, many recorded sites have at least one bowl with a turtle image, again showing the widespread distribution of all representational designs.

In general, then, researchers have discerned no clear representational design similarities or differences from site to site in the Mimbres Valley, supporting our contention that Style III (Classic) Black-on-white pottery may have been one of the elements that held Mimbres society together during the Classic period. While this may be true at the type and generalized design level, several subtler attributes of Mimbres painted pottery suggest that the painted pottery designs also represent social diversity. Relevant analyses include those of ceramic painting production groups (Gruber 2015), distinctiveness in pottery production (especially clay preparation; Creel et al. 2014; Speakman 2013), pottery distribution (Powell-Martí and James 2006), the macaw motif at the Galaz site (Gilman et al. 2014:96), paintings by individual artists (LeBlanc 2004, 2006, 2010), and the presence of Hero Twins iconography from Mesoamerica (Gilman et al. 2014).

Analyzing two specific and minute geometric (rather than larger representational) motifs on Style III Black-on-white pottery, Gruber (2015) has detected differences in the organization of ceramic painting production groups at five large Classic sites in the Mimbres Valley: Mattocks, Galaz, Swarts, NAN Ranch, and Cameron Creek. At the Mattocks, Swarts, NAN Ranch, and Cameron Creek sites, the production groups were separated in space and generally did not overlap, suggesting more rigid social boundaries between painting production groups in terms of learning and painting specific variants of the designs. Assuming that vessels from the site were painted there, the Galaz site had more painting production groups, and the groups overlapped one another in rooms and clusters of rooms. Gruber suggests that this overlap indicates less rigid social boundaries, that painters were potentially working together more frequently, and that painters were probably members of multiple painting production groups.

The Galaz site has several distinctions in terms of pottery that make it and the people who lived there stand out socially. First, Creel and Speakman (2012; chapter 6) have determined, using a large sample of pottery INAA data, that Galaz was perhaps the most prolific producer of Classic period pottery. Gruber's point about the few social boundaries among the pottery painters at Galaz as compared to other large Classic sites may relate to the fact that people were painting a lot of pottery at the site. Second, using ceramic compositional and motif data, Powell-Martí and James (2006) have proposed that Galaz was the focus of a multisite alliance, including Galaz, Old Town, Cameron Creek, and NAN Ranch, that formed after A.D. 1060. People at Galaz exported vessels to these three and many other sites but imported relatively few vessels and certainly none from these larger sites because little, if any, pottery was being made at them. Speakman (2013:37–38) has suggested, though, that a reexamination of these data indicates the presence of many more discrete compositional groups. Third, the Galaz site has more bowls (five) with macaws and parrots pictured than any other Mimbres site (although our knowledge of the vessel assemblages of several major looted sites is severely limited). These distinctions suggest that at least some people at Galaz, especially those involved with pottery production, painting, and distribution, were socially different from others in the Mimbres region.

LeBlanc (2004, 2006, 2010) has suggested that even though most people were buried with a painted bowl during the Classic period in the Mimbres Valley, not everyone actually painted pottery vessels. Examining specific motifs such as rabbits and turtles, LeBlanc and his consultants found small sets of designs that were similar enough to attribute to the same painter or household. Again, though, no designs were repeated exactly. Gruber's idea of ceramic-painting production groups, which also of course could have been individuals, fits well with LeBlanc's proposal that specific people or households may have painted specific designs. If not everyone painted pottery, then painters would likely have been a socially distinct group in the Mimbres region.

Gilman and colleagues (2014) have recently posited that some of the Classic Mimbres representational designs may depict the Hero Twins saga, the creation story common in Mesoamerica. This iconography is contemporary with the presence of scarlet macaws in Classic sites, and both may have come from the same tropical rainforest area on the southern east coast of Mexico. The Hero Twins motifs and the macaws also date somewhat after the great kivas had been burned and not replaced (Creel and Anyon 2003). As Gilman and colleagues have suggested, the scarlet macaws and the Hero Twins paintings may have been part of a new or augmented religion and as such may have served as the social structure that held people together. As we will describe, Hero Twins representations are not present in all parts of the Mimbres region, delineating another possible social distinction.

In contrast to Style III Black-on-white in the Mimbres Valley, few representational designs have been found in the Eastern Mimbres region (Karen Schollmeyer and Will Russell, personal communication 2015) or in the Gila Valley to the west of the Mimbres River, and even fewer paintings depict portions of the Hero Twins saga (Gilman 2018; Sedig, personal communication 2014; Wilson 2013). Indeed, the geometric designs differ between the Mimbres and Gila drainages (Wilson 2013), and analyses of Mogollon Red-on-brown (Powell 1991, 1996) and Style I Black-on-white (Gruber 2007) suggest that these differences began with the earliest painted pottery and continued through time. While the pottery in the Gila Valley is clearly Mimbres Black-on-white, suggesting social cohesion, it is not the same as that from the Mimbres Valley, likely representing a social distinction between the regions. The people in the Gila Valley may not have been concerned with or resisted maintaining fine-grained social cohesion with people in the Mimbres Valley, or they might not have been invited or allowed to do so. Instead, perhaps, they continued painting Style III Black-on-white bowls as if the Hero Twins saga had not been introduced nearby. That is, they made what would have been "standard" Style III Black-on-white pottery had the new religion not existed. It is important to note, however, that our knowledge of Gila drainage Classic period pottery designs is significantly less robust than that of the Mimbres drainage, and our knowledge of pottery designs actually produced in the Gila is even more limited.

Social Cohesion and Diversity During the Mimbres Classic Period

Building on previous research, both current and from long ago, we now know that large Classic period sites show overarching similarities, including the presence of room blocks, pre-Classic great kivas, and one painted pottery type—Style III Black-on-white. The room blocks, the Classic pottery, and, importantly, the practice of interring the dead beneath the floors of rooms essentially define the Mimbres Classic period, and these elements must have been part of the glue that held everyone who identified as Mimbres together for a century or a bit longer. Within this larger identification, though, were social distinctions that are important for understanding Mimbres society.

The overarching similarities often mask differences in room-block and site organization; room layout; site history; the presence, absence, and nature of ritual areas; ceramic painting production groups; pottery production and distribution; the presence of individual artists or households that painted pottery; and the presence of Hero Twins iconography. Mimbres Classic pueblos or room blocks are not all the same, and in fact they have few commonalities beyond their general pueblo structure and the interment of the dead below room floors. Room-block plans and numbers vary greatly, and this variation suggests more nuanced and complicated social roles, contexts, and relationships than we might have imagined. Site histories differ from each other, and two sites—Galaz and Old Town—have ritual precincts perhaps unlike other sites. Style III Black-on-white pottery was made at some but not all sites. LeBlanc has presented data suggesting that the same artist or household painted some designs on Style III Black-on-white pottery, but no two designs are the same, again showing the diversity of Mimbres materials. People who painted the pottery and those who did not would also have been socially distinct. Again, the Galaz site appears to stand out as the center of pottery production and distribution and as a place where ceramic-painting production groups did not have rigid social boundaries.

Given that Galaz and Old Town seem to have been different from other large Classic pueblos, some people at those two sites may have had different duties. These could have included caring for macaws and parrots (or bird keeping in general), constructing and maintaining great kivas (before the Classic period), conducting ceremonies in great kivas, and tracking the annual calendar. Continuity in the physical locations of the ceremonial precincts hints at continuity in the roles of the people tending those precincts. If indeed these sites had at least some people living at them who had specific duties related to religion and ritual, then people at other sites would have had different social relationships with them than with ordinary people. This is yet another form of social diversity in the Mimbres region.

Social distinctions were also important between people in the Mimbres Valley and those living in areas to the west and east. These differences may be shown in room-block structure and numbers, painted geometric designs, and presence or absence of representational designs. In the Mimbres Valley, the presence of new religious elements during the Classic period in the form of scarlet macaws and Hero Twins iconography on Style III Black-on-white pottery may have united people there. Scarlet macaws and Hero Twins iconography, however, were not common beyond the Mimbres Valley, and so they are not the things that symbolized Mimbres on a larger regional scale.

The Mimbres region is ideal for understanding social differentiation and similarities in an "egalitarian" society. That is, the society had no clearly demarcated leaders, although Hegmon (2010) has posited that some leaders controlled knowledge, especially in ritual matters. We can perhaps see the effects of such leaders at the Galaz and Old Town sites, and we have suggested other social differences among people that we can see archaeologically and that demonstrate the social distinctions within Mimbres society. At the same time, similarities in practice apparently united people into a Mimbres culture based on shared symbols and rituals.

Acknowledgments

Gilman thanks the College of Art and Sciences, University of Oklahoma, for support that allowed her to present an earlier version of this chapter at the 2014 Society for American Archaeology meeting in Austin. The authors appreciate the useful comments of two anonymous reviewers.

References Cited

Anyon, Roger, and Steven A. LeBlanc. 1984. *The Galaz Ruin: A Prehistoric Mimbres Village in Southwestern New Mexico*. University of New Mexico Press, Albuquerque.

Baker, Gayla. 1971. *The Riverside Site, Grant County, New Mexico*. Southwestern New Mexico Research Reports 5. Case Western Reserve University, Cleveland, Ohio.

Blake, Michael, Steven A. LeBlanc, and Paul E. Minnis. 1986. Changing Settlement and Population in the Mimbres Valley, SW New Mexico. *Journal of Field Archaeology* 13:439–464.

Bradfield, Wesley. 1931. *Cameron Creek Village: A Site in the Mimbres Area in Grant County New Mexico*. School of American Research, Santa Fe, New Mexico.

Brewington, Robbie L., Harry J. Shafer, and William D. James. 1996. Production and Distribution of Mimbres Black-on-white Ceramics: Evidence from Instrumental Neutron Activation Analysis (INAA). Paper presented at the 62nd Annual Meeting of the Society for American Archaeology, Nashville, Tennessee.

Burns, Peter. 1972. *The Heron Ruin, Grant County, New Mexico*. Southwestern New Mexico Research Reports 7. Case Western Reserve University, Cleveland, Ohio.

Cannon, Michael D. 2000. Large Mammal Relative Abundance in Pithouse and Pueblo Period Archaeofaunas from Southwestern New Mexico: Resource Depression Among the Mimbres-Mogollon? *Journal of Anthropological Archaeology* 19:317–347.

———. 2001. Large Mammal Resource Depression and Agricultural Intensification: An Empirical Test in the Mimbres Valley, New Mexico. PhD dissertation, Department of Anthropology, University of Washington, Seattle.

———. 2003. A Model of Central Place Forager Prey Choice and an Application to Faunal Remains from the Mimbres Valley, New Mexico. *Journal of Anthropological Archaeology* 22:1–25.

Cannon, Michael D., Jack Broughton, Christopher Francis, and Darrell Creel. 2015. Chapter 7: Avian Remains. In *The Old Town Project: Artifact Analyses*, by Darrell Creel. Cultural Resources Series Vol. 16(2). New Mexico Bureau of Land Management, Santa Fe. Manuscript on file, Bureau of Land Management, Las Cruces District, New Mexico.

Carlson, Roy L. 1965. *Four Mimbres Sites: The Earl Morris Excavations of 1926*. Manuscript on file, University of Colorado Museum, Boulder.

Cosgrove, H. S., and C. B. Cosgrove. 1932. *The Swarts Ruin, a Typical Mimbres Site in Southwestern New Mexico*. Report of the Peabody Museum of Archaeology and Ethnology, Harvard University Vol. 15(1). The Museum, Cambridge, Massachusetts.

Creel, Darrell. 2006a. *Excavations at the Old Town Ruin, Luna County, New Mexico, 1989–2003*. Cultural Resources Series Vol. 16(1). New Mexico Bureau of Land Management, Santa Fe.

———. 2006b. Social Differentiation at the Old Town Site. In *Mimbres Society*, edited by Valli S. Powell-Martí and Patricia A. Gilman, pp. 32–44. University of Arizona Press, Tucson.

Creel, Darrell, and Roger Anyon. 2003. New Interpretations of Mimbres Public Architecture and Space: Implications for Cultural Change. *American Antiquity* 68:67–92.

Creel, Darrell, Steven A. LeBlanc, and Robert J. Speakman. 2014. Neutron Activation Analysis of Mimbres Pottery from the Swarts Ruin. Paper presented at the 18th Biennial Mogollon Archaeology Conference, Las Cruces, New Mexico.

Creel, Darrell, and Charmion McKusick. 1994. Prehistoric Macaws and Parrots in the Mimbres Area, New Mexico. *American Antiquity* 59:510–524.

Creel, Darrell, and Robert J. Speakman. 2012. The Mimbres Vessel Project: An Update on the Neutron Activation Analysis Effort. Paper presented at the 17th Biennial Mogollon Conference, Silver City, New Mexico.

Dahlin, Eleanor. 2003. INAA and Distribution Patterns of Classic Mimbres Black-on-white Vessels during the Classic Period. Master's thesis, Department of Anthropology, Texas A&M University, College Station.

Dahlin, Eleanor, D. L. Carlson, William D. James, and Harry J. Shafer. 2007. Distribution Patterns of Mimbres Ceramics Using INAA and Multivariate Statistical Methods. *Journal of Radioanalytical and Nuclear Chemistry* 271:461–466.

Fewkes, J. Walter. 1914. *Archaeology of the Lower Mimbres Valley, New Mexico*. Smithsonian Miscellaneous Collections Vol. 63(10). Smithsonian Institution, Washington, D.C.

———. 1915. *Prehistoric Remains in New Mexico: Explorations and Field-Work of the Smithsonian Institution in 1914*. Smithsonian Miscellaneous Collections Vol. 65(6):62–72. Smithsonian Institution, Washington, D.C.

———. 1916a. Animal Figures in Prehistoric Pottery from Mimbres Valley, New Mexico. *American Anthropologist* n.s. 18:535–545.

———. 1916b. *Explorations and Field-Work of the Smithsonian Institution in 1915*. Smithsonian Miscellaneous Collections Vol. 66(3):84–89. Smithsonian Institution, Washington, D.C.

———. 1923. *Designs on Prehistoric Pottery from the Mimbres Valley, New Mexico*. Smithsonian Miscellaneous Collections Vol. 74(6). Smithsonian Institution, Washington, D.C.

———. 1924. *Additional Designs on Prehistoric Mimbres Pottery*. Smithsonian Miscellaneous Collections Vol. 76(8). Smithsonian Institution, Washington, D.C.

Fitting, James E. 1971a. *Excavations at MC 110, Grant County, New Mexico*. Southwestern New Mexico Research Reports 2. Case Western Reserve University, Cleveland, Ohio.

———. 1971b. *The Hermanas Ruin, Luna County, New Mexico*. Southwestern New Mexico Research Reports 3. Case Western Reserve University, Cleveland, Ohio.

———. 1972. Preliminary Notes on Cliff Valley Settlement Patterns. *Artifact* 10(4):15–30.

———. 1973. An Early Mogollon Community: A Preliminary Report on the Winn Canyon Site. *Artifact* 11(1–2):1–94.

Gilman, Patricia A. 2006. Social Differences at the Classic Period Mattocks Site in the Mimbres Valley. In *Mimbres Society*, edited by Valli S. Powell-Martí and Patricia A. Gilman, pp. 66–85. University of Arizona Press, Tucson.

———. 2018. Long-term, Constant, and Stable Identities and Social Relationships with and within the Mimbres Region of Southwestern New Mexico. In *Social Identity in Frontier and Borderland Communities of the North American Southwest*, edited by Karen G. Harry and Sarah Herr. University Press of Colorado, in press.

Gilman, Patricia A., and Steven A. LeBlanc. 2017. *Mimbres Life and Society: The Mattocks Site of Southwestern New Mexico*. University of Arizona Press, Tucson.

Gilman, Patricia A., and Tammy Stone. 2013. The Role of Ritual Variability in Social Negotiations of Early Communities: Great Kiva Homogeneity and Heterogeneity in the Mogollon Region of the North American Southwest. *American Antiquity* 78:607–623.

Gilman, Patricia A., Marc Thompson, and Kristina C. Wyckoff. 2014. Ritual Change and the Distant: Mesoamerican Iconography, Scarlet Macaws, and Great Kivas in the Mimbres Region of Southwestern New Mexico. *American Antiquity* 79:90–107.

Gottshall, Julia Munoz, Harry J. Shafer, and William D. James. 2002. Neutron Activation Analysis of Mimbres Corrugated Pottery from the NAN Ranch Ruin. In *Mogollon Archaeology: Collected Papers from the Eleventh Mogollon Conference*, edited by Patrick Beckett, pp. 121–128. COAS Publishing and Research, Las Cruces, New Mexico.

Gruber, Thomas E. 2007. The Regional Diversity of Mimbres Boldface (Style I) Bowl Designs. Master's thesis, Department of Anthropology, University of Oklahoma, Norman.

———. 2015. Social Boundaries between Ceramic Design Production Groups at Classic Mimbres Sites, Southwestern New Mexico, A.D. 1000–1130. PhD dissertation, Department of Anthropology, University of Oklahoma, Norman.

Halbirt, Carl D. 1985. Pollen Analysis of Metate Wash Samples: Evaluating Techniques for Determining Metate Function. Master's thesis, Department of Anthropology, Northern Arizona University, Flagstaff.

Haury, Emil W. 1936a. *The Mogollon Culture of Southwestern New Mexico*. Medallion Papers No. 20. Gila Pueblo, Globe, Arizona.

———. 1936b. *Some Southwestern Pottery Types, Series IV*. Medallion Papers No. 19. Gila Pueblo, Globe, Arizona.

Hegmon, Michelle. 2010. Mimbres Society: Another Way of Being. In *Mimbres Lives and Landscapes*, edited by Margaret C. Nelson and Michelle Hegmon, pp. 39–45. School for Advanced Research Press, Santa Fe, New Mexico.

———. 2017. *Las Animas Village (LA3949): A Large Multicomponent Site in the Eastern Mimbres Area*. Report on file, School of Human Evolution and Social Change, Arizona State University, Tempe.

Hegmon, Michelle, Jennifer A. Brady, and Margaret C. Nelson. 2006. Variability in Classic Mimbres Room Suites: Implications for Household Organization and Social Differences. In *Mimbres Society*, edited by Valli S. Powell-Martí and Patricia A. Gilman, pp. 45–65. University of Arizona Press, Tucson.

Hill, Mara. 1997. Sociocultural Implications of Large Mimbres Sites: Architectural and Mortuary Behavior at Swarts Ruin, New Mexico. Master's thesis, Department of Anthropology, Texas A&M University, College Station.

Holliday, Diane Y. 1996. Were Some More Equal? Diet and Health at the NAN Ranch Pueblo, Mimbres Valley, New Mexico. PhD dissertation, Department of Anthropology, University of Wisconsin, Madison.

James, William D., Robbie L. Brewington, and Harry J. Shafer. 1995. Compositional Analysis of American Southwestern Ceramics by Neutron Activation Analysis. *Journal of Radioanalytical and Nuclear Chemistry* 192(1):109–116.

Lancaster, James W. 1984. Groundstone Artifacts. In *The Galaz Ruin: A Prehistoric Mimbres Village in Southwestern New Mexico*, by Roger Anyon and Steven A. LeBlanc, pp. 247–262. Maxwell Museum of Anthropology and University of New Mexico Press, Albuquerque.

———. 1986. Ground Stone. In *Short-Term Sedentism in the American Southwest: The Mimbres Valley Salado*, by Ben A. Nelson and Steven A. LeBlanc, pp. 177–190. Maxwell Museum of Anthropology and University of New Mexico Press, Albuquerque.

LeBlanc, Steven A. 1976. Mimbres Archaeological Center: Preliminary Report of the Second Season of Excavation, 1975. *Journal of New World Archaeology* 1(6):1–23.

———. 2004. *Painted by a Distant Hand: Mimbres Pottery from the American Southwest*. Peabody Museum Press, Harvard University, Cambridge, Massachusetts.

———. 2006. Who Made the Mimbres Bowls? Implication of Recognizing Individual Artists for Craft Specialization and Social Networks. In *Mimbres Society*, edited by Valli S. Powell-Martí and Patricia A. Gilman, pp. 109–150. University of Arizona Press, Tucson.

——. 2010. The Painters of the Pots. In *Mimbres Lives and Landscapes*, edited by Margaret C. Nelson and Michelle Hegmon, pp. 75–81. School for Advanced Research Press, Santa Fe, New Mexico.

Lehmer, Donald. 1948. *The Jornada Branch of the Mogollon*. University of Arizona Social Science Bulletin 17. University of Arizona, Tucson.

Lekson, Stephen H. 1978. Settlement Patterns in the Redrock Valley, Southwestern New Mexico. Master's thesis, Department of Anthropology, Eastern New Mexico University, Portales.

——. 1982. Architecture and Settlement Plan in the Redrock Valley of the Gila River, Southwestern New Mexico. In *Mogollon Archaeology: Proceedings of the 1980 Mogollon Conference*, edited by Patrick H. Beckett, pp. 61–74. Acoma Books, Ramona, California.

——. 1990. *Mimbres Archaeology of the Upper Gila, New Mexico*. University of Arizona Anthropological Paper No. 52. University of Arizona Press, Tucson.

Marek, Marianne. 1990. Lone Bone Growth of Mimbres Subadults from the NAN Ranch (LA15049), New Mexico. Master's thesis, Department of Anthropology, Texas A&M University, College Station.

Mayo, Jill E. 1994. Garfield Revisited: Further Research on a Mimbres Site in the Southern Rio Grande Valley. Master's thesis, Department of Anthropology, New Mexico State University, Las Cruces.

Minnis, Paul E. 1985. *Social Adaptation to Food Stress: A Prehistoric Southwestern Example*. University of Chicago Press, Chicago.

Nelson, Margaret C. 1984. Food Selection at Galaz: Inferences from Chipped Stone Analysis. In *The Galaz Ruin: A Prehistoric Mimbres Village in Southwestern New Mexico*, by Roger Anyon and Steven A. LeBlanc, pp. 225–246. Maxwell Museum of Anthropology and University of New Mexico Press, Albuquerque.

——. 1986. Chipped Stone Analysis: Food Selection and Hunting Behavior. In *Short-Term Sedentism in the American Southwest: The Mimbres Valley Salado*, by Ben A. Nelson and Steven A. LeBlanc, pp. 141–176. Maxwell Museum of Anthropology and University of New Mexico Press, Albuquerque.

——. 1999. *Mimbres during the Twelfth Century: Abandonment, Continuity, and Reorganization*. University of Arizona Press, Tucson.

Nesbitt, Paul. 1931. *The Ancient Mimbreños: Based on Investigations at the Mattocks Ruin, Mimbres Valley, New Mexico*. Logan Museum, Beloit College, Beloit, Wisconsin.

Olive, Ben. 1989. The Oral Health and Dental Characteristics of a Mimbres Population from Southwest New Mexico. Master's thesis, Department of Anthropology, Texas A&M University, College Station.

Ownby, Mary, Deborah Huntley, and Matthew Peeples. 2014. A Combined Approach: Using NAA and Petrography to Examine Ceramic Production and Exchange in the American Southwest. *Journal of Archaeological Science* 52:152–162.

Patrick, Suzanne. 1988. Description and Demographic Analysis of a Mimbres Mogollon Population from LA15049 (NAN Ruin). Master's thesis, Department of Anthropology, Texas A&M University, College Station.

Powell, Valli S. 1991. Regional Diversity in Mogollon Red-on-brown Pottery. Master's thesis, Department of Anthropology, University of Oklahoma, Norman.

———. 1996. Regional Diversity in Mogollon Red-on-brown Pottery. *Kiva* 62:185–203.

———. 2000. Iconography and Group Formation during the Late Pithouse and Classic Periods of the Mimbres Society, A.D. 970–1140. PhD dissertation, Department of Anthropology, University of Oklahoma, Norman.

Powell-Martí, Valli S., and William D. James. 2006. Ceramic Iconography and Social Asymmetry in the Classic Mimbres Heartland, A.D. 970–1140. In *Mimbres Society*, edited by Valli S. Powell-Martí and Patricia A. Gilman, pp. 151–173. University of Arizona Press, Tucson.

Schollmeyer, Karen Gust. 2009. Resource Stress and Settlement Pattern Change in the Eastern Mimbres Area, Southwest New Mexico. PhD dissertation. Arizona State University, Tempe.

Schriever, Bernard A. 2008. Informal Identity and the Mimbres Phenomenon: Identity and Archaeological Cultures in the Mimbres Mogollon. PhD dissertation, Department of Anthropology, University of Oklahoma, Norman.

Sedig, Jakob W. 2015. The Mimbres Transitional Phase: Examining Social, Demographic, and Environmental Resilience and Vulnerability from A.D. 900–1000 in Southwest New Mexico. PhD dissertation, Department of Anthropology, University of Colorado, Boulder.

Shafer, Harry J. 1982. Classic Mimbres Phase Households and Room Use Patterns. *Kiva* 48:17–37.

———. 1999. The Classic Mimbres Phenomenon and Some New Interpretations. In *Sixty Years of Mogollon Archaeology: Papers from the Ninth Mogollon Conference, Silver City, New Mexico, 1996*, edited by Stephanie M. Whittlesey, pp. 95–105. SRI Press, Tucson, Arizona.

———. 2003. *Mimbres Archaeology at the NAN Ranch Ruin*. University of New Mexico Press, Albuquerque.

———. 2006. Extended Families to Corporate Groups: Pithouse to Pueblo Transformation of Mimbres Society. In *Mimbres Society*, edited by Valli S. Powell-Martí and Patricia A. Gilman, pp. 15–31. University of Arizona Press, Tucson.

Shafer, Harry J., and Robbie L. Brewington. 1995. Microstylistic Changes in Mimbres Black-on-white Pottery: Examples from the NAN Ruin, Grant County, New Mexico. *Kiva* 61:5–29.

Snow, Meradeth, Harry J. Shafer, and David G. Smith. 2011. The Relationship of the Mimbres to Other Southwestern and Mexican Populations. *Journal of Archaeological Science* 38:3122–3133.

Speakman, Robert J. 2013. Mimbres Pottery Production and Distribution. PhD dissertation. Department of Prehistory, Ancient History, and Archaeology, University of Barcelona.

Taliaferro, Matthew S. 2014. The Black Mountain Phase Occupation at Old Town: An Examination of Social and Technological Organization in the Mimbres Valley of Southwestern

New Mexico, ca. A.D. 1150–1300. PhD dissertation, Department of Anthropology, University of Texas, Austin.

Wilson, Michelle L. 2013. Powers Ranch, a Mimbres Site in East Central Arizona: A Question of Identity. Master's thesis. Department of Anthropology, University of Oklahoma, Norman.

Wyckoff, Kristina C. 2009. Mimbres-Mesoamerican Interaction: Macaws and Parrots in the Mimbres Valley, Southwestern New Mexico. Master's thesis, Department of Anthropology, University of Oklahoma, Norman.

5

Small Pueblo Sites of the Mimbres Classic Period

New Views and Interpretations

ROBERT J. STOKES, AARON R. WOODS,
AND ELIZABETH TONEY

S MALL PUEBLO SITES in the Mimbres area are ubiquitous across the landscape. In fact, pueblo sites containing twenty rooms or fewer represent over 75 percent of the known pueblo sites in the Mimbres and Sapillo Valleys of southwestern New Mexico (Stokes 2003). Of those, pueblos with ten or fewer rooms—the traditionally defined "field house" in Mimbres archaeology—comprise over 80 percent of what we define as small pueblo sites (figure 5.1). Clearly, use of small pueblo sites during the Mimbres Classic period (A.D. 1000–1140) was an important component of social, settlement, and subsistence systems (Stokes 2003; Toney 2012). Yet archaeological studies focusing on these small sites have been few and far between, as demonstrated in chapter 4 of this volume, where Gilman and colleagues discuss the major research projects that have defined the Mimbres over the past century. Almost without exception, these projects focused on the large pueblo sites in the Mimbres and Gila River valleys.

Prior to the work of the Mimbres Foundation in the Mimbres Valley during the 1970s, small-site research was limited to highway salvage excavations (Hammack 1964, 1966; Hammack et al. 1966; Ice 1968) and amateur archaeological association excavations (Parsons 1955), typically published with minimal information and little interpretation. The Mimbres Foundation published the results of fieldwork at a seven- to ten-room site (LA 12109) in the Mimbres Valley that subsequently came to define these structures as short-term, agriculture-related domiciles (Nelson et al. 1978). Mimbres Foundation researchers also observed a range of small pueblo sites up and down the valley and in many of its tributaries (Blake et al. 1986; Minnis 1985), but few were excavated other than LA 12109. With so few small sites systematically investigated, it is not surprising that we still know very little about this important site type in the Mimbres cultural system.

FIGURE 5.1 A one-room Mimbres Classic period field house in the Gila National Forest, southwestern New Mexico. Photograph by Elizabeth Toney.

Since these earlier excavations, small pueblo sites, no matter where they are located on the landscape, have come to be viewed as short-term and/or seasonal domiciles related to resource extraction, whether the resources were agriculturally produced or gathered from the landscape. Function seemed to be clear cut and largely unvarying. In a sense, therefore, data derived from small sites were considered either redundant or of limited interpretative value, especially since the sites typically contained little material cultural and few burials and were lightly built. An important exception comes from Arizona State University's research at Mimbres sites along the eastern side of the Black Range—the Eastern Mimbres Archaeological Project—in which Nelson (1999) argued that small pueblos functioned as isolated full-time hamlets. These sites, however, are part of what the researchers describe as a "Reorganization phase" of the Mimbres after A.D. 1150 (Hegmon et al. 1999) and therefore shed little light on small-site use prior to this reorganization. Because of the traditional limited-activity view of small pueblo sites in the Mimbres Valley and its immediate environs, interpretations of them, or even the study of them, remain inadequate despite almost one hundred years of professional research focused on the Mimbres region.

We suggest this way of thinking about small pueblo sites needs to change. We need to fully understand their histories and roles in Mimbres society, not just their limited roles in agricultural cycles and resource-extraction systems. In this chapter, we bring new data and ways of interpreting small sites to bear on questions related not only to agriculture and subsistence, but also to duration and intensity of occupation, patterns in how the sites are spread across the landscape, and their roles in Mimbres society and communities beyond just agriculture. We argue that much more is going on with small Mimbres pueblo sites than was previously known. This statement mirrors in a way the ethos of the Mimbres Foundation and its researchers' belief that the devastatingly pothunted Mimbres sites still held great potential and that much more could still be learned about the Mimbres culture and its people (LeBlanc 1983). We agree completely that much remains to be learned about the Mimbres more than forty years on. We argue that a better understanding of small pueblo sites—which are sometimes not as badly pothunted as the larger village sites—will contribute to the study of Mimbres cultural dynamics, as we demonstrate in this chapter.

Approaches to Understanding Small Mimbres Pueblos

Typical interpretations of small pueblo sites are hampered by the lack of a broader view of the Mimbres and their sociocultural systems; that is, small sites are so narrowly interpreted that we cannot see beyond their agricultural roles. In this chapter, we argue that small pueblo sites are often more than short-term agricultural sites or places of convenience at distant farm fields (sensu Haury 1956; see Moore 1978). This traditional view ignores contradictory data that suggest many small sites were occupied for long periods of time (Woods 2012). In addition, not all are located at distant fields (Toney 2012). Large-scale survey has shown that small pueblo sites occur adjacent to larger sites and that they occur in a wide variety of locations (Stokes 2003; Toney 2012). Distant farm fields and structures of convenience alone cannot explain why so many small sites are located within easy walking distance of large sites and often of each other; something else is clearly going on with small sites. We acknowledge that defining contemporaneity among these small sites is critical and that many could be sequentially occupied. The sheer number of small sites argues for a high degree of contemporaneity, however, and many must have been used at the same time.

To understand the explanatory possibilities of small sites in the Mimbres survey and excavation databases generated from decades of earlier research and from current research, we investigate several issues related to small sites. First, we examine the distribution of small sites across the landscape in the Mimbres area. Second, we investigate the social ramifications of small sites in Mimbres society by looking at how they integrate into larger-scale Mimbres communities. We ask how land use and tenure may have led to the building of so many small sites near large villages and at distant places.

Third, we investigate variation in duration and intensity of occupation of these sites by presenting new excavation research results from two sites. By exploring these issues, we can begin the process of broadening our understanding of the many socioeconomic functions of small pueblo sites, and we can build a more inclusive view of Mimbres culture and its many components.

Specifically, we attempt to delve more deeply into the meanings behind site placement across the landscape beyond previously offered explanations related to agriculture and food stresses (e.g., Blake et al. 1986; Minnis 1985). We have more sophisticated tools now at our disposal, such as geographic information systems (GIS) programs, Global Positioning Systems to more accurately plot sites, a wider array of tools for dating sites beyond cross-seriation and radiocarbon assay, and a better integration of the latest social theory that expands our ability to think in new ways. This research includes a reexamination of survey data compiled from the 1960s to today in which we use GIS and plot pueblo sites by size rather than simply occurrence, as well as data from excavations at two small sites along the Mimbres River and one of its tributaries. The approaches to and results of these recent research projects demonstrate the utility of using a wide array of tools and techniques to better understand small pueblo sites in the Classic Mimbres world. In doing so, we show how our conclusions and insights can be applicable to small-site research in general across the Southwest.

The Study of Small Sites in Southwestern Archaeology

The role of small sites in our understanding of larger behavioral patterns has been understudied to a degree in southwestern archaeology due to a focus on "big" sites and the resulting marginalized context of small sites (Sutton 1977; see chapters in Ward 1978). Moore (1979:22) notes that early Spanish descriptions of small pueblo sites suggest they were primarily agricultural in function and that they were seasonally occupied. The early Spanish described small sites clustering around the main villages but also noted far-flung small sites that marked individual land claims (Moore 1979:22–23). However, early southwestern archaeologists were primarily interested in large pueblos that were likely to produce the data they needed to define ancient southwestern cultures and to amass large artifact collections for their museum sponsors (Snead 2001), a trend true for the Mimbres Valley as well (e.g., Cosgrove and Cosgrove 1932; Nesbitt 1931).

Attention was sometimes focused on the "field house," described as a one- to three-room structure associated with agriculture that served as a summer shelter and for temporary storage of the harvest (Pilles and Wilcox 1978:3; Woodbury 1961:xiii). Room counts used by other researchers varied beyond the three-room limit if the sites were viewed as seasonally used and/or agriculture-related domiciles (Nelson et al. 1978). Artifact content (few in number and restricted or task-specific types), architectural investment (typically low or minimal), and length of occupation (typically short duration) were also issues discussed by researchers studying small sites. However, a review of small Hohokam sites led Stone (1993) to conclude that there was no clear-cut relationship between small habitation sites and artifact types and counts. This led her to argue that occupational duration was a more important factor to consider than functional differentiation defined by artifacts.

In contrast to the traditionally defined field house, Pilles and Wilcox (1978) and Kohler (1992) suggest that evidence of larger, more permanent sites (typically containing more than ten rooms) may be reflected in the quality of construction, variable domestic activities, and the existence of hearths, trash, ceramics, and burials. Factors such as the number of rooms and larger room sizes also suggest a more permanent occupation (McGregor 1951). Location likewise plays a factor in assessing site function and architectural investment; small sites exhibiting a high architectural labor investment tend to be situated in areas with consistently high agricultural yields or potential (Kohler 1992). In addition to facilitating access to fields and encouraging the management of agricultural resources, the ubiquity of smaller habitation sites may have been part of a burgeoning system of land ownership and resource-control mechanisms (Herrington 1979; Kohler 1992; Neely 1995; Stokes 2003; Sutton 1977; Wilcox 1978). Some scholars have argued that communities were organized in hierarchical clusters within social and economic systems (Harry 2003). Others have suggested that communities were created to buffer risk and regulate land-tenure claims, as is argued for the Sand Canyon–Goodman Point area of southwestern Colorado (Adler 2002).

These broader-scale views of interconnected, contemporary sites of all shapes and sizes across large swaths of the landscape have resulted in a retooling of the community concept at the landscape scale (Fish et al. 1992; Kohler and Van West 1996). This concept encompasses, and indeed emphasizes, the interconnectedness of a wide range of site types that functioned to keep the larger cultural and social systems going, including those focused on agricultural landscapes (e.g., Adler 1996; Graham 1994; Kohler 1992; Wills and Leonard 1994). In defining concepts of community, Hegmon (2002) states that communities influence regular interactions with their members and that these interactions occur on different scales from small to large—unit, cluster, supra, and community. Based on Hegmon's model of community, individual sites represent residential communities and collectives of sites represent political communities. Despite their size, these smaller sites do play an important role in the overall system of community, politics, and social relations when issues of scale and hierarchy are considered.

These concepts are beginning to have an effect on Mimbres studies as well. Typical interpretations of large Mimbres pueblos see each as largely autonomous, egalitarian, and self-supporting while participating within a larger social-economic-religious overlay (e.g., Anyon and LeBlanc 1984; Gilman et al., chapter 4; Shafer 2003). The community concept provides Mimbres archaeologists with a better way of understanding the components of the Mimbres cultural system at a larger scale than the single site. In other words, it allows researchers to refocus on what was going on around the big sites and investigate the function and meaning of small sites. For example, at Stewart Pueblo, a ten- to twelve-room Classic Mimbres site along the Mimbres River, Woods (2012) documented a surprisingly complex history that in many ways is similar to Nelson's (1999) findings from the Eastern Mimbres Project's Reorganization phase hamlets.

Clearly, some small pueblo sites along the margins of the Mimbres Valley were short-term occupations focused on resource extraction (e.g., Brown 1999), and others produce evidence for longer occupations and a richer array of artifact types (Stokes 1997; Woods 2012) than a typical agricultural field house should produce (Nelson et al. 1978). With the understanding that small pueblo sites represent a wide range of functions and many, by all appearances, resemble long-term occupations, attention is shifting to understanding the roles of small sites in larger Mimbres community systems (Stokes 1997, 2000, 2003). These roles may include landscape location choices made for nonagricultural reasons (Toney 2012), including locating permanent homes on or near ancestral sites, typically dating back to the Late Pithouse period, as a way to connect with the past and keep it alive and current in the minds and memories of the descendants (Woods 2012; see Basso 1996; Meskell 2003; Schlanger 1992) and marking land claims in a land-tenure system that appears to have developed during the Classic period (Stokes 2003). We will examine these new interpretations in more detail.

Distribution of Small Mimbres
Sites Across the Landscape

Examining the distribution of small pueblo sites across the landscape will provide important insights useful for understanding Mimbres settlement, subsistence, and food procurement systems. These insights then contribute to understanding aspects of Classic Mimbres community systems by defining probable site function based on location and distance from large villages. In order to model large-scale settlement systems across portions of the Mimbres region, Toney (2012) recently undertook a GIS-based study of small site locations. She examined the locations of 632 small sites in the

Mimbres Valley, Fort Bayard area, and Burro Mountains within the central Mimbres region (figure 5.2). Her research focused on understanding the geographic placement of small sites in relationship to agricultural potential. The agricultural potential of an area depends on both physical and social variables. To explore the placement of small sites within the social environment, she investigated ethnographically established cost-equivalent distances from larger settlements and visual relationships between sites to model the social aspects of agricultural practices. The physical landscape (i.e., slope, landform type, landform stability, soil characteristics, and arability) was characterized to evaluate the agricultural potential of the small-site locations. The initial results demonstrated that the majority of small sites were not located in areas of greatest agricultural potential. Rather, most were in areas at or beyond a one-day round-trip walking distance (18 km cost-equivalent distance) from larger settlements.

This finding differs from the more common assumptions of small-site placement and use typically made for field houses that were occupied on a part-time, seasonal basis at agricultural fields both near and far from the main villages. While agriculture was obviously a salient feature of the Mimbres Classic period, other organized tasks were also important in shaping features of the built environment. Factors other than agriculture were part of the decision to construct small pueblos at certain locations.

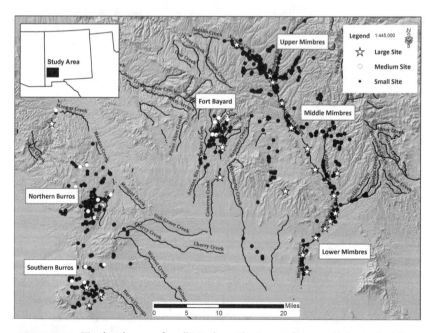

FIGURE 5.2 The distribution of small Mimbres Classic period structural sites in the Mimbres Valley, Burro Mountains, and Fort Bayard/Silver City study areas (Toney 2012).

As Minnis (1985) previously noted, the Classic period Mimbres did not rely solely on agriculture but also on gathering wild resources and hunting game. Other potential resources that might draw people repeatedly to distant places included lithic raw material and wood. In addition, non-resource factors might include connections to the past and reuse of important space, spiritual journeys, and connecting with sacred places (see Basso 1996; Meskell 2003; Schlanger 1992).

Further, Toney's (2012) research demonstrated that Mimbres communities in different locations across southwestern New Mexico may have been organized differently with regard to the placement of small pueblo sites across the landscape. Of the three study areas she examined, the Fort Bayard area may conform best to the notion that most activity taking place at small sites was focused on agriculture. Conversely, among areas that have the potential for agricultural use, the Burro Mountains area has the smallest number of sites directly associated with arable land, indicating to us that other factors were drawing people here. As opposed to the Fort Bayard area and sections of the Mimbres River study area, where broad alluvial floodplains afforded greater agricultural potential, basins and low mountain ranges, such as the Burro Mountains, may have remained primarily wild resource–procurement zones that were strategically and seasonally exploited. These findings, demonstrated through GIS modeling, open avenues for specific research geared toward understanding why the one-day walking distance was so important and what was obtained at the end of the day's journey. Such research would include directed excavations at these far-flung small sites to obtain critical research data. These preliminary results would not only help us to better understand how and why small sites were organized and used across the Mimbres landscape and within their community systems, but also to understand the roles that small sites play across the Southwest.

Mimbres Small Sites in Mimbres Communities

As we have discussed, small Mimbres pueblo sites were traditionally thought to be ubiquitous and widespread habitation structures used for short-term and seasonally related tasks. In that sense, they were mostly disconnected from the larger Mimbres villages and had more limited potential for helping us to understand Mimbres cultural systems, a position we have been disputing in this chapter. In the past, the large villages were viewed as the real communities, and the small sites were noise in the data. Although the larger-scale community system concept has been around for several decades, it has not been used until recently for understanding the constellation of Mimbres sites throughout the Mimbres Valley, its tributaries, and nearby large drainages (Stokes 2003).

For example, Stokes (1997, 2000, 2003, 2004, 2006) began a series of investigations in several side drainages of the Mimbres River with the intent of better understanding Mimbres communities and the types of sites that comprise them. The side
drainages typically contain a single, discrete community system compared to the main
Mimbres Valley, which contains a multitude of seemingly overlapping communities.
Thus, the side drainage communities allow for a better controlled data set. Stokes
recorded a variety of surface-structure sites and conducted test excavations at small,
medium, and large pueblos at two side-drainage communities: the Middle Fork of the
Mimbres River and Noonday Canyon (figure 5.3). The results of field investigations
in these two tributary drainages demonstrate a similar clustering of sites that include
a single, centrally located larger pueblo (typically at least forty rooms), several smaller
farmstead-sized pueblos (about ten to twenty rooms), and numerous field house–
sized pueblos (fewer than ten rooms). Stokes argued that if these side drainages were
used for short-term and seasonal farming and resource extraction (e.g., Blake et al.
1986; Minnis 1985), then scattered field houses and perhaps some farmsteads would
have sufficed. Yet in each case, a larger pueblo was present that mimicked the large
pueblos in the main valley in most respects except size.

The presence of these communities demonstrated that Mimbres society was potentially organized at a level analogous in many ways with that of the Hohokam, around
which the larger-scale community concept was originally developed for the Southwest
(Fish et al. 1992). In the Hohokam area of the Phoenix and Tucson Basins, many
communities were organized along canal systems that required a level of cooperation
among people to ensure an adequate flow of irrigation water for all users. Because of
the variable nature of river flow in the Salt and Gila Rivers, the Hohokam communities also extended their reach into adjacent desert and foothill areas to maintain their
ability to acquire natural food resources, resulting in a variety of site types across the
landscape (Doyel 1989; Doyel and Fish 2000; Fish et al. 1992; Howard 1987). In the
Mimbres Valley, water is also limited and variable (Creel 2006a), and the communities
along the river must have had cooperative agreements and procedures to negotiate
water usage. Mimbres sites also occur across the landscape beyond the immediate
riverine environment (Stokes 2003; Toney 2012).

Stokes (2003) also reviewed survey data for the upper Mimbres Valley and the
adjacent upper Sapillo Valley (Graybill 1975). The Sapillo Valley data were supplemented with Stokes's (1995) sample survey data of the middle and upper valley sections. After reviewing pueblo site location and size distribution, community clusters
were identified in both areas (see figure 5.3; table 5.1). Clearly, the community cluster
system is a common occurrence in the Mimbres Valley, its side drainages, and the
adjacent Sapillo. Additionally, Stokes found that the community clusters were all 3 to
5 km apart along the Mimbres River and 5 to 7 km apart upstream from the Mimbres

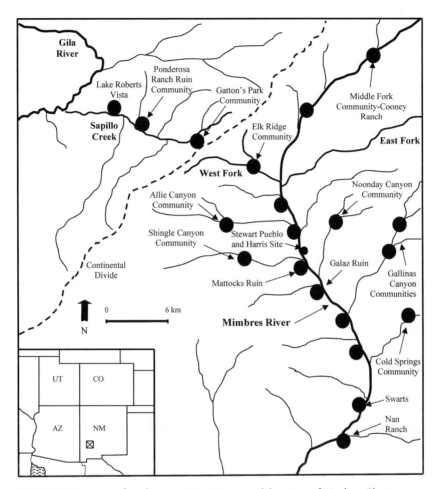

FIGURE 5.3 A map of southwestern New Mexico with locations of Mimbres Classic period community clusters (solid circles) and major Mimbres sites along the Mimbres River, its tributaries, and Sapillo Creek (major tributary communities are labeled). Map prepared by Robert Stokes.

River in the side drainages (see figure 5.3). Over 50 percent of the major tributaries contained community clusters. Another important observation was that many of the small pueblos were located close to the main villages and were probably not shelters of convenience in the traditional sense.

The idea of land tenure in the Southwest has been more influential since the 1990s (e.g., Adler 1996; Schriever 2012; Varien 1999), and the Classic Mimbres period provides an excellent case study on the development and physical expressions of land tenure because of the level of site documentation and previous research focusing on

TABLE 5.1 Comparison of Site-Size Categories Expressed by Number of Rooms and Number of Identified Community Clusters for the Three Survey Areas

Survey Area	Number of Identified Community Clusters	Site-Size Category Expressed as Number of Rooms					
		Field House	Small Farmstead	Large Farmstead	Medium Pueblo	Large Pueblo	Very Large Pueblo
Lower and Middle Mimbres Valley[a]	7[b] (Allie Canyon, Cold Springs Canyon, Gallinas Canyon [2 clusters], Noonday Canyon, Shingle Canyon, Gavilan Canyon)	1–9 (71 sites)	10–21 (20 sites)	24–27 (7 sites)	40–57 (9 sites)	80–85 (2 sites)	120–200+ (5 sites)
Upper Mimbres Valley[c]	6[d] (Elk Ridge, Cottonwood, Cooney Ranch, East Fork, Graybill Sites 41, 52, and potentially 134)	1–9 (94 sites)	10–17 (19 sites)	20–28 (6 sites)	39–53 (3 sites)	68 (1 site)	102–120+ (2 sites)
Sapillo Valley[e]	6 (Ponderosa Ranch, Gatton's Park, Lake Roberts Vista, LA 104089, LA 75046, LA 99841)	1–11 (18 sites)	16 (1 site)	20–33 (7 sites)	46–61 (4 sites)	0	120+ (1 site)
Total number of sites		183	40	20	16	3	8

Source: Stokes 2003.

[a]Primarily Mimbres Foundation and Laboratory of Anthropology data, plus information supplied by Harry Shafer for Gavilan Canyon.

[b]For the Lower and Middle Mimbres River, these are side drainages only; five other major side drainages do not appear to contain community clusters as described here. Six of the seven large main river valley sites (Montezuma, Martocks, Galaz, Perrault, Swarts, and NAN Ranch) also contain satellite site communities, but it is unclear if Old Town does from the available survey data (though it likely does). The data columns to the right include both the main valley and side drainage sites.

[c]Primarily Graybill (1975) data, supplemented with data from the Laboratory of Anthropology and the Gila National Forest.

[d]For the Upper Mimbres, Graybill Site 134, a sixty-eight-room pueblo, is listed in his data table, but its location is unknown. Therefore, a seventh community cluster may exist if Site 134 is not a data table error.

[e]From the Sapillo Valley Survey Project data (Stokes 1995, 2003).

arable land and water limitations (Creel 2006a; Minnis 1985), population estimates over time (Blake et al. 1986; Stokes 1995), and food and water shortages leading to social stresses (Minnis 1985; Shafer 2003; Stokes 2003, 2004). With the detection of Mimbres communities comprised of large-, medium-, and small-sized pueblo sites, we must ask what those communities meant to the ancient people living in the Mimbres region. If Stokes (2003, 2004) and Shafer (2003) are correct in supposing that by the beginning of the Classic period the best farmland was claimed by long-established families, either through corporate groups (Shafer 2003) or land-tenure rules of inheritance (Stokes 2003, 2004) under the conditions previously listed, then it would seem strange to see nearby sites used by unrelated or noncorporate group households so close to "land claimed by others."

Based on ethnographic examples from a variety of farming societies around the world, including Puebloan groups in the Southwest, Stokes (2003, 2004) demonstrated that small sites are often used as physical signs of land use and land claims (like early Spanish observations discussed previously in this chapter), if not outright ownership, along with other forms of land improvement, including border walls, ditches, cairns, check dams, and terraces (Herrington 1982; Sandor 1983). Thus, small sites are often very close to larger villages and are often full-time residences themselves, or at least occupied for longer durations than the typical "structure of convenience." What results is a mix of site sizes covering a range of functions that serves to protect the interests and land claims of nearby villages and the households, household clusters, lineages, or corporate groups that live there. A similar process may explain many of the isolated small sites spread throughout the Mimbres region's highlands, lowlands, deserts, and dry valleys (Toney 2012), although the level and effectiveness of land claims at these far-flung sites remain unknown.

Variation in Occupation of Small Mimbres Pueblos

To build on the preceding discussions, we present recent excavation data from a small pueblo site along the Mimbres River, Stewart Pueblo (LA 18952), that demonstrates the variability present in small-site use and function, and we supplement this with excavation data from a small site in the Noonday Canyon community. The Mimbres Foundation originally recorded Stewart Pueblo in the 1970s as a small field house with a limited number of rooms. It is located on the first low terrace just above the Mimbres River at a location where the river is perennial and the valley is relatively wide. It is directly below the Harris site, a large Late Pithouse period site, which is on the much higher second terrace (see figure 5.3). At the initiation of the excavations, it was expected that this small (ten to twelve rooms) pueblo site would exhibit the functional hallmarks of an agricultural field house, much like the Mimbres Foundation's LA 12109 (Nelson et al. 1978) and the Montoya site (Parsons 1955). These hallmarks include minimal material culture, a lithic assemblage geared toward processing agricultural foods, limited pottery (much of which would be plain and corrugated utility ceramics), limited evidence for traded and exotic goods, and low investment in architecture and building materials.

After three seasons of excavations, Stewart Pueblo has confounded all of these expectations. Despite significant hand and mechanical potting, the site exhibited traits consistent with a much larger pueblo, and it met few of the expectations for a limited-activity agricultural field house (Woods 2012). In fact, Stewart Pueblo had evidence of at least two remodeling phases: it was built of substantial stone architecture with several large rooms; it had numerous floor and subfloor features that are typically seen at larger pueblos, including a stone-lined hearth, large postholes, storage pits, ash pits, and burials; and it had varied and substantial material culture, including trade pottery and effigy vessels (figure 5.4; table 5.2). Many artifacts are clearly associated with agriculture, such as ground stone and an ax-head, and the site lacked bifacial tools typically associated with hunting and butchering animals. The assemblage as a whole is remarkably different than that reported for LA 12109. For example, Nelson and colleagues (1978:204) state that the LA 12109 lithic assemblage reflects activities heavily focused on plant processing at a special-use site. The lithic assemblage at Stewart Pueblo appears to represent a wider range of activities, including domestic tasks and animal processing. Additionally, although not quantified in their report, Nelson and colleagues (1978:197, 199) note that no pottery or ground stone was found in the backfill of the potted rooms and was virtually absent from surface contexts and that only three sherds were recovered from the excavated rooms. Stewart Pueblo could not be more different with its large ceramic and ground-stone assemblage.

The presence of Mimbres Style II/III Black-on-white pottery, sherds from the entire Classic period sequence (Early, Middle, and Late Style III), and sherds associated with a Terminal to Postclassic time frame, including El Paso Polychrome, Chupadero Black-on-white, and Reserve Black-on-white, indicate that this site experienced a much longer use-life than anticipated and participated in the full spectrum of Mimbres society, including obtaining the three nonlocal pottery types listed previously. Varied ceramic assemblages similar to that at Stewart Pueblo are often associated with the large Classic sites up and down the Mimbres River (e.g., Anyon and LeBlanc 1984; Cosgrove and Cosgrove 1932).

The partial excavation of two rooms and the delineation of a third large room partially impacted by severe pothunting revealed important architectural and material-culture information about this small pueblo. The two remodeling phases demonstrated a high level of architectural investment. For example, two of the three floors

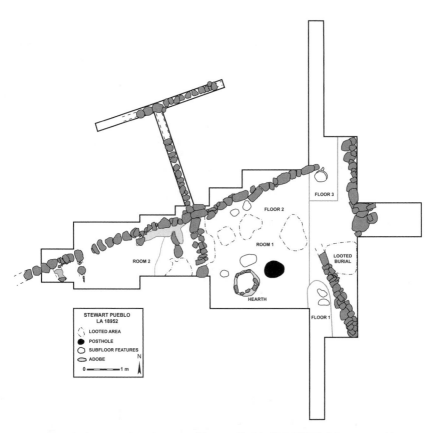

FIGURE 5.4 An excavation plan map of Stewart Pueblo (LA 18952). Map prepared by
Aaron Woods.

were plastered, and a rock-lined and collared hearth was found on the lowest floor.
At least one room was subdivided during a remodeling phase based on an interior
rock wall that was poorly constructed compared to surrounding walls. Compared
to LA 12109, which had packed-earth floors, unprepared hearths, and the limited,
task-specific lithic artifacts discussed earlier, Stewart Pueblo is an exception to the
low-investment, short-term agricultural site, or at least it appears that way due to the
dearth of comparable excavated small sites along the river. Based on excavations at a
three- to four-room pueblo site (LA 119343) in the Noonday Canyon Community on
a large tributary of the Mimbres River above the Galaz site, Stokes (1997, 2003) also
found more substantial architecture and material culture than expected for a small site,
especially for one that, unlike Stewart Pueblo, was at a poor location for agriculture.

　　In sum, we argue that the excavations at Stewart Pueblo and LA 119343 clearly
demonstrate that small pueblos in the Mimbres Valley exhibit a much wider range of

TABLE 5.2 Painted Pottery from Stewart Pueblo (LA 18952)

Mimbres Painted Series[a]	Count	Date Range (A.D.)	Painted Trade Wares[b]	Count	Date Range (A.D.)	Mimbres Black-on-white Microseriation[c]	Count	Date Range (A.D.)
Three Circle Red-on-white	1	740–780	Reserve Black-on-white	21	1100–1200	Style I	1	750–900
Style I Black-on-white	3	750–950	El Paso Polychrome	17	1100–1350	Style II–Early	4	880–980
Style II Black-on-white	3	950–1050	Chupadero Black-on-white (bird effigy)	1	1150–1550	Style II–Late	4	970–1020
Style II/III Black-on-white Indeterminate	10	950–1050	Indeterminate Cibola White Ware	9		Style II/III	5	970–1020
Style III Black-on-white	143	1000–1150				Style III–Early	12	1010–1080
Indeterminate Black-on-white	374					Style III–Middle	147	1060–1110
						Style III–Late	29	1110–1140
Totals	534			48			202	

[a] Adapted from Scott 1983, although the Mimbres Foundation never explicitly offered precise date ranges for pottery types.
[b] Dyer and Constan 2011; Reid et al. 1995.
[c] Shafer and Brewington 1995.

variation than previously seen by earlier researchers and that some of these sites appear
to be multifunctional. Yes, there is an agricultural component to Stewart Pueblo. Its
location adjacent to potential farm fields would demonstrate this fact, but clearly
more was happening socially and economically at this site than previously suspected.
One potential reason for the location of this small pueblo is the presence of the large
Late Pithouse period Harris site directly above Stewart Pueblo. Harris appears to have
been abandoned shortly before Stewart Pueblo was first occupied (Roth 2015; Woods
2012). Perhaps the occupants of Stewart Pueblo were the descendants of the people
living at Harris, and by locating near the abandoned site, they maintained a connection to their past. This "connection to the past" has been demonstrated at the Harris
site itself (Roth and Baustian 2015) and in general by the Mimbres practice of burying
their dead beneath the floors of their occupied houses and, in a sense, living with their
ancestors (Shafer 1995; see also McAnany 1995 for a discussion of the Maya practice
of living with their ancestors). This is important to note as it potentially demonstrates
why some smaller sites in the Mimbres Valley are located where they are, why they
appear to be full-time occupations, why this location was persistently occupied during
the Classic period (sensu Schlanger 1992), and that living with ancestors was powerful in this society (Shafer 1995). Additional investigations at small sites like Stewart
Pueblo will help us to further understand the social roles of small sites in Mimbres
society and belief systems.

Summary and Conclusions

The examples we have presented serve to demonstrate the importance of studying
small pueblo sites, not just in the Mimbres area but across the Southwest. At the
beginning of the chapter, we posed three important questions to consider in the data:
(1) what is the distribution of small sites at a larger regional scale; (2) what roles do
small sites play in Mimbres communities and land-tenure systems; and (3) are duration and intensity of occupation at small sites the same for all or do they vary? We
used several recent GIS, survey, and excavation examples to address these questions.
With the results, we can now better investigate the fundamental question pertaining
to small sites in general: what are their functional roles? As with most data sets, we
have intriguing patterns and insights based on strong results and hints or suggestions
of other socioeconomic processes at work in Mimbres society that clearly require more
research, as demonstrated by the intriguing results regarding small sites that may be
associated with aspects of the past and social memory.

Using GIS spatial analysis, we demonstrated that many small pueblo sites are
located at and beyond a one day's journey from the main valleys and that many of the

site locations are not in areas that can be considered prime agricultural zones. Other factors must have been drawing the Mimbres to these remote locations. We suspect that they include collecting natural resources (e.g., food, stone, wood) and hunting, but they also may relate to spiritual journeys, sacred locations, and connections to the past. Conversely, we also demonstrated that many of the small pueblos are located close to the large sites in both the main valley and side drainages, and many of these may represent land-tenure markers at owned or controlled farmland, ownership of infrastructure (e.g., water-control systems), and control of traditionally used resource areas. Certainly, many of these small sites were directly related to the agricultural cycle and were likely seasonally used as described previously by others (Nelson et al. 1978), but many small sites either had different functions altogether or were a palimpsest of functions at a single location that included agriculture.

Excavations at Stewart Pueblo and LA 119343 revealed a surprising array of architectural and artifact patterns that run counter to expectations of what an agricultural small pueblo should be. Stewart Pueblo was occupied for well over one hundred years, possibly not continuously but certainly on a sustained basis. With multiple episodes of remodeling documented at the site, we know that the occupants spent a good deal of energy to build a substantial and comfortable dwelling. LA 119343 also revealed a more diverse artifact assemblage and more elaborate architectural details than expected. This is quite different than what has been found at the few other small Mimbres pueblo sites investigated in the Mimbres Valley area (e.g., Brown 1999). The variation and amount of material culture speaks to a group of people well connected to the "outside" world who undertook a variety of tasks at these small sites, similar to patterns observed at the large pueblo sites. Stewart Pueblo, along with a handful of other excavated small sites that did not completely conform to expectations, such as LA 119343, have shown that duration and intensity of occupation can be much more substantial than previously thought.

Lastly, we have demonstrated that Mimbres communities comprised of tiers of site sizes are a common pattern in the Mimbres Valley, its side drainages, and in the Sapillo Valley. Some of these small sites in communities away from the main river may be related to economic and social aspects of Mimbres society not directly tied to agriculture (Toney 2012), and Mimbres archaeology would benefit greatly from investigating a sample of the small sites in these settings. We argue that the communities themselves are likely physical expressions of a land-tenure system in which the close-by small sites marked land claims for residents at the central or main villages, and they also demonstrate the extension of this form of land ownership to outlying areas (e.g., the side drainages). The land-tenure system may have begun in the Mimbres Valley proper at the beginning of the Classic period (Shafer 2003; Stokes 2003), but it was carried to outlying settlements later by the migrating landless and was replicated at the new communities. Mimbres archaeologists typically view people living in the Mimbres region as egalitarian (although see Creel 2006b). This is a concept argued for the main villages, which are seen as largely self-supporting and autonomous (i.e., other than a shared religious system and cultural traits, archaeologists find little evidence for political organization or social or class distinctions). However, the advent of land-tenure systems during the Classic period speaks to a significant change in Mimbres culture, society, and world view or belief systems (Shafer 2003, 2006; Stokes 2003). Land tenure arises to protect valued resources for one's core group, a system that by its nature excludes others. The fact that "others" who have less or do without existed during the Classic period speaks to people undergoing society-wide changes. We have documented aspects of this process in Mimbres communities and small pueblo sites.

Based on these discussions, we have demonstrated that small pueblo sites have a wider range of socioeconomic roles and functions associated with them than previously suspected, including associations with nonagricultural locations and landforms (perhaps spiritual places?), with land-tenure systems, and perhaps with places evoking memories of ancestors. We have also shown that many of the small pueblos may have been full-time domiciles or at least occupied for longer periods of time than previously suspected. Nelson and her colleagues (1999) have shown that small Reorganization phase pueblos along the eastern slope of the Black Range were full-time domiciles, but smaller, earlier Classic period pueblos were thought to be something else. We need to research small sites further to understand them better. For example, was the "reorganization" of the Reorganization phase occurring earlier than previously suspected? That is, the post-Classic hamlet sites that Nelson and her colleagues investigated and the important social changes they documented (e.g., Nelson 1999) may have had their roots in the Mimbres Valley prior to A.D. 1140. Clearly, these small sites were often multifunctional and certainly encompassed agriculture-related functions (the Mimbres were, after all, an agrarian society), but they are also much more than that.

Many of these functions are likely situational, but the main point is that we cannot presuppose the function of a small site. Instead, we must look carefully at specific contexts and situations to understand function(s). Steven LeBlanc understood this back in the 1970s and sought to include small pueblo sites in his Mimbres Foundation research program. We are pleased to carry on this aspect of his earlier research, and we encourage other archaeologists interested in the Mimbres to envelope small-site excavations into their research programs. If we want to better understand how economic and social systems were organized in the Mimbres area, and how scale affected these systems from specific habitation locations to larger regional studies, then we need to focus more on small sites. As shown here, context is critical for understanding the various roles that small pueblo sites played in ancient Mimbres society; preconceived notions need not apply.

Acknowledgments

The authors wish to thank Barbara Roth, Patricia Gilman, and Roger Anyon for inviting us to participate in their Mimbres Foundation symposium at the 2014 SAA meeting held in Austin, Texas. This chapter represents the important research of the three authors for their MA and PhD theses and dissertations, which built upon the solid and innovative research agenda of the Mimbres Foundation and others. We also wish to thank the editors and two anonymous reviewers for their insightful comments on earlier drafts of this chapter.

References Cited

Adler, Michael A. 1996. Land Tenure, Archaeology, and the Ancestral Pueblo Social Landscape. *Journal of Anthropological Archaeology* 15:337–371.

———. 2002. The Ancestral Pueblo Community as Structure and Strategy. In *Seeking the Center Place: Archaeology and Ancient Communities in the Mesa Verde Region*, edited by Mark D. Varien and Richard H. Wilshusen, pp. 3–23. University of Utah Press, Salt Lake City.

Anyon, Roger, and Steven A. LeBlanc. 1984. *The Galaz Ruin: A Prehistoric Mimbres Village in Southwestern New Mexico*. Maxwell Museum of Anthropology and the University of New Mexico Press, Albuquerque.

Basso, Keith H. 1996. *Wisdom Sits in Places: Landscape and Language Among the Western Apache*. University of New Mexico Press, Albuquerque.

Blake, Michael, Steven A. LeBlanc, and Paul E. Minnis. 1986. Changing Settlement and Population in the Mimbres Valley, SW New Mexico. *Journal of Field Archaeology* 13:439–464.

Brown, Gary M. (editor). 1999. *South Waste Rock Expansion: Archaeological Data Recovery in the Buckhorn Gulch Area at the Continental Mine, Grant County, New Mexico*. Report No. WCRM(F)140. Western Cultural Resource Management, Farmington, New Mexico.

Cosgrove, H. S., and C. B. Cosgrove. 1932. *The Swarts Ruin: A Typical Mimbres Site in Southwestern New Mexico*. Papers of the Peabody Museum of Archaeology and Ethnology. Harvard University, Cambridge, Massachusetts.

Creel, Darrell G. 2006a. Environmental Variation and Prehistoric Culture in the Mimbres Area. In *Environmental Change and Human Adaptation in the American Southwest*, edited by David E. Doyel and Jeffrey S. Dean, pp. 204–213. University of Utah Press, Salt Lake City.

———. 2006b. Evidence for Mimbres Social Differentiation at the Old Town Site. In *Mimbres Society*, edited by Patricia A. Gilman and Valli Powell-Martí, pp. 32–44. University of Arizona Press, Tucson.

Doyel, David E. 1989. Hohokam Social Organization and the Sedentary to Classic Transition. In *Current Issues in Hohokam Prehistory*, edited by David E. Doyel and Fred Plog, pp. 23–40. Anthropological Research Papers No. 23. Arizona State University, Tempe.

Doyel, David E., and Suzanne K. Fish. 2000. Prehistoric Villages and Communities in the Arizona Desert. In *The Hohokam Village Revisited*, edited David E. Doyel, Suzanne K. Fish, and Paul R. Fish, pp. 1–36. Southwestern and Rocky Mountain Division of the American Association for the Advancement of Science. Colorado Mountain College, Glenwood Springs.

Dyer, Jennifer Boyd, and Connie Constan. 2011. *Lower Rio Grande Ceramic Reference Manual: Elephant Butte to Las Cruces, NM*. Prepared for and published by the U.S. Bureau of Reclamation, Albuquerque, New Mexico.

Fish, Suzanne K., Paul R. Fish, and John H. Madsen. 1992. *The Marana Community in the Hohokam World*. Anthropological Papers No. 56. University of Arizona Press, Tucson.

Graham, Martha. 1994. *Mobile Farmers: An Ethnoarchaeological Approach to Settlement Organization Among the Raramuri of Northwestern Mexico*. Ethnoarchaeological Series 3. International Monographs in Prehistory, Ann Arbor, Michigan.

Graybill, Donald A. 1975. *Mimbres-Mogollon Adaptations in the Gila National Forest, Mimbres District, New Mexico*. USDA Archaeological Report No. 9. USDA Forest Service Southwestern Region, Albuquerque, New Mexico.

Hammack, Laurens C. 1964. *The Mangas Highway Salvage Project*. Laboratory of Anthropology Notes 34. Museum of New Mexico, Santa Fe.

———. 1966. *Diablo Highway Salvage Project*. Laboratory of Anthropology Notes No. 41. Museum of New Mexico, Santa Fe.

Hammack, Laurens C., Stanley D. Bussey, Ronald Ice, and Alfred E. Dittert Jr. 1966. *The Cliff Highway Salvage Project*. Laboratory of Anthropology Notes 40. Museum of New Mexico, Santa Fe.

Harry, Karen. 2003. *Economic Organization and Settlement Hierarchies: Ceramic Production and Exchange Among the Hohokam*. Praeger Press, Westport, Connecticut.

Haury, Emil W. 1956. Speculations on Prehistoric Settlement Patterns in the Southwest. In *Prehistoric Settlement Patterns in the New World*, edited by Gordon Willey, pp. 3–10. Wenner-Gren Foundation for Anthropological Research, New York.

Hegmon, Michelle. 2002. Concepts of Community in Archaeological Research. In *Seeking the Center Place: Archaeology and Ancient Communities in the Mesa Verde Region*, edited by Mark D. Varien and Richard H. Wilshusen, pp. 263–280. University of Utah Press, Salt Lake City.

Hegmon, Michelle, Margaret C. Nelson, Roger Anyon, Darrell Creel, Steven A. LeBlanc, and Harry J. Shafer. 1999. Scale and Time-Space Systematics in the Post-A.D. 1100 Mimbres Region of the North American Southwest. *Kiva* 65:143–166.

Herrington, S. LaVerne. 1979. Settlement Patterns and Water Control Systems in the Mimbres Classic Phase, Grant County, New Mexico. PhD dissertation, Department of Anthropology, University of Texas, Austin.

———. 1982. Water-Control Systems of the Mimbres Classic Phase. In *Mogollon Archaeology: Proceedings of the 1980 Mogollon Conference*, edited by Patrick H. Beckett and Kira Silverbird, pp. 75–90. Acoma Books, Ramona, California.

Howard, Jerry B. 1987. The Lehi Canal System: Organization of a Classic Period Irrigation Community. In *The Hohokam Village: Site Structure and Organization*, edited by David E. Doyel, pp. 211–222. Southwestern and Rocky Mountain Division of the American Association for the Advancement of Science. Colorado Mountain College, Glenwood Springs.

Ice, Ronald J. 1968. *West Fork Ruin: A Stratified Site near Gila Cliff Dwellings National Monument*. Laboratory of Anthropology Notes 48. Laboratory of Anthropology, Santa Fe, New Mexico.

Kohler, Timothy A. 1992. Field Houses, Villages, and the Tragedy of the Commons in the Early Northern Anasazi Southwest. *American Antiquity* 56:617–634.

Kohler, Timothy A., and Carla Van West. 1996. The Calculus of Self-Interest in the Development of Cooperation: Sociopolitical Development and Risk Among the Northern Anasazi. In *Evolving Complexity and Environmental Risk in the Prehistoric Southwest*, edited by Joseph Tainter and Bonnie B. Tainter, pp. 169–196. Addison-Wesley, Reading, Massachusetts.

LeBlanc, Steven A. 1983. *The Mimbres People: Ancient Pueblo Painters of the American Southwest*. Thames and Hudson, London.

McAnany, Patricia A. 1995. *Living with the Ancestors: Kinship and Kingship in Ancient Maya Society*. University of Texas Press, Austin.

McGregor, John C. 1951. *The Cohonina Culture of Northeastern Arizona*. University of Illinois Press, Champaign.

Meskell, Lynn. 2003. Memory's Materiality: Ancestral Presence, Commemorative Practice, and Disjunctive Locales. In *Archaeologies of Memory*, edited by Ruth M. Van Dyke and Susan E. Alcock, pp. 34–55. Blackwell, Malden, Massachusetts.

Minnis, Paul E. 1985. *Social Adaptation to Food Stress: A Prehistoric Southwestern Example*. University of Chicago Press, Chicago.

Moore, Bruce M. 1978. Are Pueblo Field Houses a Function of Urbanization? In *Limited Activity and Occupation Sites: A Collection of Conference Papers*, edited by Albert E. Ward, pp. 9–16. Contributions to Anthropological Studies No. 1. Center for Anthropological Studies, Albuquerque, New Mexico.

———. 1979. Pueblo Isolated Small Structure Sites. PhD dissertation, Department of Anthropology, Southern Illinois University, Carbondale.

Neely, James A. 1995. Mogollon/Western Pueblo Soil and Water Control Systems of the Reserve Phase: New Data from West-Central New Mexico. In *Soil, Water, Biology, and Belief in Prehistoric and Traditional Southwestern Agriculture*, edited by H. Wolcott Toll, pp. 239–262. Special Publication 2. New Mexico Archaeological Council, Albuquerque, New Mexico.

Nelson, Ben A., Margaret C. Rugge, and Steven A. LeBlanc. 1978. LA 12109: A Small Classic Mimbres Ruin, Mimbres Valley. In *Limited Activity and Occupation Sites: A Collection of Conference Papers*, edited by Albert E. Ward, pp. 191–206. Contributions to Anthropological Studies No. 1. Center for Anthropological Studies, Albuquerque, New Mexico.

Nelson, Margaret C. 1999. *Mimbres During the Twelfth Century: Abandonment, Continuity, and Reorganization*. University of Arizona Press, Tucson.

Nesbitt, Paul. 1931. *The Ancient Mimbreños, Based on Investigations at the Mattocks Ruin, Mimbres Valley, New Mexico*. Logan Museum Bulletin 4. Beloit College, Beloit, Wisconsin.

Parsons, Francis B. 1955. A Small Mimbres Ruin near Silver City, New Mexico. *El Palacio* 62:283–289.

Pilles, Peter J., and David R. Wilcox. 1978. The Small Sites Conference: An Introduction. In *Limited Activity and Occupation Sites: A Collection of Conference Papers*, edited by Albert E. Ward, pp. 1–8. Contributions to Anthropological Studies No. 1. Center for Anthropological Studies, Albuquerque, New Mexico.

Reid, J. Jefferson, Barbara Klie Montgomery, and Maria Nieves Zedeño. 1995. Refinements in Dating Late Cibola White Ware. *Kiva* 61:31–44.

Roth, Barbara J. 2015. Archaeological Investigations at the Harris Site, LA 1867, Grant County, Southwestern New Mexico. Manuscript on file. Department of Anthropology, University of Nevada, Las Vegas.

Roth, Barbara J., and Kathryn M. Baustian. 2015. Kin Groups and Social Power at the Harris Site, Southwestern New Mexico. *American Antiquity* 80:451–471.

Sandor, Jonathan. 1983. Soils at Prehistoric Agricultural Terracing Sites in New Mexico. PhD dissertation, Department of Soil Sciences, University of California, Berkeley.

Schlanger, Sarah. 1992. Recognizing Persistent Places in Anasazi Settlement Systems. In *Space, Time, and Archaeological Landscapes*, edited by Jacqueline Rossignol and LuAnn Wandsnider, pp. 91–112. Plenum Press, New York.

Schriever, Bernard A. 2012. Mobility, Land Tenure, and Social Identity in the San Simon Basin of Southeastern Arizona. *Kiva* 77:413–438.

Scott, Catherine J. 1983. The Evolution of Mimbres Pottery. In *Mimbres Pottery: Ancient Art of the American Southwest*, edited by J. J. Brody, Catherine J. Scott, and Steven A. LeBlanc, pp. 39–68. American Federation of Arts, Hudson Hills Press, New York.

Shafer, Harry J. 1995. Architecture and Symbolism in Transitional Pueblo Development in the Mimbres Valley, SW New Mexico. *Journal of Field Archaeology* 22:23–47.

———. 2003. *Mimbres Archaeology at the NAN Ranch Ruin*. University of New Mexico Press, Albuquerque.

———. 2006. Extended Families to Corporate Groups: Pithouse to Pueblo Transformation of Mimbres Society. In *Mimbres Society*, edited by Patricia A. Gilman and Valli Powell-Martí, pp. 15–31. University of Arizona Press, Tucson.

Shafer, Harry, and Robbie Brewington. 1995. Microstylistic Changes in Mimbres Black-on-white Pottery: Examples from the NAN Ruin, Grant County, New Mexico. *Kiva* 61:6–27.

Snead, James E. 2001. *Ruins and Rivals: The Making of Southwest Archaeology*. University of Arizona Press, Tucson.

Stokes, Robert J. 1995. Prehistoric Settlement Patterns in the Sapillo Creek Valley, Gila National Forest, New Mexico. Master's thesis, Department of Anthropology, Eastern New Mexico University, Portales.

———. 1997. The Development of Interactive Mimbres Communities: Strategies for Resource Control in Peripheral Areas. Manuscript on file, Laboratory of Anthropology, Santa Fe, New Mexico.

———. 2000. Late Mimbres Pueblos in Peripheral Areas: Final Report on Test Excavations at LA 5841 (Cooney Ranch #1), Middle Fork of the Mimbres River, Southwestern New Mexico, August 7–9, 1999. Manuscript on file, Laboratory of Anthropology, Santa Fe, New Mexico.

———. 2003. Aspects of Land Tenure in an Ancient Southwestern Farming Society in the Mimbres Valley, New Mexico. PhD dissertation, Department of Anthropology, University of Oklahoma, Norman. UMI Dissertation Services, Ann Arbor, Michigan.

———. 2004. Private Property, Land Tenure, and Landless Subgroups in Classic Mimbres Society. In *Proceedings of the 13th Mogollon Archaeology Conference, October 1–2, 2004*, compiled by Lonnie Ludeman, on disk. New Mexico State University, Las Cruces.

———. 2006. News from the Mimbres Periphery: Recent Test Excavations at Cooney Ranch #1 in the Upper Mimbres. In *Mostly Mimbres: A Collection of Papers from the 12th Biennial Mogollon Conference*, edited by Marc Thompson, Jason Jurgena, and Lora Jackson, pp. 55–60. El Paso Museum of Archaeology, El Paso, Texas.

Stone, Tammy. 1993. Small Site Function and Duration of Occupation in the Hohokam Northern Periphery. *Kiva* 59:65–82.

Sutton, Mark. 1977. *The Archaeological Concept of a Field House*. Master's thesis, Department of Anthropology, California State University, Sacramento.

Toney, Elizabeth. 2012. Small Sites in the Mimbres Region: A GIS and Landscape Theory Approach. Master's thesis, Department of Anthropology, University of Oklahoma, Norman.

Varien, Mark D. 1999. *Sedentism and Mobility in a Social Landscape: Mesa Verde and Beyond*. University of Arizona Press, Tucson.

Ward, Albert E. (editor). 1978. *Limited Activity and Occupation Sites: A Collection of Conference Papers*. Contributions to Anthropological Studies No. 1. Center for Anthropological Studies, Albuquerque, New Mexico.

Wilcox, David R. 1978. The Theoretical Significance of Field Houses. In *Limited Activity and Occupation Sites: A Collection of Conference Papers*, edited by Albert E. Ward, pp. 25–34. Contributions to Anthropological Studies No. 1. Center for Anthropological Studies, Albuquerque, New Mexico.

Wills, W. H., and Robert D. Leonard (editors). 1994. *The Ancient Southwestern Community: Models and Methods for the Study of Prehistoric Social Organization*. University of New Mexico Press, Albuquerque.

Woodbury, Richard B. 1961. *Prehistoric Agriculture at Point of Pines, Arizona*. Society for American Archaeology, Memoirs, Contributions to Point of Pines Archaeology No. 16. University of Utah Press, Salt Lake City.

Woods, Aaron. 2012. Preliminary Investigations at the Stewart Pueblo: A Small Mimbres Pueblo in the Mimbres River Valley. In *Collected Papers from the 16th Biennial Mogollon Archaeology Conference, October 8–10, 2010*, edited by Lonnie C. Ludeman, pp. 119–127. Friends of Mogollon Archaeology, Las Cruces, New Mexico.

6

Mimbres Pottery

New Perspectives on Production and Distribution

DARRELL CREEL AND ROBERT J. SPEAKMAN

THE MIMBRES AREA IS PROBABLY best known for its pottery, particularly black-on-white and polychrome vessels with geometric and naturalistic designs. Our knowledge of the production and distribution of that pottery has undergone dramatic and fundamental changes as a result of chemical compositional analyses in the years since the pioneering neutron activation analysis (NAA) of Mimbres pottery by Gilman and colleagues (1994). We now know that production locales changed over time: some communities ceased to make ceramics while others continued centuries-long traditions of making pottery for internal use, as well as for distribution. The distribution of Mimbres pottery beyond production locales appears to have been largely a matter of proximity, with people acquiring pottery mostly from the nearest sources, but the movement of many pottery vessels may well have resulted from their use by individuals attending feasting events and other ceremonies at more distant communities. Over time, some communities appear to have specialized in pottery production, including a focus on corrugated jars in the southern Burro Mountains. The research and interpretations herein are an outgrowth of the ceramic compositional analysis based on petrography conducted by the Mimbres Foundation and substantially expand on that original effort.[1]

The Mimbres NAA Sample

The Mimbres area has a complex geologic history and is heavily mineralized, the fortunate result being that naturally occurring clays and tempering materials can, and do, differ chemically over short distances. Consequently, chemical compositional groups are reasonably well defined, some more so than others.

Since the initial study by Gilman and colleagues (1994), NAA has been conducted on nearly five thousand Mimbres pottery and raw clay samples from several hundred sites in the Mimbres, Jornada, and San Simon areas. Most have been sherd samples, but as of now, nearly one-third are whole or nearly whole vessels, and it is these that are being used to go beyond site-level questions. The sample derives from all portions of the Mimbres area, although it is dominated by the Mimbres Valley itself. A significant portion of the sample is from Jornada sites, particularly around El Paso. Temporally, the sample extends from the Early Pithouse period through the Cliff phase, a range of about A.D. 500–1400, but it is dominated by Mimbres Black-on-white pottery made from about A.D. 850 to 1150.

Most of the NAA samples are of painted, textured, and plain types in the Mimbres series (Alma Plain, Alma Neck Banded, San Francisco Red, Mogollon Red-on-brown, Three Circle Red-on-white, Three Circle Neck Corrugated, Mimbres Black-on-white Styles I–III, Mimbres Polychrome, and Mimbres Corrugated), the remainder being primarily types such as Chupadero Black-on-white, the Playas Red series, and El Paso Polychrome that occur on Mimbres Classic and Postclassic sites. A smaller portion consists of Salado and Chihuahuan polychromes and the textured wares occurring with them from Cliff phase sites.

The large set of data on these samples is a composite of many separate analyses conducted mostly for unrelated research objectives. This data set comes from more than two hundred sites and, in general, the Mimbres Valley has been heavily sampled; most of the large sites are represented by substantial numbers of samples. A large and critical portion of the sample derives from the long-term NAN Ranch Project, with significant contributions by Brewington and colleagues (1996), Dahlin (2003), Dahlin and colleagues (2007), Gottshall and colleagues (2002), James and colleagues (1995), and Shafer (2003). Additional substantial contributions come from Miller's (1997, 2005) data on Mimbres Black-on-white pottery from Jornada sites, the Laboratory of Anthropology research in the Gila Forks area (Turnbow and Huelster 2014), the Cañada Alamosa project (Ferguson et al. 2016), the AT&T Nexgen/Core project (Myers 2012), the Old Town project (Chandler 2000; Creel 2015; Creel et al. 2002), and thesis and dissertation research projects by Powell (2000; Powell-Martí and James 2006), Sedig (2015), and Schriever (2008). Most of the whole-vessel sampling effort was undertaken by the senior author and Steven LeBlanc at the Peabody Museum, Harvard University (Creel et al. 2014).

Speakman (2013) describes the data, its significant biases, and its complex analysis. He has defined three macrogroups and thirty-six compositional groups or subgroups for the Mimbres pottery sample, and Taliaferro (2014) has defined an additional six groups in a "Playas" series that appears to have been made in certain Late Classic Mimbres and Black Mountain phase sites (not discussed in this chapter). The reader is referred to Speakman 2013 and Taliaferro 2014 for detailed discussions of the statistical

TABLE 6.1 Mimbres Pottery Compositional Groups and Possible Production Locales

Compositional Group	Macrogroup	Probable Production Locale	Production Locale ID Confidence	Primary Ceramic Types	Clays	Number of Members
Mimbres-01	A	East side of Black Range (Rio Grande drainage)	high	Mimbres Style III B/w		243
Mimbres-02A	B-2	Mimbres Valley (Middle): Swarts	high	Mimbres Style III B/w		387
Mimbres-02B	B-2	Mimbres Valley (Middle): Swarts	high	Mimbres Style III B/w		24
Mimbres-02C	B-2	Mimbres Valley (Middle): Swarts	high	Mimbres Style III B/w		17
Mimbres-03	A	Gila River Forks	high	Gila white ware (Mimbres design with Cibola paste)		111
Mimbres-04A	B-1	Mimbres Valley (Upper): Galaz	high	Mimbres Style III B/w		341
Mimbres-04B	B-1	Mimbres Valley (Middle): Perrault	medium	Mimbres Style III B/w		189
Mimbres-04C	B-1	Mimbres Valley (Upper): Harris/Galaz/Gonzales area	high	Mimbres Style II B/w and earlier		158
Mimbres-05A	B-1	Gila River Valley: Woodrow locality	medium	Mimbres Style I–III B/w and Post-classic types	Yes	131
Mimbres-05B	B-1	Gila River Forks (TJ site area)	medium	Alma, Reserve, and plain/corrugated	Yes	81
Mimbres-05C	B-1	Uncertain	N/A	Corrugated		4
Mimbres-07A	A	Deming Plain, LA 59652 area	medium	Alma		48
Mimbres-07B	A	Deming Plain, LA 59652 area	medium	Alma		8
Mimbres-08	B-2	Mimbres Valley (Upper): Mattocks	medium	Mimbres Style III B/w		127

Mimbres-09	B-1	Gila River Forks (XSX or Main Diamond B)	low	Mimbres Style III B/w		25
Mimbres-10	A	Burro Mountains: Power site area	medium	Corrugated and Alma	Yes	116
Mimbres-11	B-2	Mimbres Valley (Middle): Perrault?	medium	Mimbres Style III B/w		121
Mimbres-13	A	Rio Grande drainage (possibly the Mesilla area)	medium	Mimbres Style III B/w		4
Mimbres-14	A	Uncertain	N/A	Mimbres Style III B/w		2
Mimbres-15	A	Uncertain	N/A	Corrugated and plain		2
Mimbres-21	C-1	Gila River Valley: Woodrow	medium	Mimbres Style III and II B/w		206
Mimbres-22	C-1	Gila River Valley: Saige-McFarland	medium	Mimbres Style III and II B/w		42
Mimbres-23	C-1	Rio Grande Valley: Rio Vista	medium	Mimbres Style III B/w		26
Mimbres-24	C-1	Burro Mountains/Gila River Valley: Wind Mountain	medium	Mogollon R/b, Three Circle R/w, Mimbres Style I B/w	Yes	107
Mimbres-27	C-1	Cedar Mountain: Otto and the Snake site	medium	Mimbres Style I–III B/w		5
Mimbres-28	C-1	Uncertain	N/A	Mimbres Style I B/w		4
Mimbres-41	C-2b	Mimbres Valley (Middle): NAN Ranch	high	Mimbres Style II and I B/w	Yes	57
Mimbres-42	C-2a	Mimbres Valley (Lower or Middle): unknown	N/A	Mimbres Style III and II B/w		26
Mimbres-43	C-2b	Arenas Valley: Treasure Hill	medium	Mimbres Style III B/w		4
Mimbres-44	C-2b	Cameron Creek	low	Mimbres Style III B/w		9

(continued)

TABLE 6.1 (continued)

Compositional Group	Macrogroup	Probable Production Locale	Production Locale ID Confidence	Primary Ceramic Types	Clays	Number of Members
Mimbres-46	C-2a	Mimbres Valley (Lower): Old Town?	low	Mogollon R/b and Three Circle R/w		4
Mimbres-47	C-2b	Mimbres Valley (Middle): NAN Ranch	medium	Corrugated and Alma		33
Mimbres-48	C-2c	Deming Plain, LA 59652 area	medium	Alma		9
Mimbres-49	C-2a	Mimbres Valley (Upper): Elk Ridge	medium	Plain and red-slipped plain brown		18
Mimbres-49A	C-2a	Mimbres Valley (Upper): Elk Ridge	high	Entire Mimbres sequence	Yes	162
Mimbres-49B	C-2a	Mimbres Valley (Upper): Elk Ridge	medium	Mimbres Style I B/w		5
Unassigned	A					28
Unassigned	B					577
Unassigned	B-1					9
Unassigned	B-2					1
Unassigned	C					11
Unassigned	C-1					53
Unassigned	C-2					80
Unassigned	C-2a					4

techniques used to define the groups. Table 6.1 presents a list of the Mimbres compositional groups currently defined and, to the extent that they are known, their production locales. (Note: this group definition/structure has been significantly refined since this chapter was written.) Table 6.1 does not include Jornada compositional groups defined by Miller and Ferguson (2014) in their comprehensive analysis of the large set of El Paso Brown NAA data, nor does it include the compositional groups defined by Clark (2006) and Clark and Creel (2006) for Chupadero Black-on-white or groups defined by Echinique (2013), Ownby and Huntley (2013), and Ownby and colleagues (2014) for Cliff phase ceramics from the Mimbres area. Despite clear overlap, no effort has yet been made to integrate fully all data sets, although the Mimbres, Chupadero, and Jornada data sets have been integrated through about 2013.

As noted in table 6.1, the Mimbres chemical compositional groups are reasonably well defined, although some are quite small at present, and the majority of samples are readily assignable to groups and subgroups. There are, however, a large number of samples that cannot currently be assigned to a specific compositional group, though most are assignable to a macrogroup. A large portion apparently derives from the major middle and upper Mimbres Valley production locales (macrogroups B-1 and B-2). It is likely that many unassigned samples are simply statistical outliers of defined groups. As sample size increases, particularly from undersampled parts of the region, new groups and subgroups may be defined and will likely incorporate some samples that had been previously unassigned (similarly, some unassigned samples may become assignable as groups are refined).

We would like to emphasize the biases and limitations of the current data set. Despite its impressive size, several possible or probable production localities have yet to be sampled. Equally important, several tentatively identified production sites have comparatively small samples. As a result, several compositional groups cannot be provisionally assigned to a geographic location, and others are linked with only a low level of confidence. Indeed, some of the problems with linking compositional groups to specific sites or locales are indicated by the varying level of confidence for such linkages in table 6.1. Moreover, site sample sizes vary rather considerably: some sites have only one or two samples, whereas others, such as Old Town and Swarts, have several hundred.

Overview of Mimbres Ceramic
Production Based on NAA

Generally speaking, pottery was made widely in the Mimbres area, but so far as is currently known, pottery was made over more of the area earlier rather than later (until the mid–A.D. 1100s). Unfortunately, the sampling of pottery from the Late Pithouse period is comparatively modest and derives from far fewer sites than the Classic period sample. For later Black Mountain phase ceramics, our sample again is smaller and derives from substantially fewer sites. Obviously, because of a much larger and widespread sample for the Classic period, we know considerably more about pottery production during that time.

During the San Francisco and early Three Circle phases, about A.D. 750–850, the earliest for which we have enough data for meaningful interpretation, pottery (including San Francisco Red, Alma series, Mogollon Red-on-brown, and Three Circle Red-on-white) was made throughout much of the Mimbres area and was widely moved. In the following Three Circle phase, about A.D. 850–1000, as best we can determine from current data, pottery production was probably still widespread in the Mimbres area but was becoming more restricted to higher elevations. Types include Mimbres Style I and II Black-on-white and Three Circle Neck Corrugated. Movement of vessels continued to be widespread, and even sites producing ceramics acquired fair quantities of Mimbres pottery from other sources, including the unslipped white-paste black-on-white (Gila White Ware as per Turnbow and Huestler 2014) from the Gila Forks area, as well as some El Paso Brown vessels from the El Paso area, Hohokam pottery in small quantities, and Red Mesa Black-on-white from the Cibola area.

By the Classic period (A.D. 1000–1130), pottery production in the Mimbres Valley appears to have become restricted to elevations above about 1645 m, at least in the Mimbres drainage, there being little if any substantive evidence of production in the lower elevations at sites such as Old Town. Some compositional groups tentatively linked to lower elevation production locales such as Old Town contain only early ceramic types, suggesting that production in those sites ceased prior to the Classic period.

Being above 1645 m in elevation, Galaz appears to have been a major ceramic production locale for much of its long history, especially during the Classic period. Classic period pottery production apparently was minimal south of Swarts (just above 1645 m), although there appears to have been limited production at NAN Ranch just a couple of miles south of Swarts. Movement of vessels occurred on a substantial level, and even the major producing sites appear to have acquired many vessels from other sources. The Spiral Rubbed Corrugated (Cosgrove and Cosgrove 1932:82) and Playas that first occur near the end of the Classic period appear to have been locally made in the lower Mimbres Valley (Taliaferro 2014). Late in the Classic period, El Paso Bichrome and Polychrome, Wingate Black-on-red, Reserve Black-on-white, Reserve Smudged Corrugated, Chupadero Black-on-white, and Three Rivers Red-on-terracotta were imported.

We suggest that the restriction of pottery production to elevations above 1645 m reflects the depletion of fuelwood plants in the more xeric, lower elevation locales, where sites had long histories and most or all of them had been occupied for several centuries prior to the Classic period. One can readily see the basic modern differences in woody plant density from the desert to the forest. The difference in desert-to-forest nonriparian woody fuel availability today is likely a general representation of how it had been depleted around A.D. 1150, although much of the depletion apparently occurred by about A.D. 1000. We suggest that this is in part a human modification of the natural elevational differences in vegetation. This inference of fuel depletion at lower elevations is supported by evidence reflecting the related, increasing need to import nearly all construction timber from higher elevation areas (see Creel 2006:89). Minnis (1985) came to a similar conclusion about the prehistoric modification of vegetation a number of years ago using different kinds of data, and a more recent analysis has reached the same conclusion (Schollmeyer 2005).

Thus, it is entirely possible that by the Classic period people simply did not have enough extra fuel to fire pottery at lower elevation sites and so had to import all of their pottery, mostly from the nearest production sources at higher, more wooded elevations up the Mimbres Valley or other drainages. Potters in the higher elevation sites (primarily from Swarts and upriver) raised their production levels to accommodate the increased need from people living in lower elevation sites.

Moreover, the potters in these major producing sites were responsible for much, if not most, of the design inventory that we see throughout the Mimbres area, beyond into the Jornada, and to a lesser extent, into southeastern Arizona. Creel and Speakman (2012) conducted a preliminary analysis of the whole-vessel NAA data to see if any patterns, designs, or motifs seem to be restricted to specific compositional groups and, by inference, production locale. To be sure, the groups have some interesting design clusters, but in general, one is struck by the overall similarity in designs among the various compositional groups for which there are at least several vessels. Surely, the remarkable overall similarity from group to group, at least within the major drainages of the Mimbres area, is evidence of substantial interaction on a general level, and probably interaction of many different kinds.

Late in the Classic period, new ceramic types were made in the Mimbres area, and others were acquired from surrounding areas, particularly the Jornada and Cibola regions to the southeast and north, respectively. Along with Playas, which was perhaps the most abundant of these non-Mimbres ceramic series types, El Paso Polychrome, Wingate Black-on-red, Reserve Black-on-white, Reserve Smudged Corrugated, Chupadero Black-on-white, and Three Rivers Red-on-terracotta occur consistently. All of these types continue into the Black Mountain phase, but production of Mimbres Black-on-white ceased at that point. Tularosa Smudged Corrugated, Tularosa Black-on-white, St. Johns Polychrome, and modest quantities of Chihuahuan polychromes also occur in Black Mountain phase sites, and Tucson Polychrome occurs late. Playas, including Playas red-slipped and unslipped varieties, appears to have been made locally in multiple localities in the Mimbres Valley (Taliaferro 2014).

Because of NAA of substantial numbers of Chupadero Black-on-white and El Paso Polychrome sherds and a few whole vessels, we know quite a bit about their production and importation into the Mimbres area, but far less about the other types. Virtually all of the Chupadero Black-on-white in Mimbres sites was made in the Sierra Blanca–Sacramento Mountains area east of the Tularosa Basin, which is east of the Rio Grande, with only a small amount from the Salinas district northeast of the Mimbres region and also east of the Rio Grande (Clark 2006; Clark and Creel 2006). Three Rivers Red-on-terracotta apparently derives from the Carrizo Mountains area and other locales in the northeastern Tularosa Basin (Miller and Graves 2012). El Paso Polychrome, which is a common type in the Black Mountain phase and following Cliff phase, is confidently attributed to multiple production locales around El Paso (Miller and Ferguson 2014). At least some of the Tularosa Smudged Corrugated seems to have been made in the Mimbres area (Mimbres-25, production locale not yet determined), perhaps by immigrants from the Cibola area (see also Ennes 1999; Hegmon et al. 2000).

The recent NAA and petrographic analysis of Cliff phase pottery from Gila and Mimbres Valley sites suggests that the Maverick Mountain series and Roosevelt Red Ware pottery was made in upper Gila sites such as 3-Up, Ormand, and Dinwiddie but not in the Mimbres Valley (Echenique 2013; Ownby and Huntley 2013). The results of these studies suggest further that plain utility pottery was being made in Cliff phase sites in the Mimbres area, including the Mimbres Valley.

Changing Pottery Production in the Mimbres Valley: Case Studies

To flesh out these general observations on Mimbres pottery production, we summarize our assessment of production and acquisition at three large sites in the Mimbres Valley: Galaz, Swarts, and Old Town. Galaz is in the upper Mimbres Valley, Swarts is in the middle valley, and Old Town is in the lower valley. Of these, Galaz has by far the smallest sample, whereas Swarts and Old Town have the two largest samples in the entire data set.

Galaz apparently produced most of its own painted pottery during the San Francisco and early Three Circle phases and acquired only modest amounts from other sources. Substantial numbers of vessels made at Galaz, both painted and corrugated, were moved to other sites throughout the Mimbres and Jornada areas. During the Three Circle phase, much of the painted pottery found at the Galaz site was still produced there, but with continued import of modest quantities from several other production locales, as well as substantial export of painted and corrugated pottery.

During the Classic period, Galaz still produced much of its own painted pottery, and in fact, our current understanding based on all NAA data indicates that Galaz was one of the largest producers of Classic period pottery, particularly painted, but also including some corrugated. Galaz acquired pottery from most producing sites in the middle and upper Mimbres Valley, as well as the upper Gila Valley and Eastern Mimbres area.

Swarts, like Galaz, appears to have been a major production locale for Mimbres pottery. However, we currently have no evidence for production of pottery at Swarts until Mimbres Style II Black-on-white, probably in the late A.D. 800s. None of the Swarts Style I vessels analyzed so far were made there, and most were made farther up the Mimbres Valley, from Perrault to the Harris site area. And while some Style II pottery was made at Swarts, the majority found there was made elsewhere, most from other Mimbres Valley sources, but some from both the Gila River and Eastern Mimbres areas. Not indicated by Swarts vessels due to lack of sampling, but clearly indicated by samples from other sites, is the production of at least some corrugated and some plain smudged pottery at Swarts. Corrugated and smudged pottery made at Swarts is not, however, common in the current Mimbres data set, largely because comparatively little of either type, especially the smudged, has been analyzed.

During the Classic period, the residents of Swarts acquired about one-fourth of their painted pottery from on-site producers and the remainder from virtually all known Mimbres Classic production locales. If we have correctly identified production locales, then the sources for most Style III found at Swarts were nearby Perrault, then Galaz, and then Mattocks. Very little Classic period pottery was produced south of Swarts, as it was the southernmost major pottery-producing site on the Mimbres River during the Classic period, as far as we know. There was some production at the nearby NAN Ranch site, two miles downriver, but apparently not at the level of Swarts production.

By the late Three Circle phase, if not earlier, in the lower Mimbres Valley, Old Town apparently ceased producing any pottery and depended entirely on imported ceramic containers. Most pottery there came from the major producing sites in the Mimbres Valley, especially NAN Ranch and the Galaz/Gonzales area, with lesser numbers of vessels from other production locales. One of the biggest changes here, as at Swarts, Galaz, and other Mimbres Valley sites, was importation of roughly one-third of the Style II Black-on-white from the relatively distant Woodrow and Saige-McFarland sites in the Gila Valley above Cliff. Much of the corrugated pottery came from the Burro Mountains to the west.

During the Classic period, Old Town apparently imported all its pottery, with most coming from the nearest major producing sites, Swarts and Perrault, and fewer vessels from most known production locales, although none came from NAN Ranch. The acquisition of painted vessels from Gila Valley sites decreased substantially, whereas acquisition from the Eastern Mimbres area increased. And as in earlier periods, much of the corrugated pottery apparently came from the Burro Mountains to the west.

Intrasite Differences

Having outlined changing pottery production in the Mimbres area, we now summarize the two efforts to date that investigate intrasite differences in pottery acquisition, both using whole vessels. Compositional analysis of whole vessels allows one to address research questions well beyond what is possible with just sherds. Context and design are among the sample attributes that make whole vessels so much more preferable and informative than sherds.

At the Old Town site, four pit structures had floor assemblages that included multiple vessels, all dating to about A.D. 900, and all vessels in each pit structure were sampled via NAA. Distinct differences *and* commonalities were found in the sources of pottery acquired by residents of these contemporary pithouses very close to one another in a single courtyard group (Creel 2013, 2015). What the differences mean is unclear, but they suggest that links with producers of pottery in other sites varied substantially between individual households, even closely affiliated households. For example, Rooms B4 and B8 were contemporary domestic pit structures in that courtyard group. Almost all of the vessels associated with Room B4 were from NAN Ranch. In contrast, the vessels from Room B8 were mostly from the upper Mimbres Valley in the Galaz/Gonzales site area. Both pithouses, however, had one corrugated jar each from the southern Burro Mountains to the west.

The second effort to address intrasite variation focused on the Swarts site and is a much more substantial undertaking that has analyzed more than seven hundred vessels (Creel et al. 2014). Swarts was investigated under the auspices of the Peabody Museum at Harvard University from 1924 to 1927. Two surface room blocks and a number of underlying pithouses were excavated, resulting in what is probably the single best sample of ceramics for NAA from a Mimbres site. That is, the sample is extensive, more or less complete for this part of the site, and well documented. It is not without its limitations, of course, but no other site offers the same combination of sample size and contextual quality.

The NAA sample of 719 comprises essentially all the Mimbres Black-on-white vessels and a few of the 300 or so vessels of other types. The data are most numerous and strongest for the Classic period. The ratio of whole pottery vessels for the north and south room blocks is 7:5, and in general, the distribution of NAA samples and most chemical compositional groups mirrors this ratio. Locally made pottery vessels occurred rather evenly throughout the community, and apparent clusters in some rooms seem mostly to be a function of the larger number of vessels in those rooms, not a disproportionate preference. In Mimbres Style III Black-on-white, only a few compositional groups deviate significantly from the 7:5 ratio, suggesting little perceptible difference in the preference for pottery vessels from different producers. The south room block shows, however, a slight preference for pottery from the Gila drainage sources, and there is a noticeable difference in the occurrence of pottery acquired from Mattocks: thirty-three vessels from the south room block compared to just twenty-six from the north room block (essentially a reverse of the 7:5 north:south room-block ratio).

With robust data, such as those from Swarts, we can begin to ask what these intrasite differences mean. Are we seeing some indication of differences in family or household preferences, perhaps based in part on kinship? Were the south room-block residents more closely related with Mattocks and the north room-block residents with Perrault, the next large Mimbres site upriver (poorly known, mechanically looted; several whole vessels and a number of sherds have been analyzed)? Or did people simply choose pots that they liked, much as we do today?

Discussion

One of our major observations based on the entire data set is that, in general, proximity to production locales was the primary factor affecting pottery acquisition even in sites that actually made ceramics. When one examines the data by subregion and drainage, it is clear that pottery distribution was largely, but not exclusively, determined by proximity. That is, most of the Mimbres Black-on-white pottery used in upper Gila drainage sites was made on-site or at another production site in the same drainage. The same is true of the Mimbres Valley and the Eastern Mimbres area. By contrast, there clearly was much interdrainage acquisition of pottery, and some was moved long distances. Most of the Mimbres Black-on-white pottery in Jornada sites was made in the middle and upper Mimbres Valley, with a small amount possibly from the Eastern Mimbres area. Similarly, nearly all of the Mimbres pottery found in Arizona was made at sites in the vicinity of Cliff, New Mexico.

One of the more interesting aspects of Mimbres pottery distribution is the movement of vessels between the Gila and Mimbres valleys over time. Though samples are small for earlier painted types such as Mogollon Red-on-brown and Three Circle Red-on-white, it is reasonably clear that much more pottery was moved from Gila

Valley sources (including the Gila Forks area) to Mimbres Valley communities (ca. 37 percent) than vice versa (< 10 percent) until the Classic period. During the Classic period, this pattern reversed dramatically, and nearly one-fourth of painted vessels in Gila Valley communities came from Mimbres Valley sources, whereas only 4 percent of vessels in Mimbres Valley sites came from Gila Valley sources. Why this was the case is unknown, but it is a topic for ongoing research, including design analysis.

This rather substantial level of pottery movement has significant implications for how we assess interaction among people living in the Mimbres region, from the movement of objects to the movement of people and ideas. By far, more pots moved than stayed where they were made, with only one-fourth to one-third of the analyzed pottery being locally made at producing sites (which has sobering implications for how we use the criterion of abundance to infer production locale). Taking a broad perspective, one can easily see that there had to be a pervasive, household-level domestic demand for pottery on the part of nonproducing families regardless of where they lived. Superimposed on this domestic provisioning was surely a range of other socioeconomic behaviors that resulted in the movement of pottery vessels from producing to nonproducing sites, and possibly from one nonproducing site to another. Several researchers have discussed the distribution of pottery vessels via ceremonies and feasting events, and Shafer (2013) has discussed a possible mechanism in the movement of alcoholic beverage containers, most of which are corrugated jars. Perhaps we can use whole vessel design information to delve deeper into the nature of such inter- and intrasite social links.

What are the implications of short-distance vessel movement on the order of the few kilometers between Perrault and Swarts as opposed to movement over the 200 km between Galaz and Hueco Tanks, east of El Paso? And what are the implications of import differences between producing sites on the one hand and nonproducing sites on the other? Surely, there were variances in the items, materials, or services exchanged. So, for example, what did the residents of Old Town exchange for all the pottery they acquired from other sites? Was it food, textiles, ritual performance, or something else?

Taliaferro (2014) has approached the NAA data set from a different perspective, looking at the organization of Mimbres pottery production. His interpretation holds that production was organized as "individual/household specialization as well as community specialization during the Pithouse and Classic periods" (Taliaferro 2014:404). He suggests that the early painted pottery and utilitarian ceramics were produced through individual or household specialization. Production of Mimbres Black-on-white, by contrast, changed over time from individual- or household-level to community-level specialization. Moreover, Taliaferro posits that pottery produced in a community specialization system will likely be more widely distributed because production is more restricted and must meet an increased demand. Such analyses need to be repeated as new samples are analyzed, particularly large sets with intrasite provenience differences.

No matter what, the economic underpinnings of Mimbres communities presumably changed as local fuel resources became depleted and as populations grew, and so it is reasonable to infer that socioeconomic relationships changed as well. We firmly believe that the analysis of ceramic compositional data, vessel design, and contextual data will allow us to investigate and learn more about these relationships, and we therefore strongly advocate continued sampling of whole vessels, particularly those with good provenience and context.

Note

1. As a result of new data sets and new analyses made since this chapter was written, the NAA group structure and definitions, as well as interpretations based on them, have been and continue to be expanded and refined.

References Cited

Brewington, Robbie, Harry J. Shafer, and Dennis James. 1996. Production and Distribution of Mimbres Black-on-white Ceramics: Evidence from Instrumental Neutron Activation Analysis (INAA). Paper presented at the 62nd Annual Meeting of the Society for American Archaeology, Nashville, Tennessee.

Chandler, Shari. 2000. Sourcing Three Circle Phase Ceramics from Old Town (LA 1113), Luna County, New Mexico. Master's thesis, Department of Sociology and Anthropology, New Mexico State University, Las Cruces.

Clark, Tiffany. 2006. Production, Exchange, and Social Identity: A Study of Chupadero Black-on-white Pottery. PhD dissertation, Department of Anthropology, Arizona State University, Tempe.

Clark, Tiffany, and Darrell Creel. 2006. Sourcing Chupadero Black-on-white Pottery from the Post–A.D. 1130 Mimbres Region. Poster presentation, 71st Annual Meeting of the Society for American Archaeology, San Juan, Puerto Rico.

Cosgrove, H. S., and C. B. Cosgrove. 1932. *The Swarts Ruin, a Typical Mimbres Site in Southwestern New Mexico*. Report of the Peabody Museum of Archaeology and Ethnology, Harvard University Vol. XV(1). The Museum, Cambridge, Massachusetts.

Creel, Darrell. 2006. *Excavations at the Old Town Ruin, Luna County, New Mexico, 1989–2003*. Volume 1. Bureau of Land Management, New Mexico State Office, Santa Fe.

———. 2013. The Mimbres Vessel Sourcing Project. Paper presented at the Annual Meeting of the Archaeological Society of New Mexico, Albuquerque.

————. 2015. *The Old Town Project: Artifact Analyses*. Cultural Resources Series No. 16, Vol. 2. Bureau of Land Management, New Mexico State Office, Santa Fe.

Creel, Darrell, Steven A. LeBlanc, and R. J. Speakman. 2014. Neutron Activation Analysis of Mimbres Pottery from the Swarts Ruin. Paper presented at the 18th Mogollon Conference, Las Cruces, New Mexico.

Creel, Darrell, and R. J. Speakman. 2012. The Mimbres Vessel Project: An Update on the Neutron Activation Analysis Effort. Paper presented at the 17th Mogollon Conference, Silver City, New Mexico.

Creel, Darrell, Matthew Williams, Hector Neff, and Michael Glascock. 2002. Black Mountain Phase Ceramics and Implications for Manufacture and Exchange Patterns. In *Ceramic Production and Circulation in the Greater Southwest: Source Determination by INAA and Complementary Mineralogical Investigations*, edited by Donna Glowacki and Hector Neff, pp. 37–46. Monograph 44. Cotsen Institute of Archaeology, University of California, Los Angeles.

Dahlin, Eleanor. 2003. INAA and Distribution Patterns of Classic Mimbres Black-on-white Vessels during the Classic Period. Master's thesis, Department of Anthropology, Texas A&M University, College Station.

Dahlin, Eleanor, David Carlson, Dennis James, and Harrt Shafer. 2007. Distribution Patterns of Mimbres Ceramics using INAA and Multivariate Statistical Methods. *Journal of Radioanalytical and Nuclear Chemistry* 271:461–466.

Echenique, Ester. 2013. *Neutron Activation Analysis of Polychromes: Ceramic Circulation in the Mimbres Valley, Southwestern New Mexico*. Petrographic Report 2013–05. Desert Archaeology, Tucson, Arizona.

Ennes, Mark. 1999. Evidence for Migration in the Eastern Mimbres Region, Southwestern New Mexico. In *Sixty Years of Mogollon Archaeology: Papers from the Ninth Mogollon Conference, Silver City, New Mexico, 1996*, edited by Stephanie M. Whittlesey, pp. 127–134. SRI Press, Tucson, Arizona.

Ferguson, Jeffery R., Karl W. Laumbach, Stephen H. Lekson, Toni S. Laumbach, and Virginia T. McLemore. 2016. You Get It Here, I'll Get It There: Examining the Divergent Long Distant Exchange Patterns Throughout the Pithouse and Pueblo Occupation of the Cañada Alamosa. In *Exploring Cause and Explanation: Historical Ecology, Demography, and Movement*, edited by Cynthia L. Herhahn and Ann F. Ramenofsky, pp. 231–256. University Press of Colorado, Boulder.

Gilman, Patricia, Veletta Canouts, and Ronald Bishop. 1994. The Production and Distribution of Classic Mimbres Black-on-white Pottery. *American Antiquity* 59:695–709.

Gottshall, Julia Munoz, Harry J. Shafer, and Dennis James. 2002. Neutron Activation Analysis of Mimbres Corrugated Pottery from the NAN Ranch Ruin. In *Mogollon Archaeology: Collected Papers from the Eleventh Mogollon Conference*, edited by Patrick H. Beckett, pp. 121–128. COAS Publishing and Research, Las Cruces, New Mexico.

Hegmon, Michelle, Margaret Nelson, and Mark Ennes. 2000. Corrugated Pottery, Technological Style, and Population Movement in the Mimbres Region of the American Southwest. *Journal of Anthropological Research* 56:217–240.

James, Dennis, Robbie Brewington, and Harry J. Shafer. 1995. Compositional Analysis of American Southwestern Ceramics by Neutron Activation Analysis. *Journal of Radioanalytical and Nuclear Chemistry* 192:109–116.

Miller, Myles R. 1997. Ceramic Production and Distribution in the Jornada and Mimbres Mogollon Regions of Southern New Mexico, West Texas, and Northern Chihuahua. Paper presented in the symposium "Chemical Sourcing of Ceramics in the Greater Southwest," 62nd Annual Meeting of the Society for American Archaeology, Nashville, Tennessee.

———. 2005. Peripheral Basins and Ephemeral Polities: INAA of Mimbres Black-on-White Ceramics and Insights into Mimbres and Jornada Mogollon Social Relationships. Paper presented in the symposium "Using Nuclear Chemistry to Answer Cultural Questions: Recent Applications of INAA in the American Southwest," 70th Annual Meeting of the Society for American Archaeology, Salt Lake City, Utah.

Miller, Myles R., and Jeffery Ferguson. 2014. Classification of Brown Wares, Textured Wares, and Red Wares from Southern New Mexico and Western Texas. Unpublished documents and digital data files on file with authors, Austin, Texas.

Miller, Myles R., and Tim B. Graves. 2012. *Sacramento Pueblo: An El Paso and Late Glencoe Phase Pueblo in the Southern Sacramento Mountains*. Cultural Resources Report No. 10–22. Environmental Division, Fort Bliss Garrison Command, Fort Bliss, Texas.

Minnis, Paul. 1985. *Social Adaptation to Food Stress: A Prehistoric Southwestern Example*. University of Chicago Press, Chicago.

Myers, Tori L. 2012. Appendix F: Ceramic Analysis. In *Archaeological Investigations for the AT&T Nexgen/Core Project: New Mexico Segment*, by Joshua G. Jones, Timothy M. Kearns, and Janet L. McVickar. Western Cultural Resource Management, Farmington, New Mexico.

Ownby, Mary, and Deborah Huntley. 2013. Production and Exchange of Polychrome Pottery in the Upper Gila and Mimbres Valleys: Results from Neutron Activation and Petrographic Analyses. Paper presented at the Annual Meeting of the Society for American Archaeology, Honolulu, Hawaii.

Ownby, Mary, Deborah Huntley, and Matthew Peeples. 2014. A Combined Approach: Using NAA and Petrography to Examine Ceramic Production and Exchange in the American Southwest. *Journal of Archaeological Science* 52:152–162.

Powell, Valli. 2000. Iconography and Group Formation During the Late Pithouse and Classic Periods of the Mimbres Society, A.D. 970–1140. PhD dissertation, Department of Anthropology, University of Oklahoma, Norman.

Powell-Martí, Valli, and Dennis James. 2006. Ceramic Iconography and Social Asymmetry in the Classic Mimbres Heartland, A.D. 970–1140. In *Mimbres Society*, edited by Valli S. Powell-Martí and Patricia A. Gilman, pp. 151–173. University of Arizona Press, Tucson.

Schollmeyer, Karen. 2005. Prehispanic Environmental Impact in the Mimbres Region, South-western New Mexico. *Kiva* 70:375–398.

Schriever, Bernard A. 2008. Informal Identity and the Mimbres Phenomenon: Investigating Regional Identity and Archaeological Cultures in the Mimbres Mogollon. PhD disserta-tion, Department of Anthropology, University of Oklahoma, Norman.

Sedig, Jakob W. 2015. The Mimbres Transitional Phase: Examining Social, Demographic, and Environmental Resilience and Vulnerability from A.D. 900–1000 in Southwest New Mex-ico. PhD dissertation, Department of Anthropology, University of Colorado, Boulder.

Shafer, Harry J. 2003. *Mimbres Archaeology at the NAN Ruin*. University of New Mexico Press, Albuquerque.

———. 2013. Possible Archaeological Evidence for Classic Mimbres Use of Tesquino at the NAN Ranch Ruin, Southwest New Mexico. In *Collected Papers of the 17th Biennial Mogol-lon Archaeology Conference*, edited by Lonnie Ludeman, pp. 109–117. Las Cruces, New Mexico.

Speakman, Robert J. 2013. Mimbres Pottery Production and Distribution. PhD dissertation, Departamento de Prehistoria, Historia Antigua I Arqueologia, Universitat de Barcelona, Barcelona.

Taliaferro, Matthew. 2014. The Black Mountain Phase Occupation at Old Town: An Examina-tion of Social and Technological Organization in the Mimbres Valley of Southwestern New Mexico, ca. A.D. 1150–1300. PhD dissertation, Department of Anthropology, University of Texas, Austin.

Turnbow, Christopher, and Richard Huelster. 2014. In Search of the Seventh Parrot: A Tale of Looting, Archaeology, and a Missing Bird. Paper presented at the 18th Biennial Mogollon Conference, Las Cruces, New Mexico.

7

Mimbres Pottery Designs in Their Social Contexts

MICHELLE HEGMON, JAMES R. MCGRATH,
F. MICHAEL O'HARA III, AND WILL G. RUSSELL

ARCHAEOLOGICAL RESEARCH IN the Mimbres region has contributed to knowledge on myriad weighty topics ranging from the pithouse-to-pueblo transition to regional reorganization to subsistence stress. Nevertheless, it is the beautiful pottery—especially the designs that depict animals and humans—that makes the region famous. The pottery designs are sometimes realistic and sometimes impossible. Some are horrific and others humorous, and some are so risqué that Hattie Cosgrove censored parts of them in her reproductions (Cosgrove and Cosgrove 1932:Plate 228f). Some layouts focus attention on a single motif, portrait style; in other cases, motifs are intertwined in complex ways. Despite the fame of the designs and the attention they have garnered, archaeologists know very little about their meanings for the people who made and used the pottery. The research presented in this chapter addresses this gap by investigating the social significance of Mimbres animal designs. Specifically, we use newly available provenience data to examine the distribution of these designs spatially (across the region and within sites) and in relation to personal identity (the age and sex of individuals in burials).

What We Know, and Still Need to Know, About Mimbres Designs

Most research to date on what are called "representational" designs (i.e., those that depict specific figures, in contrast to "geometric" designs) has concentrated on identifying what was painted on Mimbres pottery and how the depictions can be interpreted. Many of these studies focus on particular kinds of designs that appear to have ritual or cosmological significance. For example, the Hero Twins and ritually important macaws have been linked to the Classic period ritual economy (Gilman et al. 2014; chapter 4), and many of the parrotlike birds (usually depicted with humans) are identified as scarlet macaws from distant sources in southern Mexico (Creel and McKusick 1994; chapter 11). These are important insights, and much remains to be done in this vein.

Other studies scrutinize the depictions for details about animal species or human activities. Thus, scholars have debated whether some of the depicted fish are saltwater species (Bettison et al. 1999; Jett and Moyle 1986). Some studies identify indicators of gender, such as clothing and body ornaments, and use these to consider the division of labor (Munson 2000; although see Hegmon et al. 2017). Some of the animals depicted (such as turkey and rabbits) were commonly eaten, but others (e.g., swallows) were not (Hegmon 2010a). These kinds of questions and topics are also worthy of more attention and perhaps can be linked to research on ecology and subsistence.

Archaeological research on style suggests another line of questioning (Hegmon 1992). While some designs have very specific iconographic meanings that can usually be verbalized, others are socially meaningful in a more general way (i.e., what Plog [1990] calls "symbolic variation"). Examples of styles with specific iconographic meanings include the Christian cross or Mesoamerican Quetzalcoatl, and examples of styles that are more generally meaningful include a feminine-cut T-shirt or a technological sequence associated with a particular area (Van Keuren 2000). Many designs are likely to have layers of meanings, such as Quetzalcoatl-like feathered serpents painted on Mimbres bowls with Mimbres stylistic conventions. Meanings also change over time or with circumstances. In Wiessner's (1983) study of the San, arrow-making traditions were simply unremarked-upon ways of doing, but these traditions became signals of ethnic differences as groups interacted. In Northwest Coast art, certain conventions signal the type of animal that is being portrayed—such as the large teeth of a beaver— and those animals also have certain cosmological meanings (Holm 1965). Very often, in both archaeological analyses and today's world, the meaningful nature of designs or styles is best understood contextually, in part because it is the context that gives them meaning. For example, many pottery painting traditions in the Southwest use some kind of hachure, but as hachure came to be associated with Chaco, including the famous cylinder jars, it took on a more specific meaning as a symbol of Chaco or even of turquoise (Plog 2003). In the Western Pueblo region, Mills (2007) notes the association between the size and visibility of designs on the exterior of pottery vessels and the use of those vessels in interhousehold feasts. Although her analysis focuses on design visibility in relation to proxemics, she concludes that the designs communicated with various audiences during performances and feasts (Mills 2007:234).

Until recently, researchers have rarely addressed these kinds of issues in Mimbres archaeology, in large part because it has been difficult to link provenience and contextual information to design analyses. One important exception is the work of Powell-Martí, which we discuss in more detail below (Powell 1996; Powell-Martí and James 2006). The Mimbres Pottery Images Digital Database (MimPIDD) makes this kind of research much more practical. It is now possible to ask if deer designs are concentrated at some sites or room blocks and rabbits at others, and thus whether they might symbolize group identity. Gilman and colleagues (2014:98) have discussed similarities between the Maya *Popol Vuh* and Mimbres iconography, suggesting that in both cases rabbits symbolize the younger, more feminine Hero Twin. With MimPIDD, it is now possible to investigate whether there is an association between rabbit designs and female burials.

The research presented in this chapter investigates the social significance of the meaning(s) and meaningfulness of Mimbres designs by analyzing their spatial and contextual distributions. The term *social significance* encompasses both specific and general meaningfulness and allows for flow between these categories.

More specifically, this research focuses on the social significance of the designs with reference to both group or kinship affiliation and personal identity (age and gender). In many societies, including those of the Pueblo peoples, clans have associated animal symbols or totems. In his study of ancestral Hopi sites, Bernardini (2005) found that clan or lineage symbols were clustered at certain sites and thus marked the different migration pathways of subclans. In ethnographically known pueblos, clans and other descent groups, sodalities, and other social units sometimes crosscut one another (Ware 2014) and are not spatially isolated (Cameron 1992; Mindeleff 1891). However, they also are not distributed evenly, and many villages are dominated by one or a few founding clans (Eggan 1950:Table 2). Thus, any material symbols that are linked to specific descent groups are likely to be distributed unevenly across space.

Most or even all societies materially mark some differences between genders and ages. Such differences are depicted on Mimbres pottery: head feathers and masklike facial decorations are associated with men, and string aprons are associated with women (Hegmon et al. 2017; Munson 2000). Some of the females are even depicted with butterfly hair whorls known to signal maiden status among a number of Puebloan societies. Elsewhere in the Southwest, male and female burials are associated with different materials (e.g., Howell 1996). Thus, if animal motifs or other designs were linked to particular sex and gender or age categories, vessels depicting those designs might be unevenly distributed in burials.

Our research asks two empirical questions to begin an investigation into these theoretical issues:

1. Are certain kinds of designs or design elements clustered in particular places? If yes, then they likely indicate something about group affiliation.
2. Are certain kinds of designs or design elements associated with buried individuals of a certain age or sex? If yes, then they likely indicate something about personal identity.

Designs depicting different animals co-occur on sites and even in the same burial (Brody 2004:167); therefore, it is unlikely that the analysis will reveal simple patterns such as rabbits at Swarts and deer at Mattocks, as C. LeBlanc (1977) demonstrated long ago. Thus, we focus here on more subtle lines of investigation including relative frequencies and intrasite distributions. The designs are also classified in various ways. It is possible that some animals have a straightforward and specific meaning, such as the bear as the symbol or totem of the Bear Clan. It is also possible that some animals are meaningful in a more general way. For example, if a potter consistently made one kind of design (a supposition supported by Powell-Martí and James 2006), then that design could come to be associated with her village (see Longacre et al. 2000). It is also possible that the meaningfulness of the animals is not captured by Western classification systems. The analysis therefore considers other attributes of the animals, including their symbolic and cosmological significance and their habitat.

This research has been made possible by the vision and energy of Steven LeBlanc. As part of his work with the Mimbres Foundation in the 1970s, he and others working for the Mimbres Foundation traveled across the country photographing and recording data on Mimbres pottery. That collection became the Mimbres Archive, and the order of vessels in the archive is a sort of record of these travels. Numbers 30–168 are in the Arizona State Museum, 169–184 in the Heard Museum, 185–268 in the Museum of Northern Arizona, 269–560 in the Western New Mexico University Museum, and on and on across the country, including material in the Heye Foundation (nos. 1639–1934), Harvard's Peabody Museum (nos. 2025–2349), and many other institutions. LeBlanc provided a copy of the archive—which originally consisted of color slides, black-and-white negatives, and paper notes—to the Maxwell Museum, where many researchers have had the opportunity to use it. He then worked to digitize the collection and added information on many more vessels. Together with Michelle Hegmon, he created a new digital and much larger database called the Mimbres Pottery Images Digital Database (MimPIDD). MimPIDD now contains photographs of and data on nearly all known decorated Mimbres vessels, as well as some undecorated and non-Mimbres types ($N > 10,500$ in early 2016). It is stored permanently on the Digital Archaeological Record (tDAR, https://core.tdar.org/collection/22070), where it is available to researchers and parts are open to the general public.

Seeing the Designs from Multiple
Perspectives: Assembling the Database

Our two research questions investigate the possible meaning of Mimbres designs by assessing their distribution at inter- and intrasite levels and in association with different types of burials. To address these research questions, we need to analyze the specific content of the designs in relation to possible systems of meaning and to assess the spatial distribution of the designs. Thus, the analysis draws on two resources: MimPIDD and a comprehensive study of how ethnographically known southwestern people used and understood a wide range of animal species (O'Hara 2007).

Of the more than 10,500 vessels in MimPIDD, 4,486 have site-level provenience data and about 25 percent of these (almost all bowls) have representational designs. (Most Mimbres Black-on-white vessels are bowls; the few jars that are decorated have relatively simple geometric designs.) The analysis considers only vessels that depict what appear to be real animals as their primary focus. A small number of designs depict unreal transformational creatures such as a bird with a fish tail, narrative scenes, or humans; these uncommon designs are not included in the analysis. We analyzed a total of 971 bowls depicting animals for this project. Most are classified as Mimbres Style III (aka Classic) and thus are generally associated with the Classic period (A.D. 1000–1130), although all Mimbres Black-on-white types are included.

The analysis classifies the designs according to three sets of variables: kind of animal, symbolic association, and habitat. The three sets of variables are summarized in table 7.1 and some examples are shown in figure 7.1. In general, the term *design* refers to the entire design painted on a vessel and *motif* refers to a part of that design that depicts an animal or some other specific form. Kind of animal (e.g., fish, turkey, tadpole) is in part a product of Western taxonomies, although Pueblo stories also refer to many of the animals we recognize today (e.g., coyote, snake, rabbit). Symbolic association and habitat are other ways people in the past may have classified animals, based on their meaning in stories or where they live. The analysis does not assume that any of these variables are necessarily meaningful. On the contrary, it is exploratory and asks if potentially meaningful patterns can be discerned if the designs are classified in these various ways. For example, if all infant burials were found to have bowls depicting water animals, then that would point to a need to explore possible meanings, such as water as primordial, as a source of life, or as a point of origin.

Kind of animal is the most obvious characteristic and was coded according to Linnaean categories, as well as best-fit description. The Linnaean classification served as a baseline against which to compare other kinds of taxonomies, and it provided a useful means of classifying motifs that were more or less specific. For example, an

TABLE 7.1 Summary and Examples of Variables Coded for This Analysis

General Category	Specific Variables	Examples			
		Figure 1b MimPIDD 2222	Figure 1f MimPIDD 2788	Figure 1h MimPIDD 7861	Figure 1k MimPIDD 4566
Kind of animal	class	Aves	Amphibia	Mammalia	Reptilia
	order	Galliformes	Anura	Chiroptera	Testudines/Chelonii
	family	Phasianidae			
	genus	*Meleagris*			
	species				
	best fit	turkey	tadpole	bat	turtle
Symbolic association	phenomena	rain, death	water		water
	direction	Underworld		Underworld	
Habitat	habitat	terrestrial	aquatic	aerial	aquatic

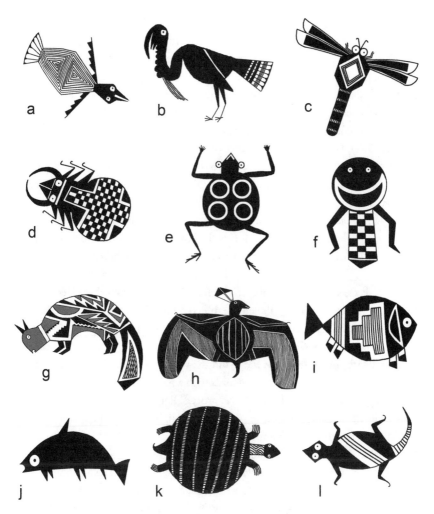

FIGURE 7.1 Examples of motifs coded for this study: (a) after MimPIDD 4621, Lower Hyatt site; (b) after MimPIDD 2222, Swarts site; (c) after MimPIDD 2694, Swarts site; (d) after MimPIDD 201, Treasure Hill site; (e) after MimPIDD 4568, Eby site; (f) after MimPIDD 2788, Galaz site; (g) after MimPIDD 139, McSherry site; (h) after MimPIDD 7861, Eby site; (i) after MimPIDD 4652, Perrault site; (j) after MimPIDD 4625, Old Town site; (k) after MimPIDD 4566, Eby site; (l) after MimPIDD 2886, Galaz site. Drawn by Will G. Russell.

indeterminate fish (figure 7.1j) could be classified by class (Actinopterygii), whereas some other animals, depicted with more detail, could be narrowed to genus and species, such as *Castor canadensis* (beaver, figure 7.1g).

Symbolic association is concerned with the cosmological meanings of the animal motifs, derived from ethnographic accounts and stories (O'Hara 2007). Several authors have made specific links between Mimbres designs and Puebloan or Mesoamerican cosmologies (Brody and Swentzell 1996; Carr 1979; Gilman et al. 2014; Kabotie 1982). Drawing on these sources does not presume that such belief systems necessarily extend back into the Mimbres past. Rather, information about these cosmologies suggests different ways of classifying the animals so that possible patternings of those categories can be explored. For example, black birds with large curving beaks (ravens) and quadrupeds with fluffy tails (coyotes) might both be Trickster. Thus, the analysis can investigate if Trickster motifs (including certain birds and certain quadrupeds) are associated with a particular room block or type of burial.

We identified three symbolic association variables: process, direction, and "birds of the . . ." Process refers to phenomena such as rain (linked to turkey, deer, bighorn sheep, and others) or fertility (linked to rabbits). Direction refers to the cardinal and primary intercardinal directions, along with zenith and nadir (which are often associated with the Upper World and Underworld, respectively). For example, bears are associated with the southwest at Hopi and the west at several other pueblos. "Birds of the . . ." is the association of certain birds with a particular realm and phenomena, which may or may not be redundant with process. For example, raptors are said to be birds of the sky and are commonly associated with lightning and thunder.

Habitat refers to where an animal is usually found—aquatic, terrestrial, or aerial. This variable recognizes that animals can be categorized in various ways, and it was coded based on our (Western) knowledge of the animal. Habitat is sometimes linked to symbolic association. For example, many aquatic animals (including frogs, turtles, and fish) are symbolically associated with water, but others (such as some water birds) are not. Interestingly, some terrestrial animals (e.g., bighorn sheep and deer) are symbolically associated with rain.

The three categories of variables—kind of animal, symbolic association, and habitat—group the motifs in various ways. For example, use of Linnaean class would group together figure 7.1a and b (hummingbird and turkey, both birds), figure 7.1c and d (ant lion or dragonfly and ant-lion larva [see Trask and Russell 2011 regarding ant lions]), figure 7.1e and f (frog and tadpole, which is an immature frog), figure 7.1g and h (beaver and bat, both mammals), figure 7.1i and j (fish), and figure 7.1k and l (turtle and lizard, both reptiles). In contrast, consideration of habitat would group the bat, hummingbird, and flying insect as aerial animals but group the other bird (turkey) with terrestrial animals, including the lizard. Classification according to symbolic association would produce far different groups, such as linking larval ant lions, bats, and fish together as Underworld creatures.

The analytical data set is available in tDAR (https://core.tdar.org/project/399095 /documents-and-data-from-hegmon-et-al-mimbres-pottery-designs-in-their-social -context). It includes catalogue and provenience data (from MimPIDD), general type of design and layout (also from MimPIDD), and the three sets of variables coded for this analysis.

The Spatial Distribution of Mimbres Designs

If the different animals or their meanings were associated with certain social groups, then we would expect them to exhibit some kind of spatial clustering at inter- or intrasite levels. We used a variety of quantitative techniques to examine intra- and intersite patterns in all three sets of variables (i.e., kind of animal, symbolic association, habitat). The results in all cases were the same. No matter how they are classified, designs bearing animal motifs are distributed homogeneously and display no discernable clustering.

To demonstrate, we show one part of the analysis here: the distribution of motifs grouped by Linnaean class (mammal, insect, arachnid, reptile, bird, fish, amphibian, gastropod). Ten sites have fourteen or more bowls coded in this system, and these form the foundation of the analysis. The distribution of motifs by site is shown in table 7.2 (which also includes the rare category "plant"). With ten sites and nine motif classes, table 7.2 comprises a total of ninety cells. The more common classes (fish, bird, insect, mammal, and reptile) are found at all sites in fairly similar percentages, and even the less common categories (amphibians and arachnids) are widely distributed. The analysis by class is a useful starting point because it draws on a large sample. Similar procedures were used to analyze the distribution of designs classified by symbolic association and habitat, with the same results: there is no discernable clustering.

The homogenous distribution of Mimbres animal motifs suggests that they were not associated with distinct social groups. It is instructive, however, to compare these distributions to a different case in which animal motifs are closely linked to group identity, specifically, the distribution of clan symbols in ancestral Hopi rock art presented by Bernardini (2005). The Hopi rock art symbols, such as bear paws and deer, cluster strongly; most are found at only a few sites and only two are found at all sites. This pattern stands in stark contrast to the widely distributed Mimbres motifs we have analyzed. The difference between distributions of Mimbres motifs and Hopi symbols can be assessed statistically with Allison's Z-scores. This statistic is based on binomial probabilities; it determines the expected count in each tabular cell and calculates how

TABLE 7.2 Distribution of Bowls Depicting Classes of Animals

	Mammalia N (%)	Aves (birds) N (%)	Actinopterygii (fish) N (%)	Insecta N (%)	Reptilia N (%)	Amphibia N (%)	Arachnida (spiders) N (%)	Gastropoda (snail) N (%)	Plants N (%)	Site Totals N
Baca	10 (23)	6 (14)	5 (12)	5 (12)	6 (14)	0	0	0	1 (2)[a]	33
Cameron Creek	20 (21)	25 (26)	14 (15)	10 (10)	7 (7)	1 (1)	1 (1)	1 (1)[b]	0	79
Eby	12 (24)	10 (20)	3 (6)	6 (12)	5 (10)	3 (6)	1 (2)	0	0	40
Galaz	55 (26)	39 (18)	28 (13)	23 (11)	24 (11)	9 (4)	2 (1)	0	0	180
Mattocks	20 (25)	22 (27)	8 (10)	6 (7)	6 (7)	1 (1)	1 (1)	0	0	64
McSherry	5 (33)	3 (20)	1 (7)	2 (13)	2 (13)	1 (7)	0	0	0	14
NAN Ranch	19 (28)	11 (16)	10 (15)	8 (12)	2 (3)	2 (3)	0	0	0	52
Old Town	6 (19)	9 (28)	6 (19)	1 (3)	1 (3)	1 (3)	0	0	0	24
Pruitt	11 (39)	4 (14)	1 (4)	5 (18)	2 (7)	0	0	0	0	23
Swarts	54 (24)	40 (17)	25 (11)	23 (10)	28 (12)	14 (6)	0	0	0	184
Class Totals	212	169	101	89	83	32	5	1	1	693

Note: Percentages indicate proportion of animal at a given site. The counts are of bowls with a particular kind of design; for example, a bowl depicting several fish and a bowl depicting one fish are both counted as a single case of a fish depiction.

[a] Allison's Z-score > 4.

[b] Allison's Z-score > 2.

much the observed count deviates from the expected count (in standard deviations). In the Mimbres case, observed counts differ from expected counts by more than two standard deviations in only two of ninety cells (each with a rare motif). In contrast, the ancestral Hopi observed counts differ from expected counts by at least two standard deviations in 28 of 180 cells.

Some kinds of Mimbres designs or motifs may have had social significance that would be swamped by the broad categories considered so far. For example, hummingbirds, although tiny, are fierce fighters who defend their territories vigorously, and the Aztec god of war, Huitzilopochtli, is sometimes depicted as a hummingbird. This kind of significance in Mimbres belief might not be revealed analytically if hummingbirds are simply included in a broad "bird" category. We used two strategies to examine whether particular kinds of animals had discernable meanings in Mimbres society. The first considered the distribution of much narrower categories, such as hummingbirds, caterpillars, and north-affiliated animals, asking if they were found at particular sites or in particular areas within sites. Again, we found no clustering, and narrowly defined groups are distributed evenly. For example, six bowls depict bears, and they were found at five different sites.

The second strategy focused on macaws, which were both portrayed on Mimbres bowls and interred at Mimbres sites. The distribution of bowls that depict macaws can be considered in relation to the actual distribution of macaw remains (table 7.3). Skeletons of these birds, most of which were formally buried, are found primarily at the large sites of Galaz and Old Town. In contrast, bowls depicting macaws are found at a number of sites and are not especially common at sites where actual macaws were buried, especially when considered as a percentage of all bowls with representational designs. Sites with the highest percentages of macaw designs (McSherry, Mattocks, and Baca) have no known burials of macaw skeletons.

We used data from the Swarts site to examine the intrasite distribution of animal motifs because it has two well-defined room blocks. Thanks to careful excavations in the early twentieth century, we have good data on the provenience of hundreds of bowls from Swarts (Cosgrove and Cosgrove 1932). The bowls considered in this analysis ($N = 229$) were found in good contexts. Most were associated with subfloor burials, a few were found under room floors, and only one was recovered from room fill.

Figure 7.2 shows the distributions of the most common animal motifs across Swarts. All four classes (fish, birds, insects, and mammals) are spread fairly evenly across both room blocks. What appear to be concentrations in figure 7.2 were examined in more detail. Room 31, in the South Room Block, has four bowls depicting birds, but the birds are of different types (a white-faced ibis, a swift or swallow, and two indeterminate birds), and the room also has two bowls with turtles and one each with an ant lion, bighorn, pronghorn, and fish. Room 84, in the northern part of

TABLE 7.3 Distribution of Bowls Depicting Parrots/Macaws in Relation to Parrot/Macaw Skeletons

Site	Macaw Skeletons (N)	Bowls Depicting Macaws (N)[a]	All Representational Bowls (N)	Frequency of Macaw Bowls
Galaz	11	3[b]	277	1.08
Old Town	2	1	40	2.50
Cameron Creek	3	2	95	2.11
McSherry	0	1	16	6.25
Mattocks	0	3[c]	93	3.22
Baca	0	2	43	4.65
Pruitt	0	0	31	0
Eby	0	0	57	0
NAN Ranch	0	0	70	0
Swarts	0	0	253	0

[a] Many macaws are depicted with humans, and bowls depicting humans were not included in the general database used for most of the analyses in this chapter. Therefore, data in this table were derived directly from MimPIDD rather than the database extracted specifically for this chapter.
[b] This number is different from that in Gilman et al. 2014:Table 3 because we classify two of the birds they identify as macaws (bowls 2766 and 2840) as raptors.
[c] This number is different from that in Gilman et al. 2014:Table 3 because we also include bowl 3676 as a macaw.

the North Room Block, has three mammals, but again they are of different types (deer, rabbit, carnivore), and it also has a dragonfly and a swift or swallow. Similarly, Room 20 in the South Room Block has three mammals of different types (rabbit, carnivore, bighorn), as well as a lizard. Some concentration of like species is evident in Room 55, in the southwest corner of the North Room Block. It has two bowls with bighorn sheep and one with a carnivore, as well as three with birds. Although burials are concentrated in some rooms, bowls depicting specific kinds of animals are widely distributed among those burials and across the site.

The Distribution of Mimbres Designs in Burials

In Puebloan and Mesoamerican world views, some animals are associated with certain personages or kinds of people. Gilman and colleagues (2014) note that among the Quiche Maya, for example, rabbits are linked to the younger and more feminine of the

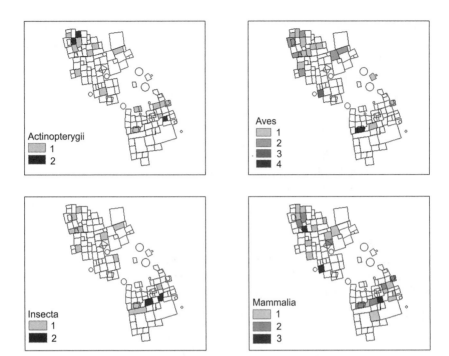

FIGURE 7.2 The distribution of bowls depicting given animal classes across the Swarts site. Map prepared by James R. McGrath after Cosgrove and Cosgrove 1932.

Hero Twins. If certain kinds of animals were associated with certain identity categories in Mimbres society, then we would expect them to be associated with particular kinds of burials. Data on burial age and sex in relation to certain kinds of motifs and other design variables can be used to investigate these possibilities. Using the same techniques applied in the spatial analysis, we examined all three sets of variables and arrived at the same conclusion. However they are classified, the designs are distributed evenly across age and sex classes and display no discernable clustering.

Of the 971 bowls in the data set used in this project, 445 are associated with burials. Unfortunately, biological sex is known for only 43 of these. Following the procedures described for the inter- and intrasite analyses, we explored the distribution of numerous motifs and motif classes within the subsets of male and female burials. Once again, we found no discernable patterning. Consideration of specific motifs with a higher likelihood of association with one sex or the other, such as rabbits (with females) or large game animals (with males), yielded the same results: no patterning.

The analysis comparing design layout and decedent sex is used as an example, since layout could be coded for all forty-three bowls associated with burials of known sex.

The general style of design layout is coded as either portrait (the motif is centered in the design field) or rotational (two or more motifs are repeated with rotational symmetry). As is evident in figure 7.3, female and male burials have very similar proportions of layouts.

MimPIDD includes all available information on the general age range of individuals buried with vessels. For this analysis, these individuals are grouped into four categories: adult, adolescent, child, and infant. Of the 971 bowls in the data set, 400 are associated with burials for which age class could be determined. We explored the distribution of designs in relation to age classes and again found no discernable patterning. This is demonstrated by one example that explores the association between animal habitat and decedent age. There are 349 bowls that depict animals for which habitat could be determined and that are associated with individuals whose age is known. Figure 7.4 shows that the four age classes have very similar distributions. Bowls depicting terrestrial, aquatic, and aerial animals are all associated, in roughly equal proportions, with adults, adolescents, children, and infants. A preliminary analysis, mentioned in Hegmon (2010a), had found that depictions of fish are rarely found with infants. This may relate to two beliefs held by a number of Southwest and Mesoamerican cultures.

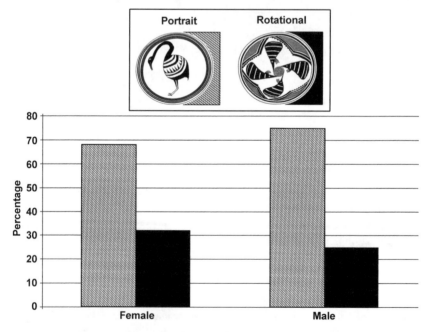

FIGURE 7.3 The proportions of bowls in burials of a given sex with a given design layout. Portrait example after MimPIDD 4640, Old Town site; rotational example after MimPIDD 162, McSherry site.

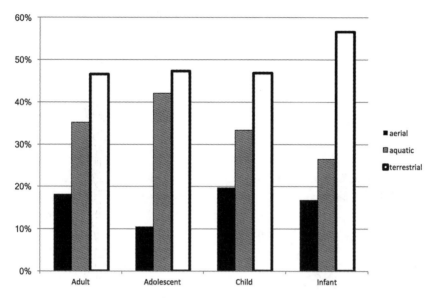

FIGURE 7.4 The proportions of bowls in burials of a given age class that have motifs associated with a given habitat.

First, the souls of deceased infants often remain in the household and will soon be reborn. Second, fish are, or represent, the (permanently) dead. Thus, it was thought, mortuary references to fish may have been inappropriate in situations where the soul was expected to return shortly. However, the more detailed analysis presented here finds that fish motifs are indeed associated with all age categories, including infants.

No Patterning or a Very Strong Pattern?

Archaeological research often involves multiple analyses of many lines of evidence with the expectation (or hope) that a majority will point in a consistent direction and thus support a conclusion. Often the minority that do not support this conclusion are explained away. It is rare to find unanimity in archaeological data analysis. We undertook the analyses described here with the expectation that we would find Mimbres designs differentially distributed across space or among burials in some consistent ways. Earlier work had investigated the distribution of different kinds of animals and found no clear patterning. Thus, our research classified the designs in multiple ways, considering not just kinds of animals but also their possible symbolic associations and habitats. We hoped that one of our classifications would parallel the way the designs were viewed in Mimbres society and would thus reveal some sort of patterning. Initially, our results were frustrating. Analysis after analysis revealed no spatial patterning. However they were classified, the designs were distributed homogeneously. Every site, and often every room block, had the same suite of designs. Burials of males and females, and of people of various ages, also had the same suites of designs. We found no support for the idea that the designs symbolized or were otherwise linked to social group or individual identity.

In describing the individual analyses, we consistently concluded that they revealed "no patterning." Taken together, however, the many individual analyses reveal a very strong pattern. With no exceptions, every single analysis found that the designs are distributed homogeneously, and this homogeneity is supported statistically by the Allison's Z-score analysis. Although contrary to what we expected, and even contrary to what we were looking for, the results are among the strongest we have ever seen in our years of archaeological analyses—there are no minority outliers to be explained away. The evidence is clear: Mimbres designs are distributed homogeneously. This empirical conclusion has important implications for our understanding of the meanings and meaningfulness of Mimbres designs, and for understanding Mimbres society.

Recent research, including some described in other chapters in this volume, provides an increasingly detailed understanding of the production of Mimbres pottery. Multiple analyses and lines of evidence indicate that the production was not homogeneous. Mimbres pottery was produced at a limited number of locations, especially during the Classic period (chapter 6). One study found an association between certain motifs and production sources (Powell-Martí and James 2006), although this conclusion was not supported by Creel and Speakman (chapter 6). Other studies have discerned the work of individual artists, and there is some indication that these ancient artists specialized in certain motifs (e.g., LeBlanc 2006; Russell and Hegmon 2015). Overall, it is likely that different designs were produced in different places, and if all pottery had been used and ultimately deposited where it was made, then we would have found some kind of patterning across space.

This information on production reinforces the conclusion that our analyses revealed: a "very strong pattern," that of homogeneity. Furthermore, that homogeneity was not simply a byproduct of other processes. Rather, it was created, possibly deliberately, through people's actions. Different designs were produced in different places and then they were distributed homogeneously, so that every village had the same suite of designs. This conclusion leads to at least two more questions and avenues for further research. What mechanisms distributed the pottery? What does the distribution suggest about the meaning and meaningfulness of Mimbres designs?

Considerable research, including that discussed in chapter 6, has traced the production and movement of Mimbres pottery. Shafer (2003) suggests that it was distributed as part of ceremonial exchanges in the context of feasts. But otherwise we know little about the social and economic processes behind the movement of pottery. To date, most research on pottery movement has analyzed sherds and thus has not considered design (the work of Powell-Martí and James [2006] is an important exception). Detailed information on where certain designs were produced and where they were ultimately deposited would add nuance to our conclusions and might suggest mechanisms whereby they were distributed.

The general assumption underlying our work is that Mimbres designs are meaningful in some way. The assumption is suggested, and supported, by many lines of evidence. Mimbres pottery is special—the artistry of the designs, the creative use of representational motifs, and the white-slipped brown-ware technology were all unique in the Southwest at the time. Mimbres Black-on-white was the only painted ware common in the Mimbres region during the Late Pithouse and Classic periods. The pottery also depicts cosmologically important scenes and characters including macaws, the Hero Twins, horned serpents, and possible deities (Brody 2004; Gilman et al. 2014; Thompson et al. 2014; Trask and Russell 2011). Many authors have suggested that the pottery, which accompanied many people into their graves, signaled membership in Mimbres society, which in turn gave people access to the productive agricultural land along the Mimbres River (e.g., Brody and Swentzell 1996; Hegmon et al. 2016; LeBlanc 1983). At the same time, researchers have noted considerable diversity across the Mimbres region, including the many different motifs painted on pottery (chapter 4; Hegmon 2010b).

The results of our analyses contribute to a more dynamic understanding of how the pottery and its designs could have been part of social life, including both diversity and unity, and thus provide insights into the meaningfulness of the designs. Different artists and production groups made pottery with different motifs, but the pottery was then distributed homogeneously, such that all sites have all the common motifs. Thus, the pottery could have signaled a community's membership and participation in Mimbres society at two levels: (1) the general style, what we recognize as "Mimbres"; and (2) the suite of designs, which might connote a suite of meanings or connections to various production areas. There is already good evidence that certain potters or groups of potters produced certain kinds of designs, and our analyses indicate that the different designs were distributed to villages across the valley and region.

This patterning, which can be further evaluated empirically, suggests social processes that help explain both the strong unity of Mimbres society during the Classic period and the rapid depopulation of many sites at the end of the Classic (chapter 9). Being a part of what we recognize as Mimbres society likely required specific intercommunity relationships, relationships that were created, demonstrated, and strengthened over time through the exchange of ritually charged decorated pottery. If every community had to have a certain suite of pottery designs, then the exchange necessary to distribute those designs would have created strong bonds up and down the Mimbres Valley and across the region. At the same time, this kind of network might be fragile and susceptible to failure if production or exchange could not continue in an area or if some people moved away. Thus, the apparently sudden end of the Classic might have resulted from, or have been aggravated by, a breakdown of this network instead of, or in addition to, subsistence issues.

Acknowledgments

This research was done as part of the Long-Term Vulnerability and Transformation Project, funded by NSF-CNH BCS-1113991. It relied heavily on MimPIDD, which was created and is being maintained with support from numerous institutions including the Mimbres Foundation, Turner Foundation, Archaeology Division of the American Anthropological Association, and tDAR. We are enormously grateful for Steven LeBlanc's pioneering and continuing work, which made MimPIDD possible. Keith Kintigh provided the analysis of the Allison's Z-scores. Cathy Cameron helped with some references. Karen Gust Schollmeyer and Gary Schwartz provided assistance with some details of the coding. We are thankful for all of this support.

References Cited

Bernardini, Wesley. 2005. *Hopi Oral Tradition and the Archaeology of Identity*. University of Arizona Press, Tucson.

Bettison, Cynthia Ann, Roland Shook, Randy Jennings, and Dennis Miller. 1999. New Identifications of Naturalistic Motifs on Mimbres Pottery. In *Sixty Years of Mogollon Archaeology: Papers from the Ninth Mogollon Conference, Silver City, New Mexico, 1996*, edited by Stephanie M. Whittlesey, pp. 119–125. SRI Press, Tucson, Arizona.

Brody, J. J. 2004. *Mimbres Painted Pottery*. Rev. ed. School of American Research Press, Santa Fe, New Mexico.

Brody, J. J., and Rina Swentzell. 1996. *To Touch the Past: The Painted Pottery of the Mimbres People*. Hudson Hills Press, New York.

Cameron, Catherine M. 1992. An Analysis of Residential Patterns and the Oraibi Split. *Journal of Anthropological Archaeology* 11:173–186.

Carr, Pat M. 1979. *Mimbres Mythology*. Texas Western Press, El Paso.

Cosgrove, Harriet S., and Cornelius B. Cosgrove. 1932. *The Swarts Ruin: A Typical Mimbres Site of Southwestern New Mexico*. Papers of the Peabody Museum of Archaeology and Ethnology, Harvard University Vol. 15(1). Peabody Museum, Cambridge, Massachusetts.

Creel, Darrell, and Charmion McKusick. 1994. Prehistoric Macaws and Parrots in the Mimbres Area, New Mexico. *American Antiquity* 59:510–524.

Eggan, Fred. 1950. *Social Organization of the Western Pueblo*. University of Chicago Press, Chicago.

Gilman, Patricia A., Marc Thompson, and Kristina C. Wyckoff. 2014. Ritual Change and the Distant: Mesoamerican Iconography, Scarlet Macaws, and Great Kivas in the Mimbres Region of Southwestern New Mexico. *American Antiquity* 79:90–107.

Hegmon, Michelle. 1992. Archaeological Research on Style. *Annual Review of Anthropology* 21:517–536.

———. 2010a. Expressions in Black-on-White. In *Mimbres: Lives and Landscapes*, edited by Margaret C. Nelson and Michelle Hegmon, pp. 65–74. School of Advanced Research Press, Santa Fe, New Mexico.

———. 2010b. Mimbres Society: Another Way of Being. In *Mimbres: Lives and Landscapes*, edited by Margaret C. Nelson and Michelle Hegmon, pp. 39–45. School of Advanced Research Press, Santa Fe, New Mexico.

Hegmon, Michelle, James R. McGrath, and Marit K. Munson. 2017. The Potential and Pitfalls of Large Multi-source Collections: Insights from the Analysis of Mimbres Gender Imagery. *Advances in Archaeological Practice* 5(2):138–146.

Hegmon, Michelle, Margaret C. Nelson, and Karen Gust Schollmeyer. 2016. Experiencing Social Change: Life During the Mimbres Classic Transformation. In *The Archaeology of the Human Experience*, edited by Michelle Hegmon, pp. 54–73. Archeological Papers of the American Anthropological Association No. 27. John Wiley & Sons, Malden, Massachusetts.

Holm, Bill. 1965. *Northwest Coast Indian Art: An Analysis of Form*. University of Washington Press, Seattle.

Howell, Todd L. 1996. Tracking Zuni Gender and Leadership Roles Across the Contact Period. *Journal of Anthropological Research* 51:125–148.

Jett, Stephen C., and Peter B. Moyle. 1986. The Exotic Origins of Fishes Depicted on Prehistoric Mimbres Pottery from New Mexico. *American Antiquity* 51:688–720.

Kabotie, Fred. 1982. *Designs from the Ancient Mimbreños with a Hopi Interpretation*. Northland Press, Flagstaff, Arizona.

LeBlanc, Catherine J. 1977. Design Analysis of Mimbres Pottery. Paper presented at the 42nd Annual Meeting of the Society for American Archaeology, New Orleans, Louisiana.

LeBlanc, Steven A. 1983. *The Mimbres People: Ancient Painters of the American Southwest*. Thames and Hudson, London.

———. 2006. Who Made the Mimbres Bowls? Implications of Recognizing Individual Artists for Craft Specialization and Social Networks. In *Mimbres Society*, edited by Valli S. Powell-Martí and Patricia A. Gilman, pp. 109–150. University of Arizona Press, Tucson.

Longacre, William A., Jingfeng Xia, and Tao Yang. 2000. I Want to Buy a Black Pot. *Journal of Archaeological Method and Theory* 7:273–293.

Mills, Barbara J. 2007. Performing the Feast: Visual Display and Suprahousehold Commensalism in the Puebloan Southwest. *American Antiquity* 72:210–239.

Mindeleff, Victor. 1891. *A Study of Pueblo Architecture in Tusayan and Cibola*. Extract from the Eighth Annual Report of the Bureau of Ethnology. Government Printing Office, Washington, D.C.

Munson, Marit K. 2000. Sex, Gender, and Status: Human Images from the Classic Mimbres. *American Antiquity* 65:127–143.

O'Hara, F. Michael. 2007. Faunal Species Descriptions and Ethnographic Uses and Beliefs. Compiled for SWCA Environmental Consultants. Electronic document, https://core.tdar .org/project/399095/documents-and-data-from-hegmon-et-al-mimbres-pottery-designs -in-their-social-context.

Plog, Stephen. 1990. Sociopolitical Implications of Stylistic Variation in the American Southwest. In *The Uses of Style in Archaeology*, edited by Margaret Conkey and Christine Hastorf, pp. 61–72. Cambridge University Press, Cambridge.

———. 2003. Exploring the Ubiquitous Through the Unusual: Color Symbolism in Pueblo Black-on-White Pottery. *American Antiquity* 68:665–695.

Powell, Valli S. 1996. Regional Diversity in Mogollon Red-on-brown Pottery. *Kiva* 62:185–203.

Powell-Martí, Valli S., and William D. James. 2006. Ceramic Iconography and Social Asymmetry in the Classic Mimbres Heartland, AD 970–1140. In *Mimbres Society*, edited by Valli S. Powell-Martí and Patricia Gilman, pp. 151–173. University of Arizona Press, Tucson.

Russell, Will G., and Michelle Hegmon. 2015. Identifying Mimbres Artists: A Quantitative Approach. *Advances in Archaeological Practice* 3:358–377.

Shafer, Harry J. 2003. *Mimbres Archaeology at the NAN Ranch Ruin*. University of New Mexico Press, Albuquerque.

Thompson, Marc, Patricia A. Gilman, and Kristina C. Wyckoff. 2014. The Hero Twins in the Mimbres Region: Representations of the Mesoamerican Creation Saga Are Seen on Mimbres Pottery. *American Archaeology* 18(2):38–43.

Trask, Garrett, and Will G. Russell. 2011. Liminal and Transformation Ideology Within the Mimbres Tradition. In *Patterns in Transition: Papers from the 16th Biennial Jornada Mogollon Conference*, edited by Melinda R. Landreth, pp. 113–134. El Paso Museum of Archaeology, El Paso, Texas.

Van Keuren, Scott. 2000. Ceramic Decoration as Power: Late Prehistoric Design Change in East-Central Arizona. In *Alternative Leadership Strategies in the Greater Southwest*, edited by Barbara J. Mills, pp. 79–94. University of Arizona Press, Tucson.

Ware, John A. 2014. *A Pueblo Social History: Kinship, Sodality, and Community in the Northern Southwest*. School for Advanced Research Press, Santa Fe, New Mexico.

Wiessner, Polly. 1983. Style and Social Information in Kalahari San Projectile Points. *American Antiquity* 49:253–276.

8

Variability in Mimbres Food and Food Procurement

KAREN GUST SCHOLLMEYER, MICHAEL W. DIEHL,
AND JONATHAN A. SANDOR

ARCHAEOLOGISTS WORKING IN the Mimbres region have made important contributions to the study of prehistoric subsistence and social organization, engaging questions of broad anthropological interest regarding the relationships between humans, plants, animals, and soils. Mimbres Foundation researchers were among the first to recognize temporal changes in subsistence in the area and link them to climate, environmental, and social change, and they were the first to document spatial patterns in resource availability.

In this chapter, we review subsequent research that has explored similar themes in the broader spatial and temporal context of the entire Mimbres Mogollon region, including the Eastern Mimbres region, the Mimbres River valley, the upper Gila River, and the tributaries of the Mimbres and Gila. Recent research has revealed differences between the Mimbres Valley and the Eastern Mimbres region, along with diachronic changes in subsistence and food procurement that may have occurred throughout the Mimbres Mogollon region. We summarize major trends of research into paleoethnobotany, zooarchaeology, and soils and farming practices, and we focus on patterns of meaningful spatial and temporal variability related to issues that include diversity in resource selection and use, long-term patterns in farming and hunting, soil nutrient depletion caused by ancient farming, and large mammal population suppression caused by ancient hunting. Despite the passage of more than nine centuries since dryland farm locations were used for agriculture and despite the continued presence of prehistoric features designed to promote soil nutrient recapture, soils associated with ancient dryland farming sites remain somewhat depleted. Where prey suppression occurred, large mammal populations required decades to recover from the effects of Mimbres Classic period hunting. Understanding the conditions under which resources were resilient to centuries of human use and anthropogenic landscape change, were impacted by these forces, and in some cases recovered from those impacts remains an important direction for future studies. These avenues of research have interesting implications for archaeologists and for broader ecological research as contemporary populations strive to balance human demands with long-term environmental effects.

Paleoethnobotany

Prior to Mimbres Foundation efforts, the goal of area archaeologists was to classify people as either foragers or farmers. They worked by listing the species that were identified among haphazardly collected animal bones and bits of charred plants and concocting an appealing scenario based on chipped- or ground-stone artifacts and examining the various resources available in the area today (e.g., Bradfield 1931:10; Fitting 1973:80; Haury 1985:147). The result was often a suite of internally inconsistent monologues about the nature of Mimbres Mogollon subsistence. Among those working in the Mimbres area from 1927 through 1973, Emil Haury came closest to articulating middle range theory in his work on the Harris site and Mogollon village. Forced to equivocate on which label to choose, he decided that specialized hunting skills implied more reliance on foraging (Haury 1936:92–93):

> Charred corn cobs and milling stones are ample evidence that agriculture must be included in the Mogollon culture. . . . Even though agriculture was practiced, a rich fauna suggests a heavy reliance on game as well, possibly more than was the case with the northern Pueblos, and certainly more than with the Hohokam whose specialty was farming. Only vigorous hunters could have brought in the abundance of game indicated, or dared to tackle the bear and bison.

The Mimbres Foundation brought osteofaunal and paleobotanical data to the forefront of subsistence discussions with an eye toward testing models of the relationship between social organization and subsistence. Minnis's (1985) *Social Adaptation to Food Stress* synthesized Mimbres Foundation data and posited an economic catastrophe: the combination of large populations, intensive farming, soil degradation, floodplain deforestation, and rainfall variability caused provisioning shortfalls, primarily owing to poor returns from farming. Mimbres social institutions that had their origins in "good times" were unable to cope with food stress, and society fell apart, resulting in the general abandonment of the Mimbres Valley.

New syntheses of the paleobotanical data presented here substantiate Minnis's findings and suggest that the crisis was worse than previously envisioned. Today, paleobotanical data are available from nineteen sites spanning just over a millennium, from the second through mid-fifteenth centuries A.D. Not all time periods are covered in equal detail among different parts of the Mimbres Mogollon. Subsistence findings drawn from paleobotanical data from throughout the Mimbres region are, therefore, synthesized diachronically rather than spatially. Table 8.1 reviews findings from Mimbres pithouse sites from the Early Pithouse period through the Three Circle phase; Table 8.2 covers early and later Classic period sites; and Table 8.3 includes Postclassic and Salado period sites from the Mimbres Valley and Eastern Mimbres area.

By inspection, it is evident that crops, especially maize, and crop weeds, such as goosefoot, pigweed, and tansy mustard, were important components of diets throughout the Mimbres sequence and during Postclassic occupations. It is also evident that with at least twenty-seven taxa or categories of wild plants available and occasionally used, residents of the Gila River and Mimbres River valleys and the Eastern Mimbres had access to a wide range of resources. Greater aridity in the Eastern Mimbres region did not substantially inhibit agricultural or wild-food foraging efforts during the Mimbres Classic period. Cactus fruit, arboreal resources, and, to a lesser extent, dispersed weeds were also used as available.

One temporal change stands out. Diet breadths contracted among all resource categories except crops during the Early Classic and Classic periods (figure 8.1). This contraction coincides with the expansion of Mimbres hamlets and field houses into most secondary drainages throughout the Mimbres region (LeBlanc and Whalen 1980). This is also the period that Minnis (1985) identifies as the interval of most intense floodplain arboreal depletion, ecological problems in the Mimbres Valley, and maximum food stress.

From Diehl's point of view, these data add new details to Minnis's (1985) findings regarding the inability of the people living during the Classic period to deal with food stress: in A.D. 1125, a farmer might have lamented that the only resource one could count on was juniper berries. During the Classic period, the combined effects of sustained soil depletion (discussed by Sandor below), precipitation shortfalls, and floodplain deforestation resulted in lower crop yields. All other plant-based foods were probably also affected. Yields declined among secondary staples such as goosefoot, pigweed, and sunflower. Deforestation in the Mimbres Valley reduced the numbers of available grapes, mesquite, and walnuts. Dispersed weeds and grasses—never very productive resources—became more important at the larger Classic sites. As Minnis (1991, 1996) notes, in times of resource stress famine foods become important. In the Mimbres Valley, even famine foods were in short supply, or else knowledge of their sustainable use had disappeared during the golden age of Mimbres Valley

TABLE 8.1 Ubiquities of Selected Charred-Food Plant Tissues from Mimbres Pithouse Period Sites

| | Early Pithouse | | | | Georgetown | San Francisco | Three Circle Phase or (late) "Late Pithouse" | | | | |
	Forest Home	McAnally	Power	Wind Mtn.	Wind Mtn.	Mogollon Village	Beargrass	Galaz	NAN Ranch	Peterson Canyon	Wind Mtn.
N^a	7	2	4	5	7	9	16	16	4	7	30
Crops											
Bean	0.14	0	0	0	0	0	0	0	0	0	0
Maize	0.71	0.50	0.50	0.80	0.86	0.77	0.75	0.69	1.00	0.29	0.47
Squash	0	0	0	0	0	0	0	0	0	0.14	0.03
Crop/Floodplain Weeds											
Buffalo gourd	0	0	0	0	0	0	0	0.13	0	0	0
Cheno-ams	0.29	0.50	0.25	0	0	0.56	0.75	0	1.00	0.43	0
Goosefoot	0.29	0	0.25	1.00	0.86	0.56	0.69	0.75	1.00	0.78	0.67
Pigweed	0	0	0	1.00	0.29	0.33	0	0.25	1.00	0	0.43
Sunflower	0	0	0	0	0	0	0.06	0.13	0.25	0	0.03
Tansy mustard	0.14	0	0	0	0.29	0	0.06	0	1.00	0	0
Cacti and Agave Family											
Prickly pear	0	0	0	0	0.14	0	0	0.13	0.50	0.14	0.10
Other cactus	0	0	0	0	0	0	0	0.13	0.25	0	0
Yucca	0	0	0	0	0	0	0	0	0.25	0	0
Trees											
Grape	0	0	0	0	0	0	0	0.06	0	0	0
Juniper	0.29	0.50	1.00	0.600	0.43	0.33	0.69	0.50	0.50	0.14	0.30

Mesquite	0	0	0.25	0	0	0	0	0	0	0
Oak-acorn	0	0	0	0	0.13	0	0	0.50	0	0.29
Piñon pine	0.13	0	0	0.06	0	0.11	0	0	0	0
Saltbush	0.07	0	1.00	0.06	0	0	0	0	0	0
Walnut	0.13	0	0	0	0	0	0	0	0	0
Dispersed Weeds										
Aster/Composite family	0	0	0.75	0	0	0	0	0	0	0
Carpetweed family	0.23	0	1.00	0	0	0	0	0.29	0	0
Dock/Knotweed type	0	0	0	0.06	0	0	0	0	0	0
Mallow type	0	0	0	0.06	0	0	0	0	0	0
Mint family	0.07	0	0	0	0	0	0	0	0	0
Purslane	0.20	0.14	1.00	0	0.06	0.22	0	0.43	0.80	0.14
Ring-wing	0	0.43	0	0	0	0.22	0.75	0	0	0
Spurge	0	0	0	0	0.06	0	0.25	0	0	0
Stick-leaf	0	0.14	0.75	0	0	0	0	0	0	0.29
Wild Grasses										
Grass family	0	0	1.00	0.25	0	0	0	0	0	0
Dropseed	0	0.57	0	0	0	0	0	0	0	0.14

[a]N = number of spatially discrete features (different pithouse, different extramural pit, or different excavation unit in extramural trash midden).

TABLE 8.2 Ubiquities of Selected Charred-Food Plant Tissues from Mimbres Classic Period Sites

	Early Classic	Classic								
	Flying Fish	Animas Village	Avilas Canyon	Buckaroo	Flying Fish	Lizard Terrace	NAN Ranch	Phelps	Wind Mtn.
N^a	7	14	8	3	8	4	19	4	6
Crops									
Cotton	0	0	0	0	0	0	0.11	0	0
Maize	0.86	1.00	0.88	1.00	0.63	0.75	1.00	0.25	0.33
Squash	0.14	0.07	0.13	0.67	0.25	0.25	0	0	0
Crop/Floodplain Weeds									
Cheno-ams	0.14	0	0.38	0.33	0.38	0.25	0.79	0	0
Goosefoot	0.29	0	0	0	0	0	1.00	0	1.00
Pigweed	0.14	0	0.13	0	0.13	0	0.68	0	0.50
Sunflower	0	0	0	0	0	0	0	0	0
Tansy mustard	0	0	0	0.67	0.13	0	0.32	0	0
Cacti									
Prickly pear	0.14	0.29	0.13	0	0.13	0	0.21	0	0
Other cactus	0.14	0.07	0	0	0	0	0.26	0	0

	1	2	3	4	5	6	7	8	9
Trees									
Grape	0	0	0	0	0	0	0.16	0	0
Juniper	0.29	0.14	0.25	0.33	0.50	0	0.05	0	0.17
Saltbush	0	0	0	0	0	0	0.21	0	0
Sumac	0.14	0	0.13	0	0.13	0	0	0	0
Walnut	0	0	0	0	0	0	0	0	0.17
Dispersed Weeds									
Aster/Composite family	0	0	0	0	0	0	0.11	0	0
Carpetweed family	0	0	0	0	0	0	0.53	0	0.67
Mint family	0	0	0.25	0	0	0	0	0	0
Purslane	0.14	0	0	0.33	0.13	0	0.79	0	0.84
Spurge	0	0	0.13	0	0	0	0	0	0
Stick-leaf	0	0	0	0	0	0	0.53	0	0
Wild Grasses									
Grass family	0	0	0.13	0	0	0	0.74	0	0.17
Dropseed	0	0	0	0.33	0	0	0	0	0

ᵃN = number of spatially discrete features.

TABLE 8.3 Ubiquities of Selected Charred-Food Plant Tissues from Postclassic, Animas, and Cliff Phase Sites

	Postclassic Mimbres						Animas Phase	Cliff Phase		
	Buckaroo	Lee Pueblo	Lizard Terrace	Mtn. Lion	Phelps	Ronnie	Animas Village	Disert	Janss	Stailey
N^a	33	11	14	11	8	10	39	21	13	3
Crops										
Bean	0.18	0.09	0.21	0.45	0.25	0.10	0.03	0.05	0.23	0
Cotton	0	0	0	0	0	0	0	0.24	0	0
Maize	0.55	0.45	0.86	1.00	0.88	0.60	0.67	0.86	0.77	1.00
Squash	0.09	0	0.36	0.64	0.25	0.10	0.05	0.05	0	0
Crop/Floodplain Weeds										
Cheno-ams	0.48	0.27	0.29	0.82	0.50	0.50	0.03	0.10	0	0
Goosefoot	0	0	0	0	0	0	0	0.62	0.46	0.67
Peppergrass	0	0	0	0	0	0	0	0	0.08	0
Pigweed	0.03	0	0	0	0	0	0	0.14	0	0.67
Sunflower	0	0	0	0.18	0.13	0.10	0.03	0	0	0
Tansy mustard	0.21	0	0.07	0	0	0.30	0.05	0.05	0	0
Cacti										
Prickly pear	0.06	0	0	0.45	0	0.10	0.27	0	0	0
Other cactus	0.09	0.09	0.07	0.18	0.13	0.10	0	0.05	0.08	0

Trees

Acacia	0	0	0	0	0	0	0	0	0.08	0
Juniper	0.06	0.09	0.07	0.55	0	0.10	0.18	0.24	0.46	0.67
Mesquite	0.15	0	0.07	0.45	0	0	0.13	0	0	0
Piñon pine	0.03	0	0	0.14	0	0	0	0	0	0
Walnut	0	0	0.07	0	0	0	0	0	0	0

Dispersed Weeds

Aster/Composite family	0	0	0	0	0	0.10	0.03	0.05	0	0
Mint family	0.03	0	0	0	0	0	0	0	0	0
Morning glory family	0	0	0	0	0	0	0	0	0.08	0
Purslane	0.33	0.27	0.07	0.18	0	0.30	0.03	0.62	0.23	0

Wild Grasses

Grass family	0.15	0	0.14	0.27	0	0.30	0.08	0.10	0.08	1.00
Dropseed	0.21	0.09	0	0.09	0	0.40	0	0	0	0

ᵃN = number of spatially discrete features.

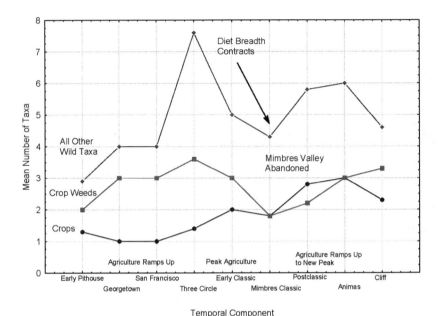

FIGURE 8.1 The mean number of plant taxa per site by resource group and temporal component.

farming initiated during the Three Circle phase of the Late Pithouse period (Diehl and LeBlanc 2001).

Classic period social and political organizations, kinship arrangements, land-tenure institutions, and labor arrangements were inadequate to the crisis, and the Mimbres Valley was mostly depopulated. In the Eastern Mimbres region, in contrast, populations remained stable during the Postclassic period and increased their use of wild resources. Human impacts on floodplain vegetation were not severe (Diehl 1992). Famine foods sustained people in the east but were insufficient to support much continuity in the Mimbres Valley. At the end of the sequence, during the Salado period, parts of the central and northern Mimbres Valley saw a small degree of population regrowth or reoccupation. Agriculture remained important, but equally importantly, secondary resource use was strong in all plant categories.

This narrative supports Minnis's (1985) observation that Mimbres social institutions were unable to cope with widespread provisioning shortfalls. Minnis focused on agricultural shortfalls, but the data now available suggest that the ecological impacts Minnis posited on farming productivity probably affected the productivity of almost every useful wild resource in the Mimbres Valley. The Mimbres Classic food provisioning crisis was more severe than previously believed.

More work needs to be done to expand the study of pre-Classic settlements along the Gila, in the Mimbres Valley, and in the Eastern Mimbres region. The research findings presented in this chapter also stand on very thin ice when it comes to empirical confidence in Early Pithouse period results owing to the very small number of samples available from that period.

Finally, we observe that trends in Mimbres Valley subsistence seem to run parallel to documented trends in Hohokam subsistence, at least in the Tucson Basin. We need to compare the data between those regions, and cooperative arrangements between institutions doing the research in both regions are desirable. We stand on the edge of recognizing and explaining trends in subsistence practices throughout southwestern New Mexico and southern Arizona.

Zooarchaeology

Studies of archaeological fauna in the Mimbres region have been particularly successful at highlighting meaningful variability in human use of animals over time and space. The results of zooarchaeological analyses have often appeared as unpublished specialist reports and student papers, but several seminal Mimbres Foundation studies combined information from multiple archaeological sites to examine broader issues, particularly changes in response to hunting and anthropogenic landscape change. Those studies set the stage for future research on these themes.

Powell (1977) compared Late Pithouse, Mimbres Classic, and Cliff phase assemblages from Mimbres Foundation sites, documenting an increase in the proportion of jackrabbits to cottontails in the Classic period compared with earlier and later assemblages. She attributed these changes to shifts in the amount of land cleared for agriculture as the area's human population increased and then decreased. Powell also noted low proportions of artiodactyls in both the Late Pithouse and Classic periods, but higher proportions in the Cliff phase.

Other Mimbres Foundation researchers using different combinations of data sets from a number of sites noted the same two patterns (Anyon and LeBlanc 1984:219). These studies, along with information from lithics, paleoethnobotany, and settlement patterns, showed increasing human population density over time linked to decreases in the availability of artiodactyls. They also suggested that very low human population densities in the centuries between the end of the Classic period and the beginning of the Cliff phase in the middle and upper Mimbres Valley allowed artiodactyl populations to rebound, increasing the ease of human access to these animals in the later period (Anyon and LeBlanc 1984; Nelson 1986; Nelson and LeBlanc 1986; Powell 1977). These themes of anthropogenic landscape change and resource responses to human demands have remained central to subsequent zooarchaeological research in the region.

More recent studies have continued to engage with the issue of large mammal resource depression in periods of dense human population. Cannon (2000, 2003) more formally linked changes in large mammal relative abundance to optimal foraging theory, reanalyzing some samples and analyzing new ones to confirm the pattern of declining abundance with human population increases across the Early and Late Pithouse and Classic periods. These changes were linked to both hunting and anthropogenic landscape change. Recent studies also indicate that large mammal population recoveries, such as that suggested for the Cliff phase, took some time. In the Eastern Mimbres area, large mammal relative abundance did not rebound immediately following the residential abandonment of Classic period sites. The delay suggests that large mammal populations may have taken decades to recover from the effects of human predation (Schollmeyer 2009, 2011).

Studies of animal use have also shown the importance of spatial variability. Mimbres Foundation studies noted differences in animal exploitation within the Mimbres Valley itself, showing that higher-elevation parts of the valley had higher proportions of large game than lower-elevation areas (Anyon and LeBlanc 1984). Sanchez (1992, 1996) expanded on this research, demonstrating that elevation differences also played a large role in the ratio of jackrabbits to cottontails in faunal assemblages within the Mimbres Valley. Sanchez relied particularly on samples from Old Town and NAN Ranch (see also Shafer 2003:129) and comparisons with other sites in the Mimbres Valley, providing an important reminder that spatial variability must be considered before attributing changes in lagomorph ratios to the effects of anthropogenic landscape alteration alone.

The expansion of research outside the Mimbres Valley has increased our appreciation for spatial variability in the zooarchaeological record. In the Eastern Mimbres area, lagomorph ratios show the effects of altitude differences and changes in land clearing associated with decreasing human population densities after the Classic period (Schollmeyer 2005). Ratios of jackrabbits to cottontails at Classic sites are higher than those from later Reorganization phase assemblages at the same elevations, more closely resembling lower-elevation sites (where jackrabbits would naturally have been more common) from the later period. Interestingly, human impacts on many plants and animals east of the Black Range appear to have been lighter than those in the Mimbres Valley, despite the eastern area's drier environment (Hegmon et al. 2006; Schollmeyer 2005). Various measures suggest land clearing there may have been less extensive, and the area remained a better habitat for cottontails than the Mimbres Valley in every period, despite some decrease in cottontail representation with increased human populations (Schollmeyer 2005).

Spatial variability in artiodactyl relative abundance also reveals interesting patterns inside and outside the Mimbres Valley. The Mimbres Valley pattern of greater artiodactyl relative abundance in assemblages from sites at higher elevations appears to hold at a regional scale as well (Schollmeyer and Driver 2013). Even after centuries of human hunting and anthropogenic landscape change, people in sites located at higher elevations and on the edges of settlement areas appear to have retained access to relatively more artiodactyls than hunters at lower-elevation sites or those with more settlements nearby (Schollmeyer and Driver 2013).

Another important theme is research on social dimensions of animal use. Researchers have been interested in analyzing the animal images painted on Mimbres Black-on-white bowls since the earliest examinations of these vessels (Fewkes 1925; Rodek 1932). Parrots and macaws, in particular, highlight the importance of animals as social symbols and the ways pottery images can complement more traditional zooarchaeological information. Parrots and macaws are shown on a number of Mimbres bowls, but their remains in the archaeological record are quite limited. We know of two examples from the Late Pithouse period, but the vast majority of known specimens are from the Classic period, and two specimens are associated with sites postdating A.D. 1130 (Creel and McKusick 1994; Gilman et al. 2014). As several researchers have discussed, the logistics of transporting these birds long distances out of their native habitats were challenging, and their presence in Mimbres area sites shows the importance of connections to Mesoamerica and Mesoamerican ideology (Gilman et al. 2014; Wyckoff 2009). The possible identification of marine fish on Mimbres Black-on-white bowls also indicates long-distance travel and social connections not easily traceable through other means (Jett and Moyle 1986), although the methods of identification in that study have been contested (Thompson 1999).

Pottery images also hint at differences between the economic and social importance of other species. Although images of birds and fish are found on a relatively high proportion of bowls at the Galaz site, for example, the bones of these taxa are uncommon in the site's faunal assemblage (Anyon and LeBlanc 1984:218; Kulow and Schollmeyer 2005), a pattern also seen in Mimbres assemblages more generally (Schollmeyer and Coltrain 2010). Similarly, artiodactyl images comprise a higher proportion of the animals on bowl assemblages at Galaz and NAN Ranch (which have large samples of published bowl images) than their contribution to the faunal assemblage, a pattern probably linked to their importance not only as highly ranked foods in terms of foraging efficiency, but as animals highly desirable for social reasons (Schollmeyer and Coltrain 2010; figure 8.2, table 8.4). Finally, pottery images have been used to examine hunting techniques. Images of hunters using bows and arrows, rabbit sticks, and hunting nets provide an interesting complement to zooarchaeological studies (Shafer 2003:129–131; Shaffer and Gardner 1995, 1997; Shaffer et al.

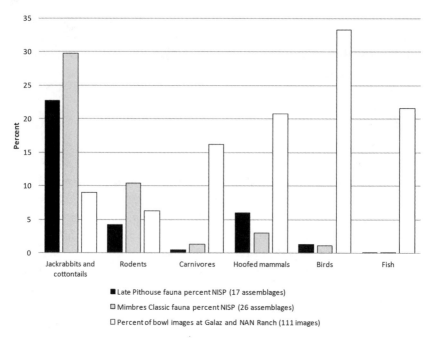

FIGURE 8.2 The major animal categories in faunal assemblages and bowl images.

1996). For example, images of net hunting may depict the types of jackrabbit drives that would have produced processing sites like the Five Feature site in southeastern Arizona (Schmidt 1999).

One of the most important themes in Mimbres zooarchaeological research has been its engagement with larger-scale questions beyond site- or region-specific issues. Researchers have tackled important issues such as resource depression, anthropogenic landscape change, and how shifts in human populations affect local animals. Research examining how animal populations might be affected by, and recover from, human hunting and land clearing has important implications for modern issues of sustainability and maintaining ecological diversity, something researchers in the Mimbres area continue to investigate today. Long-term reliance on lagomorphs may represent a sustainable hunting strategy, while artiodactyl use produced noticeable impacts at some spatial scales but was supported for centuries in the region as a whole. Understanding the apparent artiodactyl population recovery in this region after the Classic period, particularly the amount of time required and the conditions that favored such recovery, remains important for future studies from both an archaeological and an ecological standpoint as contemporary populations search for balance between human demands and impacts on vulnerable large-game species.

TABLE 8.4 Major Categories of Animals in Mimbres Area Faunal Assemblages and Bowl Images

Assemblage	Jackrabbits and Cottontails	Rodents	Carnivores	Hoofed Mammals	Birds	Fish	Total
Late Pithouse (17 assemblages)	4238	783	86	1123	244	24	18,633 faunal bone specimens
Mimbres Classic (26 assemblages)	8013	2803	358	796	311	31	26,943 faunal bone specimens
Galaz and NAN Ranch bowl images (111 images)	10	7	18	23	37	24	111 bowl images

Note: Total column displays the total number of bone specimens, including unidentified mammals and unidentified bones. Late Pithouse assemblages include Beauregard, Montezuma, Galaz, Mattocks (Powell 1977:46); Old Town (Sanchez 1992:61); NAN Ranch (Sanchez 1992:51; Shaffer 1991:91–92); Harris (Powell 2015); La Gila Encantada (Schmidt 2010); Florida Mountain (Schriever 2002:248); MC 110 (Fitting 1971:31); Wind Mountain (Olsen and Olsen 1996); Mogollon village (Cannon 1999); Woodrow (Schollmeyer 2015); Cuchillo, LA 50547 (Daniel 1991); Placitas Arroyo 2, Placitas Arroyo 8 (Butler 1984). Mimbres Classic assemblages include Mitchell, Montezuma, Mattocks (Powell 1977:46); Jackson Fraction, Badger Ruin (Kearns et al. 1999); Cooney Ranch #1 (Nisengard 2000); Old Town (Sanchez 1992:61); NAN Ranch (Sanchez 1992:51; Shaffer 1991:91–92); Columbus (Cannon 2010); Riverside (Baker 1971:41); Heron (Burns 1972:47); Wind Mountain (Olsen and Olsen 1996); Saige-McFarland (Gillespie 1987); Woodrow (Schollmeyer 2015); DeFausal/Kartchner (Sullivan and Berg 1983); Berrenda Creek (Gomolak and Ford 1976); Cuchillo, Nalda Mitchell (Daniel 1991); Avilas Canyon, Juniper Village, SJ Hamlet, Lizard Terrace, Buckaroo, Pague Well, Flying Fish, Las Animas (Schollmeyer 2009). Galaz bowl images published in Anyon and LeBlanc 1984; NAN Ranch bowl images published in Shafer 2003.

Soil Studies

Soils are a key resource for agricultural production and other subsistence strategies. Researchers have studied prehistoric Mimbres dryland (not irrigated) agricultural soils to learn about agricultural management, soil productivity, and long-term anthropogenic soil change (Sandor et al. 1986, 1990). The runoff terrace fields investigated were associated with the Classic period and located in the Black Range east of the Mimbres Valley and in the adjacent Sapillo Valley to the northwest. Although irrigation agriculture was likely the mainstay of Mimbres farming, dryland fields were studied because they were both clearly identifiable and relatively intact.

Soil studies from Mimbres Classic sites generally corroborate Minnis's (1985) findings about adverse effects from human occupation during the Classic period and subsequent findings from paleobotanical analyses already discussed. The soil studies also indicate selective use of soils and landscape settings based on field placement patterns, high potential productivity of soils for agricultural purposes in some upland locations, and evidence of long-term soil erosion and nutrient depletion caused by ancient agriculture (Sandor et al. 1990). Each of these findings is discussed in turn.

Field location patterns indicate that Mimbres farmers used only certain soils for dryland agriculture. Fields were nearly always located on Pleistocene-age soils with subsurface argillic horizons, even though such soils occupy less than 10 percent of the landscape near sites. These soils are advantageous because the coarser surface facilitates infiltration of rain and runoff, and the slowly permeable, finer subsurface promotes water retention in the crop root zone. Mimbres farmers managed soil by constructing terraces to promote topsoil aggradation. Knowledge about these soils and management techniques is relevant to current development of water harvesting and runoff agriculture in arid and drought-prone regions (Minnis and Sandor 2010; Sandor and Homburg 2015). Besides soil criteria, Mimbres agricultural strategies inferred from field location patterns include field placement at relatively high elevations to optimize moisture and temperature and on gentle slopes in small watersheds to manage runoff.

Studies of prehistoric Mimbres agricultural soils have included greenhouse tests to assess soil fertility using maize, barley, and different fertilizer regimes. Sandor and colleagues (1990) found that crop growth in the prehistoric agricultural soils was comparable to that of current agricultural soils and that these soils are potentially productive by modern standards if nitrogen levels are adequate.

Mimbres studies indicate that runoff was not only a source of supplemental water but also provided sediments and organic materials that build soil and renew fertility (Sandor 1995). A remarkable achievement of Southwest runoff agriculture, also relevant to agriculture today, is its ability to supply water and nutrients to crops in arid environments without conventional irrigation or fertilization. This is accomplished by connecting fields to hydrologic and biogeochemical processes in natural watersheds. Farmers carefully place and manage fields on certain landforms to intercept runoff and associated sediment and organic debris transported from upslope. Subsequent work at Zuni, including interviews with traditional farmers, observational studies of traditional fields, an in situ maize experiment, runoff monitoring, and soil testing, has further contributed to our understanding of these agroecological processes (Sandor et al. 2007).

Mimbres area soils also yielded evidence of long-term environmental degradation resulting from ancient agriculture, with effects that persist today (Sandor et al. 1990; Sandor and Homburg 2015). Many Mimbres Classic terraced fields exhibit accelerated sheet and gully erosion and decreased grass cover, characteristics not present in surrounding unfarmed reference areas. Prehistoric agricultural soils also show structural degradation and lighter color consistent with lower organic matter content. Two pieces of evidence indicate that the observed accelerated erosion began prehistorically: (1) gullies cut across agricultural terraces, indicating that the terraces preceded gullying; and (2) prehistoric dams were built within gullies, likely as attempts to repair damage caused by erosion. Some gullies may have started when ditches made to convey runoff got out of control during severe storms. Variations in the design of ancient agricultural terraces in the Mimbres region and other areas may indicate responses to land degradation by farmers to improve soil conservation.

Prehistoric agricultural soils further suffered from compaction and significant reductions in organic carbon, nitrogen, and phosphorus (Sandor et al. 1986, 1990). The similarity of this degradation to that of modern conventional agriculture is striking and shows that soil degradation can persist for a long time, a thousand years in the Mimbres case. Such soil degradation is likely to have reduced crop productivity in these Mimbres Classic fields, although to an unknown extent. Subsequent studies of ancient and traditional agriculture elsewhere in the Southwest and in other regions show variability in the long-term effects of farming on soils, ranging from land degradation to conservation and enhancement (Sandor and Homburg 2015). Archaeological studies are important in extending time perspectives on agricultural soil processes and change and providing a way to test for sustainability and resilience.

Going forward, important questions about Mimbres agriculture and soils remain unanswered. One area for continued research is how irrigated and dryland agriculture developed through the Mimbres cultural sequence. How did the extent of farming and agricultural strategies change over time? Although some irrigation canals and systems have been identified in Mimbres area valleys (Ellis 1995; Herrington 1979;

Shafer 2003), much more research into their scope and functioning is needed. Promising studies of southwestern irrigated fields and soils have been undertaken more recently, for example, along the Santa Cruz River in Tucson (Homburg 2015) and the middle Gila River valley (Woodson et al. 2015).

Another question for continued research about Mimbres agriculture is why there was an expansion from valley irrigation to upland dryland farming during the Classic period, considering that dryland agriculture seems marginal and riskier. Irrigation agriculture in deep alluvial valley soils is usually more productive than dryland agriculture in uplands. Most areas in the Southwest that were dryland farmed prehistorically are not farmed today, and most soil surveys do not recognize them as arable, reflecting the modern emphasis on irrigated valley agriculture. Minnis (1985) argued that needs of an increased population during the Mimbres Classic period exceeded the crop production capacity of irrigated agriculture, necessitating expansion to dryland farming. However, there are also sound agroecological reasons for this expansion involving diversification strategies to manage risk. For example, upland fields could remain productive during major valley-flooding episodes. Also, valley floors are more prone to freezing than valley edges and uplands, and some valley-floor soils lose productivity due to excess clay, salt, or sodium. Better estimates of dryland farming area are needed; its extent in the Southwest is likely much greater than currently recognized.

To what extent did soil degradation in Mimbres dryland agriculture affect society? Was it a factor in the major social changes and population movement at the end of the Classic period? Perhaps not, given the apparently limited extent of dryland agriculture, but the question remains open. Dryland agricultural soil degradation parallels other Mimbres Classic anthropogenic environmental changes, such as altered riparian vegetation and changes in animal species composition and distribution, but investigation into whether intensified Mimbres irrigation agriculture may have also degraded soils has not yet been done.

Conclusions

Mimbres Foundation and subsequent scholars have identified interesting patterns in the use of plants, animals, and soils. These combined analyses suggest that changes in Mimbres food production and population increases were complexly linked to soil-nutrient degradation in agricultural soils and faunal-resource depletion through prey suppression. Setting aside the relatively undersampled Early Pithouse period, paleobotanical data show that reliance on agriculture increased through the Late Pithouse and Mimbres Classic periods. Soil studies indicate that as populations grew and reliance on maize expanded, Mimbres farmers made greater use of dryland agriculture yield-improvement technologies, especially terraces. Osteofaunal analyses indicate that concurrent with population growth, large-bodied mammals like deer were less frequently consumed. Other changes include increases in jackrabbit-to-cottontail rabbit ratios through time, consistent with increased agricultural land clearing. The combined phenomena of population growth, increased agricultural dependence, greater land clearing, soil nutrient depletion, and large mammal prey suppression seem to have peaked during the Mimbres Classic period in the Mimbres Valley. Our findings are consistent with Minnis's (1985) conclusion that anthropogenic landscape alteration was sufficiently extreme to overtax extant social organization and food production and distribution mechanisms. Anthropogenic landscape effects were likely a strong force that promoted Mimbres Valley depopulation at the end of the Mimbres Classic period. Furthermore, our research suggests that the demographic hiatus that occurred in the Mimbres Valley promoted a partial recovery in landscape vegetation and large mammal abundance. Despite that partial recovery, adverse effects on soil quality caused by farming that ceased more than 950 years ago are still evident in Mimbres Classic period dry-farming fields.

This research has important implications for both our archaeological understanding of the circumstances behind dramatic changes like the depopulation of Classic sites and for modern issues surrounding soil and animal conservation. Our findings are, however, currently based on just a few sites from most regions and elevation zones. Adding data sets from a more representative sample of sites (particularly sites outside the Mimbres Valley, samples from the Pithouse period, and small sites) should be a high priority in future research. Ongoing research by Diehl (paleobotany) and Schollmeyer (osteofaunal analysis), supported by funding from the National Science Foundation, is expected to substantially increase the amount of data from Mimbres area pithouse and pueblo sites. Furthermore, we need to evaluate the anthropogenic impact on the Mimbres Mogollon landscape by sampling floodplain soils along the Mimbres and upper Gila rivers and from the Eastern Mimbres region to assess the degree of prehistoric soil nutrient depletion and subsequent recovery.

Acknowledgments

We thank other Mimbres researchers for their help and friendship over the years. KGS particularly thanks Margaret Nelson and Michelle Hegmon. MWD particularly thanks Paul Minnis for training and guidance and Steven LeBlanc for support on research related to the McAnally and Thompson sites. JAS is especially indebted to John Hawley for his mentorship during the Mimbres soils research and beyond. Research related to this paper was supported by the National Science Foundation (DBS 1524079, CNH-1113991, and Dissertation Improvement Grant 0542044).

References Cited

Anyon, Roger, and Stephen A. LeBlanc. 1984. *The Galaz Ruin: A Prehistoric Mimbres Village in Southwestern New Mexico*. Maxwell Museum of Anthropology and University of New Mexico Press, Albuquerque.

Baker, Gayla S. 1971. *The Riverside Site, Grant County, New Mexico*. Southwestern New Mexico Research Reports No. 5. Department of Anthropology, Case Western Reserve University, Cleveland, Ohio.

Bradfield, Wesley. 1931. *Cameron Creek Village: A Site in the Mimbres Area in Grant County, New Mexico*. School of American Research Monographs No. 1. El Palacio Press, Santa Fe, New Mexico.

Burns, Peter E. 1972. *The Heron Ruin, Grant County, New Mexico*. Southwestern New Mexico Research Reports No. 7. Department of Anthropology, Case Western Reserve University, Cleveland, Ohio.

Butler, Barbara H. 1984. Identified Fauna from Placitas Arroyo. In *Archaeological Investigations in the Placitas Arroyo, New Mexico*, edited by E. Pierre Morenon and T. R. Hays, pp. C1–13. Archaeology Program, Institute of Applied Sciences, North Texas State University, Denton.

Cannon, Michael D. 1999. The Faunal Remains from Mogollon Village (LA 11568). Report submitted to the USDA Forest Service, Gila National Forest, Silver City, New Mexico.

———. 2000. Large Mammal Relative Abundance in Pithouse and Pueblo Period Archaeofaunas from Southwestern New Mexico: Resource Depression Among the Mimbres-Mogollon? *Journal of Anthropological Archaeology* 19:317–347.

———. 2003. A Model of Central Place Forager Prey Choice and an Application to Faunal Remains from the Mimbres Valley, New Mexico. *Journal of Anthropological Archaeology* 22:1–25.

———. 2010. Introduction to the Faunal Analysis. In *Archaeological Excavations at Columbus Pueblo (LA 85774), a Southern Mimbres Occupation in Luna County, New Mexico*, edited by Nancy A. Kenmotsu, Tabitha L. Griffith, Lora J. Legare, William Russell, and Myles R. Miller, pp. 9.3–9.9. Geo-Marine, El Paso, Texas.

Creel, Darrell, and Charmion R. McKusick. 1994. Prehistoric Macaws and Parrots in the Mimbres Area, New Mexico. *American Antiquity* 59:510–524.

Daniel, Carolyn L. 1991. Faunal Analysis. In *The Cuchillo Negro Archaeological Project: On the Periphery of the Mimbres-Mogollon*, edited by Jeanne A. Schutt, Richard C. Chapman, and June-el Piper, pp. II6:1–II6:77. Office of Contract Archaeology, University of New Mexico, Albuquerque.

Diehl, Michael W. 1992. Preliminary Analysis of Archaeobotanical Samples from 83NM400, 85NM612, 85NM613, Palomas Creek Drainage, Sierra County, New Mexico. tDAR ID:399234. DOI:10.6067/XCV8W66N44, accessed October 2017.

Diehl, Michael W., and Stephen A. LeBlanc. 2001. *Early Pithouse Villages of the Mimbres Valley and Beyond: The Thompson and McAnally Sites in their Cultural and Ecological Contexts.* Papers of the Peabody Museum of Archaeology and Ethnology 83. Harvard University, Cambridge, Massachusetts.

Ellis, G. Lain. 1995. An Interpretive Framework for Radiocarbon Dates from Soil Organic Matter from Prehistoric Water Control Features. In *Soil, Water, Biology, and Belief in Prehistoric and Traditional Southwestern Agriculture*, edited by H. Wolcott Toll, pp. 155–186. Special Publication 2. New Mexico Archaeological Council, Albuquerque.

Fewkes, Jesse Walter. 1925. Designs on Prehistoric Pottery from the Mimbres Valley, New Mexico. *Smithsonian Miscellaneous Collections* 74(6):1–47.

Fitting, James E. 1971. *Excavations at MC 110, Grant County, New Mexico.* Southwestern Research Reports 2. Department of Anthropology, Case Western Reserve University, Cleveland, Ohio.

———. 1973. An Early Mogollon Community: A Preliminary Report on the Winn Canyon Site. *Artifact* 11(1 and 2). El Paso Archaeological Society, El Paso, Texas.

Gillespie, William B. 1987. Vertebrate Remains from LA 5421, the Saige-McFarland Site. Manuscript on file, Archaeology Southwest, Tucson, Arizona.

Gilman, Patricia A., Marc Thompson, and Kristina C. Wyckoff. 2014. Ritual Change and the Distant: Mesoamerican Iconography, Scarlet Macaws, and Great Kivas in the Mimbres Region of Southwestern New Mexico. *American Antiquity* 79:90–107.

Gomolak, Andrew R., and Dabney Ford. 1976. Reclamation of a Vandalized Prehistoric Settlement Site: Berrenda Creek Project 1976. Manuscript on File, New Mexico State University, Las Cruces.

Haury, Emil W. 1936. *The Mogollon Culture of Southwestern New Mexico.* Medallion Papers 20. Gila Pueblo, Globe, Arizona.

———. 1985. *Mogollon Culture in the Forestdale Valley, East-Central Arizona.* University of Arizona Press, Tucson.

Hegmon, Michelle, Margaret C. Nelson, Karen G. Schollmeyer, Michelle Elliott, and Michael W. Diehl. 2006. Agriculture, Mobility, and Human Impact in the Mimbres Region of the United States Southwest. In *Managing Archaeological Data and Databases: Essays in Honor of Sylvia W. Gaines*, edited by Jeffrey L. Hantman and Rachel Most, pp. 107–121. Archaeological Research Paper 57. Arizona State University, Tempe.

Herrington, Selma L. C. 1979. Settlement Patterns and Water Control Systems of the Mimbres Classic Phase, Grant County, New Mexico. PhD dissertation, Department of Anthropology, University of Texas, Austin.

Homburg, Jeffrey A. 2015. Anthropogenic Effects on Soil Quality of Irragric Soils at Las Capas, AZ, AA:12:111 (ASM). In *The Anthropogenic Landscape of Las Capas, an Early Agricultural Irrigation Community in Southern Arizona*, edited by James Vint and Fred L. Nials, pp. 193–225. Anthropological Papers 50. Archaeology Southwest and Desert Archaeology, Tucson, Arizona.

Jett, Stephen C., and Peter B. Moyle. 1986. The Exotic Origins of Fishes Depicted on Prehistoric Mimbres Pottery from New Mexico. *American Antiquity* 51:688–720.

Kearns, Timothy M., Cherie K. Walth, Gary M. Brown, and Kate McDonald. 1999. Osteological Analyses. In *South Waste Rock Expansion: Archaeological Data Recovery in the Buckhorn Gulch Area at the Continental Mine, Grant County, New Mexico*, edited by Gary M. Brown, pp. 491–519. Western Cultural Resource Management, Farmington, New Mexico.

Kulow, Stephanie, and Karen G. Schollmeyer. 2005. Mimbres Animal Representations and Faunal Resources in the Mimbres Valley, New Mexico. Paper presented at the 13th Mogollon Conference, Silver City, New Mexico.

LeBlanc, Steven A., and Michael E. Whalen (editors). 1980. *An Archaeological Synthesis of South-Central and Southwestern New Mexico*. Office of Contract Archaeology, University of New Mexico, Albuquerque.

Minnis, Paul E. 1985. *Social Adaptation to Food Stress: A Prehistoric Southwestern Example*. University of Chicago Press, Chicago.

——. 1991. Famine Foods of the Northern American Desert Borderlands in Historical Context. *Journal of Ethnobiology* 11:231–257.

——. 1996. Notes on Economic Uncertainty and Human Behavior in the Prehistoric North American Southwest. In *Evolving Complexity and Environmental Risk in the Prehistoric Southwest*, edited by Joseph A. Tainter and Bonnie Bagley Tainter, pp. 57–78. Proceedings 24. Santa Fe Institute, Santa Fe, New Mexico.

Minnis, Paul E., and Jonathan Sandor. 2010. Mimbres Potters' Fields. In *Mimbres Lives and Landscapes*, edited by Margaret C. Nelson and Michelle Hegmon, pp. 82–89. School for Advanced Research Press, Santa Fe, New Mexico.

Nelson, Ben A., and Stephen A. LeBlanc. 1986. *Short-Term Sedentism in the American Southwest: The Mimbres Valley Salado*. University of New Mexico Press, Albuquerque.

Nelson, Margaret C. 1986. Chipped Stone Analysis: Food Selection and Hunting Behavior. In *Short-Term Sedentism in the American Southwest: The Mimbres Valley Salado*, edited by Ben A. Nelson and Steven A. LeBlanc, pp. 141–176. University of New Mexico Press, Albuquerque.

Nisengard, Jennifer E. 2000. Faunal Analysis at LA 5841. In *Late Mimbres Pueblos in Peripheral Areas: Final Report on Test Excavations at LA 5841 (Cooney Ranch #1), Middle Fork of the Mimbres River, Southwestern New Mexico, August 7–19, 1999*, edited by Robert J. Stokes, pp. 69–81. Report to the Laboratory of Anthropology, Santa Fe, New Mexico.

Olsen, Sandra L., and John W. Olsen. 1996. An Analysis of Faunal Remains from Wind Mountain. In *Mimbres Mogollon Archaeology: Charles C. Di Peso's Excavations at Wind Mountain*, edited by Anne I. Woosley and Allan J. McIntyre, pp. 389–406. Amerind Foundation, Dragoon, Arizona, and University of New Mexico Press, Albuquerque.

Powell, Doss. 2015. Preliminary Analysis of Faunal Remains from the Harris Site. In Archaeological Investigations at the Harris Site (LA 1867), Grant County, New Mexico, edited by Barbara J. Roth, pp. 364–380. Report on file, University of Nevada, Las Vegas.

Powell, Susan. 1977. Changes in Prehistoric Hunting Patterns Resulting from Agricultural Alteration of the Environment: A Case Study from the Mimbres River Area, New Mexico. Master's thesis, Department of Anthropology, University of California, Los Angeles.

Rodek, Hugo G. 1932. Arthropod Designs on Prehistoric Mimbres Pottery. *Annals of the Entomological Society of America* 25:688–693.

Sanchez, Julia L. J. 1992. Mimbres Faunal Subsistence A.D. 200–1150, Mimbres Valley, Grant and Luna Counties, New Mexico. Master's thesis, Department of Anthropology, Texas A&M University, College Station.

———. 1996. A Re-evaluation of Mimbres Faunal Subsistence. *Kiva* 61:295–307.

Sandor, Jonathan A. 1995. Searching Soil for Clues about Southwest Prehistoric Agriculture. In *Soil, Water, Biology, and Belief in Prehistoric and Traditional Southwestern Agriculture*, edited by H. W. Toll, pp. 119–137. New Mexico Archaeological Council Special Publication 2. New Mexico Archaeological Council, Albuquerque.

Sandor, Jonathan A., Paul L. Gersper, and John W. Hawley. 1986. Soils at Prehistoric Agricultural Terracing Sites in New Mexico: I. Site Placement and Soil Morphology and Classification. II. Organic Matter and Bulk Density. III. Phosphorus, Micronutrients, and pH. *Soil Science Society of America Journal* 50:166–180.

———. 1990. Prehistoric Agricultural Terraces and Soils in the Mimbres Area, New Mexico. *World Archaeology* 22:70–86.

Sandor, Jonathan A., and Jeffrey A. Homburg. 2015. Agricultural Soils of the Prehistoric Southwest: Known Unknowns. In *Arid Lands Agriculture*, edited by Scott. E. Ingram and Robert C. Hunt, pp. 54–88. University of Arizona Press, Tucson.

Sandor, Jonathan A., Jay B. Norton, Jeffrey A. Homburg, Deborah A. Muenchrath, Carleton S. White, Stephen E. Williams, Celeste I. Havener, and Peter D. Stahl. 2007. Biogeochemical Studies of a Native American Runoff Agroecosystem. *Geoarchaeology* 22:359–386.

Schmidt, Kari M. 1999. The Five Feature Site (AZ CC:7:55 [ASM]): Evidence for a Prehistoric Rabbit Drive in Southeastern Arizona. *Kiva* 65:103–124.

———. 2010. Faunal Remains from Excavations at La Gila Encantada. In Archaeological Investigations at La Gila Encantada (LA 113467), Grant County, New Mexico, edited by Barbara J. Roth, pp. 133–143. Report submitted to The Archaeological Conservancy, Albuquerque, New Mexico.

Schollmeyer, Karen G. 2005. Prehispanic Environmental Impact in the Mimbres Region, Southwestern New Mexico. *Kiva* 70:375–397.

———. 2009. Resource Stress and Settlement Pattern Change in the Eastern Mimbres Area, Southwest New Mexico. PhD dissertation, Arizona State University, Tempe. University Microfilms, Ann Arbor.

———. 2011. Large Game, Agricultural Land, and Settlement Pattern Change in the Eastern Mimbres Area, Southwest New Mexico. *Journal of Anthropological Archaeology* 30:402–415.

———. 2015. Vertebrate Fauna from Woodrow Ruin, LA 2454. Report on file, Archaeology Southwest, Tucson, Arizona.

Schollmeyer, Karen Gust, and Joan Brenner Coltrain. 2010. Anthropogenic Environments, Resource Stress, and Settlement Pattern Change in the Eastern Mimbres Area. In *The Archaeology of Anthropogenic Environments*, edited by R. M. Dean, pp. 266-294. Center for Archaeological Investigations Occasional Paper No. 37, Southern Illinois University, Carbondale.

Schollmeyer, Karen G., and Jonathan C. Driver. 2013. Settlement Patterns, Source-Sink Dynamics, and Artiodactyl Hunting in the Prehistoric U.S. Southwest. *Journal of Archaeological Method and Theory*, special issue, edited by Virginia L. Butler, Christyann M. Darwent, and Michael J. O'Brien, 20:448–487.

Schriever, Bernard A. 2002. Mimbres-Mogollon Mobility: The Late Pithouse Period and the Florida Mountain Site, Luna County, New Mexico. Master's thesis, Department of Anthropology, University of Oklahoma, Norman.

Shafer, Harry J. 2003. *Mimbres Archaeology at the NAN Ranch Ruin*. University of New Mexico Press, Albuquerque.

Shaffer, Brian S. 1991. *The Economic Importance of Vertebrate Faunal Remains from the NAN Ruin (LA 15049), a Classic Mimbres Site, Grant County, New Mexico*. Master's thesis, Department of Anthropology, Texas A&M University, College Station.

Shaffer, Brian S., and Karen M. Gardner. 1995. The Rabbit Drive Through Time: Analysis of the North American Ethnographic and Prehistoric Evidence. *Utah Archaeology* 8(1):13–25.

———. 1997. Reconstructing Animal Exploitation by Puebloan Peoples of the Southwestern United States Using Mimbres Pottery, A.D. 1000–1150. *Anthropozoologica* 25, 26: 263–268.

Shaffer, Brian S., Karen M. Gardner, and Barry W. Baker. 1996. Prehistoric Small Game Snare Trap Technology, Deployment Strategy, and Trapper Gender Depicted in Mimbres Pottery. *Journal of Ethnobiology* 16(2):145–155.

Sullivan, Norman C., and Deborah Berg. 1983. Faunal Remains at the Kartchner Site: A Mimbres-Mogollon Pueblo in Southwestern New Mexico. *Kiva* 49:105–110.

Thompson, Marc. 1999. Mimbres Iconology: Analysis and Interpretation of Figurative Motifs. PhD dissertation, University of Calgary, Alberta. University Microfilms, Ann Arbor.

Woodson, M. Kyle, Jonathan A. Sandor, Colleen Strawhacker, and Wesley D. Miles. 2015. Hohokam Canal Irrigation and the Formation of Irragric Anthrosols in the Middle Gila River Valley, Arizona, USA. *Geoarchaeology* 30:271–290.

Wyckoff, Kristina C. 2009. Mimbres-Mesoamerican Interaction: Macaws and Parrots in the Mimbres Valley, Southwestern New Mexico. Master's thesis, Department of Anthropology, University of Oklahoma, Norman.

9

Continuity and Change in the Eastern Mimbres Area After A.D. 1130

KAREN GUST SCHOLLMEYER, MARGARET C. NELSON, AND MICHELLE HEGMON

T HE END OF THE MIMBRES CLASSIC PERIOD around A.D. 1130 is a water-shed in Mimbres archaeology. Before this, the region shared the widespread attributes of material culture (particularly ceramic and architectural styles) that archaeologists traditionally use to define culture areas. After 1130, the region became a patchwork of different ceramic and architectural traditions, population changes and settlement patterns, and archaeological phase names distributed across what was formerly considered an easily defined region (also see chapter 10). Decades of research focused on examining what changed and what remained the same across the Mimbres Classic to Postclassic transition and beyond have given us a picture of this period, highlighting the variability in material culture, land use, and social patterns characteristic of the former Mimbres region after A.D. 1130.

The long-term research discussed here owes much to the Mimbres Foundation's pioneering work in the Mimbres Valley. In the 1980s, archaeologists trained on Mimbres Foundation projects began expanding on what was then known of Mimbres archaeology by investigating archaeological sites east of the Mimbres Valley (Nelson 1989). The Eastern Mimbres Archaeological Project, directed by Margaret Nelson and Michelle Hegmon, had its first official field season in 1993. Several years of study followed, the results of which are summarized here. The project trained many students, some of whom eventually led fieldwork in the area as part of the Mogollon Prehistoric Landscapes Project (Schollmeyer et al. 2010; Swanson et al. 2008). Both projects used field methodology and approaches adapted from the Mimbres Foundation. We have also used the Mimbres Foundation's original metal screens throughout this work (figure 9.1); their continued use in the archaeological field schools now

FIGURE 9.1 Field-school students use original Mimbres Foundation screens on a 2014 excavation with Archaeology Southwest and the University of Arizona outside Cliff, New Mexico.

conducted by Archaeology Southwest is a testament to the Mimbres Foundation's enduring legacy of long-lasting ideas, approaches, and field equipment.

In this chapter, we discuss evidence for continuity and change in the decades following the end of the Mimbres Classic period. We also discuss thirteenth- and fourteenth-century developments in which continuity is more difficult to trace in the Eastern Mimbres area. This area, between the Black Range and the Rio Grande (see figure I.1), has seen some of the most sustained and intensive research on this period. It is also a particularly diverse area and contains several different ceramic and architectural styles within its four most heavily studied drainages. The first half of this chapter focuses on the Early Postclassic period (A.D. 1130–early 1300s) in the Eastern Mimbres area and the second half on the Late Postclassic period (A.D. 1300–1450). Postclassic period developments in the Mimbres Valley are discussed in chapter 10.

The post–A.D. 1130 era is troublesome from the perspective of phase names across the region and the Eastern Mimbres area is no exception. A multitude of phase names are currently in use, some of which are difficult to distinguish based on surface evidence (see table I.1). Early Postclassic (A.D. 1130–early 1300s) sites include Reorganization phase (A.D. 1130–early 1200s) hamlets immediately postdating the end of the Mimbres Classic and later sites contemporary with the Black Mountain, Tularosa, Early Animas, and Late Doña Ana phases (e.g., Douglas 2004; Hegmon et al. 1999;

Lekson 1996; Miller and Kenmotsu 2004). Late Postclassic (A.D. 1300–1450) sites are contemporary with the Cliff phase (Salado), Magdalena, Late Animas, and El Paso phases. Eastern Mimbres sites share some, but not all, attributes of several of these phases. We refer to post-1130 developments generally as Early and Late Postclassic because sites in the area we discuss do not fit neatly into the phase definitions currently in use. The area's position at the edges of multiple cultural phenomena, along with the diversity in pottery and architectural styles found there, is one of its most interesting characteristics after A.D. 1130.

The Early Postclassic Period in the Eastern Mimbres Area (A.D. 1130–early 1300s)

The Reorganization Phase (A.D. 1130–early 1200s)

Until A.D. 1130, material culture in the Eastern Mimbres area fit patterns characterizing the broader region. Most excavated Mimbres Classic villages show evidence of underlying pithouses. Cobble-masonry sites of twenty to sixty-five rooms are located on low terraces above floodplains along drainages descending from the Black Range to the Rio Grande. Larger villages may have been built along the Rio Grande (Lekson 1989; Mayo 1994), but destruction has made estimating their size difficult.

Many smaller (one- to three-room) sites are dispersed along major drainages, side drainages with little floodplain land, and upland areas. These were probably field houses or other special-use sites, and many were not occupied year-round (Nelson 1999:55–65). These small sites show a mix of cobble masonry and adobe or jacal construction. Decorated pottery is almost entirely Mimbres Classic Black-on-white, typical of the region at this time (Hegmon et al. 1999).

Around A.D. 1130, people in the Eastern Mimbres area stopped living in these villages. Some people left the region altogether and other former village residents dispersed into hamlets, a pattern of living that lasted a generation or two until the early A.D. 1200s. This time is called the Reorganization phase. The phase lacks a precise end date and is plagued by the same dating problems (particularly a lack of datable tree-ring samples) characterizing much of the Postclassic period. It is roughly contemporary with the Terminal Mimbres Classic phase (A.D. 1130–late 1100s) occupations of some Mimbres Valley sites (Creel 1999).

Some of the strongest evidence for population continuity between Mimbres Classic villages and Reorganization phase hamlets in the Eastern Mimbres area comes from architecture. A number of Reorganization phase hamlets were constructed in the same locations as Mimbres Classic field houses or small special-use sites, and sometimes these earlier structures were remodeled into Reorganization phase rooms

(Nelson 1993). Hamlets are groups of three to fifteen cobble-masonry or jacal rooms (Schollmeyer 2009:226–227). The largest, Lizard Terrace (LA 37727/37728), has twenty-four rooms. Households consist of single habitation rooms joined into blocks, a contrast with the varied array of multiroom suites and other household architecture configurations characteristic of the Mimbres Classic period (Hegmon et al. 2006).

Ceramic assemblages indicate both continuity and change. Mimbres Classic Black-on-white pottery was still used and perhaps was still being manufactured during the first part of this period (Hegmon et al. 1998). In contrast to Mimbres Classic ceramic assemblages, Reorganization phase assemblages are dominated by pottery associated with other traditions and often made for long periods, including El Paso Polychrome, St. Johns Polychrome, Chupadero Black-on-white, Playas Red Incised, and Tularosa Patterned Corrugated (Hegmon et al. 1999). This array of types includes imported vessels and locally made ones and combines Mimbres Classic pottery with types made after A.D. 1150 (Hegmon et al. 2000; Hegmon et al. 1998). The combination of jacal and cobble-masonry architecture and ceramic assemblages composed of types made for long periods makes Reorganization phase sites difficult to identify based on surface evidence, particularly in comparison to Mimbres Classic sites. That is, Mimbres Classic sites with a later Postclassic (after A.D. 1250) reoccupation can produce very similar surface signatures. Excavation, however, reveals a mix of Mimbres Classic and later ceramic types in use contexts (e.g., floor and roof assemblages) in Reorganization phase sites, a combination not seen in Mimbres Classic sites with later reoccupations (Nelson 1999:56–57).

Our initial (1990s) interpretations of Reorganization phase settlement size and location, combined with what was then known about the Mimbres Valley, supported the idea that population in the Eastern Mimbres area increased after A.D. 1130 and that the area may have been a destination for people leaving the Mimbres Valley. As data quality from survey and excavation increased, however, it has become clear that the Eastern Mimbres population declined between the late Mimbres Classic period and the Reorganization phase (Schollmeyer 2011). Residential mobility also increased over this time interval. Hamlets were probably occupied regularly but intermittently over an extended period. Domestic roof-support posts (which required periodic replacement regardless of occupation intensity) were replaced or repaired at similar rates in Mimbres Classic villages and Reorganization phase hamlets, but floor wear and replastering (linked in part to continuous use of rooms by residents walking on floors) was substantially less frequent in Reorganization phase rooms than in Mimbres Classic ones (Nelson et al. 2006). This is particularly interesting given the smaller size of Reorganization phase hamlets and lack of clear division between villages and special-use sites in that phase (as opposed to the villages and field houses we see in the Mimbres Classic period), implying a shift between greater emphasis on logistical mobility between villages and field houses before A.D. 1130 and more residential mobility between hamlets during the Reorganization phase.

Site settings also show aspects of both continuity and change. Mimbres Classic villages are generally located near large tracts of land suitable for farming, particularly places where drainages briefly narrow just above a broad floodplain and underlying bedrock forces water to the surface. Other settings held small special-use sites, but not villages. In contrast, Reorganization phase hamlets occur in a variety of settings, including former field-house locations. Initially, this variability in site setting raised the issue of whether resource use (including dependence on farming and the suite of plants and animals used) changed after A.D. 1130. However, charred seeds from Reorganization phase hearths demonstrated continued heavy reliance on cultigens. Noncultigens from these contexts showed that the most common taxa did not change between the Mimbres Classic and Reorganization phases (Nelson and Diehl 1999; Nelson et al. 2006; Schollmeyer 1999). Faunal remains showed similar continuity, with no changes in the range of taxa used or in access to important species like deer and pronghorn (Schollmeyer 2011; Schollmeyer and Coltrain 2010).

The advent of widespread GIS technology has enabled new spatial analyses revealing some reasons for this continuity. Although Reorganization phase hamlets are located in more diverse settings, most are 3 km or less from Mimbres Classic villages (Schollmeyer 2009:210–211). Consequently, the areas where residents would have located their fields and done the bulk of their day-to-day foraging for wild foods (commonly thought to be 5 km or less from residences) would have been quite similar across the two periods (Schollmeyer 2011). The biggest change in settlement location after A.D. 1130 was an overall movement downstream; the upper reaches of the Eastern Mimbres drainages with Mimbres Classic villages do not contain Reorganization phase sites, while the middle and lower stretches have sites from the Mimbres Classic and Reorganization phases.

In the Eastern Mimbres area, movement from Mimbres Classic villages to Reorganization phase hamlets does not appear to have occurred primarily as a response to food stress. Although we know of a substantial climatic downturn from the A.D. 1120s to 1140s, GIS analyses suggest there would still have been enough arable land to support the area's Mimbres Classic population if residents had been willing to walk slightly farther to field areas than was necessary in earlier decades (Schollmeyer 2011). Shifting residence from villages to hamlets after A.D. 1130 did not improve resource access, at least not in ways that could not have been accomplished by moving some of the area's population between existing Mimbres Classic villages, nor did moving improve hunters' access to large mammal resources (Schollmeyer 2011). This shift was not a response to starvation conditions or to any archaeologically visible population-resource imbalance, but to conditions farmers probably perceived as below average.

Declining productivity, though not catastrophic in a nutritional sense, may have been perceived as part of a larger problem with the social context of which Mimbres Classic period farmers were a part (Hegmon et al. 2016; Schollmeyer 2011; Schollmeyer and Coltrain 2010). Resource stress had a larger role in the depopulation of Mimbres Classic villages in the Mimbres Valley (Minnis 1985; Pool 2002), and people's perceptions of events there surely played an important role in post-1130 changes in the Eastern Mimbres area also.

Some of our recent work has focused on the experiences of the people who lived through the transformation at the end of the Mimbres Classic period (Hegmon et al. 2016). People in the densely populated Mimbres Valley saw social and ritual institutions dissolve as nearly three-quarters of their neighbors left (Nelson et al. 2010). People privileged by the land-tenure system might have lost their advantages, while those previously on the margins would have had new opportunities. In the Eastern Mimbres area, the changes would have been less dramatic since many people stayed in the general area but simply relocated to dispersed hamlets. Although the coherence and symbolism of the Mimbres Classic came to an end across the entire region, there would have been considerable demographic, and probably also social and institutional, continuity (Creel 1999; Hegmon et al. 2016).

Other Early Postclassic Occupations (early 1200s–1300s)

Sites immediately postdating the Reorganization phase are less common than those from earlier periods and have been comparatively less well studied in the Eastern Mimbres area. Only three sites with thirteenth-century occupations are known from the Animas, Palomas, and Seco drainages (LA 3948, LA 3949, and LA 44996; see figure I.1). Ceramic assemblages consist largely of El Paso Polychrome and Chupadero Black-on-white, as well as smaller quantities of Playas Red Incised. Each site has adobe architecture around a plaza adjacent to a preexisting Mimbres Classic village. Of these three sites, only Las Animas village (LA 3949) has been excavated. This site consists of a masonry pueblo depopulated at the end of the Mimbres Classic and an adobe pueblo built in the later 1200s and used most extensively in the 1300s and probably into the 1400s (Hegmon 2017). This site is discussed in more detail in the next section of this chapter due to its largely later date.

The Rio Alamosa drainage to the north (see figure I.1) has a different form of Early Postclassic period occupation. Small dispersed linear-masonry pueblos were used between the mid-twelfth and early thirteenth centuries. The only excavated example, the Kelly Canyon site (LA 1125), has architecture and ceramics dominated by Socorro Black-on-white decorated ceramics with Los Lunas Smudged and Pitoche Rubbed Ribbed utility wares characteristic of Socorro phase sites to the north (Clark and Laumbach 2011). These northern-affiliated sites were partially contemporary with Mimbres Classic pueblos nearby (Clark and Laumbach 2011), although it is also possible that they were constructed shortly after the Mimbres Classic sites were residentially abandoned, or perhaps they are examples of farmers transitioning between Mimbres-linked and Socorro-linked cultural affiliations (Laumbach and Laumbach 2006).

From the early A.D. 1200s until 1300, the entire population of the Rio Alamosa drainage was probably aggregated in the Victorio site (LA 88889). This five-hundred-room village combines unshaped-cobble masonry in some room blocks (resembling local Socorro-affiliated sites) and adobe and cobble architecture with upright foundation stones (resembling local Mimbres Classic sites) in others; rooms of both types contain a similar mix of Tularosa Black-on-white, St. Johns Polychrome, and Tularosa Corrugated series ceramics (Clark and Laumbach 2011). This combination of two styles of architecture with a shared set of ceramics suggests that people leaving both Mimbres Classic–affiliated and Socorro-affiliated sites settled at Victorio (Clark and Laumbach 2011).

The Late Postclassic Period in the Eastern Mimbres Area (A.D. 1300–1450)

The Late Postclassic (A.D. 1300–1450) is contemporary with the Cliff (Salado), Magdalena, Late Animas, and El Paso phases. Several Eastern Mimbres sites do not fit well into any of these traditions, and so we refer to them as Late Postclassic. These sites include cobble-masonry architecture (probably sometimes two-story) and adobe and sometimes a mix of both on the same site. On the Palomas, Seco, and Animas drainages, the numerically dominant pottery types on these sites include El Paso Polychrome/Bichrome and Tularosa Black-on-white, plus smaller quantities of Magdalena Black-on-white, Heshotauthla Polychrome, Rio Grande Glaze Ware, and very rarely Roosevelt Red Ware and Chihuahuan polychromes. Survey data indicate that these sites occur only in the lower-elevation portions of the three drainages, within 15 km of the Rio Grande (Swanson et al. 2008). The Rio Alamosa has a different pattern, as we will discuss.

Two sites from the early part of this period have been excavated by the Mogollon Prehistoric Landscapes Project: Phyllis Pueblo (LA 45160) and Roadmap Village (LA 45157), both on the Palomas drainage. The two have different ceramics and architecture. Like other Postclassic sites, a lack of tree-ring dates hampers interpretations concerning whether these differences are social, temporal, or both. Phyllis Pueblo includes about sixty rooms, primarily of cobble masonry. Rooms are arranged into one or two blocks. An arroyo currently separates the architecture into two blocks, but it may not have existed in the past. One or two partially enclosed plazas are present. The dominant decorated wares are El Paso Polychrome and Chupadero Black-on-white with smaller amounts of Playas Red, Cibola White Ware, St. Johns Polychrome, and Three Rivers Red-on-terracotta (table 9.1). Rooms were remodeled numerous times, as shown in repeated floor replastering events and remodeling episodes that involved removing and reconfiguring walls and floors (Russell et al. 2010). Several early walls are preserved only as adobe stubs under later cobble-masonry walls. These may have been either full-height adobe walls or adobe footings for masonry walls. Excavated rooms consist of domestic rooms (which have hearths and postholes) and smaller rooms that lack floor features; the latter may have been storage rooms. Hearths include basin-shaped hearths and more formal square and circular adobe-collared hearths.

Roadmap Village, less than 1 km upstream from Phyllis Pueblo on the Palomas drainage, includes at least eighty rooms arranged in two blocks around two partially enclosed plazas. Walls are cobble masonry, although several have adobe-wall footings. We strongly suspect many rooms were once two story; some rooms have a preserved standing wall height over 2 m and coursed wall fall suggesting original room heights of at least 3.9 m, but only two surfaces (either a floor and a roof or a lower- and upper-story floor with no preserved roof surface) have been found in any one room. These tall walls are thin for their height (30–40 cm) and composed of courses of medium-sized (approximately 20 × 40 cm) unshaped river cobbles with smaller (roughly 3 × 8 cm) coursed chinking stones, held in place with mud plaster. Many walls rest on trash fill. Unfortunately, the sherds in this fill are plain, making it difficult to assess whether this fill comes from an earlier occupation at the site or refuse discarded by the residents of the first rooms constructed in the A.D. 1300s. Some rooms have slightly larger foundation cobbles, while others do not. Only one excavated room has evidence of remodeling (with a newer floor constructed several centimeters above the older one), and there is very little evidence of floor replastering or posthole repair, an interesting contrast to Phyllis Pueblo. The decorated ceramic assemblage is dominated by El Paso Polychrome (see table 9.1). Other common decorated ceramics include Magdalena Black-on-white and Chupadero Black-on-white, with smaller amounts of Playas Red and Cibola White Ware. Interesting types found in very small quantities include Kwakina Polychrome, Rio Grande Glaze A, and Gila Polychrome.

The presence of Magdalena Black-on-white is particularly interesting. This carbon-painted pottery is the dominant decorated type at two sites interpreted as linked to Mesa Verde migrants: Gallinas Springs (LA 1178) and Pinnacle Ruin (LA 2292; Knight and Gomolak 1985; Lekson et al. 2002; see figure I.1). Compositional data from neutron activation analysis indicate some Magdalena Black-on-white found at Roadmap and Pinnacle Ruin was made at Gallinas Springs, and some at each site was also made locally (Ferguson et al. 2016). The presence of this pottery along with

TABLE 9.1 Decorated Ceramics from Selected Thirteenth- and Fourteenth-Century Sites in the Eastern Mimbres Area

Site	Contribution to decorated ceramic assemblage								
	Magdalena B/w	El Paso Polychrome	Chupadero B/w	Cibola White Ware	St. Johns Polychrome	Other White Mountain Red Ware	Three Rivers Red-on-terracotta	Playas Red	Ramos Polychrome
Las Animas Village[a] (LA 3949)	None	Common	Common	None	Present	None	None	Present	Rare
Phyllis Pueblo (LA 45160)	None	34%, 209 sherds	25%, 156 sherds	3%, 17 sherds	1%, 7 sherds	None	1%, 6 sherds	6%, 37 sherds	None
Roadmap Village (LA 45157)	9%, 456 sherds	41%, 2079 sherds	5%, 243 sherds	1%, 70 sherds	Rare	Rare	Rare	2%, 77 sherds	None
Pinnacle Ruin[b] (LA 2292)	48%	16%	Present	None	Present	14%	None	Present	Rare
Gallinas Springs[b] (LA 1178)	74%–80% (two different excavations)	None	Present	None	Present	Present	None	None	None

[a]Hegmon 2002.
[b]Ferguson et al. 2016.

two-story masonry at Roadmap Village also suggests some level of connection to the Mesa Verde region far to the north in southwest Colorado or to the migrants argued to have inhabited the other two sites. However, there are also substantial differences between Roadmap and those more clearly Mesa Verde–affiliated sites. Gallinas Springs and Pinnacle have slab-masonry walls and site layouts resembling the architecture of the Mesa Verde region (Bertram et al. 1990; Lekson et al. 2002), a pattern not seen at Roadmap. Magdalena Black-on-white is the dominant decorated pottery type at both Pinnacle and Gallinas Springs, comprising 48 percent of the painted pottery at Pinnacle (Lekson et al. 2002), whereas Roadmap is dominated by El Paso Polychrome and contains only 9 percent Magdalena Black-on-white (see table 9.1). Roadmap Village has a mix of cultural influences from northern and southern traditions rather than a substantial Mesa Verde presence.

Las Animas Village (LA 3949) was partially contemporary with Roadmap and Phyllis, but its use continued considerably later, probably into the fifteenth century (Hegmon 2017). The Postclassic adobe pueblo at Las Animas Village consists of about one hundred rooms that enclose a single plaza. One side of the pueblo was two story. Construction techniques varied, but most walls were made of adobe with embedded cobbles; often vertical cobbles were set into an adobe base to anchor the walls. Nearly every area that was excavated revealed evidence of extensive remodeling. Most simply, some rooms had multiple floors. In one area the first-story floors were filled in prehistorically, the second story was remodeled into a series of small closet-sized spaces, and use of the second story continued. In another area one layer of adobe architecture was allowed to collapse and was replaced by another, aligned differently. Chronometric dates indicate building and use primarily during the fourteenth century, although some construction may have begun before 1300 and use may have continued into the fifteenth century. A wide range of ceramics was found at Las Animas Village, including smudged obliterated corrugated, El Paso Polychrome, Chupadero, and small quantities of Cibola types, Ramos Polychrome, Roosevelt Red Ware, Rio Grande Glaze, and Biscuit.

None of these sites fit well into established Late Postclassic archaeological phases. Their ceramic assemblages differ, but all show a mix of northern and southern influences. Roadmap and Phyllis have ceramic assemblages dominated by El Paso Polychrome, but their use of substantially more cobble masonry than adobe is atypical of the sites generally classified as El Paso or Animas phase. Masonry walls may suggest either a more northern influence or some degree of continuity with earlier Mimbres cobble masonry, but these sites contain far more southern ceramics than are normally associated with Tularosa phase or other northern-influenced sites. Roadmap may date slightly later than Phyllis Pueblo, which has less White Mountain Red Ware and lacks Rio Grande Glaze Ware. El Paso Polychrome jar rims also suggest a relatively later date for Roadmap, which has sherds from both large and small jars and more flared rims (in contrast to the fewer flared rims and lack of small jars at Phyllis Pueblo; Russell 2010). Architecturally, Las Animas Village appears to conform to expectations for the Black Mountain phase (Early Postclassic), but its dates and ceramics clearly indicate that it is later.

Late Postclassic occupation is quite different in the Rio Alamosa drainage. Pinnacle Ruin (LA 2292) lies just upstream from the Victorio site, on a high butte above fertile floodplains (Lekson et al. 2002). The site has up to 150 rooms constructed of carefully coursed slab masonry around an enclosed plaza (Clark and Laumbach 2011; Lekson et al. 2002). This architecture is unlike that of earlier sites in the area but compares favorably with Mesa Verde. Magdalena Black-on-white composes 48 percent of the decorated assemblage, with substantially less El Paso Polychrome and White Mountain Red Ware (Ferguson et al. 2016). At Pinnacle and the Gallinas Springs sites discussed previously, decoration on the Magdalena Black-on-white pottery closely resembles McElmo Black-on-white (Clark and Laumbach 2011; Lekson et al. 2002). These architectural and ceramic similarities suggest these two sites were founded by migrants from the northwest affiliated with Mesa Verde (Lekson et al. 2002).

Interestingly, accelerator mass spectrometry (AMS) dates indicate that the occupation of Pinnacle Ruin may have partially overlapped with that of the Victorio site (Clark and Laumbach 2011). However, there is almost no evidence of shared decorated ceramics. Only one sherd of Magdalena Black-on-white was found at Victorio, and very little Tularosa Black-on-white was present at Pinnacle (Clark and Laumbach 2011). Pinnacle's occupation continued much later, probably through the late A.D. 1300s (Lekson et al. 2002). Pinnacle Ruin is argued to have been home to migrants affiliated with the Mesa Verde region who moved into the Rio Alamosa drainage, either near the end of the Victorio site's occupation or shortly after it ended (Clark and Laumbach 2011; Lekson et al. 2002). The differences in abundance of Magdalena Black-on-white, El Paso Polychrome, and Tularosa Black-on-white at Pinnacle Ruin, Victorio, and Roadmap Village are intriguing and suggest very different social connections at these three sites.

Continuity and Change

The variability in site layouts, architecture, and ceramics in the Eastern Mimbres area exemplifies the variability seen throughout the former Mimbres region after the late 1100s. Not surprisingly, this variability has contributed to differing interpretations of how much continuity (in population, culture, or both) there was between farmers in the Mimbres Classic period and those in the diverse villages of later periods. In the

Mimbres Valley, Creel (1999) sees population and cultural continuity between Black Mountain phase and earlier occupations. Although the frequencies of practices (such as cremation versus inhumation and use of masonry versus adobe) change over time, he sees an overall stability in the range of architectural forms and mortuary practices. We see the Eastern Mimbres area similarly. Cobble masonry and adobe or jacal construction are present in both the Mimbres Classic and Early Postclassic periods, and the range of pottery types is similar although frequencies change substantially (mortuary data are unavailable here). The placement of sites in the A.D. 1200s also suggests continuity. These sites are located immediately adjacent to Mimbres Classic sites in the Eastern Mimbres area, a pattern also seen in many Black Mountain phase sites in the Mimbres Valley (Creel 1999; Hegmon et al. 1999). Other researchers argue that cultural changes at the end of the twelfth century marked a complete break between Mimbres and Postclassic period traditions (LeBlanc 1989; Shafer 1999). In this view, people who left the Mimbres Valley after A.D. 1130 spent decades or generations elsewhere, but their descendants reoccupied the valley in the Black Mountain phase (Shafer 1999). Others see population continuity at a regional scale but not a local one, with people moving between the Cliff Valley, Mimbres Valley, and other areas fairly often over the long term (Nelson and Anyon 1996).

Continuity in populations, cultural practices, or both is even more difficult to trace between the Early (pre-1300) and Late (post-1300) Postclassic periods. In the Mimbres Valley, pueblos in both periods have coursed-adobe architecture and a broadly similar site layout, and the range of mortuary practices includes a mix of inhumations, primary cremations, and urn cremations (Creel 1999; Lekson 2002; Nelson and Anyon 1996). In the Eastern Mimbres area, a tradition of revisiting sites and making special deposits after their residential use ended may also hint at some continuity. At the Mimbres Classic Flying Fish Village (LA 37767), such deposits included a ring of cobbles surrounding a polished green stone placed high in the post-occupational fill of one room and a turkey vulture (*Cathartes aura*) cranium buried high in similar fill in another room. Roadmap Village also had such deposits from the 1300s or early 1400s. One room held a turkey vulture burial, again placed high in post-occupational fill. The use of turkey vulture is relatively rare in the Puebloan Southwest and may indicate some continuity in beliefs or cultural practices. Another room at Roadmap Village held a series of three pronghorn skulls: one was located in fill near floor level, a second in post-occupational room fill but in the same area of the room, and a third higher up in post-occupational fill but again in the same area of the room. Although these shared patterns are suggestive, it is difficult to say what they mean in terms of the degree of continuity in culture or population in the area. Other researchers maintain that the dramatic population decline after A.D. 1130 makes continuity unlikely and that the many differences in material culture between phases do not suggest cultural continuity across this long time period (LeBlanc 1989; Shafer 1999). The case for a lack of continuity is particularly strong for sites like Pinnacle Ruin, where both architecture and pottery differ markedly from local developments from earlier time periods and from contemporaneous sites nearby (Clark and Laumbach 2011; Lekson et al. 2002).

In conclusion, an examination of the Postclassic period from the perspective of the Eastern Mimbres area highlights some of the most interesting attributes of this time period across the broader region. The decades immediately following the end of the Mimbres Classic period are probably better known for this area than in any other part of the region. In contrast, the late 1200s remain poorly understood here, and sites from the 1300s in particular defy characterization according to the archaeological phases currently in use. The diversity in architecture and ceramics after 1130 reflects the diversity seen in this time period across the region more generally, but the existence of so much diversity across just four drainages is particularly striking. The Eastern Mimbres area transitions from being near the eastern edge of the Mimbres Classic region before 1130 to a position at or just beyond the edge of multiple traditions (Black Mountain, Tularosa, El Paso, and Magdalena phases) after 1130. As other chapters in this volume show, part of the Mimbres Foundation's contribution to archaeology in this region has been to give us a base or core from which to build an increasing appreciation for intraregional diversity in many aspects of material culture over time and space. The Eastern Mimbres area is an example of this, and we hope the work summarized here will follow that tradition of providing a springboard for future studies of continuity and change.

References Cited

Bertram, Jack B., Andrew R. Gomolak, Steven R. Hoagland, Terry L. Knight, Emily Garber, and Kenneth J. Lord. 1990. Excavations in the South Room Block of Gallinas Springs Pueblo (LA 1178), a Large Town of the Gallinas Mountain Phase (Late Pueblo III–Early Pueblo IV) on the Mogosazi Frontier. Manuscript on file, USDA Forest Service, Albuquerque, New Mexico.

Clark, Jeffery J., and Karl W. Laumbach. 2011. Ancestral Pueblo Migrations in the Southern Southwest: Perspectives from Arizona and New Mexico. In *Movement, Connectivity, and Landscape Change in the Ancient Southwest*, edited by Margaret C. Nelson and Colleen Strawhacker, pp. 297–320. University Press of Colorado, Boulder.

Creel, Darrell G. 1999. The Black Mountain Phase in the Mimbres Area. In *The Casas Grandes World*, edited by Curtis F. Schaafsma and Carroll L. Riley, pp. 107–120. University of Utah Press, Salt Lake City.

Douglas, John E. 2004. A Reinterpretation of the Occupational History of the Pendleton Ruin, New Mexico. *Journal of Field Archaeology* 29:425–436.

Ferguson, Jeffrey R., Karl W. Laumbach, Stephen H. Lekson, Margaret C. Nelson, Karen Gust Schollmeyer, Toni S. Laumbach, and Myles R. Miller. 2016. Characterization of Carbon-Painted Ceramics from Southwestern and South Central New Mexico and Implications for Migration. *Kiva* 82:22–50.

Hegmon, Michelle. 2002. Reaggregation: The Black Mountain Phase Occupation of Las Animas Village. Paper presented at the Mogollon Archaeology Conference, Las Cruces, New Mexico.

———. 2017. *Las Animas Village (LA3949): A Large Multicomponent Site in the Eastern Mimbres Area*. Electronic document, https://core.tdar.org/document/433579/las-animas-village-la3949-a-large-multicomponent-site-in-the-eastern-mimbres-area, accessed November 2017.

Hegmon, Michelle, Jennifer A. Brady, and Margaret C. Nelson. 2006. Variability in Classic Mimbres Room Suites: Implications for Household Organization and Social Differences. In *Mimbres Society*, edited by Valli S. Powell-Martí and Patricia A. Gilman, pp. 45–65. University of Arizona Press, Tucson.

Hegmon, Michelle, Margaret C. Nelson, Roger Anyon, Darrell Creel, Steven A. LeBlanc, and Harry J. Shafer. 1999. Scale and Time-Space Systematics in the Post–A.D. 1100 Mimbres Region of the North American Southwest. *Kiva* 65:143–165.

Hegmon, Michelle, Margaret C. Nelson, and Mark J. Ennes. 2000. Corrugated Pottery, Technological Style, and Population Movement in the Mimbres Region of the American Southwest. *Journal of Anthropological Research* 56:217–240.

Hegmon, Michelle, Margaret C. Nelson, and Susan M. Ruth. 1998. Abandonment and Reorganization in the Mimbres Region of the American Southwest. *American Anthropologist* 100:148–162.

Hegmon, Michelle, Margaret C. Nelson, and Karen Gust Schollmeyer. 2016. Experiencing Social Change: Life During the Mimbres Classic Transformation. In *Archaeology of the Human Experience*, edited by Michelle Hegmon, pp. 54–73. Archaeological Papers 27. American Anthropological Association, Washington, D.C.

Knight, Terry L., and Andrew R. Gomolak. 1985. Ceramics. In *Social and Economic Organization of Gallinas Springs Pueblo: A Report on the 1977 Excavations*, edited by Joseph A. Tainter, pp. 100–149. Manuscript on file, Cibola National Forest and Grasslands Supervisor's Office, Albuquerque, New Mexico.

Laumbach, Karl W., and Toni S. Laumbach. 2006. Cañada Alamosa in the Late Eleventh and Early Twelfth Centuries: Perspectives from the Montoya and Kelly Canyon Sites. In *Mostly Mimbres: A Collection of Papers from the 12th Biennial Mogollon Conference*, edited by Marc Thompson, Lori Jackson, and Jason Jurgena, pp. 61–67. El Paso Museum of Archaeology, El Paso, Texas.

LeBlanc, Steven A. 1989. Cultural Dynamics in the Southern Mogollon Area. In *Dynamics of Southwestern Prehistory*, edited by Linda S. Cordell and George. J. Gumerman, pp. 179–208. Smithsonian Institution Press, Washington, D.C.

Lekson, Stephen H. 1989. An Archaeological Reconnaissance of the Rio Grande Valley in Sierra County, New Mexico. *Artifact* 27(2):1–102.

———. 1996. Southwestern New Mexico and Southeastern Arizona, A.D. 900–1300. In *The Prehistoric Pueblo World, A.D. 1100–1300*, edited by Michael A. Adler, pp. 170–176. University of Arizona Press, Tucson.

———. 2002. *Salado Archaeology of the Upper Gila, New Mexico*. Anthropological Papers of the University of Arizona No. 67. University of Arizona Press, Tucson.

Lekson, Stephen H., Curtis P. Nepstad-Thornberry, Brian E. Yunker, Toni S. Laumbach, David P. Cain, and Karl W. Laumbach. 2002. Migrations in the Southwest: Pinnacle Ruin, Southwestern New Mexico. *Kiva* 68:73–101.

Mayo, Jill E. 1994. Garfield Revisited: Further Research on a Mimbres Site in the Southern Rio Grande Valley. Master's thesis, Department of Anthropology, New Mexico State University, Las Cruces.

Miller, Myles R., and Nancy A. Kenmotsu. 2004. Prehistory of the Jornada Mogollon and Eastern Trans-Pecos Regions of West Texas. In *The Prehistory of Texas*, edited by Timothy K. Perttula, pp. 205–265. Texas A&M University Press, College Station.

Minnis, Paul E. 1985. *Social Adaptation to Food Stress: A Prehistoric Southwestern Example*. University of Chicago Press, Chicago.

Nelson, Ben A., and Roger Anyon. 1996. Fallow Valleys: Asynchronous Occupations in Southwestern New Mexico. *Kiva* 61:275–292.

Nelson, Margaret C. 1989. The 1985 Survey on Lower Palomas Creek: An Appendix from an Archaeological Reconnaissance of the Rio Grande Valley in Sierra County, New Mexico. *Artifact* 27(2):89–96.

———. 1993. Changing Occupational Pattern Among Prehistoric Horticulturalists in SW New Mexico. *Journal of Field Archaeology* 20:47–57.

———. 1999. *Mimbres During the Twelfth Century: Abandonment, Continuity, and Reorganization*. University of Arizona Press, Tucson.

Nelson, Margaret C., and Michael W. Diehl. 1999. Foraging and Farming. In *Mimbres During the Twelfth Century: Abandonment, Continuity, and Reorganization*, edited by Margaret C. Nelson, pp. 142–166. University of Arizona Press, Tucson.

Nelson, Margaret C., Michelle Hegmon, Stephanie Kulow, and Karen Gust Schollmeyer. 2006. Archaeological and Ecological Perspectives on Reorganization: A Case Study from the Mimbres Region of the US Southwest. *American Antiquity* 71:403–432.

Nelson, Margaret C., Keith W. Kintigh, David R. Abbott, and John M. Anderies. 2010. The Cross-Scale Interplay Between Social and Biophysical Context and the Vulnerability of Irrigation-Dependent Societies: Archaeology's Long-Term Perspective. *Ecology and*

Society 15(3):31. Electronic document, http://www.ecologyandsociety.org/vol15/iss3/art31/, accessed November 2017.

Pool, Michael David. 2002. Prehistoric Mogollon Agriculture in the Mimbres River Valley, Southwestern New Mexico: A Crop Simulation and GIS Approach. PhD dissertation, University of Texas, Austin. University Microfilms, Ann Arbor.

Russell, Will G. 2010. The Role of El Paso Polychrome in Refining Site Chronology at Roadmap Village and Las Animas Village, New Mexico. *Kiva* 76:7–32.

Russell, Will G., Karen Gust Schollmeyer, Margaret C. Nelson, and Steve Swanson. 2010. Phyllis Pueblo (LA45160): Report on the 2009–10 Excavation Seasons. Report on file, Arizona State University School of Human Evolution and Social Change, Tempe.

Schollmeyer, Karen Gust. 1999. Settlement Size, Environmental Impact and Large Mammal Use in the Mimbres Region, Southwest New Mexico. Master's thesis, Department of Anthropology, Arizona State University, Tempe.

———. 2009. Resource Stress and Settlement Pattern Change in the Eastern Mimbres Area, Southwest New Mexico. PhD dissertation, Arizona State University, Tempe. University Microfilms, Ann Arbor.

———. 2011. Large Game, Agricultural Land, and Settlement Pattern Change in the Eastern Mimbres Area, Southwest New Mexico. *Journal of Anthropological Archaeology* 30:402–415.

Schollmeyer, Karen Gust, and Joan Brenner Coltrain. 2010. Anthropogenic Environments, Resource Stress, and Settlement Pattern Change in the Eastern Mimbres Area. In *The Archaeology of Anthropogenic Environments*, edited by Rebecca M. Dean, pp. 266–294. Occasional Paper No. 37. Center for Archaeological Investigations, Southern Illinois University, Carbondale.

Schollmeyer, Karen Gust, Will G. Russell, and Margaret C. Nelson. 2010. Excavations at Two Thirteenth-Century Villages West of Truth or Consequences. *NewsMAC* 2010-4:2–13.

Shafer, Harry J. 1999. The Mimbres Classic and Postclassic: A Case for Discontinuity. In *The Casas Grandes World*, edited by Curtis F. Schaafsma and Carroll L. Riley, pp. 121–133. University of Utah Press, Salt Lake City.

Swanson, Steve, Karen Gust Schollmeyer, and Margaret C. Nelson. 2008. *Mogollon Prehistoric Landscapes Project: Report of the 2007 Survey*. Bureau of Reclamation Albuquerque Area Office, Albuquerque, New Mexico.

10

Continuity and Change in the Early Postclassic (A.D. 1130 to 1300) in the Mimbres Valley

KATHRYN PUTSAVAGE AND MATTHEW TALIAFERRO

AROUND A.D. 1130, PEOPLE LIVING in the Mimbres Valley, and more broadly in the Mimbres region, dramatically changed their material culture and possibly reorganized their social structures (Creel 1999; Hegmon et al. 1999; LeBlanc 1977, 1980; Nelson 1999; Nelson and Hegmon 2001; Shafer 1999). In the Mimbres Valley, these changes are evidenced by a perceived decrease in population, the cessation of Mimbres Black-on-white pottery production, the introduction of new ceramic types, a change from cobblestone masonry to coursed-adobe architecture, and an apparent shift in mortuary behavior. During the late 1970s, Mimbres Foundation archaeologists were some of the first researchers to note these changes at sites along the Mimbres River (e.g., LeBlanc 1977; LeBlanc and Whalen 1980; Nelson and LeBlanc 1986). From excavation and survey data, the foundation proposed two new Postclassic phases for the Mimbres Valley: the Black Mountain phase (ca. A.D. 1130–1300)[1] and the Cliff phase (ca. A.D. 1300–1450).

More recent research has shown that changes in material culture likely began at the end of the Mimbres Classic period (A.D. 1000–1130) and continued during what is now termed the Terminal Classic (A.D. 1130–1180), a period of transition from the Mimbres Classic to the Early Postclassic or Black Mountain phase (see table I.1; Creel 1999, 2006; Hegmon et al. 1999). The Black Mountain phase is currently suggested to start in the late A.D. 1100s and end around A.D. 1300 (Hegmon et al. 1999; Putsavage 2015:150–192).

For the past forty years, archaeologists have debated the social processes behind the changes in material culture. As noted by Schollmeyer and colleagues in chapter 9, who focus on similar questions for the Postclassic in the Eastern Mimbres region, these debates center on whether the shifts represent population continuity or change. On the one hand, proponents of population continuity argue that resident populations remained in the Mimbres Valley after A.D. 1130 and restructured the organization of their social networks (Creel 1999, 2006; see also Nelson 1999; Nelson and Hegmon 2001). On the other hand, proponents of population change argue that the valley was abandoned at the end of the Mimbres Classic and that migrant populations moved into the region after A.D. 1180, bringing new material culture and social structures (LeBlanc 1977, 1980; Shafer 1999).

While there are numerous social processes that cause change in material culture, we chose to condense these complex processes into an investigation focused on continuity and change in the social systems of the region's Postclassic period occupants. We did this for two reasons. First, previous research in the Mimbres Valley has focused on processes of population continuity versus change and thus provides a framework for the discussion. Second, because several social processes appear to be at play in the changes seen between the Mimbres Classic and Postclassic, the use of continuity and change provides an overarching theory for interpreting these diverse data sets.

In this chapter, we review earlier research to contextualize the debate, focusing mainly on research in the Mimbres Valley (see figure I.1). At the heart of the debate rests the timing of these shifts. New excavation data are helping to refine the Black Mountain phase chronology (Putsavage 2015:150–192). We use data from recent excavations at Old Town (LA 1113) and the Black Mountain site (LA 49; see Figure I.2; Putsavage 2015; Taliaferro 2014) as a proxy for understanding whether the shifts in material culture represent continuity or change in social organization. For example, shifts in mortuary practices are used as a measure of changing ceremonial practices, which may indicate social or political differentiation. Thus, *social organization* refers to the ways in which this society remained stable or restructured its cultural networks and systems at the end of the Classic period. Although changes can be seen in material, many cultural systems provide evidence of continuity. At the same time, there are indications of social reorganization and cultural change. We suggest that both scenarios played a role in material change and indicate the reformation of group identities at the end of the Classic and into the Early Postclassic.

Previous Work on the Early Postclassic Period in the Mimbres Valley

The Mimbres Foundation survey covered over 10,000 ha with greater coverage in the upper and middle Mimbres Valley (Blake et al. 1986). The survey data suggested that during the Black Mountain phase, the lower Mimbres was more heavily populated than the upper and middle portions of the valley. However, since there was less survey coverage in the lower Mimbres Valley, we still do not have a clear picture of site density and population estimates for the Early and Late Postclassic periods. While this sampling bias affects site estimates for all periods in the Mimbres Valley, if people were relocating to the lower Mimbres after A.D. 1130, then the Postclassic period data would be skewed the most.

These site density estimates are further complicated by several factors. Since the Mimbres Foundation survey was one of the first large-scale surveys in the region, site attributes of each period were not fully understood and, therefore, may not have captured the full chronological range at individual sites (Taliaferro 2014:111–114). This is particularly true for Terminal Classic, Black Mountain phase, and Cliff phase sites, which frequently contain adobe architecture and similar diagnostic pottery types (see table I.1; Lekson 2006; Taliaferro 2014). The adobe construction does not preserve as well as the cobble masonry of Mimbres Classic sites and is more difficult to see during survey (Nelson and LeBlanc 1986; Taliaferro 2014; see also Ackerly et al. 1988). Additionally, there is a clear trend through time of locating sites closer to perennial streams (LeBlanc and Whalen 1980; Lekson 2006). Due to this trend in settlement patterns, some Postclassic sites are likely buried by alluvial deposits.

Even with these challenges, the Mimbres Foundation located a total of four hundred sites, seventeen of which were recorded as Black Mountain phase.[2] Of these, only two were excavated: Walsh and Montoya (Blake et al. 1986; LeBlanc 1977, 1980; Ravesloot 1979). Based on material correlates from the Walsh and Montoya sites, such as adobe room blocks, burial practices, and the presence of Chihuahuan polychrome pottery, Mimbres Foundation researchers suggested that people living in the Mimbres Valley during the Early Postclassic had social ties to the Casas Grandes regional system (Blake et al. 1986; LeBlanc 1977, 1980). However, since few chronometric dates have been collected from sites with Terminal Classic and Black Mountain phase components (Hegmon et al. 1999; LeBlanc and Whalen 1980; Putsavage 2015; Taliaferro 2014), it is still not clear if Early Postclassic sites were contemporaneous with the Casas Grandes regional system. Thus, social links between inhabitants of the Mimbres Valley and the Casas Grandes regional system are still tenuous.

The limited chronometric data available for the Terminal Classic and Black Mountain phase have also made it challenging to define the timing of the transition from the Classic to Postclassic (figure 10.1; Anyon et al. 2017). Mimbres Foundation excavations, as well as later projects, recovered about twenty chronometric dates from Terminal Classic and Black Mountain phase structures at Mattocks, Swarts, Old Town, and NAN Ranch (Anyon and LeBlanc 1984:143, 147–148, 316; Creel 2006; LeBlanc and Whalen 1980; Shafer 2003). These archaeomagnetic and radiocarbon dates, along

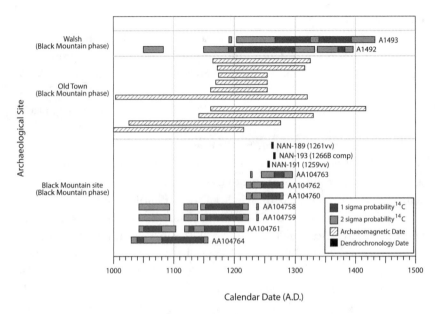

FIGURE 10.1 Chronometric dates for Black Mountain phase sites.

with one tree-ring date, cluster in the A.D. 1120s. The absolute dates recovered from sites in the Mimbres area led Hegmon and colleagues (1999:154–155) to place the beginning of the Terminal Classic period, which represents the transition between the Mimbres Classic and Black Mountain phase, at A.D. 1130 (see also Creel 2006; LeBlanc and Whalen 1980; Shafer 2003).

Archaeomagnetic and two radiocarbon samples collected from Black Mountain phase hearths at the Walsh site (LeBlanc and Whalen 1980:515; Lekson 2011; Taliaferro 2014), as well as seventeen "tentative" tree-rings dates from the Montoya site, cluster in the A.D. 1180s (Hegmon et al. 1999:161; LeBlanc and Whalen 1980:532). These data led LeBlanc (1977) to suggest a start date of A.D. 1180 for the Black Mountain phase (see Hegmon et al. 1999). However, many of these data came from non-stratigraphic contexts, such as backfill, and the dendrochronology samples do not overlap with the master tree-ring chronology for the region. Thus, these dates may best be understood as indicating that the A.D. 1180s were included in the span of the Black Mountain phase.

While some chronometric data are available for the Terminal Classic and Black Mountain phase, most samples have not allowed for the chronological refinement necessary to answer questions surrounding the fifty- to seventy-five-year period of the social transformation. Moreover, many of the ceramics common in Terminal Classic, Black Mountain phase, and Cliff phase assemblages, such as the Playas series,

Chupadero Black-on-white, and El Paso Polychrome, were produced over long time spans and are therefore not useful for refining the phase chronology (Nelson and LeBlanc 1986:105). Clearly, one of the foci for future research is the establishment of a more fine-grained Postclassic chronology (Anyon et al. 2017).

Debates Surrounding Postclassic Change and Continuity in the Mimbres Valley

As we have highlighted, the Terminal Classic period and Black Mountain phase in the Mimbres Valley encompass some of the most poorly investigated phases of southwestern New Mexico (Hegmon et al. 1999; Nelson and LeBlanc 1986; Shafer 2006:31). While this is partially due to the relative lack of excavation and high amount of diversity present at sites postdating A.D. 1130, lack of chronometric data and slightly different chronologies for the subregions further complicate discussions concerning the timing of the transition (see table I.1). Differences in the chronologies proposed by archaeologists seem to represent the various ways in which populations addressed the shifts at the end of the Mimbres Classic. For example, there appear to be differences in material culture and exchange networks, especially after the twelfth century, among people in the Mimbres Valley, Eastern Mimbres, and upper Gila (chapter 9; Dungan 2015:127–168; Fitting 1973; Nelson and LeBlanc 1986).

A key issue for this chapter is whether the shifts in material culture around A.D. 1130 represent population continuity, change, or a combination of these scenarios. Initially, Mimbres Foundation researchers suggested that only some parts of the Mimbres Valley were completely depopulated after A.D. 1130 and that Classic period populations reaggregated in the lower Mimbres Valley and southern portions of the region (LeBlanc 1977; LeBlanc and Whalen 1980). LeBlanc (1977:16) specifically notes that the populations inhabiting Black Mountain phase sites were "made up of an agglomeration of previously unrelated peoples . . . [and that] the presence of flexed inhumations with 'killed' bowls represents a continuation of the Mimbres tradition." However, because of the decreased site density and marked differences in material culture and settlement patterns, research began to focus on the "abandonment" of the Mimbres region. Anyon and colleagues (1981:220), for example, proposed that "with the end of the Mimbres Classic phase, the long Mogollon-Mimbres sequence also terminates." The authors suggest that the Black Mountain phase represents a cultural break and that new populations moved into the Mimbres Valley around A.D. 1180 (see also LeBlanc 1989; Shafer 1999). Thus, subsequent research has debated whether this fifty- to seventy-five-year period (A.D. 1130–late 1100s/early 1200s) was characterized primarily by continuity or change of social structures.

Several scholars (Anyon and LeBlanc 1984:24; LeBlanc 1980, 1989; Shafer 1999) have proposed that the Mimbres Valley was depopulated during the Terminal Classic for about fifty years after the Mimbres Classic period. They argue that the Black Mountain phase began in the early A.D. 1200s and new populations, possibly from the Jornada Mogollon to the east or Chihuahua, Mexico, to the south, settled in the southern parts of the Mimbres Valley. Although these scholars acknowledge that some traits show a connection between the people living during the Black Mountain phase and the Mimbres Classic period, they argue that the Black Mountain phase represents a cultural and, in part, a demographic break (Blake et al. 1986; LeBlanc 1989:192–194; Shafer 1999:131–133). The decrease in flexed inhumations with "killed" bowls and the increase in cremations, the shift from masonry to adobe architecture, and most importantly, the cessation of Mimbres Classic Black-on-white pottery signified an abandonment of Classic period ideologies (Shafer 1999:131–133).

Creel (1999, 2006) and Taliaferro (2014), on the other hand, have argued that populations continued to inhabit the valley, at a greatly reduced density, during the Terminal Classic period (A.D. 1130–1180) and Black Mountain phase (A.D. 1180–1300). Creel (2006) proposes that the Terminal Classic is a short period marking the beginning of significant changes in material culture. Many Classic period practices persisted during the Terminal Classic and Black Mountain phase, such as the use of killed bowls in burials and the organization of lithic and ceramic technologies. In the Mimbres Valley, there is strong evidence that some of the ceramic types (Playas Red, Chupadero Black-on-white, and El Paso Polychrome) the Mimbres Foundation noted as particular to the Black Mountain phase first appear at the end of Mimbres Classic and beginning of the Terminal Classic (Creel 1999:108–110, 116–117). Additionally, adobe-lined circular hearths, an architectural trait that the Mimbres Foundation used to suggest a connection to Casas Grandes, are documented at Late Pithouse and Classic period sites in the Mimbres region (Creel 1999). Thus, the scholars who are proponents of continuity argue that although changes are apparent in material culture, some populations remained in the valley.

For the Eastern Mimbres, Hegmon and colleagues (1999) call the period immediately following the Mimbres Classic the Reorganization phase (Nelson and Hegmon 2001). As summarized in chapter 9, there are important differences between the events in the Mimbres Valley and the Eastern Mimbres area from A.D. 1130 to A.D. 1200. Unlike in the Mimbres Valley, where food stress appears to have played a role in depopulation (Minnis 1985; Pool 2002), in the Eastern Mimbres people had access to more resources even in the face of environmental stress (Schollmeyer 2011). Additionally, in the Eastern Mimbres, researchers propose that the Black Mountain phase began in the early A.D. 1200s and ended at 1300, but it may have lasted until the 1400s. Since the focus of this chapter is the Mimbres Valley, we will not elaborate on events in the Eastern Mimbres beyond noting that research in the area also provides evidence of both population continuity and change (see chapter 9).

Evidence for Early Postclassic Continuity and Change in the Mimbres Valley

As we have emphasized, the Mimbres Valley contains evidence for population continuity and change around A.D. 1130. In the following sections, we review new research at Old Town (Taliaferro 2014) and the Black Mountain site (Putsavage 2015) and examine previous compositional analyses on obsidian and ceramic samples from several sites in the Mimbres Valley (see figure I.2). These new investigations track obsidian and ceramic exchange, architectural patterns, and mortuary practices from the Mimbres Classic through the Black Mountain phase as a proxy for examining cultural continuity or change.

Old Town is in the lower Mimbres Valley on a small bluff overlooking the Mimbres River. The presence of Pithouse period, Mimbres Classic period, Terminal Classic period, and Black Mountain phase occupations make the Old Town site an important case study for this chapter. Black Mountain is the type site for the Black Mountain phase. It is located in the lower Mimbres Valley, roughly 15 km northwest of Deming, New Mexico. The site includes three distinct areas of architecture: a Late Pithouse period component, a Black Mountain phase room block with Black Mountain phase pit structures built below the room block, and a large Cliff phase pueblo, which appears to be built over earlier, presumably Black Mountain phase, structures (Putsavage 2015:150–192). The Black Mountain site does not contain Mimbres Classic or Terminal Classic occupations. Chronometric data suggest that the Black Mountain site was first occupied in the late A.D. 1100s with habitation ending around 1320 (Putsavage 2015:150–192). Thus, Old Town and the Black Mountain site provide a snapshot of the Mimbres Valley prior to and well after the social reorganization beginning around A.D. 1130. While both sites have been extensively disturbed by hand and mechanical looting or grading, data recovered from these sites are revealing new insights about the Postclassic period and represent the lasting impact of the Mimbres Foundation's preservation work at heavily looted sites.

Taliaferro's (2014) research at Old Town and Putsavage's (2015) work at the Black Mountain site focus on several classes of data: chronometric, architectural, lithic, ceramic, and mortuary. These attributes were examined for the Mimbres Classic period, the Terminal Classic period, and the Black Mountain phase and compared through time. Generally, we suggest that if these suites of attributes show consistency through time, then we have evidence of cultural continuity, whereas changes in attributes could indicate the influx of migrants. Yet during fluid, liminal periods such as the Postclassic, it can be difficult for archaeologists to detect and define the population composition of sites and regions (see Cabana 2011; Cameron 2008, 2014; Ortman and Cameron 2008). How can we distinguish resident groups (people who continued to live in the Mimbres Valley) from migrants (those who moved in from surrounding communities) during periods of change and population decline? Although the picture is far more complex than this overly simplified dichotomy (resident versus migrant) suggests, by building on previous research (Anyon and LeBlanc 1984; Creel 1999, 2006; Hegmon et al. 1999; LeBlanc 1980, 1989; Shafer 1999), these extensive data sets from Old Town and the Black Mountain site are helping to further clarify the lives of Postclassic peoples.

Evidence for Continuity

In the following section, we summarize evidence for population continuity through the investigation of architectural layout and construction, lithic and ceramic technologies, and mortuary practices. Research at Old Town shows that many social structures remained fairly constant from the Mimbres Classic through the Black Mountain phase (Taliaferro 2014). Yet there is evidence, such as the termination of Mimbres Black-on-white pottery production, that may be linked to Classic period ideologies (Brody 2004; Gilman et al. 2014; Moulard 1984; Shafer 2003), suggesting that populations who remained in the valley were reforming group identities. Thus, population continuity does not suggest complete stability in social structures (see Putsavage 2015).

Several researchers note a change in construction materials from cobble masonry to coursed adobe from the Mimbres Classic period to Black Mountain phase (Creel 1999; LeBlanc 1977; Shafer 1999). While Early Postclassic architecture at both Old Town and the Black Mountain site follows this trend, the construction of the Black Mountain phase room-block walls demonstrate technological continuity with Mimbres Classic construction. Taliaferro (2014:179–186) notes large quantities of masonry cobbles in wall fall at Old Town and proposes that the lower portions of the Black Mountain phase walls may have contained masonry architecture in some wall sections. At the Black Mountain site, excavation of adobe room-block walls revealed that they were made with large footing stones placed in wall trenches (Putsavage 2015:187–192). The adobe coursings above the footing stones contained coursings of cobbles (figure 10.2). Construction techniques at Old Town and Black Mountain thus show similarities to earlier Classic period structures (Cosgrove and Cosgrove 1932; Creel 2006; Shafer 2003). While Mimbres Classic period structures used footing stones, the use of footing stones and coursed adobe may also demonstrate similarities

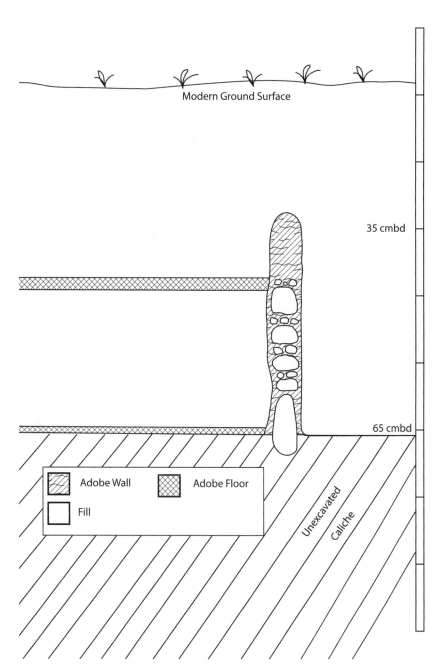

FIGURE 10.2 Mimbres-like footer stones in Black Mountain component adobe walls at the Black Mountain site.

to construction techniques in northern Chihuahua and northern Sonora, Mexico (Lekson 2002:72). Wall-construction techniques are just one of the many technological attributes that could suggest affinity to more than one cultural area. As we will discuss, attributes associated with other technological systems (i.e., ceramic and lithic technologies) are not clearly differentiated along cultural lines.

Although room size tended to increase from the Classic period through the Black Mountain phase, the size of room suites remained consistent (Taliaferro 2014:179–185). Additionally, intramural features show consistency in location and use through time. Since Shafer (1982) proposes that these room suites represent family or household units during the Mimbres Classic period, the consistent size of room suites and similar location of room features provide evidence of similar social groups occupying these structures during both the Mimbres Classic and Early Postclassic.

The analysis of informal and formal chipped-stone tool use at Old Town also provides preliminary evidence of social continuity (Taliaferro 2014:188–302). For informal tool production and use, we have limited comparative data for the Classic period (but see Dockall 1991; Nelson 1981). Overall, lithic technology was organized as a generalized strategy. People in the Mimbres region predominantly used easily accessible raw materials from the immediate vicinity of settlements (Nelson 1996; Taliaferro 2014). The fact that raw material exploitation shows relatively little fluctuation through time suggests that groups inhabiting the area from the Late Pithouse period through the Black Mountain phase used similar design strategies in their organization of informal tool production.

The formal stone tool assemblages demonstrate that the inhabitants of the Mimbres Valley implemented a specialized design strategy in the fabrication of some tools, specifically projectile points (Nelson 1996; Taliaferro 2014). The most common raw material for formal tools was obsidian, and the use of obsidian increased through time. While the production of lithic materials was commonly organized in this manner, with easily accessible materials used for informal tools and higher quality materials used for more formal tools (Andrefsky 2009; Arakawa et al. 2011; Clark et al. 2011; Clark et al. 2012; Shackley 2002), the consistency in the organization of lithic technology through time indicates population continuity as opposed to population replacement.

An examination of pottery production and use from the Late Pithouse period through the Black Mountain phase also provides evidence of continuity (Putsavage 2015:193–249; Taliaferro 2014:303–339, 404–414). Focusing on ceramics from Old Town, Taliaferro (2014) considered production sequence, organization of production, use-wear, and vessel form and function. Part-time specialists made pottery during the Mimbres Classic period (Gilman 1989; Gilman et al. 1994; LeBlanc 1983:138–139, 2006; but see Shafer 1985, 2003), and this practice continued during the Black Mountain phase based on similarities in the context, concentration, scale, and intensity of pottery production within the Mimbres area through time (Taliaferro 2014:303–339, 404–414).

Ceramic use characteristics and the form and function of ceramics from the Black Mountain phase occupation at Old Town also point to continuity in the use of ceramics during the Classic and Postclassic periods. Specifically, the contexts of vessel forms (jars and bowls) were similar during the Classic period and the Black Mountain phase. During the Classic period, bowls were more common in burials, domestic contexts, and midden deposits at NAN Ranch, whereas jars were more frequently associated with domestic and midden deposits (Lyle 1996). Lyle (1996) attributes these differences to the more varied functions of bowls (food serving, preparation, storage, and semiotic signaling) when compared to jars, which were primarily used for food preparation and storage. The occurrence of vessel forms in similar contexts from the Late Pithouse period through the Black Mountain phase suggests that the social practices dictating the appropriate use of different vessel forms were similarly structured through these periods.

Neutron activation analysis (NAA) data on ceramic production and exchange suggest that Black Mountain phase inhabitants continued to rely on clay sources that had been widely used during the Mimbres Classic (Putsavage 2015:193–239; Taliaferro 2014:340–414). In the context of Taliaferro's (2014) study, the long-term use of clay resources provides preliminary evidence that some potters who lived in the Mimbres Valley before A.D. 1130 remained in the valley and procured clay resources used by previous generations (also see Shafer 2006, which suggests that residential spaces were passed on through kinship base groups). Since clays are socially constituted resources (Jones 2005) and there were a range of physically appropriate clays in the Mimbres Valley (Creel et al. 2002; Gilman et al. 1994; Taliaferro 2014), the long-term use of clays may provide additional evidence for continuity.

While the investigation of mortuary practices through time reveals changes between the Mimbres Classic and Black Mountain phase with an increase in cremations (LeBlanc 1977; Shafer 1999), burial practices also showed several similarities (Creel 1999; Taliaferro 2014:415–440). Subfloor inhumations, which were the most common burial method during the Late Pithouse and Mimbres Classic periods (Creel 1989; Shafer 1995), greatly outnumber cremations during the Black Mountain phase by a ratio of 5:1. Many of these inhumations had killed vessels placed over the individuals' heads (Creel 1999; Taliaferro 2014: 415–440), a practice that was common during the Late Pithouse and Classic periods (Creel 1989; Shafer 1995). Although the ceramics used in burials during the Black Mountain phase change to later types, such as Playas Red and Chupadero Black-on-white, the persistence of this practice suggests a historical and social link to Mimbres Classic populations.

Taken individually, these lines of evidence provide a tenuous link between Mimbres Classic and Black Mountain phase populations. As a whole, they suggest that at least some resident populations remained in the Mimbres Valley during the Terminal Classic and into the Black Mountain phase (after A.D. 1130). Some residents may have stayed in the region until at least the early 1300s. The evidence for continuity is complicated by the numerous changes in architecture, compositional studies, and mortuary data. These data, as we will discuss, indicate social reorganization by resident populations and/or migrants moving into the region sometime after A.D. 1130. Importantly for archaeological investigations of cultural change, these data highlight how stability and continuity may accompany what otherwise appears to be radical change.

Evidence for Change

Research by the Mimbres Foundation on the Early Postclassic suggested the possibility that migrant populations moved into the valley as early as A.D. 1180 (Hegmon et al. 1999; LeBlanc 1977). Recent research supports the idea that some resident populations remained during the Terminal Classic and Black Mountain phase (Creel 1999, 2006; Putsavage 2015; Taliaferro 2014) and, at the same time, also highlights that changes in social organization were simultaneously occurring (Putsavage 2015). Although this investigation has not been able to delineate the exact social processes behind the material culture changes (shifting exchange networks, immigration, or some other process), several lines of evidence hint at the possibility that migrant populations may have moved into the valley after A.D. 1130. Below we discuss shifts in ceramic production and exchange, obsidian procurement and exchange, and burial practices to illuminate possible changes in social organization after 1130.

Compositional analyses demonstrate change as well as stability. While several clay sources were exploited during the Mimbres Classic through the Postclassic, several were first used during the Early Postclassic (Putsavage 2015:193–239; Speakman 2013; Taliaferro 2014:340–414). At the Black Mountain site, two of these new clay sources (Group 2a and 2b) were used to make most Black Mountain phase Chihuahuan polychromes (Putsavage 2015:193–239). Petrographic analyses suggest that these vessels were made in the Mimbres Valley (Britton 2014) and could indicate either the appearance of migrants or closer ties to the Casas Grandes region. While the use of new clay sources may imply the influx of new populations who did not have access to sources used by resident populations, there are a number of other processes that could explain the reliance on new sources. These include, but are not limited to, population fluctuations, stream-channel dynamics, the availability of adequate fuels for vessel firing, shifting ideas about which clay sources were acceptable for making pottery, and changes in pottery-exchange networks.

Putsavage's (2015:240–284) study of the history of obsidian procurement and exchange also provides insight into changes around A.D. 1130. She collated obsidian data from eighteen sites in the Mimbres region (figure 10.3; table 10.1; see also Taliaferro et al. 2010). Some samples from previous analyses (Putsavage 2015:table 7.3) were collected from multicomponent sites and often lack provenience data that allow for the assignment of a sample to a specific temporal period. Taliaferro and colleagues (2010:544–545) propose that exchange patterns first seen in the Late Pithouse period continued through the Classic; therefore, the samples from these two periods were combined for all sites. Because previous research has shown differences in the environment, in the diversity of ceramic assemblages, and in obsidian-exchange networks for sites north and south of Old Town (Dolan 2016; Minnis 1985; Taliaferro et al. 2010), the obsidian analyses were grouped by sites north of Old Town (middle/lower Mimbres Valley) and sites south of Old Town (lower Mimbres Valley basin and range; Dolan 2016; Putsavage 2015; Taliaferro et al. 2010).

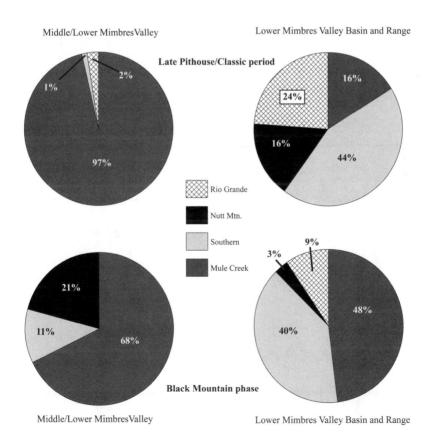

FIGURE 10.3 The percentage of obsidian source use through time.

TABLE 10.1 Obsidian Totals for the Late Pithouse/Classic Period and the Black Mountain Phase

	Mule Creek	Southern	Nutt Mtn.	Rio Grande	Unknown	Total Sample
Late Pithouse/Classic period Total	*339*	*68*	*24*	*43*	*1*	*475*
Lower Mimbres Total	24	65	24	35	—	148
Black Mountain	3	3	1	—	—	7
Florida Mountain	9	29	—	1	—	39
Kipp	11	33	1	16	—	61
LA 173885	1	—	4	17	—	22
LA 176740	—	—	18	1	—	19
Middle/Lower Mimbres Total	*315*	*3*	*—*	*8*	*1*	*327*
Galaz	87	—	—	3	—	90
LA 111395	17	—	—	—	—	17
LA 111413	21	—	—	—	—	21
Old Town	166	3	—	5	1	175
Swarts	24	—	—	—	—	24
Black Mountain phase Total	*87*	*48*	*14*	*10*	*9*	*168*
Lower Mimbres Total	51	42	3	10	9	115
Black Mountain	51	42	3	10	9	115
Middle/Lower Mimbres Total	*36*	*6*	*11*	*—*	*—*	*53*
Montoya	7	—	7	—	—	14
Old Town	12	2	—	—	—	14
Walsh	17	4	4	—	—	25
Total Sample	**426**	**116**	**38**	**53**	**10**	**643**

Note: Lower Mimbres includes Lower Mimbres Valley basin and range (sites south of Old Town) and Middle/Lower Mimbres Valley includes sites north of Old Town.

Compositional analyses show variation in obsidian-exchange networks between the middle/lower Mimbres Valley and lower Mimbres Valley basin and range through time. They also show a shift in obsidian-source use between and among regions from the Late Pithouse and Mimbres Classic periods to the Black Mountain phase: an overall decrease in the amount of obsidian from the Mule Creek sources for the middle/lower Mimbres and an increase in Mule Creek for the lower Mimbres basin and range (figure 10.4; see table 10.1; Putsavage 2015:240–284). An important consideration is the frequency of the Nutt Mountain source. The Nutt Mountain obsidian source was first identified in 2008 and has not been considered in many recent studies (Shackley 2014). Therefore, earlier studies (e.g., Putsavage 2015:table 7.3; Taliaferro et al. 2010) may not have captured this source in their analyses. While low samples sizes may be driving some of the variation among geographic regions and periods, these data currently suggest a shift in obsidian exchange from the Late Pithouse and Classic periods to the Black Mountain phase.

Since Mule Creek was the most common source of obsidian in the Mimbres Valley from the Late Archaic through the Classic period (Taliaferro et al. 2010:544–545), the shift in procurement and exchange patterns for the middle/lower Mimbres may signify that new populations were moving into the valley after A.D. 1130. It may also indicate population influx into the source area as opposed to the valley or changes in socioeconomic arrangements. For the lower Mimbres Valley basin and range, the increase in Mule Creek obsidian may indicate populations moving south from northern portions of the valley (see Blake et al. 1986). In an earlier study, Taliaferro and colleagues (2010) suggested that the common occurrence of Mule Creek obsidian material could have been related to socio-ideological practices and therefore deeply tied to identity. Thus, the shifting use of Mule Creek obsidian in both subregions may also hint at local resident populations who continued to live in the Mimbres Valley.

There was a noticeable shift in mortuary practices between the Mimbres Classic period and the Black Mountain phase, and this also provides preliminary evidence of changing social organization and possibly the influx of populations from outside of the Mimbres Valley. During the Late Pithouse and Classic periods, deceased individuals were commonly interred beneath floors in the Mimbres Valley (Shafer 1995). While cremations were not an entirely new practice before the Black Mountain phase, they became far more common during this period, and they indicate changing ideas about how to care for the dead (Taliaferro 2014:415–425). The increase in cremations may also indicate the migration of nonresident populations into the Mimbres Valley (LeBlanc 1977). Sampling strategies on Late Pithouse and Classic sites, however, have biased these data. Several researchers have established that cremations are more commonly located in extramural areas at these earlier sites (Creel 1989; Shafer 1991, 2003). Since most excavations in the Mimbres have targeted intramural areas, cremations are

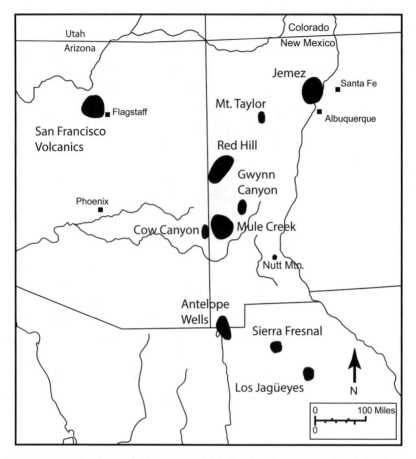

FIGURE 10.4 Southwest obsidian sources: Mule Creek exchange network includes all the Mule Creek sources, Cow Canyon, and Gwynn Canyon; southern exchange network includes Antelope Wells, Sierra Fresnal, and Los Jagüeyes; Rio Grande exchange network includes Jemez sources and Mount Taylor. Adapted from Shackley 2005.

likely underrepresented in the data set. Thus, the examination of mortuary practices suggests a link to practices from earlier periods, as well as a shift in mortuary practices with an increase in cremations.

Conclusion and Future Research

Highlighting the need for further research on the Black Mountain phase, Shafer (2006:31) comments, "Archaeologists know so little about the Black Mountain phase sites that follow the Mimbres Classic phase that one cannot even begin to speculate on how the society may have been structured." While recent research has greatly contributed to our understanding of the Early Postclassic period in the Mimbres Valley, the data are still limited.

There is strong evidence that population continuity and change played a role in the events that occurred after A.D. 1130. Small groups of resident Classic period people continued to inhabit several sites throughout the Mimbres Valley into the Early Postclassic period, while others established sites, such as Black Mountain, Walsh, and Montoya, that were not adjacent to Classic period sites. As evidenced by architectural construction and layout, lithic and ceramic production and exchange, and mortuary practices, some individuals in these groups continued Classic period economic, social, and political practices even in the face of other transformations.

These same data also highlight changes that could indicate transforming social processes, including the restructuring of exchange networks and the immigration of new groups. Previous research has shown that ceramic type variability increased at the end of the Classic period (Hegmon et al. 1998; Nelson and Hegmon 2001). Recent compositional analyses demonstrate shifts from the Classic period through the Black Mountain phase in the procurement and exchange of clay, pottery, and obsidian. Mortuary practices were also changing as cremations increased. At present, it is unclear where these practices originated. Additionally, the shift from cobble masonry to adobe could suggest links to Casas Grandes. Because delineating the social processes behind these changes in material culture is difficult, we need to further operationalize what they mean for social organization and when these changes occurred in the Early Postclassic.

We suggest that during periods of population decline and social reorganization it is especially difficult to discern evidence of migrant groups (see Abbott 2003; Ortman and Cameron 2008). Importantly, evidence for an overall population decrease does not eliminate the possibility that migrants may have played a role in this transition. In the case of the transition from Mimbres Classic to the Terminal Classic and Black Mountain phase, we need more accurate regional, subregional, and site-level population histories to determine whether immigrant groups were involved in the transition. The current evidence suggests that resident group continuity was not antithetical to the changes seen around A.D. 1130. The continuation of practices from the Classic to the Early Postclassic periods and the immigration of new populations during the Postclassic, which were both situated in long-term practices, may have informed the reorganization of social, economic, and political networks and played a role in the reinvention or reformation of group identities—the central question of the Postclassic social reorganization.

While recent data are helping to refine the timing and social processes behind the reorganization, work is still needed. In particular, we need chronometric data to develop a more precise timing of the transition to the Early Postclassic. While research at the Black Mountain site has shown that the Black Mountain phase likely continued, at least at this site, into the early A.D. 1300s, the transitions between the Classic period, Terminal Classic period, and Black Mountain phase are still open areas of research. The chronometric data are key to unraveling the possible connections between people in the Mimbres Valley and the rise of the Casas Grades regional system. The Late Postclassic period in the Mimbres Valley (Cliff phase), which has even less chronometric resolution, is also significant for understanding connections to the Casas Grandes regional system and the large-scale social reorganization seen throughout the southern Southwest after A.D. 1300. For these Late Postclassic period sites, especially in the Mimbres Valley, similar questions concerning continuity versus change remain.

Notes

1. Early researchers in southern New Mexico had a variety of phase designation for sites that contained polychrome pottery and adobe architecture. In extreme southwestern New Mexico, sites with these characteristics were labeled as Animas phase (Kidder et al. 1949), whereas sites in southeastern New Mexico were El Paso phase (Lehmer 1948). Some sites in the Mimbres Valley were initially labeled as Animas phase. In 1977 LeBlanc called for renaming the Early Postclassic period in the Mimbres region the Black Mountain phase. The main differences between Black Mountain phase sites and contemporaneous sites in the surrounding areas is the higher proportion of Playas Red Ware, architectural and settlement patterns, and mortuary patterns (see table I.1).

2. Only twelve Black Mountain phase sites were used in the Mimbres Foundation's population reconstruction because it was not possible to gauge room sizes for five of the sites with Black Mountain phase occupations (Blake et al. 1986).

References Cited

Abbott, David R. 2003. *Centuries of Decline During the Hohokam Classic Period at Pueblo Grande.* University of Arizona Press, Tucson.

Ackerly, Neal W., Cody B. Browning, Mary G. Canavan, and Michael Johnson. 1988. *A Preliminary Evaluation of Prehistoric Settlement Patterns in Grant and Luna Counties, New Mexico: Results of a Sample Survey on State of New Mexico Lands.* Report No. 657. Center for Archaeological Research, New Mexico State University, Las Cruces.

Andrefsky, William. 2009. The Analysis of Stone Tool Procurement, Production, and Maintenance. *Journal of Archaeological Research* 17:65–103.

Anyon, Roger, Darrell Creel, Patricia A. Gilman, Steven A. LeBlanc, Myles R. Miller, Stephen E. Nash, Margaret C. Nelson, Kathryn J. Putsavage, Barbara J. Roth, Karen Gust Schollmeyer, Jakob W. Sedig, and Christopher A. Turnbow. 2017. Re-evaluating the Mimbres Region Prehispanic Chronometric Record. *Kiva* 83:316–343.

Anyon, Roger, Patricia A. Gilman, and Steven A. LeBlanc. 1981. A Reevaluation of the Mogollon-Mimbres Archaeology Sequence. *Kiva* 46:209–225.

Anyon, Roger, and Steven A. LeBlanc. 1984. *The Galaz Ruin: A Prehistoric Mimbres Village in Southwestern New Mexico*. Maxwell Museum of Anthropology and University of New Mexico Press, Albuquerque.

Arakawa, Fumiyasu, Scott G. Ortman, M. Steven Shackley, and Andrew I. Duff. 2011. Obsidian Evidence of Interaction and Migration from the Mesa Verde Region, Southwest Colorado. *American Antiquity* 76:773–795.

Blake, Michael, Steven A. LeBlanc, and Paul E. Minnis. 1986. Changing Settlement and Population in the Mimbres Valley, SW New Mexico. *Journal of Field Archaeology* 13:439–464.

Britton, Emma. 2014. Petrographic Analysis Report: Black Mountain Site, New Mexico. Manuscript on file, Anthropology Department, University of California, Santa Cruz.

Brody, J. J. 2004. *Mimbres Painted Pottery*. Rev. ed. School of American Research Press, Santa Fe, New Mexico.

Cabana, Graciela S. 2011. The Problematic Relationship Between Migration and Culture Change. In *Rethinking Anthropological Perspectives on Migration*, edited by Graciela S. Cabana and Jeffery J. Clark, pp. 16–30. University Press of Florida, Gainesville.

Cameron, Catherine M. 2008. Introduction: Captives in Prehistory as Agents of Social Change. In *Invisible Citizens: Captives and Their Consequences*, edited by Catherine M. Cameron, pp. 1–24. University of Utah Press, Salt Lake City.

———. 2014. Commodities or Gifts? Captive/Slaves in Small-Scale Societies. In *The Archaeology of Slavery: A Comparative Approach to Captivity and Coercion*, edited by Lydia Wilson Marshall, pp. 24–40. Southern Illinois University Press, Carbondale.

Clark, Jeffery J., M. Steven Shackley, J. Brett Hill, W. Randy Haas Jr., and Matthew Peeples. 2012. Long Distance Obsidian Circulation in the late Pre-contact Southwest: Deviating from Distance-Decay. Paper presented at the 77th Annual Meeting of the Society for American Archaeology, Memphis, Tennessee.

Clark, Jeffery J., M. Steven Shackley, Robert Jones, and Stacy Ryan. 2011. Through Volcanic Glass: Measuring the Impact of Ancestral Puebloan Immigration on the Hohokam World. Paper presented at the 76th Annual Meeting of the Society for American Archaeology, Sacramento, California.

Cosgrove, C. B., and H. B. Cosgrove. 1932. *The Swarts Ruin, A Typical Mimbres Site in Southwestern New Mexico*. Papers of the Peabody Museum of American Archaeology and Ethnology Vol. 15(1). Harvard University, Cambridge, Massachusetts.

Creel, Darrell. 1989. A Primary Harvard Cremation at the NAN Ranch Ruin, with Comparative Data on Other Cremations in the Mimbres Area, New Mexico. *Journal of Field Archaeology* 16:309–329.

———. 1999. The Black Mountain Phase in the Mimbres Area. In *The Casas Grandes World*, edited by Curtis Schaafsma and Carroll Riley, pp. 107–120. University of Utah Press, Salt Lake City.

———. 2006. *Excavations at the Old Town Ruin Luna County, New Mexico, 1989–2003.* Cultural Resource Series 16, Vol. 1. Bureau of Land Management, New Mexico State Office, Santa Fe.

Creel, Darrell, Matthews Williams, Hector Neff, and Michael D. Glascock. 2002. Black Mountain Phase Ceramics and Implications for Manufacture and Exchange Patterns. In *Ceramic Production and Circulation in the Greater Southwest: Source Determination by INAA and Complementary Mineralogical Investigations*, edited by Donna M. Glowacki and Hector Neff, pp. 37–46. Cotsen Institute of Archaeology, University of California, Los Angeles.

Dockall, John E. 1991. Chipped Stone Technology at the NAN Ruin, Grant County, New Mexico. Master's thesis, Department of Anthropology, Texas A&M University, College Station.

Dolan, Sean G. 2016. Black Rocks in the Borderlands: Obsidian Procurement in Southwestern New Mexico and Northwestern Chihuahua, Mexico, A.D. 1000 to 1450. PhD dissertation, Department of Anthropology, University of Oklahoma, Norman.

Dungan, Katherine. 2015. Religious Architecture and Borderland Histories: Great Kivas in the Prehispanic Southwest, 1000 to 1400 CE. PhD dissertation, School of Anthropology, University of Arizona, Tucson.

Fitting, James E. 1973. *Four Archaeological Sites in the Big Burro Mountains of New Mexico.* COAS Monograph No. 1. COAS Publishing & Research, Las Cruces, New Mexico.

Gilman, Patricia A. 1989. Households, Communities, and Painted Pottery in the Mimbres Region of Southwestern New Mexico. In *Households and Communities: Proceedings of the 21st Annual Conference of the Archaeological Association of the University of Calgary*, edited by Scott MacEachern, David J. W. Archer, and Richard D. Garvin, pp. 218–226. University of Calgary, Calgary, Alberta.

Gilman, Patricia A., Veletta Canouts, and Ronald L. Bishop. 1994. The Production and Distribution of Classic Mimbres Black-on-white Pottery. *American Antiquity* 59:695–709.

Gilman, Patricia A., Marc Thompson, and Kristina C. Wyckoff. 2014. Ritual Change and the Distant: Mesoamerican Iconography, Scarlet Macaws, and Great Kivas in the Mimbres Region of Southwestern New Mexico. *American Antiquity* 79:90–107.

Hegmon, Michelle, Margaret C. Nelson, Roger Anyon, Darrell Creel, Steven A. LeBlanc, and Harry J. Shafer. 1999. Scale and Time-Space Systematics in the Post–A.D. 1100 Mimbres Region of the North American Southwest. *Kiva* 65:143–166.

Hegmon, Michelle, Margaret C. Nelson, and Susan M. Ruth. 1998. Abandonment and Reorganization in the Mimbres Region of the American Southwest. *American Anthropologist* 100:148–162.

Jones, Andrew. 2005. Lives in Fragments? Personhood and the European Neolithic. *Journal of Social Archaeology* 5:193–224.

Kidder, A. V., H. Cosgrove, and C. Cosgrove. 1949. *The Pendleton Ruin, Hidalgo County, New Mexico*. Carnegie Institution of Washington Contributions to American Anthropology and Archaeology Vol. 10(50). Carnegie Institution, Washington, D.C.

LeBlanc, Steven A. 1977. The 1976 Field Season of the Mimbres Foundation in Southwestern New Mexico. *Journal of New World Archaeology* 2(2):1–23.

———. 1980. The Post-Mogollon Periods in Southwestern New Mexico: The Animas/Black Mountain Phase and the Salado Period. In *An Archaeological Synthesis of South-Central and Southwestern New Mexico*, edited by Steven A. LeBlanc and Michael E. Whalen, pp. 271–316. Office of Contract Archaeology, University of New Mexico, Albuquerque.

———. 1983. *The Mimbres People: Ancient Pueblo Painters of the American Southwest*. Thames and Hudson, London.

———. 1989. Cultural Dynamics in the Southern Mogollon Area. In *Dynamics of Southwest Prehistory*, edited by Linda S. Cordell and George J. Gumerman, pp. 179–208. Smithsonian Institution Press, Washington, D.C.

———. 2006. Who Made the Mimbres Bowls? Implications of Recognizing Individual Artists for Craft Specialization and Social Networks. In *Mimbres Society*, edited by Valli S. Powell-Marti and Patricia A. Gilman, pp. 109-150. University of Arizona Press, Tucson.

LeBlanc, Steven A., and Michael E. Whalen. 1980. *An Archeological Synthesis of South-Central and Southwestern New Mexico*. University of New Mexico, Office of Contract Archeology, Albuquerque.

Lehmer, Donald H. 1948. *The Jornada Branch of the Mogollon*. University of Arizona Social Science Bulletin No. 17. University of Arizona, Tucson.

Lekson, Stephen H. 2002. *Salado Archaeology of the Upper Gila, New Mexico*. Anthropological Paper of the University of Northern Arizona 67. University of Arizona Press, Tucson.

———. 2006. *Archaeology of the Mimbres Region, Southwestern New Mexico, U.S.A*. British Archaeological Reports International Series 1466. Archaeopress, Oxford.

———. 2011. Black Mountain and Paquimé: Dating the Medio Period of Casas Grandes. Electronic Document, https://stevelekson.files.wordpress.com/2011/07/black-mountain-and-paquime.pdf, accessed December 10, 2011.

Lyle, Robyn P. 1996. Functional Analysis of Mimbres Ceramics from the NAN Ruin (LA 15049), Grant County, New Mexico. Master's Thesis, Department of Anthropology, Texas A&M, College Station.

Minnis, Paul E. 1985. *Social Adaptation to Food Stress: A Prehistoric Southwestern Example*. University of Chicago Press, Chicago.

Moulard, Barbara. 1984. *Within an Underworld Sky: Mimbres Ceramic Art in Context.* Twelve-trees Press, Pasadena, California.

Nelson, Ben A., and Steven LeBlanc. 1986. *Short-Term Sedentism in the American Southwest: The Mimbres Valley Salado.* University of New Mexico Press, Albuquerque.

Nelson, Margaret C. 1981. Chipped Stone Analysis in the Reconstruction of Prehistoric Subsistence Practices: An Example from Southwestern New Mexico. PhD dissertation, Department of Anthropology, University of California, Santa Barbara.

———. 1996. Technological Strategies Responsive to Subsistence Stress. In *Evolving Complexity and Environmental Risk in the Prehistoric Southwest*, edited by Joseph A. Tainter and Bonnie Bagley Tainter, pp. 107–144. Westview Press, Reading, Massachusetts.

———. 1999. *Mimbres During the Twelfth Century: Abandonment, Continuity, and Reorganization.* University of Arizona Press, Tucson.

Nelson, Margaret C., and Michelle Hegmon. 2001. Abandonment Is Not as It Seems: An Approach to the Relationship Between Site and Regional Abandonment. *American Antiquity* 66:213–235.

Ortman, Scott G., and Catherine M. Cameron. 2008. A Framework for Controlled Comparisons of Ancient Southwestern Movement. In *Movement, Connectivity, and Landscape Change in the Ancient Southwest*, edited by Margaret C. Nelson and Colleen A. Strawhacker, pp. 233–252. University Press of Colorado, Boulder.

Pool, Michael David. 2002. Prehistoric Mogollon Agriculture in the Mimbres River Valley, Southwestern New Mexico: A Crop Simulation and GIS Approach. PhD dissertation, University of Texas, Austin. University Microfilms, Ann Arbor.

Putsavage, Kathryn J. 2015. Social Reorganization in the Mimbres Region of Southwestern New Mexico: The Classic to Postclassic Mimbres Transition (A.D. 1150 to 1450). PhD dissertation. Department of Anthropology, University of Colorado, Boulder.

Ravesloot, John C. 1979. The Animas Phase: The Post-Classic Mimbres Occupation of the Mimbres Valley, New Mexico. Master's thesis, Department of Anthropology, Southern Illinois University, Carbondale.

Schollmeyer, Karen Gust. 2011. Large Game, Agricultural Land, and Settlement Pattern Change in the Eastern Mimbres Area, Southwest New Mexico. *Journal of Anthropological Archaeology* 30:402–415.

Shackley, M. Steven. 2002. More than Exchange: Pre-Ceramic Through Ceramic Period Obsidian Studies in the Greater North American Southwest. In *Geochemical Evidence for Long-Distance Exchange*, edited by Michael D. Glascock, pp. 53–88. Bergin and Garvey, Westport, Connecticut.

———. 2005. *Obsidian: Geology and Archaeology in the North American Southwest.* University of Arizona Press, Tucson.

———. 2014. Source Provenance of Obsidian Artifacts from Archaeological Sites near Lake Roberts, Southern New Mexico. Manuscript on file, Department of Anthropology, University of California, Berkeley.

Shafer, Harry J. 1982. Classic Mimbres Phase Households and Room Use Patterns. *Kiva* 48:17–37.

———. 1985. A Mimbres Potter's Grave: An Example of Mimbres Craft Specialization. *Bulletin of the Texas Archaeology Society* 56:185–200.

———. 1991. Archaeology at the NAN Ruin: The 1989 Season. *Artifact* 29(4):1–43.

———. 1995. Architecture and Symbolism in Transitional Pueblo Development in the Mimbres Valley, SW New Mexico. *Journal of Field Archaeology* 22:23–47.

———. 1999. The Mimbres Classic and Postclassic: A Case for Discontinuity. In *The Casas Grandes World*, edited by Curtis Schaafsma and Carroll Riley, pp. 121–133. University of Utah Press, Salt Lake City.

———. 2003. *Mimbres Archaeology at the NAN Ranch Ruin*. University of New Mexico Press, Albuquerque.

———. 2006. Extended Families to Corporate Groups: Pithouse to Pueblo Transformation of Mimbres Society. In *Mimbres Society*, edited by Valli S. Powell-Martí and Patricia A. Gilman, pp. 15–31. University of Arizona Press, Tucson.

Speakman, Robert J. 2013. Mimbres-Mogollon Pottery Production and Distribution in the American Southwest, USA. PhD dissertation, Departamento de Historia y Arqueología, Universitat de Barcelona.

Taliaferro, Matthew S. 2014. The Black Mountain Phase Occupation at the Old Town Ruin: An Examination of Social and Technological Organization in the Mimbres Valley of Southwestern New Mexico, ca. 1150–1300. PhD dissertation. Department of Anthropology, University of Texas, Austin.

Taliaferro, Matthew S., Bernard A. Schriever, and M. Steven Shackley. 2010. Obsidian Procurement, Least Cost Path Analysis, and Social Interaction in the Mimbres Area of Southwestern New Mexico. *Journal of Archaeological Science* 37:536–548.

11

Connectivity of Social Change in Mimbres and Points South

BEN A. NELSON AND PAUL E. MINNIS

T HE WORK OF THE MIMBRES FOUNDATION showed that in comparison to earlier and later populations in the Mimbres Valley, the Classic period experienced anomalous population growth, aggregation, and artisanal production. Between A.D. 1000 and 1130, a dozen or more large sites and hundreds of smaller "outliers" appear to have been occupied in the Mimbres Valley at any given time, and people of explicit Mimbres identity also inhabited or used the Gila Valley in the Redrock area and upstream, the desert area to the south of the Mimbres Valley, and the eastern slopes of the Black Range, where several east-flowing streams lead to the Rio Grande. Not only was village formation intensive, but potters developed a unique and expressive style that was often executed with masterful technological control. This occupation, presumably including some thousands of people, was radically reorganized at about A.D. 1130–1150. Population appears to have shifted to what had been small or seasonally occupied settlements, most of which were outside the Mimbres Valley proper, especially in the Eastern Mimbres area (chapter 9; Nelson 1999). The large sites in the Mimbres Valley were either abandoned or occupied by significantly fewer people. What had been a relatively rigorous conformity of ceramic style centering on Mimbres Classic Black-on-white pottery gave way to a more diversely decorated set of ceramic wares, indicating increased contact with and possibly immigration from areas as far away as east of the Rio Grande, northern Chihuahua, and southeastern Arizona (chapter 10; Hegmon et al. 1998).

The purpose of this chapter is to review archaeological sequences in north and west Mexico (figure 11.1) to see whether other coeval polities arose and declined on a schedule similar to that of the Classic Mimbres. Such synchronies would be significant

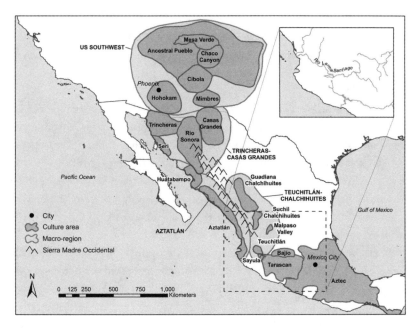

FIGURE 11.1 Mesoamerican and southwestern U.S. areas mentioned in this chapter.

because they could imply that participation in long-distance exchange networks played a role in the processes of cultural intensification we have mentioned. LeBlanc, among a few other archaeologists in the 1970s and 1980s, was open to the possibility that migration and other forms of interregional interaction stimulated local social change. For example, DiPeso (1974), Kelley and Kelley (1975), and Weigand et al. (1977) visualized imperial agents from Mesoamerica provoking the development of such centers as Paquimé and Chaco Canyon. Cordell and Plog (1979) argued that new hierarchically organized intercommunity alliances formed to solve subsistence shortages in the U.S. Southwest as population increased and mobility options became more limited.

The Mimbres Foundation certainly did its share of exploring social and environmental change in local terms. Still, the local focus seemed insufficient to account for certain rhythms in the regional history and even some of the local change. For example, why were some valleys apparently empty of population at some times and filled at others? What mechanisms brought distant objects and symbols into the Mimbres Valley? To argue that interregional interaction could have played a role in local changes was more than a little bit novel. Although LeBlanc (1983) was wisely silent on the question of hierarchy, he may have been the first to suggest that it could hardly be coincidental that the main occupations in the Mimbres Valley and Chaco Canyon areas ended so closely in time, around A.D. 1130. He also suggested (joined by one present author) that the end of the Mimbres Classic occupation might have been related to the formation of the major center of Casas Grandes in northern Chihuahua (Nelson and LeBlanc 1986; see Minnis and Whalen 2015 for a recent summation of Casas Grandes).

Within the U.S. Southwest, archaeologists have explored Classic Mimbres connections and parallels to groups to the north and west, especially Chaco Canyon and the Hohokam. While the site abandonments at the end of the Mimbres Classic period coincide closely with that of Chaco Canyon, Hegmon and Nelson (2007:78–79) conclude that there is almost no ceramic evidence of interaction between these polities. In contrast, they find considerable but changing relationships between Mimbres and Hohokam ceramics, with a decline in shared designs about A.D. 1000–1130 during the apogees of both (Hegmon and Nelson 2007:93–96).

Other nonceramic indicators of interactions with the Hohokam reveal varying degrees of connection. During the Pithouse period, while Mimbres pottery designs shared several elements with contemporary Hohokam designs, dwellings were semisubterranean, somewhat like those of the Hohokam, and the settlements were occasionally configured similarly in courtyard groups with inward-facing sets of pithouses. Mimbres sites also contain shell artifacts, the raw materials for which were presumably obtained from Mexican sources through Hohokam connections. There were other practices and patterns that the Mimbres did not share with the Hohokam, notably the use of ball courts and the practice of cremation, except in a few circumstances for the latter. By A.D. 1000, most of the previously mentioned ties appear to have diminished. The Classic pottery style emerged, dwellings changed to surface pueblos, which were loosely related to those of Ancestral Pueblo populations to the north, and Mimbres potters embarked on their highly independent odyssey into black-on-white surrealism. Various scholars (Hegmon and Nelson 2007; Minnis 1985) have concluded that Mimbres society during the period A.D. 1000–1130 was closed to outside influence and emphasized internal social conformity.

While A.D. 1130 is a seemingly important date for synchrony between Mimbres and points north, especially Chaco Canyon, Classic period developments seem to have occurred on an independent time scale from those in the Hohokam. At about A.D. 1070, when the use of ball courts ended in the Hohokam and the associated market system apparently collapsed (Abbott et al. 2007), the Mimbres Classic shows no ripple effects. When platform mounds were adopted about A.D. 1100, implying yet another very significant Hohokam institutional change, the Mimbres again evidenced no corresponding change. Nothing noticeable happened in the Hohokam to complement the Mimbres Classic collapse at about A.D. 1130.

Regarding points south in Mexico, we are in a stronger position now than were archaeologists in the 1970s and 1980s to characterize interregional relationships because of greater communication between Mexican and American scholars and the many new chronologies that have emerged from recent field projects. Do the north and west Mexican regions connect Mimbres Classic with Mesoamerica? Is Mimbres Classic part of a synchronous rise of polities to the south, or does its development adhere more closely to southwestern U.S. temporal patterns? By reviewing evidence of connectivity with these southern regions, we outline what is known and what remains to be learned if we are to understand the place of the Mimbres Classic development in a macroregional framework.

A full study of these relationships would distinguish physical exchange and acquisition of goods, sharing of ceramic and architectural styles, transmission of symbols, and the timing of important changes. Our objective is more limited: we simply wish to track the order of apogees of polities to the south to see whether the rise of the Classic period was part of that order and to note some broad stylistic similarities and possible exchange or acquisition ties to determine with which polities to the south the Classic population might have been connected, if any. We deal with iconography only tangentially. We pay especially close attention to Casas Grandes, as it is the nearest neighbor to the south, although discussion of that relationship comes near the end of our analysis.

We sketch developments in Mesoamerica in very broad terms beginning about A.D. 600 and highlight some of the most salient changes that might have affected southwestern U.S. populations, especially those who lived in the Mimbres region during the Classic period, in some way. This discussion moves from the core regions of Mesoamerica northward and from the Mesoamerican Late Classic or Epiclassic period (A.D. 600–900) onward. This order may seem odd to southwestern archaeologists, who are more accustomed to looking southward and backward in time to understand these connections, whereas we will look northward and forward. This north-forward orientation makes sense for answering the aforementioned questions because it allows us to see developments in the southwestern United States unfolding from their possible antecedents.

A fundamental aspect of Mesoamerican–southwestern U.S. relations is the adoption of Mesoamerican maize and other cultigens by southwestern U.S. peoples. This important process occurred outside the time frame considered in this chapter, yet it is important to recognize the profound economic role of maize agriculture and the evidence of maize-related ritual from the earliest occurrences of the plant in the southwestern United States. Although we do not have the space to develop the argument here, it is likely that many of the objects, symbols, and practices that constituted Mesoamerican–southwestern U.S. connections were maize related. Two observations about the introduction of Mesoamerican crops are salient here. First, nearly all the Mesoamerican crops that could have been grown in the southwestern United States were indeed grown in the pre-Hispanic southwestern United States. Second, the introduction of the various Mesoamerican-derived crops occurred at different times in different regions of the southwestern United States. These points further reinforce the general conclusions that the long-term relationships between Mesoamerica and the southwestern United States had few impediments but were flexible, complex, and contingent.

A basic point that many scholars seem to have missed is that pre-Hispanic Meso-america never had an overarching political framework. Some of the aforementioned "imperialist" views of Mesoamerican–southwestern U.S. interaction treat Mesoamer-ica as if it were a nation-state, but Mexico became a nation during the period from A.D. 1810 to 1821, when it overthrew Spanish rule. Until that time, the region was a mosaic of independent city-states, small volatile empires, and less integrated areas with diverse populations speaking numerous languages. While Teotihuacan rulers exerted political control in some regions well outside the Basin of Mexico—for exam-ple, Matacapan (Santley and Arnold 2006), Tikal (Coggins 1993; Stuart 2000), and Copan (Price et al. 2010)—the interventions documented thus far appear to have been confined primarily to the period A.D. 350–450 (Cowgill 2003). The rulers of Tula of the Toltecs (about A.D. 850–1150) probably never established an empire (Smith and Montiel 2001:259–260, 267–268). The Aztec empire, A.D. 1425–1519, known for its violent hegemony, also had a system of taxation and placed garrisons in what Berdan and colleagues (1996) call strategic provinces. Very importantly for our analysis, neither the Aztecs nor the contemporaneous Tarascan empire ever controlled areas in north or west Mexico.

The Mesoamerican time periods of concern here are listed in table 11.1. The apogees for the constituent cultural areas are in table 11.2. These areas should be considered representative rather than all-inclusive (regional specialists recognize even more). We lump them into three super-regions, which we call Teuchitlán-Chalchihuites, Aztat-lán, and Trincheras–Casas Grandes. These broad groups are only appropriate for analyses at very large spatiotemporal scales. Teuchitlán-Chalchihuites includes the northernmost large river that flows to the Pacific from central Mexico, plus the eastern flank of the Sierra Madre Occidental. The Aztatlán region includes the Pacific coastal plain west of the Sierra Madre Occidental. Trincheras–Casas Grandes includes the southern portion of the modern International Four Corners area.

Within the Teuchitlán-Chalchihuites region, the Teuchitlán tradition (200 B.C.–A.D. 400) preceded the developments of direct concern here, but it was a towering presence in its time. It is an example of apogeal demographic concentration, long-distance connection, and monumental architecture (Beekman 1997). We assume that

TABLE 11.1 Mesoamerican Periods

Period	Dates (A.D.)
Epiclassic	600–900
Early Postclassic	900–1150
Middle Postclassic	1150–1300
Late Postclassic	1300–1519

TABLE 11.2 Apogees in Selected Cultural Areas

Area	Apogee dates	Sources
Teuchitlán	100 B.C.–A.D. 150	Beekman and Weigand 2010
Bajío	A.D. 200/300–650/750	Cárdenas 1999
Sayula	A.D. 400–1000	Valdez et al. 2005
Malpaso Valley	A.D. 750–900	Nelson 1997; Trombold 1990
Chalchihuites– Suchil Branch	A.D. 750–950	Kelley 1985
Chalchihuites– Guadiana Branch	A.D. 850–1000	Punzo and Ramírez 2008
Aztatlán	A.D. 800–1400	Carpenter 2002; Mountjoy 2000
Huatabampo	A.D. 700–900	Álvarez Palma 2007
Seri	—	Braniff 2001
Trincheras	A.D. 1300–1450	McGuire and Villalpando 1991
Casas Grandes	A.D. 1200–1400/1450	Dean and Ravesloot 1993; Phillips and Gamboa 2015

Note: The areas are listed in approximate order of development and make a generally south-to-north array. Compare with Mimbres Classic, A.D. 1000–1130 (Anyon et al. 2017).

if any north or west Mexican agents strongly affected people's beliefs or institutions in the Mimbres region, it would be during some such apogee. By about A.D. 600, another common set of architectural and ceramic styles had extended over the Teuchitlán-Chalchihuites region, originating in the Bajío of Guanajuato at about A.D. 350 (Beekman 1997; Cárdenas García and Fernández-Villanueva 2004). The spread of these elements is considered by some to represent a colonization or diaspora out of central Mexico toward the north and west (Braniff Cornejo and Hers 1998; Jiménez Moreno 1959); note that *north* and *west* here refer to areas located 500–1500 km south of the Mimbres area. Decorated ceramics included red-on-buff, incised-engraved, negative, and pseudo-cloisonné wares, and settlements consisted of terraced hillsides and hilltops, often with walled enclosures, and complexes of rooms that enclosed patios, sometimes connected with staircases and causeways. Braniff Cornejo (1995) and Carot (2001) have identified striking similarities between the red-on-buff ceramics of these sites and those of the Hohokam. However, these similarities occur as much as six hundred years and 2000 km apart, from A.D. 250 in what later became the Tarascan area to A.D. 600–750 in the Malpaso and Suchil-Branch Chalchihuites areas to A.D. 800–875 in the Hohokam region of Arizona. It remains unclear how to interpret the sometimes uncannily similar ceramic motifs over such spans of time and space except to say that the producers were referencing enduring cosmological concepts that they held in common.

Along the eastern edge of the Sierra Madre Occidental, people who were in some sites within the Teuchitlán-Chalchihuites region seem to have played a prominent role in a perceived Toltec period (A.D. 900–1150) "turquoise trail" from central Mexico to the United States (Weigand 1968, 1982; Weigand and Harbottle 1992, 1993; Weigand et al. 1977). This argument is potentially relevant to the Mimbres Classic because these scholars argued that people in Mesoamerica imported turquoise from southwestern U.S. sources, while objects from Mesoamerica such as copper bells and macaws, which are found in Mimbres sites, were traded in return. More recent information makes this turquoise link questionable. Although it appeared from surface observations that La Quemada in the Malpaso area was an Early Postclassic (A.D. 1000–1150) site and would have been contemporary with the Toltecs, Chaco Canyon, and the Mimbres Classic occupation, subsequent excavations have shown the site to be earlier and probably abandoned around A.D. 900 (Nelson 1997). It also turns out that the Malpaso sites have very little turquoise (Nelson 1994). Suchil-Branch Chalchihuites sites, which were probably abandoned about A.D. 1000 (Kelley 1985), had much more turquoise (Weigand 1982), but because of recent reconsiderations of sourcing methods (Thibodeau 2012), some geochemists seem skeptical as to how much Meso-american turquoise is from southwestern U.S. sources. In sum, there is little temporal overlap and mostly only vague material-culture connections between the people of the Mimbres region and those in Chalchihuites and Malpaso sites on the eastern edge of the Sierra Madre Occidental.

The Aztatlán tradition arose in the late A.D. 800s in the western coastal flank of the Sierra Madre Occidental (Kelly 1938, 1945; Mountjoy 2000; Mountjoy and Torres M. 1985; Sauer and Brand 1932). This development was more relevant to Mesoamerican–southwestern U.S. interaction. The Aztatlán tradition included new forms of public architecture such as long tall rectangular platform mounds surrounding plazas, a visually flamboyant and sophisticated ceramic technology, and metallurgy. The earliest Aztatlán ceramics appeared on the Pacific coast and eventually spread inland to the Sayula and Guadiana-Branch Chalchihuites areas. The ceramics were very unlike

Mimbres Classic (or even Hohokam) ceramics, but this area and tradition were a probable source of the copper bells acquired by people in the Mimbres area, again probably through the Hohokam (Vargas 1995). So well connected were people in the Hohokam region with the west Mexican Aztatlán development that the earliest dates for Hohokam copper bells align very closely with the earliest credible dates for copper bells in west Mexico, probably in the late A.D. 800s (the earlier contexts cited by Hosler [1994:49–51] are not firmly dated). In contrast, the earliest dates for copper bells in central and northeastern Mexico are considerably later, about A.D. 1200 (Hosler and MacFarlane 1996). The Aztatlán tradition includes a vigorous shell industry and might potentially be the source of the Mimbres shell artifacts, although other sources lie considerably closer.

The Mimbres Classic period (A.D. 1000–1130) occurred during the wide temporal span of the Aztatlán development (A.D. 800–1400). This span includes local antecedents, apogees, and subsequent derivatives of the "principal" Aztatlán cultural pattern. If Mountjoy (2000:96) is correct in suggesting that such a principal pattern dates from about A.D. 800–1100, then one may conclude that there is an interesting synchrony among several subregions of Aztatlán and the Late Pithouse and Mimbres Classic periods (A.D. 735–1130 [Anyon et al. 2017]). Moreover, this chronological alignment matches the Early Bonito, Classic Bonito, and Late Bonito phases in Chaco Canyon (A.D. 850–1140 [Lekson 2006:Figure 1.3]) and the Colonial and Sedentary Hohokam periods (Wallace 2014:Figure 1.3). The material connections of people in the Hohokam region with inhabitants of west Mexico during Aztatlán appear extremely strong based on their adoption of modified west Mexican forms of public architecture, metallurgy, figurines, spindle whorls, and shell technology. The population in the Mimbres Valley, in contrast, seems to have shared in these connections secondarily through the Hohokam. Some of these synchronies recall the title that Hegmon and Nelson (2007) use to characterize the connections of Chaco Canyon and the Mimbres—"In Sync, but Barely in Touch"—and suggest that it has wider applicability.

Connections between the Mimbres area and Trincheras–Casas Grandes came into play primarily after the Mimbres Classic period. One might assume that these connections would continue yet farther south, but, perhaps surprisingly to those of us who think of Mexico as tropical, most of the Sonoran coastline was uninhabitable on a permanent basis because of aridity. Thus, in terms of coastal connections, there is a large gap in sedentary settlements along the coast, and the northernmost coastal area that could have played a part in connections with the southwestern United States is Huatabampo (A.D. 700–900) in far southern Sonora. Reports of that area do not mention the presence of southwestern ceramics, although they do have shell ornaments and blue-green stones (Álvarez Palma 1981, 2007).

Importantly, the Trincheras area was once thought to be a shell-production center for the southwestern United States, especially the Hohokam (Sauer and Brand 1931). However, the Trincheras area has no ceramic ties with the Mimbres area (Villalpando and McGuire 2009:244–248). The shell workshops at the Trincheras site date to the El Cerro phase, A.D. 1250–1450, and recent research has not confirmed the production of shell at a scale suitable for outside consumption (Villalpando and McGuire 2009).

Another important observation is that one might expect a corridor of connection and influence to have existed along the eastern edge of the Sierra Madre Occidental, terminating at or passing through the Mimbres area, but the evidence for such a corridor is weak. After the abandonment of the Suchil-Branch Chalchihuites and Malpaso areas no later than A.D. 1050, sedentary people did not occupy these areas for the remainder of the pre-Hispanic period. The more northerly Guadiana branch of the Chalchihuites, which continued to be occupied until about A.D. 1350, was connected to the Pacific coast rather than to the southwestern United States. Beyond that area and to the southern edge of the Casas Grandes area, there existed only a very few small hilltop sites with enclosures that lacked pottery or had very small amounts of plain brown pottery (Brooks 1971). In other words, the apparent gap between Casas Grandes and the Chalchihuites area was real.

Connections to the Casas Grandes area varied through time. Connections to the area's center of Paquimé are the most interesting and complex but mainly relate to the ultimate results of reorganization during the Postclassic period in the Mimbres region (chapters 9 and 10). More germane to this chapter, we have records of earlier "Mimbres" sites in northern Mexico (Phelps 1998; Whalen and Minnis 2001), but their nature is unclear, and none have been excavated. Mimbres Style I and III Black-on-white sherds have been recovered from Viejo period sites (now dated A.D. 800–1150/1200). For example, Di Peso (1974) notes that nearly 80 percent of nonlocal sherds on one Casas Grandes–area site were Mimbres. More recently, Jane Holden Kelley (personal communication 2014) reports finding Mimbres sherds in Viejo period sites to the south but none as far south as the Babícora Basin in central Chihuahua.

Regarding trade pottery, including Mimbres types, in northwestern Chihuahua, Brand (1933:84) suggests that "these wares increase in quantity toward their populated sources." Besides the presence of Mimbres sherds, there is little "Mimbres" about the Viejo sites. Architecture of the Late Viejo period, the time contemporary with the Mimbres Classic period (Kelley and Searcy 2015), does not look like Mimbres Classic architecture. This is the case for building technology and ritual architecture. Mimbres pueblo walls are mostly stone and mud, whereas pueblo walls common in the latest part of the Viejo period are adobe. There appear to be large "communal" pit structures in Late Viejo sites, but none from Mimbres Classic. There is also much architectural variation in Late Viejo sites. The architecture of the Viejo period Calderon site in central Chihuahua, as an example, includes large circular pit structures, while the Convento site just north of Paquimé has smaller ones, as well as surface structures (Kelley and Searcy 2015).

Therefore, it seems that Mimbres ceramics were simply acquired or made locally by communities that shared little else with the Mimbres Classic. That does not mean that no communities lived in northern Chihuahua whom we could call "Mimbres Classic." Still, it is our impression that intrusive Classic ceramics may be more common in far northern Chihuahua compared with other areas peripheral to the Mimbres Valley. If so, people whose territories lay to the south of the core Mimbres area may have identified more closely with Mimbres Classic groups than they did with other people peripheral to the core Mimbres region.

These unresolved questions about the Mimbres Classic period may ultimately have a bearing on inferences about what happened to the groups who abandoned the larger sites of the Mimbres Classic period. During the Mimbres Foundation's field seasons, LeBlanc often spoke of the "bright city lights effect," by which he meant that the rise of population and intensified activity in the Casas Grandes area attracted other people. The implication from the perspective of southwestern New Mexico would be that the apparent increase in population in the Casas Grandes world during the Medio period (A.D. 1200–1450) was due, in part, to the eventual arrival of migrants from the Mimbres Valley (Nelson and LeBlanc 1986).

Did Mimbres contribute to the rise of the Casas Grandes center of Paquimé? This question has largely revolved around the debate regarding how large the Viejo period population was in relation to that of the Medio period. Both Di Peso (1974) and Lekson (2009) argue that the Viejo population was small and that the Medio period population expanded due to significant in-migration, likely from the Mimbres area, among others. It is true that there are fewer Viejo period sites compared with those dating to the Medio period. Whalen and Minnis (2001, 2003, 2009; Minnis and Whalen 2015), in contrast, argue the apparent population-size difference between the Viejo and Medio periods is not nearly as great as Di Peso, Lekson, and others argue. Whalen and Minnis base their conclusion on three observations. First, most of the Medio period sites they have excavated contained Viejo deposits under Medio pueblos, suggesting that Viejo period sites had been obscured by later Medio structures. Second, some Medio period sites may have been partially depopulated during the early Medio as people relocated elsewhere, likely to Paquimé itself (Whalen and Minnis 2009). Thus, the large number of Medio period sites may overrepresent the population at any one time. Third, Whalen and colleagues (2010) argue that Paquimé was significantly smaller than Di Peso originally estimated, containing two thousand rather than five thousand people. Therefore, it is not obvious whether in-migration was necessary to account for the apparent population increase during the Medio period around Paquimé.

To conclude, Mesoamerica was a complex and diverse region, and its relationship to the southwestern United States, including people in the Mimbres region during the Mimbres Classic, was also complex. Mesoamerica provided maize and probably much associated ritual and cosmology to southwestern U.S. peoples in general. For people in the Hohokam region, concrete evidence of a generalized Mesoamerican connection is ubiquitous in ceramics, public architecture, and shell and copper ornaments and implements (Haury 1976). Yet for the groups living in the Mimbres Classic tradition, such material connections were more limited, although present. The Mimbres Classic development coincided closely in time with several major cultural apogees in west Mexico that are subsumed under the label of the Aztatlán tradition, possibly seeded in some way by interaction with Hohokam groups. There is no ceramic evidence of direct connection to any of the aforementioned Mesoamerican traditions. The Meso-american region did provide a reservoir of rituals, practices, symbols, and powerful objects. Evidence for distant exchange or acquisition includes copper bells, macaws, and macaw imagery (Creel and McKusick 1994; Gilman et al. 2014). Some connections with northern Mexico are seen in Mimbres Black-on-white ceramics present at Viejo period sites in the Casas Grandes region. The collapse and reorganization after the Mimbres Classic period may have set the regional stage for recruitment of people to Casas Grandes. If such recruitment occurred, it was probably almost three generations after the large Mimbres Classic communities dispersed. During those years, large settlements formed in the lower deserts of New Mexico and in Texas around El Paso. Perhaps some descendants of these populations of the Black Mountain and El Paso phases became part of the core of the Casas Grandes region.

The research directed by LeBlanc answered significant questions and posed many more, which members of the foundation crew, such as ourselves, have continued to pursue throughout our careers. LeBlanc was the name of the force that spurred many of us on forty years ago and has never faded; perhaps the only change is that we are now more conscious of its influence.

References Cited

Abbott, David R., Alexa M. Smith, and Emiliano Gallaga. 2007. Ballcourts and Ceramics: The Case for Hohokam Marketplaces in the Arizona Desert. *American Antiquity* 72: 461–484.

Álvarez Palma, Ana María. 1981. Machomoncobe, un sitio arqueológico en Huatabampo. In *Memoria del VI Simposio de Historia de Sonora*, pp. 1–7. Unison–Instituto de Investigaciones Históricas, Hermosillo, Sonora.

————. 2007. Reinterpretando Huatabampo. In *Memoria del Seminario de la Arqueología del Norte de México*, edited by Cristina García Moreno and María Elisa Villalpando, pp. 99–114. Consejo Nacional para la Cultura y las Artes e Instituto Nacional de Antropología e Historia, Hermosillo, Sonora.

Anyon, Roger, Darrell Creel, Patricia A. Gilman, Steven A. LeBlanc, Myles R. Miller, Stephen E. Nash, Margaret C. Nelson, Kathryn J. Putsavage, Barbara J. Roth, Karen Gust Schollmeyer, Jakob W. Sedig, and Christopher A. Turnbow. 2017. Re-evaluating the Mimbres Region Prehispanic Chronometric Record. *Kiva* 83(3):316–343.

Beekman, Christopher S. 1997. Recent Research in West Mexican Archaeology. *Journal of Archaeological Research* 5:345–384.

Beekman, Christopher S., and Phil C. Weigand. 2010. La secuencia cronológica de la Tradición Teuchitlán. In *El sistema fluvial Lerma-Santiago durante el Formativo y el Clásico Temprano: Precisiones cronológicas y dinámicas culturales*, edited by L. Solar Valverde, pp. 243-264. Instituto Nacional de Antropología e Historia, Mexico City.

Berdan, Frances F., Richard E. Blanton, Elizabeth Hill Boone, Mary G. Hodge, Michael Smith, and Emily Umberger. 1996. *Aztec Imperial Strategies*. Dumbarton Oaks, Washington, D.C.

Brand, Donald D. 1933. The Historical Geography of Northwestern Chihuahua. PhD dissertation. Department of Geography, University of California, Berkeley.

Braniff Cornejo, Beatriz. 1995. Diseños tradicionales mesoamericanos y norteños: Ensayo de interpretación. In *Arqueología del norte y del occidente de México: Homenaje al Doctor J. Charles Kelley*, edited by Bruce Dahlgren and Maria Soto, pp. 181–209. Instituto de Investigaciones Antropológicas, Universidad Nacional Autónoma de México, Mexico City.

———— (editor). 2001. *La Gran Chichimeca: El lugar de las rocas secas*. Jaca Book and Consejo Nacional para la Cultura y las Artes, Mexico City.

Braniff Cornejo, Beatriz, and Marie-Areti Hers. 1998. Herencias chichimecas. *Arqueología* 19:55–80.

Brooks, Richard Howard. 1971. Lithic Traditions in Northwestern Mexico, Paleo-Indian to Chalchihuites. PhD dissertation, Department of Anthropology, University of Colorado, Boulder.

Cárdenas García, Efraín. 1999. *El Bajío en el Clásico*. Colegio de Michoacán, Zamora, Michocán.

Cárdenas García, Efraín, and Eugenia Fernández-Villanueva. 2004. Apuntes para el estudio de la arqueología del Bajío. In *Introducción a la arqueología del occidente*, edited by Beatriz Braniff Cornejo, pp. 497–523. Universidad de Colima y Conaculta–Instituto Nacional de Antropología e Historia, Mexico City.

Carot, Patricia. 2001. *Le site de Loma Alta, Lac de Zacapu, Michoacan, Mexique*. Archaeopress, Oxford.

Carpenter, John. 2002. Of Red Rims and Red Wares: The Archaeology of Prehispanic Sinaloa. In *Boundaries and Territories: The Archaeology of the U.S. Southwest and Northern Mexico*, edited by E. Villalpando, pp. 143–153. Arizona State University Anthropological Research Papers Series 54. Department of Anthropology, Arizona State University, Tempe.

Coggins, Clemency Chase. 1993. The Age of Teotihuacan and Its Mission Abroad. In *Teotihuacan: Art from the City of the Gods*, edited by K. Berrin and E. Pasztory, pp. 140–155. Hudson, New York.

Cordell, Linda S., and Fred Plog. 1979. Escaping the Confines of Normative Thought: A Reevaluation of Puebloan Prehistory. *American Antiquity* 44:405–429.

Cowgill, George L. 2003. Teotihuacan and Early Classic Interaction: A Perspective from Outside the Maya Region. In *The Maya and Teotihuacan: Reinterpreting Early Classic Interaction*, edited by Geoffrey E. Braswell, pp. 315–335. University of Texas Press, Austin.

Creel, Darrel, and Charmion McKusick. 1994. Prehistoric Macaws and Parrots in the Mimbres Region, New Mexico. *American Antiquity* 59:510–524.

Dean, Jeffrey S., and John C. Ravesloot. 1993. The Chronology of Cultural Interaction in the Gran Chichimeca. In *Culture and Contact: Charles C. Di Peso's Gran Chichimeca*, edited by A. I. W. a. J. C. and J. C. Ravesloot, pp. 83–103. Amerind Foundation and University of New Mexico Press, Albuquerque.

Di Peso, Charles C. 1974. *Casas Grandes: A Fallen Trading Center of the Gran Chichimeca*, Vol. 2. Amerind Foundation, Dragoon, Arizona.

Gilman, Patricia A., Marc Thompson, and Kristina C. Wyckoff. 2014. Ritual Change and the Distant: Mesoamerican Iconography, Scarlet Macaws, and Great Kivas in the Mimbres Region of Southwestern New Mexico. *American Antiquity* 79:90–107.

Haury, Emil W. 1976. *The Hohokam: Desert Farmers of the American Southwest*. University of Arizona Press, Tucson.

Hegmon, Michelle, and Margaret C. Nelson. 2007. In Sync, but Barely in Touch: Relations Between the Mimbres Region and the Hohokam Regional System. In *Hinterlands and Regional Dynamics in the Ancient Southwest*, edited by Alan P. Sullivan II and James Bayman, pp. 70–96. University of Arizona Press, Tucson.

Hegmon, Michelle, Margaret C. Nelson, and Susan M. Ruth. 1998. Abandonment and Reorganization in the Mimbres Region of the American Southwest. *American Anthropologist* 100:148–162.

Hosler, Dorothy. 1994. *The Sounds and Colors of Power: The Sacred Metallurgical Technology of Ancient West Mexico*. MIT Press, Cambridge, Massachusetts.

Hosler, Dorothy, and Andrew MacFarlane. 1996. Copper Sources, Metal Production, and Metals Trade in Late Postclassic Mesoamerica. *Science* 273:1819–1824.

Jiménez Moreno, Wigberto. 1959. Síntesis de la historia pretolteca de Mesoamérica. In *El esplendor del México antiguo*, Vol. 2, pp. 1109–1196. Centro de Investigaciones Antropológicos, Mexico City.

Kelley, Jane H., and Michael T. Searcy. 2015. Beginnings: The Viejo Period. In *Ancient Paquimé and the Casas Grandes World*, edited by Paul E. Minnis and Michael E. Whalen, pp. 41–57. University of Arizona Press, Tucson.

Kelley, J. Charles. 1985. The Chronology of the Chalchihuites Culture. In *The Archaeology of West and Northwest Mesoamerica*, edited by Michael S. Foster and Phil C. Weigand, pp. 269–288. Westview Press, Boulder, Colorado.

Kelley, J. Charles, and Ellen Abbott Kelley. 1975. An Alternative Hypothesis for the Explanation of Anasazi Culture History. In *Collected Papers in Honor of Florence Hawley Ellis*, edited by T. F. Frisbie, pp. 178–223. Papers of the Archaeological Society of New Mexico, No. 2. Hooper, Norman, Oklahoma.

Kelly, Isabel. 1938. *Excavations at Chametla, Sinaloa*. University of California Press, Berkeley.

———. 1945. *Excavations at Culiacán, Sinaloa*. University of California Press, Berkeley.

LeBlanc, Steven A. 1983. *The Mimbres People: Ancient Painters of the American Southwest*. Thames and Hudson, London.

Lekson, Stephen H. 2006. Chaco Matters: An Introduction. In *The Archaeology of Chaco Canyon: An Eleventh-Century Pueblo Regional Center*, edited by S. H. Lekson, pp. 3–44. School of American Research Press, Santa Fe, New Mexico.

———. 2009. *A History of the Ancient Southwest*. School for Advanced Research Press, Santa Fe, New Mexico.

McGuire, Randall H., and María Elisa Villalpando. 1991. Prehistory and the Making of History in Sonora. In *Columbian Consequences*, edited by D. H. Thomas, pp. 159–178. Smithsonian Institution, Washington, D.C.

Minnis, Paul E. 1985. *Social Adaptation to Food Stress: A Prehistoric Southwestern Example*. University of Chicago Press, Chicago.

Minnis, Paul E., and Michael E. Whalen. 2015. *Ancient Paquimé and the Casas Grandes World*. University of Arizona Press, Tucson.

Mountjoy, Joseph B. 2000. Prehispanic Cultural Development Along the Southern Coast of West Mexico. In *Greater Mesoamerica: The Archaeology of West and Northwest Mexico*, edited by Michael S. Foster and Shirley Gorenstein, pp. 81–106. University of Utah Press, Salt Lake City.

Mountjoy, Joseph B., and Luis Torres M. 1985. The Production and Use of Prehispanic Metal Artifacts in the Central Coastal Area of Jalisco, Mexico. In *The Archaeology of West and Northwest Mesoamerica*, edited by Michael S. Foster and Phil C. Weigand, pp. 133–152. Westview Press, Boulder, Colorado.

Nelson, Ben A. 1994. Outposts of Mesoamerican Empire and Architectural Patterning at La Quemada, Zacatecas. In *Culture and Contact: Charles C. Di Peso's Gran Chichimec*, edited by Anne I. Wooseley and John C. Ravesloot, pp. 173–190. University of New Mexico Press, Albuquerque.

———. 1997. Chronology and Stratigraphy at La Quemada, Zacatecas, Mexico. *Journal of Field Archaeology* 24:85–109.

Nelson, Ben A., and Steven A. LeBlanc. 1986. *Short-Term Sedentism in the American Southwest: The Mimbres Valley Salado*. University of New Mexico Press, Albuquerque.

Nelson, Margaret C. 1999. *Mimbres During the Twelfth Century: Abandonment, Continuity, and Reorganization.* University of Arizona Press, Tucson.

Phelps, Alan L. 1998. An Inventory of Prehistoric Native American Sites in Northwestern Chihuahua. *Artifact* 36(2):1–175.

Phillips, David A., Jr., and Eduardo Gamboa Carrera. 2015. The End of Paquimé and the Casas Grandes Culture. In *Ancient Paquimé and the Casas Grandes World*, edited by P. E. Minnis and Michael E. Whalen, pp. 148–171. University of Arizona Press, Tucson.

Price, T. Douglas, James H. Burton, Robert J. Sharer, Jane E. Buikstra, Lori E. Wright, Loa P. Traxler, and Katherine A. Miller. 2010. Kings and Commoners at Copan: Isotopic Evidence for Origins and Movement in the Classic Maya Period. *Journal of Anthropological Archaeology* 29(1):15–32.

Punzo Díaz, José Luis, and Ángel Ramírez Luna. 2008. The Chalchihuites Chronology Revisited: The Guadiana Branch. Paper presented at the 73rd Annual Meeting of the Society for American Archaeology, Vancouver, B.C.

Santley, Robert S., and Philip J. Arnold III. 2006. The Obsidian Trade to the Tuxtlas Region and Its Implications for the Prehistory of Southern Veracruz, Mexico. *Ancient Mesoamerica* 16(2):179–194.

Sauer, Carl O., and Donald Brand. 1931. *Prehistoric Settlements of Sonora, with Special Reference to Cerros de Trincheras.* University of California Publications in Geography Vol. 5(3):67–148. University of California Press, Berkeley.

——. 1932. *Aztatlán: Prehistoric Mexican Frontier on the Pacific Coast.* University of California Press, Berkeley.

Smith, Michael E., and Lisa Montiel. 2001. The Archaeological Study of Empires and Imperialism in Pre-Hispanic Central Mexico. *Journal of Anthropological Archaeology* 20:245–284.

Stuart, David. 2000. "Arrival of Strangers": Teotihuacan and Tollan in Classic Maya History. In *Mesoamerica's Classic Heritage: Teotihuacán to the Aztecs*, edited by L. J. a. S. S. D. Carrasco, pp. 465–513. University Press of Colorado, Niwot.

Thibodeau, Alyson. 2012. Isotopic Evidence for the Provenance of Turquoise, Mineral-Paints, and Metals in the Southwest United States. PhD dissertation, Department of Geosciences, University of Arizona, Tucson.

Trombold, Charles D. 1990. A Reconsideration of the Chronology for the La Quemada Portion of the Northern Mesoamerican Frontier. *American Antiquity* 55(2):308–323.

Valdez, Francisco, Susana Ramírez Urrea, and Catherine Liot. 2005. *Los asentamientos humanos en la Cuenca de Sayula. In Arqueología de la Cuenca de Sayula*, edited by F. Valdez, O. Schöndube, and J. P. Emphoux, pp. 69–124. Universidad de Guadalajara / Institut de Recherche pour le Développement, Guadalajara.

Vargas, Victoria D. 1995. *Copper Bell Trade Patterns in the Prehispanic U.S. Southwest and Northwest Mexico.* Arizona State Museum Archaeological Series 187. University of Arizona Press, Tucson.

Villalpando, M. Elisa, and Randall H. McGuire. 2009. *Entre muros de piedra: La arqueología del Cerro de Trincheras*. Gobierno del Estado de Sonora, Hermosillo, Sonora.

Wallace, Henry D. 2014. Introduction to the Land Between. In *Between Mimbres and Hohokam: Exploring the Archaeology and History of Southeastern Arizona and Southwestern New Mexico*, edited by H. D. Wallace, pp. 1–13. Archaeology Southwest, Tucson, Arizona.

Weigand, Phil C. 1968. The Mines and Mining Techniques of the Chalchihuites Culture. *American Antiquity* 33:45–61.

———. 1982. Mining and Mineral Trade in Prehispanic Zacatecas. In *Mining and Mineral Trade in Prehispanic Zacatecas*, edited by Phil C. Weigand and G. Gwynne, pp. 87–134. Special Issue of Anthropology Vol. 6. Department of Anthropology, State University of New York, Stony Brook.

Weigand, Phil C., and Garman Harbottle. 1992. Turquoise in Pre-Columbian America. *Scientific American* 266:78–85.

———. 1993. The Role of Turquoises in the Ancient Mesoamerican Trade Structure. In *The American Southwest and Mesoamerica: Systems of Prehistoric Exchange*, edited by Jonathan E. Ericson and Timothy Baugh, pp. 159–179. Plenum, New York.

Weigand, Phil C., Garman Harbottle, and Edward V. Sayre. 1977. Turquoise Sources and Source Analysis: Mesoamerica and the Southwestern U.S.A. In *Exchange Systems in Prehistory*, edited by Timothy K. Earle and Jonathan E. Ericson, pp. 15–34. Academic Press, New York.

Whalen, Michael E., Arthur C. MacWilliams, and Todd Pietzel. 2010. Reconsidering the Size and Structure of Casas Grandes, Chihuahua, Mexico. *American Antiquity* 75:527–571.

Whalen, Michael E., and Paul E. Minnis. 2001. *Casas Grandes and Its Hinterland Prehistoric Regional Organization in Northwest Mexico*. University of Arizona Press, Tucson.

———. 2003. The Local and the Distant in the Origin of Casas Grandes, Chihuahua, Mexico. *American Antiquity* 68:314–332.

———. 2009. *The Neighbors of Casas Grandes: Excavating Medio Period Communities of Northwest Chihuahua, Mexico*. University of Arizona Press, Tucson.

12

The Mimbres Foundation in the History of Nonprofit Archaeology

WILLIAM H. DOELLE

A RCHAEOLOGY IS CARRIED OUT in an institutional context, and private nonprofit corporations have had a surprisingly strong role in the history of southwestern archaeology. The Mimbres Foundation was incorporated as a nonprofit organization in the state of California in 1976. It dispersed its resources and ceased to exist as a corporation in 2013. Over the span of just thirty-seven years, the Mimbres Foundation accomplished a broad range of impressive goals. In this chapter, I provide a brief overview of southwestern nonprofits before exploring the history of the Mimbres Foundation. This is by no means a definitive history of the foundation as there are many documents and avenues one could pursue to produce a more detailed narrative of this organization. Rather, my goal is to consider the institutional context of the work of the Mimbres Foundation and Steven LeBlanc within the broader historical setting of nonprofit organizations that have contributed to southwestern archaeology for over a century.

Previous discussions of nonprofits and their impact on southwestern archaeology present brief, basic histories and descriptions of individual organizations (Cerino et al. 2016; Doelle 2013). In this chapter, I highlight the role of the individuals or institutions that established nonprofit organizations and the ways in which their attributes have changed over time. The interplay of the nonprofit institutional context with the specific attributes of the Mimbres Foundation leader, Steven LeBlanc, parallels the history of many nonprofits. Like several other Southwest nonprofits that had limited life-spans, the Mimbres Foundation and its impact extend in many ways past its formal existence.

Nonprofits and the Southwest

There has been an increase in the diversity of institutions that carry out archaeological activities in this nation over time. Museums, universities, private nonprofit organizations, and, most recently, private for-profit firms all employ professional archaeologists. Throughout this trajectory, avocational archaeologists have participated in local or state-level archaeological societies as well. The focus here is on professional nonprofits with full-time employees. Figure 12.1 shows the formation of such professional nonprofits in the Southwest by half decade. An early group of nonprofits was established between 1900 and 1940 and a second group at regular intervals beginning in the 1960s. The Mimbres Foundation falls in the early half of the second group.

Nonprofit Founders and Their Organizations

A key attribute of nearly every nonprofit organization is that it is entrepreneurial. The professional organization must communicate its mission and secure funding to be effective for the long term. As a result, nearly every nonprofit is founded by a leader with significant entrepreneurial energy and skill. Table 12.1 lists the founders of the Southwest archaeological nonprofits included in figure 12.1 along with the

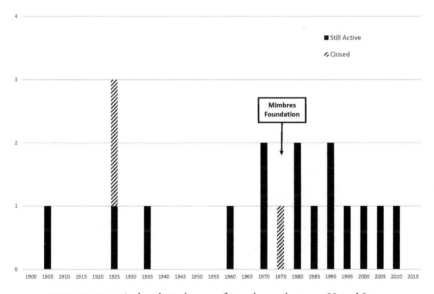

FIGURE 12.1 Archaeological nonprofits in the southwestern United States.

TABLE 12.1 The Major Archaeological Nonprofits of the Southwest with Their Founding Year and Founder or Director

Name	Founded	Founder/Director
School for Advanced Research	1907	Edgar Lee Hewett
Laboratory of Anthropology	1927	Kenneth Chapman
Gila Pueblo	1928	Harold S. Gladwin
Museum of Northern Arizona	1928	Harold S. Colton
Amerind Foundation	1937	William Shirley Fulton
Salmon Ruins	1964	Cynthia Irwin-Williams
Human Systems Research	1972	Mark Wimberly/Peter Eidenbach
Mimbres Foundation	1976	Steven A. LeBlanc
Archaeological Conservancy	1980	Mark Michel/Steven A. LeBlanc
Archaeology Southwest	1982	William Doelle
Crow Canyon Archaeological Center	1983	Stuart Struever
Santa Fe Institute	1984	Murray Gell-Mann
A:shiwi A:wan Museum and Heritage Center	1992	Zuni Tribe
Old Pueblo Archaeology Center	1993	Allen Dart
Fort Apache Heritage Center	1998	Tribal charter
SRI Foundation	2001	Jeffrey Altschul
Colorado Plateau Archaeological Alliance	2005	Jerry Spangler
Verde Valley Archaeology Center	2010	Ken Zoll (incorporator)

organization's founding date. For discussion purposes, I will consider organizational founders in two groups—the early founders of pre-1940 and the more recent group from the 1960s onward.

The early group has a common thread in that founding support came from eastern wealth. The founders of the Museum of Northern Arizona (MNA), Gila Pueblo, and the Amerind Foundation all had family wealth from the East and trained themselves in archaeology. Kenneth Chapman at the Laboratory of Anthropology in Santa Fe benefitted from the wealth of the Rockefeller family. While Edgar Lee Hewett was not wealthy, he was provided initial support by the long-established Archaeological Institute of America. Hewett quickly proved himself to be incredibly innovative and entrepreneurial as he built what is today the School for Advanced Research (SAR) in Santa Fe and multiple other institutions. Another common theme among all of these early organizations was the implementation of substantial programs of field-work. Much of the basic cultural historical background of the Southwest derived from original research conducted by these organizations (Doelle 2013:282).

The second group of nonprofits is much more diverse. The two organizations that stand out as most distinct from the rest are the A:shiwi A:wan Museum and Heritage

Center at Zuni and the Fort Apache Heritage Center. The former benefited from a million-dollar legal settlement and was established to serve the Zuni community. The Fort Apache Heritage Center was established via a tribal charter. Thus, the two tribal nonprofits do not follow the more typical pattern of entrepreneurial founders creating them.

The nontribal organizations in this modern group all had founders who exhibited strong entrepreneurial traits (Doelle 2013), and the early founders in this group all had direct connections to universities, at least at the outset. Especially significant is the even earlier pioneering work of Stuart Struever outside of the Southwest, back in Illinois. He was a professor at Northwestern University in Chicago, and in 1953 he founded a nonprofit that today is known as the Center for American Archeology (CAA). Struever initiated an intensive regional research program in southern Illinois and from 1969 through 1978 developed a massive excavation at a deeply stratified site known as Koster. It was an ambitious research program that included up to ten thousand public visitors annually at its peak, and in the late 1970s Struever laid the groundwork for a western field campus for CAA. A financial crisis at CAA led to Struever's founding of Crow Canyon Archaeological Center and leaving Northwestern to build the new nonprofit. One of the founders of Human Systems Research explicitly acknowledges the inspiration of Struever's example in his co-creation of an archaeological nonprofit in southern New Mexico in 1972 (Eidenbach 2014:12). Cynthia Irwin-Williams was also beginning her major excavation program in partnership with a nonprofit at Salmon Ruins in the early 1970s. The New Archaeology (e.g., Watson et al. 1971) of the late 1960s and early 1970s was not only stirring up archaeological methods and theory, it was also generating new institutional approaches to doing archaeology. The Mimbres Foundation was yet another example of this early pattern within the modern group of nonprofits.

Of today's nonprofits, only two, Crow Canyon and Archaeology Southwest, still emphasize regional programs of fieldwork, and the amount of fieldwork they take on is quite limited compared to the early nonprofits. In fact, large-scale research is now the domain of cultural resource management firms, which are mostly for-profit corporations. The Amerind Foundation and SAR now focus on advanced seminars and synthetic archaeological and anthropological publications. For the Mimbres Foundation, field research was a core activity including both regional survey and substantial excavations.

Archaeological advocacy is another theme of the modern nonprofits. The Archaeological Conservancy, Crow Canyon, Archaeology Southwest, SRI Foundation, and Colorado Plateau Archaeological Alliance all commit significant portions of their budgets to various aspects of advocacy. The Archaeological Institute of America and Edgar Lee Hewett played this role in achieving passage of the Antiquities Act of 1906

(Harmon et al. 2006; Thompson 2000). As I will discuss, the Mimbres Foundation played an important role in creating the Archaeological Resources Protection Act (ARPA) of 1979.

The other mission elements of the current nonprofits include synthetic research, often on regional scales and scales larger than the Southwest. Public outreach is common across all of the nonprofits, although the target audience for public education and outreach is often the local community. While several nonprofits curate collections from their past fieldwork as part of their mission, MNA is the only nonprofit providing curation as a fee-based service.

The Mimbres Foundation in the News

With increasing numbers of newspapers from around the nation being scanned and made available online, I searched for "Mimbres Foundation" and "Steven LeBlanc" and reviewed the first one hundred hits for each search. Along with some specific follow-up searches, I soon had nearly fifty articles, most dating to the mid-1970s from various New Mexico newspapers. These articles provide an interesting glimpse into the activities and impacts of the Mimbres Foundation and its president during its most active time.

Curiously, during the first field season in 1974 LeBlanc posted a classified ad in the *Silver City Daily Press* that stated: "The Mimbres Archaeological Center would like to study some membrainal [Mimbreño?] skeletons. If you have complete skeletons or parts that you would like to either donate or just let us look at we would appreciate your calling" (Peterson 1974:7).

It is clear from a variety of weekly calendar and short article announcements that LeBlanc was very active in giving talks about the work the foundation was undertaking. In 1975 an article showed a photo of LeBlanc, who announced the first successful tree-ring date of A.D. 1107 from the excavations (Peterson 1975:3). The foundation held annual open houses where information was shared with local community members, and one article notes that the students held "an impromptu ice cream social" and invited a number of neighbors (Peterson 1977a:5A). The survey work conducted throughout the valley would have brought LeBlanc and his students into regular contact with local landowners and with the consequences of long-term and ongoing pothunting activity.

In the fall of 1976, a series of five public discussions on pothunting was organized by Dr. Dale Geise, history professor at Western New Mexico University in Silver City, through a New Mexico Humanities Council grant. The two articles that covered the discussions in Deming and Silver City convey that it was a highly contentious topic.

A pair of Deming audience members (Cousland 1976:10), who were described in the article as "experienced amateur diggers," had been convicted in 1975 of looting a Mimbres site on federal land. They had been hired by an individual who was transporting artifacts to Arizona for sale on the art market in Scottsdale and the East (Collins and Michel 1985:85). The paper described how the Deming pair "excavate for bowls and jewelry, and when they come across an Indian burial, they often say a Christian prayer before 'we rebury the bones where we find them'" (Cousland 1976:10).

At the Silver City meeting, the newspaper article notes: "One Mimbres Foundation archaeologist from England said 'things in the U.S. are just too mercenary.' In England, he said, artifacts 'are considered the property of the crown.' But another unidentified member of the audience said he objected to 'the government sticking its nose into private property'" (Peterson 1976:1).

It was in this setting, where there were clear conflicts in values between professional archaeologists and local community members, that LeBlanc and others began the effort to establish a New Mexico law that would partly regulate, and slow the pace of, pothunting on private land. In early 1977, as preparations for the new bill were completed, the foundation felt increasing push back from southwestern New Mexico in particular. Some quotes from an article in the *Deming Graphic* convey these issues and the frustrations of LeBlanc:

> The director of the controversial Mimbres Foundation refuted charges that his organization seeks to strip the Mimbres valley of valuable Mimbreno Indian artifacts and ship them all to California.
>
> He (i.e. LeBlanc) said the most absurd argument centers on local objections that artifacts his team of student archaeologists remove are being shipped to California.
>
> Whereas his teams have to date removed some 40 bowls from the valley in three summers of excavation, he said last summer alone pothunters dug up more than 300 bowls which are being sold throughout the country.
>
> "If they are worried about our few pots that are gone," LeBlanc said, "then they should be worried about the hundreds and hundreds that are disappearing" [Peterson 1977b:7].

The reporter subsequently conveys LeBlanc's explanation that arrangements were being made with University of New Mexico to receive the Mimbres Foundation collections as a donation. He also notes that the collections could be loaned to an accredited museum if one were to be established locally in the future. Furthermore, he notes that the pothunting was destroying a resource with potential economic value if developed for tourism.

New Laws for Archaeological Resource Protection

In the fall of 1977 the New Mexico law was approved, and several articles note that the Mimbres Foundation and the University of New Mexico (UNM) had reached an agreement. The artifact collections did indeed go to the Maxwell Museum at UNM, and LeBlanc became a curator at the Maxwell, although his salary was paid by the Mimbres Foundation.

LeBlanc next worked with Mark Michel, the Society for American Archaeology, and a number of key politicians from Arizona and New Mexico to draft and pass the ARPA. The process is detailed nicely by Collins and Michel (1985). LeBlanc worked closely with Michel on the New Mexico law, and it is clear in the several published accounts (Collins and Michel 1985; Fowler and Malinky 2006) that LeBlanc played the role of a catalyst throughout the ARPA process. Motivated by firsthand experiences of the scale of the looting problem, LeBlanc made use of the institutional freedom that a nonprofit can provide. When the process of drafting the language for the future ARPA came to a critical point, LeBlanc stepped forward to raise the $10,000 sum that was needed, and Michel was hired as a lobbyist to move the work forward. The process was complex, but skilled leadership in the political and professional arenas brought about successful new legislation in remarkably short time. A bill introduced in February of 1979 was signed by President Carter on October 31 of the same year.

The Mimbres Foundation

While Steven LeBlanc initiated Mimbres Valley fieldwork in 1974, the Mimbres Foundation was formally incorporated in the state of California in 1976. LeBlanc brought in private donations and other funds to carry out a major research and site-protection program in the Mimbres Valley of southern New Mexico. Here I highlight six elements of the Mimbres Foundation history to illustrate the creative use of the nonprofit legal framework to accomplish objectives that might be more difficult, or even impossible, in another institutional context. In all of these, it was LeBlanc, as the president of the Mimbres Foundation, who was the prime mover.

Funding

A nonprofit organization provides an opportunity for wealthy individuals to make tax-deductible donations and can receive grants from private foundations. The critical challenge is to connect the donor to the nonprofit's mission. LeBlanc tells it best:

Unlike most archaeology in the United States, the Mimbres project was not the result of a University or other public organization using federal funds to undertake field research. Instead the impetus came from the art community. Most serious collectors of Mimbres pottery had little knowledge of Mimbres archaeology and even less of the level of site destruction. But, when made aware of the seriousness of the situation, the vast majority were only too willing to help. Thus the initial work was financed entirely by private donations from people connected with the arts, and most of our remaining work was also supported in this manner, although supplementary grants were made available by the government. In fact it was the vision of one man, Tony Berlant[,] that really made all the rest possible. An artist in his own right, Tony Berlant is also well known as a leading expert on Navajo blankets. He recognized the artistic worth of Mimbres pottery and began collecting pieces. When I subsequently explained to him the terrifying level of destruction, he took it upon himself to persuade others in the art community that something needed to be done to try and learn something about the Mimbres people before all the village sites disappeared. Fortunately, he convinced Edwin Janss of this need, and an initial grant from the Janss Foundation enabled us to begin work in the Mimbres Valley [LeBlanc 1983:12–13].

Research Methods

Despite being advised by many "to not waste my time there because all of the sites had been destroyed" (LeBlanc 2003:10), LeBlanc carried out fieldwork at multiple sites and found that there were effective ways to recover valuable information from what the looters had left behind. Initial excavations provided further insights into how to work in this area: "There was little use in working on the internal structure of a single site. Instead, the study of the relationships between sites seemed to be a more fruitful approach. It required the systematic survey of large areas, both to locate sites to excavate and to help understand how they were related to each other. Fortunately, such an approach allowed us to analyze the settlement patterns of the region and the fluctuations in population over time" (LeBlanc 1983:16).

Work with the Best and Brightest

LeBlanc managed to recruit field personnel of very high quality, and as a group they listened to and learned from LeBlanc and became part of the expansion and continuation of his vision. Wages were certainly adequate, and many of the field crew used Mimbres material in subsequent MA and PhD degrees, either directly or indirectly. Many from those early crews have continued to work in the Mimbres region and have brought second and third generations of students into the research area.

Protect Sites for the Future

Archaeological field research is expensive, and the analysis and report-preparation processes, followed by long-term curation of artifacts, have become increasingly costly over time. Fairly early on, LeBlanc had a brilliant insight that the most cost-effective way to preserve the information in Mimbres area sites was to purchase the property where a site was located and conserve the site for the future. As a result, the Mimbres Foundation was soon the owner of several archaeological sites and held conservation easements on several others. This idea of protection through ownership was expanded many times over by the Archaeological Conservancy, of which LeBlanc was a co-founder in 1980.

Advocacy and ARPA

As I have described, LeBlanc's work in the Mimbres Valley led to him working with legislators to pass an anti-looting bill in the state of New Mexico. On the heels of that success, he worked with a lobbyist and other archaeologists to draft the language of ARPA. Passed in 1979, ARPA corrected a number of the deficiencies of the Antiquities Act of 1906 and has led to the arrest and conviction of looters in the Mimbres area and other areas across the United States.

Database Development

Long before "big data" was an everyday phrase, LeBlanc had assembled a photographic database of every Mimbres vessel that he could access. That process continued with subsequent Mimbres area researchers and is now an online database with over nine thousand images (Mimbres Pottery Images Digital Database [MimPIDD; tDAR ID: 377852]).

The Mimbres Foundation in Historical Context

Nearly every nonprofit is established by a visionary. In some of the early examples, that individual was the source of the vision and had the personal wealth to launch the organization as well. Recent founders, however, have almost all brought the vision and then figured out how to raise the financial resources to get the organization running. This was clearly the case with LeBlanc and the Mimbres Foundation.

With initial success, the vision of the founder tends to expand. The Mimbres Foundation experienced rapid success in its research mission, which led to an innovative conservation strategy, advocacy to strengthen laws to protect archaeological sites, and research, publication, and expansion of the Mimbres pottery database.

If it was so successful, then why did the Mimbres Foundation close? The transition from the leadership of the founder to the next generation of leadership is one of the most difficult times in the developmental cycle of a nonprofit. Multigenerational success requires substantial preparation. While the Mimbres Foundation was both innovative and effective in fund-raising, its resources were invested almost exclusively in implementing the organization's highly focused mission. Resources were not invested in developing an administrative and fund-raising staff or in recruiting new governing board members, which are institutional necessities for a successful nonprofit. In the case of the Mimbres Foundation, it seems fair to say that the mission as defined by the founder had largely been accomplished. It was thus entirely appropriate for the founder and his board members to conclude that closing down the organization was the right thing to do.

Carrying the Legacy of the Mimbres Foundation Forward

In a brief article titled "ARPA: Some Lessons," near the end of a set of essays about ARPA, LeBlanc (1985) contemplates the collaborative success of getting the legislation passed, and he points out a number of institutional failings in the archaeological community. One is the governing structure of our primary professional society, the SAA, where the institutional memory of governing board members tends to be shallow due to three-year terms and their very part-time roles. Another is the bureaucratic insularity of government agencies like the National Park Service. LeBlanc (1985:117) asks a very important question: "Where do leadership and innovation in archaeology come from?" He concludes that the history of ARPA shows that it does not come from our established institutions: "The lesson is, if you want change or something new, do it yourself" (LeBlanc 1985:117). In the context of LeBlanc's experience in 1985, I think that conclusion is justified. However, there has been a significant advancement in the SAA through continuity in the administrative leadership and growth in its financial capacity. In addition, as summarized in this chapter, our archaeological nonprofit organizations have proliferated and diversified considerably since 1985.

Nonprofits have a mission-based focus and, when well managed, a stability of personnel that allows them to grow beyond the vision and capacity of their founders. They can play a diversity of roles. Small nonprofits often are tightly focused; larger ones have multiple goals. The role of nonprofits in advocacy seems to be increasing. With the development of new laws and regulations, monitoring those who are responsible for implementing the laws and regulations is an ongoing necessity. It is a role for increasing numbers of nonprofits, and new ways of advocating for archaeological resources continue to be developed within the nonprofit community.

When the Mimbres Foundation took on the ownership of archaeological properties in the Mimbres Valley, it took on obligations to monitor those properties to ensure that they were not damaged by looters or otherwise harmed. Prior to closing down, the Mimbres Foundation transferred the ownership of those easements and properties to Archaeology Southwest (formerly the Center for Desert Archaeology). Conservation of archaeological properties is part of the mission of Archaeology Southwest, and its staff members are now responsible for the long-term protection of those sites. At the Mattocks site, Archaeology Southwest was able to expand the protective easement by working with the landowner of the adjacent parcel to the north. In addition, Archaeology Southwest staff are working to identify and pursue additional site-protection priorities in the greater Mimbres area (Laurenzi et al. 2013).

The legacy of the Mimbres Foundation also continues with the work of the Archaeological Conservancy. From their founding in 1980 to the present, they have expanded to a national scale and own over five hundred properties. Archaeology Southwest pursues both fee ownership and conservation easements as protection measures but works only in the North American Southwest, where the two organizations collaborate on protection efforts.

The greatest legacy of the Mimbres Foundation is its body of published work, much of which is cited in the chapters here; the curated collections at the Maxwell Museum at UNM; and the massive photographic database—all of which are tangible evidence of a mission achieved. Somewhat less tangible, but perhaps even more valuable, is the transmission of the vision that Steven LeBlanc brought to the founding of the Mimbres Foundation to subsequent generations of archaeologists.

Conclusion

When Steven LeBlanc initiated work in the Mimbres Valley, he was employed in an academic position at University of California, Los Angeles. As noted, Stuart Struever was at Northwestern University and was running a major program of excavation and research through the CAA in Illinois. Struever (2007) has suggested that a nonprofit is the ideal organization to carry out a long-term research program. He established Crow Canyon Archaeological Center near Cortez, Colorado, in 1983, and that organization has been pursuing a regional research goal ever since. Cynthia Irwin-Williams was a professor at Eastern New Mexico University when she conducted her major excavations in partnership with the nonprofit that manages Salmon Ruin. That three ambitious archaeologists in academic settings found nonprofit institutions an effective way to do modern archaeology is telling.

The agility of the nonprofit was particularly well suited to LeBlanc's focused mission. His ability to communicate his vision helped an entirely new set of donors to support archaeological fieldwork and research. The low overhead of the foundation ensured that scarce resources went directly to the mission, not to a university bureaucracy. When decisions had to be made regarding purchases of property to protect archaeological sites, the foundation could act quickly. It accomplished what might have been possible in a university or museum framework, but that framework would have been much less flexible and would not likely have achieved nearly as much.

The Mimbres Foundation was an early innovator and truly made a difference in nonprofit archaeology and in the profession as a whole. That legacy is carried forward on multiple fronts by other organizations and individuals who were shaped by the Mimbres Foundation and Steven LeBlanc.

References Cited

Cerino, Katherine, William H. Doelle, and John Ware. 2016. One-Hundred Years of Southwest Nonprofits. *Kiva* 81:100–119.

Collins, Robert B., and Mark Michel. 1985. Preserving the Past: Origins of the Archaeological Resources Protection Act of 1979. *American Archaeology* 5(2):84–89.

Cousland, Harold R. 1976. Pot Hunters, Archeologists, Debate over Indian Artifacts. *Deming Graphic* 4 October:10. Deming, New Mexico.

Doelle, William H. 2013. The Role of Nonprofit Organizations in the History of Southwest Archaeology. In *Archaeology in the Great Basin and Southwest: Papers in Honor of Don D. Fowler*, edited by Nancy J. Parezo and Joel Janetski, pp. 280–289. University of Utah Press, Salt Lake City.

Eidenbach, Peter. 2014. The Origins of Human Systems Research. *NewsMAC: Newsletter of the New Mexico Archaeological Council* 2014(2):12–15.

Fowler, Don D., and Barbara Malinky. 2006. The Origins of ARPA: Crafting the Archaeological Resources Protection Act of 1979. In *Presenting Archaeology in Court*, edited by Sherry Hutt, Marion P. Forsyth, and David Tarler, pp. 1–23. AltaMira Press, New York.

Harmon, David, Francis P. McManamon, and Dwight T. Pitcaithley. 2006. The Antiquities Act: A Cornerstone of Archaeology, Historic Preservation, and Conservation. In *The Antiquities Act: A Century of American Archaeology, Historic Preservation, and Nature Conservation*, edited by David Harmon, Francis P. McManamon, and Dwight T. Pitcaithley, pp. 267–285. University of Arizona Press, Tucson.

Laurenzi, Andy, Matthew Peeples, and William H. Doelle. 2013. Cultural Resources Priority Area Planning in Sub-Mogollon Arizona and New Mexico. *Advances in Archaeological Practice: A Journal of the Society for American Archaeology* 1:61–76.

LeBlanc, Steven A. 1983. *The Mimbres People: Ancient Painters of the American Southwest.* Thames and Hudson, London.

———. 1985. ARPA: Some Lessons. *American Archaeology* 5(2):115–117.

———. 2003. Mimbres Archaeology and Site Preservation. *Archaeology Southwest Magazine* 17(4):10.

Peterson, Richard. 1974. Notices. *Silver City Daily Press* 9 October:7. Silver City, New Mexico.

———. 1975. Date Reported for Prehistoric Mimbrenos. *Silver City Daily Press* 11 July:3. Silver City, New Mexico.

———. 1976. Artifact Forum Draws Large Crowd. *Silver City Daily Press* 29 September:1. Silver City, New Mexico.

———. 1977a. Mimbres News. *Silver City Daily Press* 2 June:5A. Silver City, New Mexico.

———. 1977b. Archeologist Doesn't Dig Pothunting by Bulldozer. *Deming Graphic* 7 February:7. Deming, New Mexico. Reprinted from *Silver City Daily Press* 2 February. Silver City, New Mexico.

Struever, Stuart. 2007. Remarks by Stuart Struever to the Board of Trustees of Crow Canyon Archaeological Center, October 12, 2007. Manuscript on file, Board Minutes, Crow Canyon Archaeological Center, Cortez, Colorado.

Thompson, Raymond H. 2000. An Old and Reliable Authority: An Act for the Preservation of American Antiquities. *Journal of the Southwest* 42:191–381.

Watson, Patty Jo, Steven A. LeBlanc, and Charles L. Redman. 1971. *Explanation in Archeology: An Explicitly Scientific Approach.* Columbia University Press, New York.

13

Thoughts on Mimbres Archaeology

STEVEN A. LEBLANC

I BEGAN WORK ON MIMBRES as an undergraduate. I found a copy of the Swarts site monograph (Cosgrove and Cosgrove 1932) in the college library rather by accident and got interested in applying the idea of a generative grammar to the bowl designs. I did not get anywhere and fortunately gave up early on. But from that point, I was always interested in the bowl designs. I decided at some point to try and learn something about the Mimbres before all the sites were destroyed and was advised to look on the peripheries for a place to work because all the big sites in the Mimbres drainage had been destroyed beyond study. I am not very good at taking advice, however, and so I looked in the Mimbres Valley, as well as around the edges. I wandered around the Mimbres area for a few weeks and came across the Mattocks site (Nesbitt 1931). It did not seem completely destroyed to me, and so I started a Mimbres archaeological project. The takeaway is listen to your elders, but it is sometimes best to ignore them.

The focus of the project was to be the Mimbres Classic period, and it was more about the social system that created the pottery than anything else. Thus, I did not initially dig deeply into the extant literature on the entire sequence in the Mogollon region. But I believed then, as I do now, in a combination of survey and excavation, as one without the other does not allow for much interpretation of social systems. So we began a limited survey the very first season. Initially, it was just to find out what was around the Mattocks site and what sites existed on the land that was available to us for research. But to understand what happened, one needs to be aware of the state of knowledge at the time.

It is hard today to realize how little was known about the Mimbres region as a whole in the early 1970s. Conceptually, the sequence began with Haury's (1936)

262 • Steven A. LeBlanc

pithouse sequence that started perhaps at A.D. 600. There were hints of earlier sites of course, but the information was limited, and there had been no real attempt at synthesis. The only large project other than Haury's was the Cosgroves' work in the late 1920s, and that was before tree-ring dating was well established. As far as I can tell, the Cosgroves thought one needed wood to get dates and that charcoal did not work, which is why they threw away all the charcoal from burned rooms. Such was the state of affairs. Anything earlier than A.D. 600 was poorly understood, at best.

The later end of the sequence was every bit as enigmatic. The end of the Mimbres sequence was vaguely presumed to be in the A.D. 1200s, but later sites certainly existed. One only had to visit Kwilleylekia (LA 4937) in the upper Gila region to the west to realize this. Having been dug by a pothunter, the site was hard to make sense of, and it was over on the Gila River, not in the Mimbres Valley.

So, we had a purported six hundred years of a reasonably well-understood pottery-producing sequence in the Mimbres Valley. In the valley proper, little to nothing was appreciably earlier or later. It seems obvious that there must have been, but it was unknown and not even much thought about. I think in part this was the lure of the Mimbres pottery for generations of archaeologists, including myself.

That began to change almost immediately. Some enterprising youths on the project climbed the nearby hill. They came back after finding a pithouse site up there, with all plain pottery! Of course, farther north and west in the Mogollon area such hilltop sites were known, the Promontory site (Martin et al. 1949) being the most obvious with which to compare it. It was just that no one had connected the dots. If there were hilltop sites elsewhere, why not in the Mimbres? But who had looked? Finding what we now call the McAnally site (Diehl and LeBlanc 2001) changed that. Almost instantly, 350 years were added to the early end of the sequence.

Once survey began in an organized fashion, we quickly found the Janss site (Nelson and LeBlanc 1986). It surely looked like Kwilleylekia. These sites are what is termed Salado, what we came to call the Cliff phase, and were inhabited over two centuries after the Mimbres Classic period. Then we found sites that looked different and realized they fit in between Mimbres and these Salado–Cliff phase sites. Of course, such sites were known from the Bootheel of New Mexico (Nelson and LeBlanc 1986), but again, it took a while to realize the entire sequence existed in the Mimbres Valley. This was not an unlikely finding, but it was something that had not been thought out in a systematic way. Two hundred years or more were quickly added to the later end of the prehistoric ceramic sequence. We started with six hundred years of sequence, and now we had twelve hundred years. To add to these revelations, during the first field season we obtained some tree-ring samples from the Mattocks site, and late that winter I got the dates back from the Laboratory of Tree-Ring Research in Tucson. It seemed to me that the samples came from contexts that were late in the Mimbres sequence, but they dated only into the very beginning of the A.D. 1100s. I then made a great leap of faith that has held up to this day. I decided that Mimbres Classic was equivalent in time to the Chaco Interaction Sphere and that both ended as organized systems around A.D. 1130. Suddenly, the overall sequence was longer, but the Mimbres Classic period was shorter. In one field season, much had changed. From my perspective, that overall ceramic-period sequence has held up for now more than forty years. It has been refined but not dramatically changed. The first field season was very exciting.

Some Open Questions and Some Suggestions

My purpose here is to suggest some areas of future research. I think some are low-hanging fruit, and some are very tough. My advice is this: if you do not have tenure, stay away from the really tough ones.

The Mimbres–Post-Mimbres Transition

I will lay out what I think happened at the end of the Mimbres Classic. I cannot fully support the argument, but at least I can set up a model that is testable and makes clear where research could be focused to address it. I am not fully defending this model here, rather I am simply saying there is some evidence for it, and it seems to me to be the model most worth testing.

First, I will try to summarize what I think happened with the Chaco Interaction Sphere and later events in the northern Southwest because I think that they parallel in many ways what happened in the Mimbres area and that the events are interwoven.

Chaco started earlier than most archaeologists realize, probably prior to A.D. 800 (Plog and Heitman 2010). The sequence thus lasted for several hundred years. However, at around A.D. 1130 something really dramatic and I think traumatic happened. The Chaco system collapsed. There was probably some population decline, perhaps 50 percent or slightly more, and for two generations or so, social chaos. I think most of the extreme processing events (i.e., cannibalism) took place then. Sites became small, hard to find, and people often used kiva-like structures as domestic domiciles. After a couple of generations, the societies became more organized, people began to live in larger communities again, and what we think of as the classic Pueblo III (PIII) commenced. The regional population rebounded, perhaps not to Chaco levels, but to substantial, visible levels. Now clearly, not all the people disappeared at the beginning of this collapse. There were clear continuities, but for two to three generations, there really was a "dark age" of some kind. When habitations again become more easily recognized archaeologically, they do not seem to have been as evenly spread over the landscape as they were previously. Later during PIII times, empty zones or buffer zones opened between clusters of sites. They may have begun by the time we see sites becoming more visible, but that is not clear. I will come back to Chaco shortly.

I suspect something similar happened in the Mimbres area. Things changed gradually for several hundred years. Yes, the pottery changed. Yes, people moved to aboveground rooms. Yes, the nature of the ceremonial architecture changed, but the continuities both in terms of behavior and in site location were remarkably strong. Sites tended to stay in the same places for centuries, and their layouts followed the same patterns. Burial practices were quite stable. Vessel forms and color schemes changed very gradually, as did pottery designs. Around A.D. 1130, however, something dramatic happened. Mimbres pottery ceased to be made in the Mimbres Valley as far as we can tell; it may have been made a bit longer in the Eastern Mimbres area. But in any case, the level of production after A.D. 1130 would have been miniscule compared with earlier levels. Large sites were completely or partially abandoned. For the next two or three generations, people were hard to find on the landscape. They were there, at least in some places, but they were much less visible. Some people continued to occupy or reoccupy the larger Mimbres Classic sites, but the architecture was different, painted pottery does not seem to have been locally made, and population sizes were smaller. I think we begin to see buffer zones opening, but they are not obvious until perhaps A.D. 1200, the same as farther north in the former Chaco area.

There is a strong similarity between what occurs in the old Chaco sphere (i.e., Chaco Canyon and the larger region where Chaco outliers and roads existed) and in the Mimbres area. In both cases, something dramatic happened at A.D. 1130. Both cases include a two- to three-generation span during which it is hard to find people. Sites that do exist are small. Then the population seems to rebound, sites get larger, and sites appear to begin to cluster on the landscape.

The major difference between the two areas is that the old Chaco area is very large compared to the Mimbres, and so we can see the pattern over a broad area in the north. We can envision the Mimbres area running from just north of the Gila Cliff Dwelling region to near the present Mexican border and from just over the Arizona line near Duncan to the Rio Grande. For the Mimbres area, it appears that the southern part of the old territory became part of the Casas Grandes Interaction Sphere, the middle part seems to have been an empty zone, and the northern part may have become part of the Reserve area group of sites (but in this time range termed the Late Reserve or Tularosa phases). That is, the Mimbres cultural area no longer existed and was broken into several considerably different political systems. The old Chaco area also splintered but not nearly so dramatically.

It is the southern portion of the Mimbres area on which I now focus. We term these sites Black Mountain phase. They exist from the Mexican border up the Mimbres

Valley about to where the Swarts site was located. Farther north, the valley was mainly empty or at least empty most of the time. Over time, the empty zone widened, and the northern tier of Black Mountain phase sites retreated farther and farther south along the Mimbres River. Such Black Mountain phase sites do not exist in the Gila Valley, which seems to lie in the empty zone. Thus, I predict that it will always be hard to find sites that date to A.D. 1130–1180 anywhere in the Mimbres area. They are there, but they are small and will be hard to date. Sites do seem to exist from the Swarts area south, but I suspect most will turn out to be post–A.D. 1180.

We should find sites that are Casas Grandes–like in the southern part of the Mimbres area. They will have dates as early as A.D. 1180. The implication, of course, is that Paquimé in some form was in existence by that time. It may not have been the Paquimé we see today but some earlier version of it. Remember that if it had not been excavated so completely, we would not see the A.D. 800s portion of Pueblo Bonito either. In fact, the west wing of the early Pueblo Bonito has roof-beam tree-ring dates of A.D. 919, yet some lintel dates and some radiocarbon dates are perhaps seventy years earlier (Plog and Heitman 2010; Windes and Ford 1996). If that same type of hard-to-see early occupation existed at Paquimé, we could be seeing post–A.D. 1250 architecture on a site that was founded and important in A.D. 1180.

I think a low-hanging-fruit research project is to date Postclassic sites in the Mimbres Valley. If enough are sampled, I suspect late A.D. 1100s dates will be found, and our conception of Paquimé and the Casas Grandes Interaction Sphere and its relationship to Mimbres will change dramatically. Moreover, we should see a consolidation of sites over time; they will get larger, and the buffer zone or empty zone to the north will get wider.

I have no useful ideas about how Black Mountain relates to the Cliff phase. It is worth pointing out that, to my knowledge, the latest tree-ring dates of any sites in the Anasazi or Mogollon area that are not the locations of historic sites (i.e., Hopi, Zuni, Acoma, Rio Grande pueblos) are in the old Mimbres cultural area. These dates are from the Janss and Kwilleylekia sites at just before A.D. 1400. Whatever process led to the abandonment of so much of the Southwest, it appears at this point that it took longer in the Mimbres area than most other places. Looking more closely at this end point is another research topic that could be approached with a reasonable probability of success.

Mimbres Times

The benefits of refining our dates for the Late Pithouse through Mimbres Classic periods are obvious. Many people are working on this problem, and so little needs to be said. However, one point might be worth making. It is hard to see how the Classic is much shorter than A.D. 1000–1130. We have records of more than nine thousand complete Mimbres Style III Black-on-white bowls. Extrapolating from sherd counts to estimates of complete vessels, there must have been five times that many bowls produced (LeBlanc 2010). This is around four times the number of earlier Styles I and II Black-on-white bowls. Even if we cut just twenty-five years off the Classic period, it becomes hard to contemplate how it could be so short, based on the numbers of bowls. If we reduce the time to A.D. 1050–1130, then how could all those bowls have been produced in eighty years when Boldface (Style I) and Transitional (Style II) bowls are so much rarer and would have been made for three hundred years? I think we do not understand the A.D. 900s very well, but I think the timing of events from A.D. 1000 to 1130 will hold few surprises.

My feeling is that fieldwork will continue to focus on this Late Pithouse and Classic interval, and researchers will continue to use the collections in museums. I suspect increases in knowledge will be incremental and not revolutionary, but we might be surprised.

Earlier Times

It is the time prior to A.D. 700 that I think holds significant promise for new data and important new insights. However, it is a tough time interval to work on, and those without tenure should be careful in deciding to attack it. This is because prior to around A.D. 550, most sites were located on hilltops. These sites are hard to access, and the soil is often very compacted, making excavations very difficult (Diehl and LeBlanc 2001). We at the Mimbres Foundation found a number of hilltop sites with as many as eighty pithouse depressions (Blake et al. 1986). It now appears that at least some of these pithouses date to A.D. 200–550. The ones we tested had pottery associated with them.

We did not test many structures (Diehl and LeBlanc 2001), but if a lot of these hilltop pithouse depressions were pre-pottery, I think we should have found some of them. Perhaps our sample was small and biased, but so far there is little evidence for farmers in the Mimbres Valley prior to A.D. 200. This lack of pre-pottery sites contrasts with lower, more arid environments, including the area closer to Deming (see chapter 1) or into Arizona, where there seem to be some pre-pottery *trincheras*— hilltop sites with low stone walls or terraces—as well as sites in flatter locations, just as there are in Chihuahua, Sonora, and parts of Arizona (Hard and Roney 2007). If the early farming–pre-pottery horizon seems well established to the south of the Mimbres Valley, then why do we not find the same number or even more of these sites (either trincheras or lower lying) in the better watered, presumably more fertile Mimbres Valley during the pre-pottery–farming period?

The one obvious explanation for the lack of pre-pottery sites in the Mimbres Valley is that the sites are there, but we have not found them, perhaps because we do not have the right paradigm to locate them. The other possibility is that they are not there for some reason. Based on recent conversations with John Roney, I can propose a possible reason. What if the early agricultural adaptation focused on spreading summer monsoonal rain over river floodplains? This would not entail ditches taking water from permanent streams or rivers, but rather catching more easily controlled, more ephemeral summer rains from small side drainages. Such water could be spread over the floodplains of major drainages, such as the Gila. However, the water itself would come from more ephemeral sources such as side drainages, not from the river itself. That is, larger drainages could provide good flatland and good soils, but the permanent water flowing in them might have been too hard to control. A solution was to find a place where a side drainage enters a major tributary and use the water from the side tributary to water the crops grown in the major drainage floodplain. If a drainage is small enough, it can be used both for the water that flows in it and the floodplain it contains, but if a drainage is too large, then the side tributary method might have been used. So early farming sites might be located on a good floodplain, where the water of a small discharge drainage can be diverted onto the floodplain and easily controlled.

This might explain both where the sites are and where they are not. The Mimbres River simply might have been too large for direct water control, and perhaps it had too few (but not none) side tributaries to be useful. Only later, perhaps after around A.D. 200, was the technology developed for dealing with rivers like the Mimbres, at which point we find a larger population in the valley. The benefit of this model is that it is testable both within and outside the Mimbres Valley. There are a few possible locations in the Mimbres Valley that could have been used this way, and looking for sites near them would potentially be fruitful. Looking for sites in lower elevation areas in and beyond the Mimbres drainage that fit this criterion might also prove useful. For example, we might expect early sites between the NAN Ranch and the Swarts sites, where a small side drainage flows into the Mimbres River and the floodplain is nice and wide. Another locality might be further downstream where Cameron Creek flows into the Mimbres. This approach to farming might also explain why we can find early sites along the Gila River, where the flow must have been large and hard to control but which has good floodplains and where a number of small side tributaries could have been used as water sources.

While I do not want to get into this topic here, a strong case can be made that many hilltop sites are a response to warfare or its threat. Not all sites are located on hilltops during the late pre-pottery or early pottery periods, but many are, especially where such locations occur near farmable areas. It is thus interesting that the pre-pottery use of hillside and hilltop locations does continue into the pottery period because apparently what changed was the farming method, not the social circumstances that required people to live on hilltops. The land forms change to some degree between pre-pottery and early pottery sites. Instead of basalt outcrops often being selected for site locations as in the pre-pottery period, any knoll sufficed, and while the basalt hills provided the material to make trincheras, the hills like those in the Mimbres did not. So while the sites look different, the logic does not. This is the important point: the overall conceptual pattern remains the same, but the land form of the sites changes.

Thus, we might recognize a three-stage process: (1) pre-pottery trincheras sites initially used floodplain farming with side-drainage water; (2) then pottery-period hilltop sites without trincheras used water from larger drainages, such as the Mimbres; and (3) finally, the hilltop locations were abandoned and the focus shifted to first benches above the floodplain for the next nine hundred years. It does seem that to some degree in the Mimbres area people shifted from using lower elevations with trincheras to using higher river-valley locations with just hilltop sites. Does this mean that once the technology was developed for farming larger drainages, places like the Mimbres Valley were more desirable than the earlier locations, and so there was a population–settlement pattern shift?

Questions like these are of considerable interest both from a local perspective and from a larger "How does farming evolve?" perspective. The problem with these early sites is that they are very hard to excavate. The soil is rock hard, they are way up on hilltops, and trash would have been tossed down the slopes and is likely gone. Non-hilltop sites during this same period, to the extent they exist, are probably buried and very hard to find. Consequently, we have a great question, not easily addressed.

Mimbres and Casas Grandes Pottery

The Mimbres Pottery Images Digital Database (MimPIDD) now has pictures of about eleven thousand bowls. It surprises me how little use is made of it and how little others care about it. New bowls are still coming to light, but there is no systematic plan to incorporate them into the archive. The original focus was on complete vessels, but with that base, very large sherds or partial bowls can now be usefully included in the archive. Who has given any thought to systematically adding them?

From a larger perspective, if MimPIDD is useful, why not build a Casas Grandes pottery image archive for comparison? The same could be said for Reserve painted ceramics, but I will focus on Casas Grandes pottery here.

It is clear from MimPIDD that a small painted jar shape that is found in the Mimbres is the same shape as later Ramos Polychrome jars from the Casas Grande area. I do not believe this is a widely used shape in the rest of the Southwest. This implies a connection between the two traditions. Similarly, the famous Ramos Polychrome jar form with a human or animal face molded into the upper profile is also found in the Mimbres Classic. There are less than half a dozen Mimbres jar examples, but there are some. Again, this jar form is unique to these two traditions, also implying a link. Also, the Ramos Polychrome practice of negative painting, especially when used for figurative elements, is a common Mimbres painting style; once again, such a design concept is very rare outside the Mimbres–Casas Grandes regions. These similarities are ones that I have noticed without the benefit of a searchable Casas Grandes pottery archive to help with such comparisons. Clearly, these two painting traditions are more strongly linked than most researchers realize. With a large Casas Grandes pottery image archive, such comparisons could be investigated efficiently, and most likely additional linkages would be found.

I do think we know much more about Mimbres pottery production than we did forty years ago. Neutron activation analysis has helped, and so has MimPIDD. We still do not really understand why the Mimbres painting tradition deviated so radically from its contemporaries, but this problem seems solvable with the tools at hand. This is a promising area of research that many different people with different skills could approach, with good outcomes likely.

The Mesoamerican Connection

That there was a connection between the southwestern United States and Mesoamerica is obvious. The question is, what was it like? And what does it imply? Setting aside the Hohokam area, the most obvious place where we see such a connection prior to A.D. 1130 is between Mimbres and Chaco Canyon on the one hand and Mesoamerica on the other. While some Southwest-Mesoamerica similarities, such as the use of kilts as men's clothing and shared iconography, are widespread in space and time, some are more focused. Turquoise and macaws are found in Chaco and Mimbres, are very rare elsewhere in the non-Hohokam Southwest prior to A.D. 1130, and both relate to Mesoamerica. The macaws obviously originated there, and turquoise was highly valued there, as well. While I do not want to discuss this topic at length, the point is that Mimbres is a key area in our understanding of the early timing of this linkage, and it should be included more in the thinking about it.

Another southern connection is less thought about, although Wilcox (1986) brought it up years ago. This is the span of Uto-Aztecan speakers that runs from central Mexico to northern Arizona, ignoring for the present the Uto-Aztecan-speaking Numic of the Great Basin. In the past, this linguistic chain may have gone north as far as southeastern Utah. The historic period gap between the Piman speakers of southern Arizona and Hopi speakers much farther north (both Uto-Aztecan languages) probably did not exist prior to the late A.D. 1300s. So this long linguistic chain would have facilitated communication over these hundreds of kilometers. One example of the potential consequences of a Uto-Aztecan linguistic chain is the focus on red-slipped pottery in the western Southwest. From well into Mexico to southeast Utah, red slipping was the norm for a very long time. To the east, beyond this linguistic chain, in much of present-day New Mexico and Colorado, white slipping dominated. Only well into the A.D. 1200s and more into the 1300s did the desire for red-slipped pottery penetrate this eastern area. Was this red slipping a product in some way of the linguistic chain in the west? Whether because of some deep symbolic meaning or just emulation, it must be telling us something about how communication and related-ness worked. Interestingly, people in the Mimbres area participated in this red-slipped tradition early on via San Francisco Red and Mogollon Red-on-brown pottery. Then the red-slipped tradition died out and white slipping replaced it. Did people in the Mimbres region speak a Uto-Aztecan language? Did they speak another language and simply emulate the red-slipped tradition for a while before they rejected it? Surely, this is telling us something about Mimbres origins and cultural change, but what is it?

On a final and speculative note, Lekson's (1999) Chaco meridian, a north–south line that links Pueblo Bonito with Aztec and Paquimé, goes right through the Mim-bres area. The large, unique Mimbres site of Old Town is very close to the meridian line, as is the large Postclassic Casas Grandes period site of Black Mountain. While I am not sure I am a fan of the meridian concept, the fact that its southern extension is anchored in the south very near Guasave, Mexico, does give one pause. The Guasave area is a candidate for a core area where a Mesoamerican-southwestern U.S. connec-tion lies. Perhaps we have it backward. Perhaps the meridian is a Guasave meridian and that is why Pueblo Bonito, Paquimé, and Aztec, as well as some special sites in the Mimbres area, are all directly north of Guasave. Maybe a Guasave meridian is the ultimate expression of a Mesoamerican connection that includes the Mimbres rather than an expression of a Chaco-based conceptual center.

Conclusions

One has the feeling that after forty years of Mimbres research (which is my time frame), we have made significant headway on some fronts but little on others. Perhaps that is not surprising, but it is disappointing. Do we really think we know how the Mimbres Classic period ended? I do not. Do we really think we know the dating of Paquimé, which is very relevant to many Mimbres issues? I do not. Do we really think we know why the Mimbres painted pottery diverged so significantly and rapidly from the rest of southwestern pottery in the A.D. 900s? I do not. Thus, the answers to some questions are still quite elusive after all this time.

I am encouraged by the number of people, new and old, still interested in the Mimbres. I have hope that some of these issues will be resolved in the near future.

References Cited

Blake, Michael, Steven A. LeBlanc, and Paul E. Minnis. 1986. Changing Settlement and Population in the Mimbres Valley, SW New Mexico. *Journal of Field Archaeology* 13:439–464.

Cosgrove, H. S., and C. B. Cosgrove. 1932. *The Swarts Ruin, a Typical Mimbres Site in Southwestern New Mexico*. Papers of the Peabody Museum of Archaeology and Ethnology Vol. 15(1). Harvard University, Cambridge, Massachusetts.

Diehl, Michael W., and Steven A. LeBlanc. 2001. *Early Pithouse Villages of the Mimbres Valley and Beyond: The McAnally and Thompson Sites in their Cultural and Ecological Contexts.* Papers of the Peabody Museum of Archaeology and Ethnology 83. Harvard University, Cambridge, Massachusetts.

Hard, Robert J., and John R. Roney. 2007. Cerros de Trincheras in Northwestern Chihuahua. In *Trincheras Sites in Time, Space, and Society*, edited by Suzanne K. Fish, Paul R. Fish, and M. Elisa Villalpando, pp. 11–52. University of Arizona Press, Tucson.

Haury, Emil W. 1936. *The Mogollon Culture of Southwestern New Mexico*. Medallion Papers 20. Gila Pueblo, Globe, Arizona.

LeBlanc, Steven A. 2010. The Painters of the Pots. In *Mimbres Lives and Landscapes*, edited by Margaret C. Nelson and Michelle Hegmon, pp. 75–81. School for Advanced Research Press, Santa Fe, New Mexico.

Lekson, Stephen H. 1999. *The Chaco Meridian: Centers of Political Power in the Ancient Southwest*. AltaMira Press, Walnut Creek, California.

Martin, Paul S., John B. Rinaldo, and Ernst Antevs. 1949. *Cochise and Mogollon Sites, Pine Lawn Valley, Western New Mexico*. Fieldiana Vol. 38(1). Chicago Natural History Museum, Chicago.

Nelson, Ben A., and Steven A. LeBlanc. 1986. *Short-Term Sedentism in the American Southwest: The Mimbres Valley Salado*. University of New Mexico Press, Albuquerque.

Nesbitt, Paul H. 1931. *The Ancient Mimbrenos: Based on Investigations at the Mattocks Ruin, Mimbres Valley, New Mexico*. Logan Museum, Beloit College, Beloit, Wisconsin.

Plog, Steven, and Carrie Heitman. 2010. Hierarchy and Social Inequality in the American Southwest, A.D. 800–1200. *Proceedings of the National Academy of Sciences* 107:19619–19626.

Wilcox, David R. 1986. The Tepiman Connection: A Model of Mesoamerican-Southwestern Interaction. In *Ripples in the Chichimec Sea: New Considerations of Southwestern-Mesoamerican Interactions*, edited by Frances Joan Mathien and Randall H. McGuire, pp. 135–154. Southern Illinois University Press, Carbondale.

Windes, Thomas C., and Dabney Ford. 1996. The Chaco Wood Project: The Chronometric Reappraisal of Pueblo Bonito. *American Antiquity* 61:295–310.

CONTRIBUTORS

Roger Anyon (MA, University of New Mexico) has been active in Mimbres archaeology for over four decades, beginning with the Mimbres Foundation in 1975 and through the publication of *The Galaz Ruin* monograph with Steven LeBlanc in 1984. Between 1985 and 1996, he was the tribal archaeologist at the Pueblo of Zuni, New Mexico, where he focused on repatriation and cultural landscapes. He worked as a consultant to many southwestern tribes from 1996 to 2001. He is currently an archaeologist with the Pima County (Arizona) Office of Sustainability and Conservation, where he has worked since 2001. His primary research interests are Mimbres archaeology, cultural landscapes, and social memory as represented in the archaeological record.

Darrell Creel (PhD, University of Arizona) was an associate professor in the Department of Anthropology and director of the Texas Archeological Research Laboratory, University of Texas, Austin. He has conducted research in the Mimbres area since 1982, first on the NAN Ranch Project, then the Old Town Project, the Harris Site Project, and, most recently, the Elk Ridge Project. Much of his research has involved Mimbres pottery production and distribution.

Michael W. Diehl (PhD, University at Buffalo, SUNY) is the senior project director and paleoethnobotanist for Desert Archaeology in Tucson, Arizona. His expertise is in paleoethnobotany, human-environment interaction, and historic and prehistoric archaeology of the American Southwest.

William H. Doelle (PhD, University of Arizona) has more than forty years of experience as a professional archaeologist. He has worked in Mexico, Guatemala, and extensively in the North American Southwest. His primary research interests include the demographic history of the greater Southwest and the history of private-sector archaeology in the United States. He is the founder of two Tucson-based organizations dedicated to respectfully exploring the Southwest's past and sharing that story broadly. He now focuses on one of these organizations, the nonprofit Archaeology Southwest, where he serves as president and CEO.

Patricia A. Gilman (PhD, University of New Mexico) has done archaeological fieldwork and research in the Mimbres region of southwestern New Mexico and southeastern Arizona for more than forty years. Her initial research interests included architecture and the transition that ancient people made from living in pithouses to inhabiting pueblos. Recently, Dr. Gilman and her colleagues have been investigating two topics—Mimbres chronometrics and the scarlet macaws in Mimbres sites. She has published on both topics, as well as on social variations within the Mimbres region, Mogollon great kivas, and Mimbres iconography and religion. Dr. Gilman recently retired from the Department of Anthropology at the University of Oklahoma, where she taught for twenty-five years.

Thomas E. Gruber (PhD, University of Oklahoma) is the co-owner and principal investigator at Open Range Archaeology, LLC. His research focuses on social boundaries and ceramic design style. He has worked with Mimbres ceramics for fifteen years. Currently, he works primarily in the Great Plains, Southeast, and Rocky Mountain regions of the United States. His most recent research focuses on the practical application of remote sensing technology in cultural resource management.

Robert J. Hard (PhD, University of New Mexico) is a professor of anthropology at the University of Texas, San Antonio. His research has focused on long-term change among hunter-gatherers and the adoption and spread of agriculture. He has conducted projects in northwest Chihuahua, southern New Mexico, Texas, and most recently in southeastern Arizona. His interests include variability in the transition to farming, warfare, subsistence intensification, and stable isotope ecology. He has collaborated extensively with John Roney in the examination of Early Agricultural period *cerros de trincheras*, including Cerro Juanaqueña in Chihuahua. Hard's publications include articles in *Science, Proceedings of the National Academy of Sciences, American Antiquity*, and *American Anthropologist* and a forthcoming book from the University of Utah Press.

Michelle Hegmon (PhD, University of Michigan) is a professor of anthropology in the School of Human Evolution and Social Change at Arizona State University. In the early 1990s she began working in the Mimbres region with the Eastern Mimbres Archaeological Project, which she co-directed with Margaret Nelson. She also collaborated with Steven LeBlanc in developing the Mimbres Pottery Images Digital Database. Her most recent focus is the archaeology of the human experience, which explores what it was like to live in the past that archaeologists study, in the Mimbres region and elsewhere. Some of her major publications include *Mimbres Lives and Landscapes* (2010 with M. Nelson), "Social Transformation and Its Human Costs in the Prehispanic U.S. Southwest" (2008), and "Setting Theoretical Egos Aside: Issues and Theory in North American Archaeology" (2003).

Steven A. LeBlanc (PhD, Washington University in St. Louis) is an archaeologist associated with Harvard's Peabody Museum. His studies of the American Southwest have focused on the Mimbres culture of southwestern New Mexico but has included work elsewhere in the region. He has written nine books and various papers on southwestern topics, especially on the results of work by the Mimbres Foundation and on Mimbres painted pottery.

Stephen H. Lekson (PhD, University of New Mexico) is the curator of archaeology and professor of anthropology at the Museum of Natural History, University of Colorado, Boulder. He has held research, curatorial, or administrative positions with the University of Tennessee, Eastern New Mexico University, the National Park Service, the Arizona State Museum, the Museum of New Mexico, and Crow Canyon Archaeological Center. Lekson has directed more than twenty archaeological projects throughout the Southwest. He was editor of the journal *Kiva* (2006–2011). His publications include a dozen books, many chapters in edited volumes, and articles in journals and magazines. Most recently, he has published *A History of the Ancient Southwest* (2009) and *Chaco Meridian* (2015, 2nd edition). *A Study of Southwestern Archaeology* is currently in press. He has curated a half-dozen exhibits, most recently *A History of the Ancient Southwest* (2014) at the University of Colorado Museum of Natural History.

James R. McGrath (BA, Arizona State University) assembled the database and carried out many of the analyses that formed the basis of chapter 7 as an undergraduate research assistant for the Long-Term Vulnerability and Transformation Project. He is currently a graduate student at the University of Iowa, working on Middle and Later Stone Age archaeological materials from Namibia and South Africa.

Paul E. Minnis (PhD, University of Michigan) is a professor emeritus of anthropology at the University of Oklahoma now living in Tucson, Arizona. He conducts research on the pre-Hispanic ethnobotany and archaeology of the U.S. Southwest and northwest Mexico. Most recently, he has co-directed research projects on Casas Grandes and Paquimé in northwest Chihuahua, Mexico. He is the author or editor of twelve books and numerous articles. He is a past president of the Society of Ethnobiology, treasurer and press editor for the Society for American Archaeology, and co-founder of the Southwest Symposium.

Ben A. Nelson (PhD, Southern Illinois University) is a professor of anthropology, School of Human Evolution and Social Change, Arizona State University. He has taught at the University of New Mexico; the University of Missouri, St. Louis; and the State University of New York, Buffalo. His field research has been conducted in the U.S. Southwest, especially the Mimbres region, and in northern Mexico, where he directs the La Quemada–Malpaso Valley Archaeological Project in Zacatecas. He is currently studying the social and environmental conditions that surrounded the northward expansion of the northern Mesoamerican frontier and the connectivity between the U.S. Southwest and Mesoamerica. He has recently published with Oxford University Press and in *Proceedings of the National Academy of Sciences* and *Quaternary Research*.

Margaret C. Nelson (PhD, University of California, Santa Barbara) is a professor in the School of Human Evolution and Social Change and vice dean of Barrett Honors College at Arizona State University. She has conducted research in the Mimbres region of southwest New Mexico for over forty years, collaborating for the past twenty-five years with Dr. Michelle Hegmon. Their work focuses primarily on the Classic to Postclassic transformation. Nelson's 1999 book, *Mimbres During the 12th Century: Abandonment, Continuity, and Reorganization*, derives from that research. Her 2010 book, *Mimbres Lives and Landscapes*, edited with Hegmon, brings many specialists together in a popular book about archaeology and Mimbres culture. Most recently, she led a comparative, interdisciplinary research team in addressing resilience and sustainability among prehistoric farmers in the U.S. Southwest and historic settlers in the North Atlantic Islands, published in *Ecology and Society*, as well as *Proceedings of the National Academy of Sciences*. Nelson was elected a fellow of the American Association for the Advancement of Science in 2008. She has been named Centennial Professor, Parents Association Professor of the Year, and ASU President's Professor in recognition of her teaching.

F. Michael O'Hara III (PhD, Arizona State University) is a consulting archaeologist and ethnographer for Cornerstone Environmental and Ecoplan Associates. Much of the coding done to establish the database used in chapter 7 was based on his compilation (2007) of southwestern peoples' beliefs about and uses of animals, as well as his knowledge of birds. His primary research is on the archaeology of the Flagstaff region with a focus on communal ritual.

Kathryn Putsavage (PhD, University of Colorado, Boulder) was an assistant professor in the Department of Anthropology and Applied Archaeology at Eastern New Mexico University from 2015 to 2017. Her research interests include late prehistoric archaeology in the American Southwest with an emphasis on the Mogollon/Mimbres and northern San Juan regions, ceramic analysis, museum anthropology, social transformation, migration, social identity, and connections between the American Southwest and northern Mexico between A.D. 1150 and 1450. She has worked at the Smithsonian's National Museum of the American Indian, the Anasazi Heritage Center, and the University of Colorado Museum of Natural History. She has also worked on field projects in New Mexico, northern Mexico, and Belize.

John R. Roney (MA, Eastern New Mexico University) retired after a full career as an archaeologist for the Bureau of Land Management in Nevada and New Mexico, and he is now employed as a cultural resources consultant in Albuquerque, New Mexico. Along with his co-authors, he has worked for many years in New Mexico, Arizona, and northwestern Mexico, investigating the early spread of agriculture and other topics. Roney's interests also include prehistoric and historic roads and post-Chacoan developments in the greater San Juan Basin of northwestern New Mexico. Results of his research have appeared in *Science*, *Proceedings of the National Academy of Sciences*, *Journal of Anthropological Archaeology*, and other venues.

Barbara J. Roth (PhD, University of Arizona) is a professor and chair of the Department of Anthropology at the University of Nevada, Las Vegas. She is an archaeologist who specializes in prehistoric cultures of the southwestern United States. Her main areas of interest include the transition from hunting and gathering to farming, the social changes (household organization, gender roles) that result from this transition, and the role of household organization in community development. She has conducted research at several sites in the Mimbres Mogollon region of southwestern New Mexico, including the Lake Roberts Vista site, La Gila Encantada, the Harris site, and more recently the Elk Ridge site, a large Classic period pueblo located in the Mimbres River Valley.

Will G. Russell (PhD, Arizona State University) is the cultural resources manager, state park archaeologist, tribal liaison, and site steward program coordinator for Arizona State Parks and Trails. He is a research affiliate with Arizona State University's Center for Archaeology and Society, where his research is focused on ritual practice and social integration in the Mimbres region of New Mexico and north-central Arizona.

Jonathan A. Sandor (PhD, University of California, Berkeley) is an emeritus professor of agronomy and soil science at Iowa State University and is now a consultant living in New Mexico. He studies ancient and current agricultural soils in the Americas and also explores knowledge of soils and agriculture among traditional farmers.

Karen Gust Schollmeyer (PhD, Arizona State University) is a preservation archaeologist for Archaeology Southwest. Her research interests include zooarchaeology, long-term human-environment interactions, and food security and landscape use. She is also interested in how archaeologists' long-term insights can be applied to contemporary issues in conservation and development. Much of her fieldwork has focused on southwest New Mexico, especially the "edges" of the Mimbres-Mogollon area along the Rio Grande and the upper Gila. Her recent publications include articles on the Mimbres area and zooarchaeology in the journal *Kiva* and on animals in *The Oxford Handbook of Southwest Archaeology*.

Jakob W. Sedig (PhD, University of Colorado, Boulder) conducts archaeological research in the Mimbres region of southwest New Mexico and studies human resilience and vulnerability during times of environmental change. He is also the consulting archaeologist for the Reich Lab at the Harvard Medical School, which examines ancient DNA.

Robert J. Speakman (PhD, University of Barcelona) is the director of the Center for Applied Isotope Studies at the University of Georgia and holds faculty appointments in UGA's Departments of Anthropology and Geology. Prior to coming to UGA in 2011, Speakman was a research scientist and department head at the Smithsonian Institution's Museum Conservation Institute (2006–2011) and a researcher at the University of Missouri's Archaeometry Laboratory (1997–2006). Over more than twenty-five years of archaeological research experience in the Americas and the Russian Far East, he has managed over one hundred projects and authored or co-authored over 150 publications. Speakman has been at the forefront of geochemical-based research on archaeological ceramic, obsidian and alloys in the United States for almost two decades and is an internationally recognized expert in radiocarbon dating, neutron activation analysis, X-ray fluorescence spectrometry, and inductively coupled plasma mass spectrometry. His research has been funded by the National Science Foundation, European Union, National Park Service, Smithsonian Institution, and various other state and federal agencies. He is on the editorial board or is an associate editor for several journals, including *Geoarchaeology*, is a registered professional archaeologist, and is active in multiple professional associations and societies.

Robert J. Stokes (PhD, University of Oklahoma) has been practicing archaeology since 1988. His research interests include settlement patterns and landscape use, social transformations, and Spanish colonial period and historic archaeology. After working for fourteen years in Arizona as a principal investigator with several cultural resource management firms, he is now the New Mexico State Parks archaeologist and lives in Santa Fe.

Matthew Taliaferro (PhD, University of Texas, Austin) has over fifteen years of archaeological experience throughout the southern United States. He currently works as an archaeologist with the U.S. Forest Service. His research interests include technological organization, household and community studies, social change, and human ecology.

Elizabeth Toney (MA, University of Oklahoma) is employed as an archaeologist with the U.S. Forest Service. Her interests include small architectural sites in the Mimbres area, the application of geographic information systems to look at landscape scale trends through time, and the transition from foraging to farming in southwestern prehistory.

Christopher A. Turnbow's (MA, University of Kentucky) early experience focused on Fort Ancient and contact-period populations in the Ohio Valley prior to his moving to the Southwest, where he conducted research on Paleo-Indian to Spanish colonial occupations and obsidian-quarry sites. His research in the Mimbres region began with excavations of nine Archaic and Pithouse sites and led to interests in preceramic transitions to farming, Mimbres diversity, and interactions on the northern edge of the region. As the associate director of the Laboratory of Anthropology/Museum of Indian Arts and Culture, he reanalyzed understudied collections from the Forks of the Gila, including West Fork Ruin and Diablo Village Complex.

Aaron R. Woods (MA, Brigham Young University) is a PhD candidate at the University of Nevada, Las Vegas. His current research focuses on the role of small sites in community systems, the importance of experimental archaeology and replicative studies, and chipped-stone tool use. He has published the preliminary results of a small pueblo excavation, a case study for implementing experimental archaeology in the classroom, and an overview of a Fremont projectile-point assemblage recovered from Utah.

INDEX